"In this gripping, entertaining and deeply thought-provoking study, Michael Tai analyses the basis of trust – or lack of it – between the Chinese and American leaderships. He asks whether these two great nations can bridge the chasm between their vastly different historical experiences and ideological legacies and build the kind of relationship that might lead us towards a cleaner planet, a more stable and fairer financial system and ultimately take us down the road to peace rather than set us on a path to war. It is impossible to exaggerate the importance of this book, for the fate of the world rests largely in their hands."

Tim Clissold, author of *Mr China* and *China Rules*

"World peace depends on sensible power sharing based on trust between the two remaining superpowers. Michael Tai's scholarly and deeply insightful book underlines the need to temper the distrustful impulses of each nation's power elites driven by historical prejudices and lack of empathy. An important contribution to the understanding of China–US relations."

Professor Hong Hai, former Dean, College of Business,
Nanyang Technological University, Singapore

"This is a masterful and probing study, of how trust in business global relations is precariously pivoted on personal probity and relationships. It should appeal to leaders and students in many disciplines."

Professor James M. Houston, Regent College, Vancouver, Canada

US–China Relations in the Twenty-First Century

The relationship between the United States and China will be of critical importance to the world throughout the twenty-first century. In the West, China's rise is often portrayed as a threat and China seen in negative terms. This book explores the dynamics of this crucial relationship. It looks in particular at what causes an international relationship to be perceived negatively, and considers what can be done to reverse this, arguing that trust is a key factor. It goes on to discuss US and Chinese rhetoric and behavior in three key areas – climate change, finance, and international security. The book contends that, contrary to much US rhetoric, China's actions in these areas are often much more flexible and accommodating than the US position, and that the Chinese are much more knowledgeable about, and understanding and appreciative of, the United States than vice versa.

Michael Tai who has had an extensive career in business and management in Asia, completed his doctorate at the University of Cambridge, UK.

Routledge Studies on the Chinese Economy

Series Editor:
Peter Nolan Director, Centre of Development Studies;
Chong Hua Professor in Chinese Development; and Director of
the Chinese Executive Leadership Programme (CELP), University
of Cambridge

Founding Series Editors:
Peter Nolan, University of Cambridge and Dong Fureng, Beijing
University

The aim of this series is to publish original, high-quality, research-level work
by both new and established scholars in the West and the East, on all aspects
of the Chinese economy, including studies of business and economic history.

**1 The Growth of Market Relations
in Post-reform Rural China**
A micro-analysis of peasants,
migrants and peasant entrepreneurs
Hiroshi Sato

2 The Chinese Coal Industry
An economic history
Elspeth Thomson

**3 Sustaining China's Economic
Growth in the Twenty-First Century**
*Edited by Shujie Yao and
Xiaming Liu*

4 China's Poor Regions
Rural-urban migration, poverty,
economic reform and urbanisation
Mei Zhang

**5 China's Large Enterprises and the
Challenge of Late Industrialization**
Dylan Sutherland

6 China's Economic Growth
Yanrui Wu

**7 The Employment Impact of
China's World Trade
Organisation Accession**
A.S. Bhalla and S. Qiu

**8 Catch-Up and Competitiveness
in China**
The case of large firms in the
oil industry
Jin Zhang

9 Corporate Governance in China
Jian Chen

**10 The Theory of the Firm and
Chinese Enterprise Reform**
The case of China International
Trust and Investment Corporation
Qin Xiao

11 Globalisation, Transition and Development in China
The case of the coal industry
Huaichuan Rui

12 China Along the Yellow River
Reflections on rural society
Cao Jinqing, translated by Nicky Harman and Huang Ruhua

13 Economic Growth, Income Distribution and Poverty Reduction in Contemporary China
Shujie Yao

14 China's Economic Relations with the West and Japan, 1949–79
Grain, trade and diplomacy
Chad J. Mitcham

15 China's Industrial Policy and the Global Business Revolution
The case of the domestic appliance industry
Ling Liu

16 Managers and Mandarins in Contemporary China
The building of an international business alliance
Jie Tang

17 The Chinese Model of Modern Development
Edited by Tian Yu Cao

18 Chinese Citizenship
Views from the margins
Edited by Vanessa L. Fong and Rachel Murphy

19 Unemployment, Inequality and Poverty in Urban China
Edited by Shi Li and Hiroshi Sato

20 Globalisation, Competition and Growth in China
Edited by Jian Chen and Shujie Yao

21 The Chinese Communist Party in Reform
Edited by Kjeld Erik Brodsgaard and Zheng Yongnian

22 Poverty and Inequality among Chinese Minorities
A.S. Bhalla and Shufang Qiu

23 Economic and Social Transformation in China
Challenges and opportunities
Angang Hu

24 Global Big Business and the Chinese Brewing Industry
Yuantao Guo

25 Peasants and Revolution in Rural China
Rural political change in the North China Plain and the Yangzi Delta, 1850–1949
Chang Liu

26 The Chinese Banking Industry
Lessons from history for today's challenges
Yuanyuan Peng

27 Informal Institutions and Rural Development in China
Biliang Hu

28 The Political Future of Hong Kong
Democracy within Communist China
Kit Poon

29 China's Post-Reform Economy -
Achieving Harmony,
Sustaining Growth
*Edited by Richard Sanders and
Chen Yang*

30 Eliminating Poverty Through
Development in China
*China Development
Research Foundation*

31 Good Governance in China - A
Way Towards Social Harmony
Case studies by China's
rising leaders
Edited by Wang Mengkui

32 China in the Wake of Asia's
Financial Crisis
Edited by Wang Mengkui

33 Multinationals, Globalisation and
Indigenous Firms in China
Chunhang Liu

34 Economic Convergence in
Greater China
Mainland China, Hong Kong,
Macau and Taiwan
Chun Kwok Lei and Shujie Yao

35 Financial Sector Reform and the
International Integration of China
Zhongmin Wu

36 China in the World Economy
Zhongmin Wu

37 China's Three Decades of
Economic Reforms
*Edited by Xiaohui Liu and
Wei Zhang*

38 China's Development Challenges
Economic vulnerability and public
sector reform
Richard Schiere

39 China's Rural Financial System
Households' demand for credit and
recent reforms
Yuepeng Zhao

40 Sustainable Reform and
Development in Post-Olympic China
*Edited by Shujie Yao, Bin Wu,
Stephen Morgan and
Dylan Sutherland*

41 Constructing a Social Welfare
System for All in China
*China Development
Research Foundation*

42 China's Road to Peaceful Rise
Observations on its cause, basis,
connotation and prospect
Zheng Bijian

43 China as the Workshop of
the World
An analysis at the national and
industry level of China in the
international division of labor
Yuning Gao

44 China's Role in Global
Economic Recovery
Xiaolan Fu

45 The Political Economy of the
Chinese Coal Industry
Black gold and blood-stained coal
Tim Wright

46 Rising China in the Changing
World Economy
Edited by Liming Wang

47 Thirty Years of China's Reform
Edited by Wang Mengkui

48 China and the Global Financial Crisis
A comparison with Europe
Edited by Jean-Pierre Cabestan, Jean-François Di Meglio and Xavier Richet

49 China's New Urbanization Strategy
China Development Research Foundation

50 China's Development and Harmonisation
Towards a balance with nature, society and the international community
Bin Wu, Shujie Yao and Jian Chen

51 Chinese Firms, Global Firms
Industrial policy in the age of globalization
Peter Nolan

52 The East Asian Computer Chip War
Ming-chin Monique Chu

53 China's Economic Dynamics
A Beijing consensus in the making?
Edited by Jun Li and Liming Wang

54 A New Development Model and China's Future
Deng Yingtao
Translated by Nicky Harman, with a foreword by Peter Nolan and an Afterword translated by Phil Hand

55 Demographic Developments in China
China Development Research Foundation

56 China's Centralized Industrial Order
Industrial reform and the rise of centrally controlled big business
Chen Li

57 China's Exchange Rate Regime
China Development Research Foundation

58 China's WTO Accession Reassessed
China Development Research Foundation

59 US–China Relations in the Twenty-First Century
A question of trust
Michael Tai

Routledge Studies on the Chinese Economy - Chinese Economists on Economic Reform

1 Chinese Economists on Economic Reform – Collected Works of Xue Muqiao
Xue Muqiao, edited by China Development Research Foundation

2 Chinese Economists on Economic Reform - Collected Works of Guo Shuqing
Guo Shuqing, edited by China Development Research Foundation

3 Chinese Economists on Economic
Reform – Collected Works of
Chen Xiwen
*Chen Xiwen, edited by China
Development Research Foundation*

4 Chinese Economists on Economic
Reform – Collected Works of
Du Runsheng
*Du Runsheng, edited by China
Development Research Foundation*

5 Chinese Economists on Economic
Reform – Collected Works of
Lou Jiwei
*Lou Jiwei, edited by China Develop-
ment Research Foundation*

6 Chinese Economists on Economic
Reform – Collected Works of
Ma Hong
*Ma Hong, edited by China
Development Research Foundation*

7 Chinese Economists on Economic
Reform – Collected Works of
Wang Mengkui
*Wang Mengkui, edited by China
Development Research Foundation*

8 Chinese Economists on Economic
Reform – Collected Works of
Yu Guangyuan
*Yu Guangyuan, edited by China
Development Research Foundation*

US–China Relations in the Twenty-First Century

A question of trust

Michael Tai

Routledge
Taylor & Francis Group

LONDON AND NEW YORK

First published 2015 by Routledge

2 Park Square, Milton Park, Abingdon, Oxon OX14 4RN
711 Third Avenue, New York, NY 10017, USA

Routledge is an imprint of the Taylor & Francis Group, an informa business

First issued in paperback 2017

British Library Cataloguing in Publication Data
A catalogue record for this book is available from the British Library

Library of Congress Cataloging in Publication Data
    US–China relations in the twenty-first century : a question of trust /
Michael Tai.
        pages cm. – (Routledge studies on the Chinese economy ; 59)
Includes bibliographical references and index.
    1. United States–Foreign relations–China. 2. China–Foreign relations–
United States. I. Title. II. Title: United States–China relations in the twenty-
first century.
    E183.8.C5T26 2015
    327.73051–dc23
                2014040501

ISBN: 978-1-138-88643-8 (hbk)
ISBN: 978-1-138-07979-3 (pbk)

Typeset in Times New Roman
by Taylor & Francis Books

To Grandma
With love and gratitude

Contents

List of illustrations   xiv
Preface   xv
List of abbreviations   xvii

1   Introduction   1

2   Generic trust   27

3   Climate change   69

4   Financial crisis   103

5   International security   137

6   Conclusion   185

    Index   203

List of illustrations

Figures

5.1 US vs other top 10 budgets combined 2011   138
5.2 Planned defense expenditure by country 2011   142
5.3 Nuclear arsenals in 2013 by country   143

Tables

2.1 History topics covered by *American Pageant*   33
2.2 Racial composition of the 112th Congress   35
4.1 Holdings of US government debt in 2011   107
4.2 US versus Chinese views on causes of the GFC   115
4.3 Bank mergers since the 1980s   118
4.4 Bank mergers since the Global Financial Crisis   119
4.5 Percentage of bank assets owned by foreign banks in 2002   120
4.6 The top 10 Banks in 2012 (ranked according to Tier 1 capital)   122
5.1 US defense related budget requests for 2011   139
5.2 US and Chinese military capability   142

Preface

This book argues that trust between states depends on History, Interests, Structures and Empathy. It uses these four dimensions (HISE) to analyze trust between the US and China with regard to climate change, global finance and international security. It holds that interstate trust boils down to trust between power elites; the views of the citizenry are important but susceptible to manipulation. As with social trust, interstate trust is never wholly rational. It is based on cognition, emotion and perception. Expectations and presuppositions color our vision and we see what we expect to see. They shape our behavior, often producing the very consequences we fear. Only by laying aside prejudices and embracing a spirit of empathy can states hope to build trust.

Humanity stands at a crossroads. One road leads to cooperation; the other to conflict. The path humanity takes will depend in no small measure on America's relationship with China. This thesis explores trust in US–China relations with respect to climate change, financial crises and international security. These are global threats that demand collective response and yet collaboration is failing for lack of trust. I consider each side's perspective by consulting Chinese and Western sources, paying attention to the voices of officials, scholars, businessmen and journalists.

Chapter 1 explores trust, human nature and the state, and proposes a framework for analyzing trust between states. Chapter 2 lays the groundwork for later chapters by discussing generic trust between the US and China. It consists of four sub-chapters comparing the way Chinese and Americans view themselves and each other. Chapters 3, 4 and 5 contrast their perspectives on climate change, financial crises and international security respectively. Chapter 6 discusses the asymmetry in US–China relations and its implication for trust.

The idea of writing this book arose from discussions about trust with Professor James Houston of Regent College. I am grateful for his encouragement to embark on this journey. I am deeply grateful to Professor Peter Nolan of Cambridge University for his diligent supervision and steadfast support, without which this book would not have seen the light of day. He broadened my perspectives with his encyclopedic knowledge, and deepened my understanding of America and China. To him I owe an apprentice's debt.

My gratitude goes also to Professor Koen Steemers, Dr. George Karekwaivanane, Professor Tahir Kamran, and Lesley Dingle of Cambridge University, and Dr. Ian Randall of Spurgeon's College, and Dr. Quyen Vo and Dr. Kiran Vijayan for their helpful comments on my drafts.

I am also grateful to Professor Kenneth Tan of the Lee Kuan Yew School of Public Policy, Professor Archon Fung, Dr. William Overholt and Ajmal Qureshi of the Harvard Kennedy School of Government, Professor Xin Qiang of Fudan University, Professor Liu Yan of the Central China Normal University, and Professor Akio Takahara of Tokyo University for sharing their valuable insights.

I thank the Harvard Kennedy School's Ash Center for Democratic Governance and Innovation and the National Chengchi University's Institute of International Relations for welcoming me as visiting fellow.

List of abbreviations

ACFTA	ASEAN–China Free Trade Area
AEI	American Enterprise Institute
AFC	Asian Financial Crisis
AIG	American International Group
API	American Petroleum Institute
ASBM	Anti-ship ballistic missile
ASEAN	Association of South East Asian Nations
BBC	British Broadcasting Corporation
BOC	Bank of China
BP	British Petroleum
CBRC	China Banking Regulatory Commission
CCP	Chinese Communist Party
CDM	Clean Development Mechanism
CEIBS	China Europe International Business School
CIA	Central Intelligence Agency
CISS	China Institute of Strategic Studies
CNCERT	Computer Network Emergency Response Technical Team
COP	Congressional Oversight Panel
DHS	Department of Homeland Security
DOD	Department of Defense
DOE	Department of Energy
DPP	Democratic Progressive Party
DVA	Department of Veteran Affairs
ECFA	Economic Cooperation Framework Agreement
EEZ	Economic Exclusion Zone
FCIC	Financial Crisis Inquiry Commission
FDI	Foreign Direct Investment
FT	*Financial Times*
GAO	General Accounting Office
GDP	Gross domestic product
GFC	Global Financial Crisis
HISE	History, Interests, Structures, Empathy
HSBC	Hong Kong and Shanghai Banking Corporation

ICBC	Industrial and Commercial Bank of China
IEA	International Energy Agency
IMF	International Monetary Fund
IR	International relations
IW	Information warfare
IWEP	Institute of World Economics and Politics
JOAC	Joint Operational Access Concept
KBR	Kellog, Brown and Root
KMT	Kuomintang
LNG	Liquid natural gas
LSE	London School of Economics and Political Science
LTCM	Long-Term Capital Management
NCCP	National Climate Change Program
NFU	No first use
NPL	Non-performing loan
NSA	National Security Agency
NYCLU	New York Civil Liberties Union
NYT	*New York Times*
OECD	Organization for Economic Cooperation and Development
PBOC	People's Bank of China
PLA	People's Liberation Army
PNAC	Project for the New American Century
ppm	Parts per million
PPP	Purchasing power parity
PRC	People's Republic of China
RMA	Revolution in military affairs
ROC	Republic of China
SDR	Special drawing right
TARP	Troubled Asset Relief Program
TPP	Transpacific Partnership
TRA	Taiwan Relations Act
UN	United Nations
UNCLOS	United Nations Convention on the Law of the Sea
UNFCCC	United Nations Framework Convention on Climate Change
US	The United States of America
USCESRC	US–China Economic and Security Review Commission
VOC	Volatile organic compound

1 Introduction

The worst periods of international history have been when trust has broken down between nations. How to build trust between the great powers is the key problem in international relations, and wise leadership is necessary to avoid conflict between established and rising powers, observes political scientist Andrew Gamble.[1] It is difficult for established powers to make concessions to the rising powers, and there is the danger of the rising powers growing too fast. Leaders must have a desire to compromise and be inclusive, but domestic forces pressing for a hard line may oppose a conciliatory posture, he cautions.

Vital as it is, trust has received scant attention in international relations theory. This chapter begins by reviewing concepts of trust and its relation to human nature. It examines the role of psychology in international politics, and argues that states behave like individuals, and that interstate trust boils down to trust between national leaders. It is a form of social trust based on cognition, emotion and perception. The chapter ends by proposing a framework to analyze trust in US–China relations.

What is trust?

When Columbus arrived off the shores of the Bahama Islands, the Arawak men and women emerged from their villages, naked and full of wonder. They ran to greet the strangers and brought them food, water and gifts. Columbus wrote in his log:

> They ... brought us parrots and balls of cotton and spears and many other things, which they exchanged for the glass beads and hawks' bells. They willingly traded everything they owned ... They were well built, with good bodies and handsome features ... They do not bear arms, and do not know them, for I showed them a sword, they took it by the edge and cut themselves out of ignorance. They have no iron. Their spears are made of cane ... They would make fine servants ... With fifty men we could subjugate them all and make them do whatever we want.[2]

The Arawaks were much like the Indians on the mainland who were remarkable for their hospitality and their belief in sharing. European observers reported this repeatedly, as these were traits uncommon in Renaissance Europe.[3] Columbus recounted that the Indians were "so naïve and so free with their possessions that no one who has not witnessed them would believe it. When you ask for something they have, they never say no. To the contrary, they offer to share with anyone ..." On the first island he found in the West Indies, Columbus took some of the natives by force "in order that they ... might give information of whatever there is in these parts." On his return to Europe, he wrote to the monarchs of Spain asking for help, promising to bring from his next voyage "as much gold as they need ... and as many slaves as they ask." In their quest for gold, Columbus and his followers proceeded to enslave and brutalize the Indians throughout the Caribbean. The men were forced to work in the mines while the women tilled the soil. In *History of the Indies* Bartolomé de las Casas (1484–1566) described how the Spaniards treated the Indians:

> Thus husbands and wives were together only once every eight or ten months and when they met they were so exhausted and depressed on both sides ... they ceased to procreate. As for the newly born, they died early because their mothers, overworked and famished, had no milk to nurse them, and for this reason, while I was in Cuba, 7,000 children died in three months. Some mothers even drown their babies from sheer desperation ... In this way, husbands died in the mines, wives died at work, and children died from lack of milk ... and in a short time this land which was so great, so powerful and fertile ... was depopulated ... My eyes have seen these acts so foreign to human nature, and now I tremble as I write ... [4]

By 1650 the entire Arawak population on Haiti had been wiped out by sword or suicide. "Thus the eternal God, our Lord, gives victory to those who follow his way over apparent impossibilities," wrote Columbus.[5]

Anyone who has ever been abused or betrayed knows what trust is. Yet like energy and money, it defies definition, and the modern study of trust has proceeded without a common understanding of what the word means. Researchers even disagree on the category to which it belongs. It is thought variously as a general outlook on human nature,[6] an emotional attitude,[7] a relationship,[8] a decision,[9] an action[10] or social capital.[11] Is trust a leap of faith beyond reason?[12] Is it programmed into our brains by evolution[13] or is it just a psychological response to chemicals in the body?[14] Russell Hardin describes trust in the following way: "To say we trust you means we believe you have the right intentions toward us and that you are competent to do what we trust you to do."[15] Delhey and Newton define trust as "the belief that others will not deliberately or knowingly do us harm, if they can avoid it, and look after our interests, if this is possible."[16] Kurt Koch sees trust as the counter-pole of fear.[17] It is also thought of as the opposite of control.[18] Trust is the absence of control, and control is a lack of trust.

Russell Hardin holds that trust is based on knowledge – knowledge of the other's trustworthiness and reliability. In his "encapsulated interest" concept of trust, Alice trusts Bob because he is motivated to act in her interest.[19] She trusts him because he includes her interest in his own, i.e. Alice's interest is "encapsulated" in Bob's. He looks after her interest because he values their relationship. He may also do so out of love and altruism. Or because he values his reputation.[20] Bob's behavior may be grounded in moral commitments or in psychological or character disposition.[21] Alice must also consider Bob's ability (freedom and competence)[22] as trust depends on domain: I may trust you with money but not with my children. I may trust you to operate the kitchen toaster but not to fly the airplane. Equally, trust is based on "social intelligence" or the ability to detect signs of untrustworthiness.[23] It rests on certain qualities which we learn to discern. Thus, trust is both cognitive and relational.

Instead of calculated trust, however, Eric Uslaner holds that trust is a general outlook on human nature not contingent on personal experiences or risk assessment, i.e. there is no link between trust and trustworthiness.[24] He argues that trust is a moral value. Behind moralistic trust is the belief that most people share certain fundamental moral values regardless of their political and religious affiliation. As Fukayama maintains: "trust arises when a community shares a set of moral values in such a way as to create regular expectations of regular and honest behavior."[25] Moralistic trust depends on a belief in the goodwill of others (that they will not try to take advantage of us). It is faith in strangers (although there are limits: would one entrust $10,000 or one's child to random strangers?) Trusting people, Uslaner claims, are more likely to volunteer, give to charity, be tolerant, and support policies that benefit the underprivileged. Countries with more trusters have better functioning governments, less corruption, more open markets, more redistributive policies and income equality, he posits.[26]

Measuring trust

How does one measure an abstract quality like trust or confidence? Measuring trust is problematic because much of the work proceeds without a clear account of what is meant by trust in the first place. Trust is measured either with a survey question ("Generally speaking, would you say that most people can be trusted or that you can't be too careful in dealing with people?") or by observing behavior in experiments such as the "investment game."[27] Some doubt the validity of the survey approach because the respondent is left to answer the question using their own understanding of the word "trust." The second approach has been challenged too because the experiments often use convenient samples such as students (it is not clear what population they represent) and involve a certain degree of self-selection. Moreover, the subject's behavior in the early stages of the experiment may not be a good indicator of trust. Some argue that the investment game measures cooperation instead of trust per se, and cooperation can be used as a proxy only if trust is a precondition for cooperation.[28] Trust is difficult to quantify. Nonetheless, human beings can sense trust, and we know when we trust one individual more than another.

Determinants of trust

It has long been argued that some countries lack trust.[29] Trust is related to social capital, which is the mutual support enabled by a social network. Some evidence suggests that trust is important for social integration and favorable economic and political outcomes. This led researchers to investigate what determines trust but no one has yet produced a general theory of trust; only a long list of possible determinants.[30] One study used thirty-five variables relating to six different theoretical views.[31] Some suggest that civic engagement and institutions play an important role in fostering trust. Robert Putnam posits that people learn trust, reciprocity and cooperation by participating in voluntary associations and other forms of civic engagement.[32] He argues that the bonds of community in America have withered because of television, two-career families, increasing hours at work, suburban sprawl, and generational changes in values.[33] Reduced participation in parent–teacher associations, card playing, choir singing, and league bowling leads to the decline in trust. But skeptics question the formative importance of voluntary associations, since most people spend relatively little time in those activities compared to time spent in other social contexts. They suggest instead that institutions create the incentive to behave in a trustworthy manner.[34] People are more likely to behave in a trustworthy fashion if there are institutions (including customs and norms) that detect and punish betrayal.[35] By lowering the risk of trusting others, institutions promote trust. Institutional fairness, especially in socially diverse societies, also promotes trust.[36] Some argue that democracy, by creating transparency, accountability and stability, fosters trust – although the decline in social capital in America challenges that assumption.[37]

Others suggest that moral norms determine the level of trust.[38] Values such as justice and egalitarianism are strongly related to trust. These are values learned early in life through education and socialization. There is also evidence of the effect of religious values and income equality,[39] while the effect of ethnic diversity has been studied with varying results. Researchers have found strong trust among Russians, Tatars and Yakuts in the republics of Tatarstan and Sakha-Yakutia,[40] as well as among non-Western immigrant groups in Denmark.[41] But mixed communities in North America show low trust.[42] One study found that the presence of "visible minorities" reduced trust among the white majority.[43] In the US, personal experiences and community characteristics influence how much people trust each other.[44] Factors that reduce trust include traumatic experiences; gender and race discrimination; low income and education level; and high income inequality.[45]

If the study of trust so far seems tentative, it is due to some degree to the methods employed. Social science's difficulty in researching trust stems partly from its reliance on rationalistic methods. Reason adopts an analytic approach and breaks a complicated subject into constituent parts, while intuition perceives a subject as a whole and grasps its essential nature directly. Some subjects are less amenable to scientific analysis and yet readily understood intuitively. Western thinkers since Aristotle have sought to compartmentalize truth, experience, life and philosophy itself into separable aspects of knowledge, but Eastern philosophers tend to look at life in its totality, not in its parts.[46] Rather than the positivism of Auguste Comte, Easterners prefer pithy proverbs ("before you embark on a journey of revenge, dig two graves")[47] accessible to the intuition rather than lengthy treatises that appeal to the intellect. The Dao De Jing (道德经) declares:[48]

We put thirty spokes together and call it a wheel;

But it is on the space where there is nothing that the usefulness of the wheel depends.

We turn clay to make a vessel;

But it is on the space where there is nothing that the usefulness of the vessel depends.

We pierce doors and windows to make a house;

And it is on these spaces where there is nothing that the usefulness of the house depends.

Therefore just as we take advantage of what is, we should recognize the usefulness of what is not.

Because the study of trust cannot be divorced from ethics, Chinese philosophy may have an important contribution to make. There is in Chinese philosophy a profound inseparability of philosophy and life and even of theory and practice, and a fundamental conviction that truth is essentially moral. All truths, whether found in nature or in human history, are meant for the purpose of moral cultivation.[49] In contrast to the Western interest in metaphysical systems, the fundamental aim of Chinese philosophy is that of achieving "sageliness within and kingliness without" (内圣外王).[50] The Chinese thinkers were moralists and political theorists concerned with the conduct of the individual and the organization of society.[51] There is more discussion on the question of good and evil than on the question of truth and falsehood.[52] According to Mencius (孟子) (372–289 BC), a leading Confucian thinker, what distinguishes man from animals is his heart (*xin*, 心).[53] Although he shares many appetites and desires with animals, these drives alone cannot be called human nature because they fail to distinguish him from animals. The heart is the thinking part of the human being, and what Mencius had in mind was moral thinking – thinking about moral duties, priorities, purpose, man's destiny and his position in the universe. Intellectual thinking constitutes only an insignificant part of thinking. Chinese philosophers may not refer explicitly to trust, but the term for ethics, *lunli* (伦理), means "the principles of relationships" and implies the importance of ethical relationships in creating trust. For Mencius, empathy is central to an ethical relationship.

What is empathy?

Mencius held that empathy is the ability to understand and share the feelings of others.[54] He famously said that anyone who suddenly sees an infant about to fall into a well would react with alarm.[55] He contrasted compassion with self-interest:

> Suppose a man were, all of a sudden, to see a young child on the verge of falling into a well. He would certainly be moved to compassion, not because he wanted to get in the good graces of the parents, nor because he wished to win the praise of his fellow villagers or friends nor yet because he disliked the cry of the child.[56]

Centuries later Adam Smith (1723–1790) made a similar observation:

> How selfish soever man may be supposed, there are evidently some principles in his nature, which interest him in the fortunes of others, and render their happiness necessary to him, though he derives nothing from it, except the pleasure of seeing it. Of this kind is pity or compassion, the emotion we feel for the misery of others, when we either see it, or are made to conceive it in a very lively manner. That we often derive sorrow from the sorrows of others, is a matter of fact too obvious to require any instances to prove it; for this sentiment, like all the other original passions of human nature, is by no means confined to the virtuous or the humane, though they perhaps may feel it with the most exquisite sensibility. The greatest ruffian, the most hardened violator of the laws of society, is not altogether without it.[57]

Mencius held that the heart had four inborn tendencies: empathy and benevolence (ren, 仁), shame and aversion (*li*, 礼), courtesy and modesty (*yi*, 仪), and a sense of right and wrong (*zhi*, 智). *Ren* has to do with love and concern for others, the reluctance to cause harm and the capacity to be moved by the suffering of others.[58] The ideogram for *ren*, 仁, consists of two parts – one meaning *person* and the other the numeral *two* – thus signifying two persons and the *relational* nature of benevolence. Aristotle (384–322 BC) concurred that benevolence or goodwill (*euonia*) is a natural human tendency:

And the affection of parent for child and of child for parent seems to be a natural instinct not only in man but in birds and most animals; and similarly the mutual friendliness between members of the same species, especially the human species; which is why we commend those who love their fellow men.[59]

Aristotle taught that the highest good was happiness or wellbeing (*eudaimonia*), and man's function (*ergon*) consisted in doing things in accordance to virtue and excellence.[60] He believed that being a good person was about doing the right thing, at the right time, in the right way. Although health and wealth are desirable, living well is but a life of virtuous activity. In this way, he linked happiness (not the same thing as pleasure) with virtue – a proposition that is gaining currency among modern social psychologists.[61] Aristotle regarded ethical virtues such as benevolence, justice, courage and temperance to be social skills central to a well-lived life.[62]

Mencius cautioned, however, that "the heart of compassion" is but a germ, which although inborn, must be nurtured if it is to become full-fledged benevolence. Virtuous activity is the highest good but it does not come by chance. We must be fortunate enough to have parents or friends who help us become virtuous, and we share the responsibility for practicing the virtues. According to Aristotle, "we become just by the practice of just actions, self-controlled by exercising self-control, and courageous by performing acts of courage."[63]

Love changes everything

While conceding the power of competition ("the invisible hand"), Adam Smith also believed that all members of society stand in need of each other's assistance, and "where the necessary assistance is reciprocally afforded from love, from gratitude, from friendship, and esteem, the society flourishes and is happy."[64] Although best remembered for his theory of evolution in *The Origin of Species*, Charles Darwin wrote about emotions in *The Descent of Man* and *The Expression of Emotions in Man and Animals*. He observed that most of the "more complex emotions are common to the higher animals and ourselves" and "animals not only love, but desire to be loved."[65] He noticed that many animals empathized with each other's distress. Toward life's end, he wrote more about the social nature and the affectionate bond among creatures, and believed that the survival of the fittest was as much about cooperation as about competition, and that human beings were just as likely to form collaborative bonds with other human beings. Indeed, mutual love and support is key to the survival of the species. Echoing Mencius, he used the example of a person rushing to rescue a stranger in a fire at great personal risk and no thought of reward. Darwin claimed that this reflected a deeply ingrained social instinct and empathetic impulse. The degree to which this impulse develops depends on early parenting experience, as well as the values and worldview of one's culture.[66]

That human beings need affection is attested by the work of John Bowlby, who studied orphaned and homeless children in the aftermath of the Second World War. His study of affection-less children and the effects of hospital and institutional care yielded important insights. His *attachment theory* revolutionized thinking about child care. Bowlby posited that "the infant and young child should experience a warm, intimate, and continuous relationship with his mother (or permanent mother substitute) in which both find satisfaction and enjoyment," the lack of which may produce irreversible mental health consequences.[67] When a child feels unloved or that its love is not accepted, it develops aberrant relationships and pathological symptoms such as withdrawal, aggression, obsession, paranoia and phobic behavior. The child learns to trust through these early interactions. Caregivers' responses shape the individual's perceptions, emotions, and expectations in later relationships. "Basic trust" (child-like trust) is foundational to the healthy development of a child.[68] Intimate attachments are the hub around which a person's life revolves, and people draw strength and enjoyment from these attachments.[69] Can empathy, essential to the human psyche, be ignored in the conduct of international relations?

Psychology of international relations

International relations theories are "rational choice theories" that assume that the state makes decisions by exploring all possible options and rationally picking the one that promises the best outcome.[70] But because of time and resource constraints, that is rarely the case. In his analysis of the Cuban Missile Crisis, Graham Allison argued that decisions taken during the stand-off were not based on rational choices but determined by organizational processes (pre-established plans and set responses) and court politics (rivalry within the administration team).[71] Humans are complex and their behavior often non-rational for a host of cognitive and affective (moods, feelings and attitudes) reasons.[72] Leaders are often carried along by flawed assumptions, miscalculations and circumstances. Reflecting on the causes of the First World War, historian A. J. P. Taylor wrote:

> Men are reluctant to believe that great events have small causes. Therefore, once the Great War started, they were convinced that it must be the outcome of profound forces. It is hard to discover these when we examine the details. Nowhere was there conscious determination to provoke a war. Statesmen miscalculated. They used the instruments of bluff and threat which had proved effective on previous occasions. This time things went wrong. The deterrent on which they relied failed to deter: the statesmen became the prisoners of their own weapons. The great armies,

accumulated to provide security and preserve the peace, carried the nations to war by their own weight.[73]

The perceptions of statesmen and generals are crucial.[74] William Fulbright noted:

> The more I puzzle over the great wars of history, the more I am inclined to the view that the causes attributed to them – territory, markets, resources, the defense or perpetuation of great principles – were not the root causes at all but rather explanations or excuses for certain unfathomable drives of human nature.[75]

He reasoned that if the source of war and peace is human nature, then the study of politics and international relations must be grounded in the study of man and his needs and fears, which is the domain of psychology. He observed:

> We know so very much more about things than we do about people, so very much more about the workings of jet planes and nuclear missiles than about our own inner needs. We are exploring the mysteries of outer space while we remain puzzled and ignorant about the mysteries of our own minds.[76]

One of the unfathomable drives of human nature is aggression.

Aggression

Man has a long history of aggression. Homer described savage warfare believed to have taken place in the twelfth century BC. Konrad Lorenz believed aggression to be innate to human beings.[77] Aggression, he posited, is an evolutionarily developed impulse that serves the survival of the individual and the species. Lorenz studied animal behavior, and observed that in the face of danger, defensive aggression kicks in.[78] Drawing a link between animal and human behavior, Lorenz argued that all human aggression is biologically driven, even the passion to kill and torture. War, crime, quarrels and all kinds of violent behavior are due to an inborn instinct waiting to discharge. Others, like Robert Ardrey and Desmond Morris, shared similar views.[79]

Thomas Hobbes concluded that humankind is condemned to violence, and the only answer to this nightmare experience is a government to keep people from killing each other.[80] Freud agreed that civilization keeps aggression in check. To be civilized, human beings must curb their two most basic instincts – sex and violence. But subordinating one's desires to the power of the community leaves the individual feeling dissatisfied (*unbehaglich*).[81] Civilization is an unresolved struggle. Does this tension explain our record of peace punctuated by war?

Erich Fromm distinguished between "benign aggression" (defensive reaction) and "malignant aggression" (the human propensity to destroy and crave absolute control).[82] Crucially, he argued that only the former is biologically conditioned, and that the latter is present only in humans and not in animals. Cain and Abel was premeditated murder, not a defensive reflex. Wanton aggression, cruelty, egotism and deceit are unseen anywhere in the animal kingdom. Indeed, there would be fewer, if any, wars if human beings were more like animals. Fromm also drew a line between character and instinct.[83] Whereas instincts are biologically determined, character, the human substitute for animal instincts, is formed through experience. Human beings have the capacity to choose their actions, and are therefore morally accountable.

Emotion

International relations theory underestimates the power of emotions.[84] Many argue that cognition, not emotion, is the main determinant of behavior but research now shows that rational decision-making is, in fact, dependent on prior emotional processing.[85] Jonathan Mercer established that emotion helps to shape behavior in systematic ways, just as cognition can.[86] Anger has been found to lead to aggression while contempt prompts dehumanization of others, and can motivate murder and massacre.[87] Anxiety heightens perceptions of threat.[88] Guilt, shame, sympathy, pity, envy, and jealousy too can affect political behavior. Eastern cultures are shame-based and focus on what other people will think, while Western cultures are guilt-based and focus on how the individual will feel about himself. Humiliation, another powerful emotion, produces a desire for revenge.[89] Foreign policy can stoke hate and mistrust by encouraging racism, prejudice and stereotyping.[90] Mercer showed that trust is as much an emotional as a cognitive process and should be treated as such in international relations theory.[91]

State actor

International relations theory treats states as unitary actors, but how do states behave? Psychologist Charles Osgood drew insights about the behavior of nations from principles of individual behavior.[92] His method of *Graduated Reciprocation in Tension-reduction* (GRIT) sought to build trust between hostile states through small reciprocal steps. The state is not an abstract entity but consists of people. The US government employs 22 million people[93] but it is the governing elite that matters.[94] Franz Oppenheimer defined the state as "an organization of one class dominating over the other classes."[95] The populace is not unimportant but its perceptions can be manipulated by its leaders.[96] They can frame issues to produce anxiety in the minds of citizens, and cultivate stereotypes to foster certain behaviors and attitudes.[97] Trust between states consists ultimately in trust between power elites.

In recalling the Cuban Missile Crisis, Robert Kennedy wrote: "The fourteen people involved were very significant ... If six of them had been President of the US, I think the world might have been blown up."[98] The fourteen men were the Executive Committee of the National Security Council – John Kennedy's inner circle of decision-makers. George W. Bush's inner circle was even smaller, as he often deferred to Donald Rumsfeld and Dick Cheney.[99] Trust between states rests eventually on a handful of core decision-makers, who tend over time to emphasize cohesion, solidarity and loyalty, resulting in groupthink.[100] Political and corporate leaders play the most important role in shaping state behavior.[101] Ralph Waldo Emerson judged that "an institution is the lengthened shadow of one man."[102] Richard Neustadt stressed the importance of the personal characteristics of the president in determining policies.[103] John Kennedy's empathy for Khrushchev determined the outcome of the Cuban Missile Crisis just as Ronald Reagan's distrust of Soviet leaders accelerated the arms race.[104] Despite the complexity of the state, trust between states boils down to trust between leaders.[105] They trust depending on what they know, how they feel and what they perceive.[106]

Empathy between states

The US and the Soviet Union came within hair's breadth of nuclear war but the crisis was defused thanks to Llewellyn Thompson's reading of Khrushchev's messages to Kennedy. Thompson had lived for a period with the Khrushchevs, and understood the Soviet leader.[107] Perception is crucial.[108] Leaders tend to suffer from distortions in their self-image and see themselves as honorable and virtuous and the enemy as diabolical ("I am cooperative but you are greedy").[109] On the brink of war, they expect the worst from their adversaries. They see their options as limited by necessity or "fate," whereas the adversary enjoys many choices. What we see is often determined by what we expect to see. Expectations and presuppositions color our vision. If A expects B to be hostile, A may treat B in such a way that B fulfills A's expectations, which sets in motion a vicious cycle.[110] Indeed, empathy was Robert McNamara's key lesson from Vietnam.[111] The Chinese practiced empathy as statecraft as early as the fifth century BC. Mozi (470–391 BC) taught inclusive care (*jian ai*, 兼爱) and rejected aggression between individuals, families and countries.[112] To achieve social order, people must show as much concern for others' families and communities as their own. Military aggression is considered wrong for the same reason that murder and robbery are: it pursues selfish gain at others' expense. The Mohists formulated China's first explicit moral and political theories, and became an influential philosophical, social and religious movement.

HISE framework

Surprisingly little has been written about trust in international relations.[113] IR theorists see the world as an anarchy of states prone to conflict.[114] In the wake of the First World War, IR thinkers emphasized the role of morality, but mainstream writers since E. H. Carr (1892–1982) have rejected the idea that ethics belong in the international arena.[115] This was not surprising in the turbulent 1930s and in the aftermath of the Second World War. During the Cold War, the IR discipline became dominated by American scholars, which led to certain types of questions being asked and certain kinds of answers being provided.[116] Realism established itself as the dominant theory, and deeply influenced policymakers. It provided a language and set of policies for operating in a world of its own making. It framed the Soviet Union as a dangerous threat, and realists failed to see that the theory which supposedly explained state behavior was in fact producing that very behavior. It was self-fulfilling.[117] Nearly half a century of geopolitical tension was not explained by realism but was the *product* of realist thinking about international politics.[118] Alexander Wendt held that state behavior depends on whether nations see each other as enemies, rivals or friends.[119] Even anarchy is socially constructed – it is what states make of it.[120] Because world views can change, nations are not condemned to war and conflict. This suggests that trust has a part to play.

Drawing from the foregoing discussion of trust, human nature and international relations, this thesis will analyze trust between states along four dimensions. First, the history of their relations: Integrity builds trust; betrayal destroys it (cf. Yamagishi's "social intelligence"). History shows the character of a state and its leaders. Second, their vested interests: States whose interests are compatible are more likely to trust each other (cf. Hardin's "encapsulated interest"). Third, the nature of structures such as institutions, treaties and alliances: Structures derive from vested interests, and the more in mutual harmony their structures, the more likely they are to trust each other (cf. Wendt's constructivism). Finally, their mutual empathy: the deeper the understanding and goodwill, the stronger the trust (cf. Mencius and Aristotle). None of the factors are static. History, Interests, Structures and Empathy influence each other and evolve over time.[121]

History (H)

When it comes to trust, history matters. Trust is based on knowledge – knowledge of the other's trustworthiness and reliability.[122] Because trust is both cognitive and relational, history is a pivotal factor in trust between states. Aggression and betrayal breed distrust and suspicion; mutual respect and assistance build trust. Surrounded by powerful neighbors, Poland bore the brunt of conflict in power struggles between Sweden, Prussia, Austria and Russia. Since the seventeenth century, the Polish state has been thrice partitioned, most recently carved up by Hitler and Stalin.[123] Millions of Poles died in German and Soviet concentration camps. The atrocities of Auschwitz, Treblinka, Dachau and Katyn left deep scars and a profound sense of humiliation. Although relations with Germany have steadily improved since the 1990s, many ordinary Poles remain ambivalent about Germans, and despite (or because of) forty-five years in the Warsaw Pact, distrust or loathe the Russians. With the exception of a brief low-level armed confrontation between Malaysia and Indonesia (1963–1966), the countries of Southeast Asia have known little interstate conflict in the modern era (except against European, American and Japanese imperialist powers). The history of good-will, political scientist Charles Kupchan believes, explains the success of ASEAN, the ten-member Association of Southeast Asian Nations, as a regional bloc consisting of 600 million people (more populous than the twenty-eight-nation European Union).[124] The United States of America emerged as a nation from an eight-year war of independence (1775–1783) against Britain but later came to the latter's aid in two devastating world wars, forging strong bonds of trust between the two states. Britain has since proven a stalwart supporter of the US, with both sides working hand-in-glove on a wide range of matters.[125]

Interests (I)

National interests often stem directly from the ambitions of society's privi-leged class, be it made up of feudal aristocrats or modern industrialists. Vested interests such as the military–industrial complex, Big Oil and Wall Street exercise powerful influence over the state to adopt policies favoring their gain and reject those that threaten their profit. Even in liberal democ-racies practicing one person one vote, the concerns of the rich frequently outweigh those of the poor. Strategic interests involve national security but are often little more than veiled business interests. The British East India Company, chartered in 1600 by the English crown for commerce, soon became the very impetus and instrument of British colonial expansion into Asia. A similar tale can be told of US involvement in Latin America.[126] Rivalry between the vested interests of one polity and another undermines trust. Where conflicts of interest arise, trust suffers, as Russell Hardin's "encapsulated interest" model implies.[127]

Structures (S)

There is a symbiotic link between vested interests and power structures. One proceeds from the other, and the two are often synonymous. Sociologist Michael Mann identifies four sources of social power, namely, ideological, economic, military and political power.[128] These sources of power take the form of networks, organizations and structures. Ideology can come from the church or the mosque but also from universities and think tanks, with the mass media playing a crucial supporting role. Economic power resides in businesses. With financial muscle, big business can steer the other branches of power. Military power represents the capacity for physical defense and aggression. It mobilizes violence and is the bluntest instrument of human power. Political power lies with the state, which is vested with broad authority to regulate and coerce. These national structures in turn shape global struc-tures such as treaties, institutions, supply chains and the worldwide division of labor. Bretton Woods and the institutions that emerged therefrom defined the postwar world order. To Mann's four sources of power may be added a fifth, namely technology, which can cast the balance of military, economic, political and even ideological power.

Empathy (E)

Empathy begets trust. Empathy is the act of putting oneself in the other person's shoes. It can be motivated by compassion but even by the mere need to correctly gauge the other person, for as the Chinese aphorism declares: "Know thyself *and* thy neighbor, and thou shalt prevail."[129] We are more apt to trust those who show they understand us, especially when it is demonstrated through deeds. Similarly, we can win trust by showing empathy. Kupchan argues that enemies start to become friends when one side makes unilateral concessions to befriend an adversary.[130] The concessions signal benign instead of hostile intent. This is followed by reciprocal restraint, with both sides trading concessions and stepping away from rivalry. Geopolitical competition soon gives way to programmatic cooperation. Examples he cited of this process of reconciliation include the fifteenth-century Iroquois Confederation of five American Indian tribes following years of debilitating warfare, and the Concert of Europe which emerged from the Congress of Vienna marking the close of the Napoleonic Wars (1803–1815).[131] Unilateral accommodation at the outset is usually prompted by a state's lack of resources to deal with existing threats. In other words, it accommodates out of need and exhaustion. But there is no reason why states cannot make concessions out of strength and empathy. Empathy conveys respect and can heal. Indeed, it has the power to turn enemies into friends.

Linkages

History, Interests, Structures and Empathy are neither static nor independent. They affect one another and their interrelationship can be best illustrated with a case. China, Taiwan and Japan form an East Asian geopolitical triangle (of which more will be said in Chapter 5). During the first half of the twentieth century, the Chinese communists, the US-backed Kuomintang (KMT) and the Japanese army battled for control of China. After Japan's surrender in 1945, the communists and the Kuomintang fought on. Four years later, the Kuomintang lost and fled to Taiwan. In 1949 the communists established the People's Republic of China (PRC) with its seat of government in Beijing. The Kuomintang under Chiang Kai-shek set up the rival Republic of China (ROC) government in Taipei. Japan meanwhile quickly became an important strategic ally of the US, serving as a forward base for the wars in Korea and Vietnam. Chiang vowed to retake the mainland, and Tokyo did not establish diplomatic ties with Beijing. History, interests and structures drew sharp divisions across East Asia, and the Cold War further dampened the prospects for mutual trust and goodwill.

But the ideological, economic, military and political power structures gradually shifted. Ideological change came first when in 1978 the Chinese Communist Party (CCP) renounced class struggle and took up economic development as its central focus.[132] Economic change followed as China's economy took off, thanks in no small measure to the infusion of capital and know-how from Taiwan. Political change followed in 1986 when President Chiang Ching-kuo of Taiwan scrapped martial law, instituted multi-party elections and lifted the travel ban to the mainland. Bilateral trade and investments skyrocketed and China has since become Taiwan's largest trading partner. With increased contact, empathy and trust have grown. While many support Taiwanese independence, the narrowing gap in living standards and civil liberties between the two sides has made reunification, once unimaginable, less improbable.

Sino–Japanese trust, on the other hand, is more complicated. History is a major factor. Japan's invasion of China and the atrocities committed by the Imperial Japanese Army are an abiding sore in East Asian relations. Japan's denial of its wartime aggression alarms the Chinese and also the Koreans, who suffered harsh and humiliating Japanese rule (1910–1945). But evolving economic interests and structures favor closer ties. Bilateral trade and investments are robust and there is enormous potential for empathy and friendship between the two neighbors. Japan is a popular destination for Chinese tourists and students. Major retail outlets hire Chinese-speaking store attendants to cater to the growing number of Chinese shoppers, while the country's universities attract more Chinese students than the UK. There is broad cultural affinity (the Japanese language is heavily influenced by Chinese) and Chinese figures like Lu Xun, Sun Yat-sen, Wang Jingwei and Zhou Enlai lived for extended periods in Japan. Political and military structures, however, stand in the way. Right-wing politics and Japan's military alliance with the US work against trust. Territorial disputes in the East China Sea pour cold water on business and threaten to spiral out of control.[133]

This book uses the HISE framework to study US–China relations in order to draw insights about trust between states. The United States is the world hegemon. China is a rising star, and some fear it may one day challenge America.[134] Power transition theorists predict conflict whenever an emerging rival challenges a hegemon. Deep mistrust bedevils US–China relations.[135] Divided into two halves, each chapter discusses the view from one side and then the other, followed by a conclusion linking the two perspectives back to the central question of trust. This study seeks to report Chinese and US perceptions of each other rather than adjudicate between them. Trust, however, relates ultimately to notions of ethics, and statements about the character of events may be unavoidable.

Notes

1   Remarks by Andrew Gamble at the 2013 CELP conference in Cambridge.
2   Howard Zinn, *A People's History of the United States: From 1492 to the Present*, 2nd ed. (London: Longman, 1996), 1.
3   Ibid.
4   Bartolomé de las Casas, *A Short Account of the Destruction of the Indies*, ed. Nigel Griffin, Penguin Classics (London: Penguin Books, 1992); Bartolomé de las Casas, *Historia de Las Indias*, ed. Lewis Hanke, Biblioteca Americana. Serie de Cronistas de Indias 15–17 (Mexico: Fondo de Cultura Económica, 1951).
5   Zinn, *A People's History of the United States*, 3.
6   Eric M. Uslaner, *The Moral Foundations of Trust* (Cambridge: Cambridge University Press, 2002).
7   Karen Jones, "Trust as an Affective Attitude," *Ethics* 107, no. 1 (1996): 4–25; Jessica Miller, "Trust: The Moral Importance of an Emotional Attitude," *Practical Philosophy* 3, no. 3 (2000): 38–49.
8   Russell Hardin, "Concepts and Explanations of Trust," in *Trust in Society* (New York: Russell Sage Foundation, 2001), 3–39.
9   I. Bohnet and R. Zeckhauser, "Trust, Risk and Betrayal," *Journal of Economic Behavior and Organization* 55, no. 4 (2004): 467–84.
10   Piotr Sztompka, *Trust: A Sociological Theory* (Cambridge: Cambridge University Press, 2000).
11   Ibid.
12   Robert Cummins, *Representations, Targets and Attitudes* (Cambridge, MA: MIT Press, 1996).
13   R. Kurzban, "Biological Foundations of Reciprocity," *Trust and Reciprocity: Interdisciplinary Lessons from Experimental Research* (New York: Russell Sage Foundation, 2003), 105–27.
14   Michael Kosfeld, M. Heinrichs, P. J. Zak, U. Fischbacher and E. Fehr, "Oxytocin Increases Trust in Humans," *Nature* 435, no. 7042 (June 2, 2005): 673–76, doi: 10.1038/nature03701.
15   Russell Hardin, *Trust*, Key Concepts in the Social Sciences (Cambridge, MA: Polity Press, 2006), 17.
16   J. Delhey and K. Newton, "Predicting Cross-National Levels of Social Trust: Global Pattern or Nordic Exceptionalism?," *European Sociological Review* 21, no. 4 (2005): 311–27.
17   Cardinal Kurt Koch, "Trust as the Basic Attitude in a Culture of Humanity" (Speech, Woolf Institute, Cambridge, February 26, 2013).
18   Henry Hexmoor, Cristiano Castelfranchi, and Rino Falcone, *Agent Autonomy* (Berlin: Springer, 2003).
19   Hardin, "Concepts and Explanations of Trust."
20   Hardin, *Trust*, 20.
21   Hardin, *Trust*, 17.
22   Margaret Levi and L. Stoker, "Political Trust and Trustworthiness," *Annual Review of Political Science* 3, no. 1 (2000): 475–507.
23   Toshio Yamagishi, "Trust as a Form of Social Intelligence," in Karen S. Cook (ed.) *Trust in Society* (New York: Russell Sage Foundation, 2001), 121–47.
24   Uslaner, *The Moral Foundations of Trust*.
25   Francis Fukuyama, *Trust: The Social Virtues and the Creation of Prosperity* (London: Hamish Hamilton, 1995), 153.
26   Eric M. Uslaner, "Civic Associations: Democratic Elixir or Democratic Illusion?," Paper presented to Joint Sessions of the European Consortium for Political Research. Turin, Italy, 2002.

27 Joyce Berg, John Dickhaut, and Kevin McCabe, "Trust, Reciprocity, and Social History," *Games and Economic Behavior* 10, no. 1 (July 1995): 122–42, doi: 10.1006/game.1995.1027.

28 Russell Hardin, "Gaming Trust," in *Trust and Reciprocity* (New York: Russell Sage Foundation, 2003), 80–101; Margaret Levi, "The Transformation of a Skeptic: What Non-Experimentalists Can Learn from Ex-Experimentalists," in *Trust and Reciprocity* (New York: Russell Sage Foundation, 2003), 373–80.

29 Peter Nannestad, "What Have We Learned about Generalized Trust, if Anything?," *Annual Review of Political Science* 11, no. 1 (2008): 422.

30 Delhey and Newton, "Predicting Cross-National Levels of Social Trust: Global Pattern or Nordic Exceptionalism?"; J. Delhey and K. Newton, "Who Trusts?: The Origins of Social Trust in Seven Societies," *European Societies* 5, no. 2 (2003): 93–137.

31 Delhey and Newton, "Predicting Cross-National Levels of Social Trust: Global Pattern or Nordic Exceptionalism?"

32 Robert D. Putnam, Robert Leonardi, and Raffaella Y. Nanetti, *Making Democracy Work: Civic Traditions in Modern Italy* (Princeton, NJ: Princeton University Press, 1993).

33 Robert D. Putnam, *Bowling Alone: The Collapse and Revival of American Community* (New York: Simon & Schuster, 2000).

34 Henry Farrell and J. Knight, "Trust, Institutions and Institutional Change," *Politics and Society* 4 (2003): 357–66; Margaret Levi, "State of Trust," in *Trust and Governance* (New York: Russell Sage Foundation, 1998), 77–101.

35 Margaret Levi, "Social and Unsocial Capital: A Review Essay of Robert Putnam's *Making Democracy Work*," *Politics and Society* 24, no. 1 (1996): 45–55.

36 J. Knight, "Social Norms and the Rule of Law: Fostering Trust in a Socially Diverse Society," *Trust in Society* 2 (2001): 354–73.

37 Piotr Sztompka, "Trust, Distrust and Two Paradoxes of Democracy," *European Journal of Social Theory* 1, no. 1 (1998): 19–32.

38 Eric M. Uslaner, "Trust as a Moral Value," in D. Castiglione, J. van Deth, and G. Wolleb, eds, *The Handbook of Social Capital* (New York: Routledge, 2008), 101–121.

39 Delhey and Newton, "Predicting Cross-National Levels of Social Trust: Global Pattern or Nordic Exceptionalism?"

40 D. Bahry, M. Kosolapov, P. Kozyreva, and R. K. Wilson, "Ethnicity and Trust: Evidence from Russia," *American Political Science Review* 99, no. 4 (2005): 521–32.

41 P. Nannestad, G. L. H. Svendsen, and G. T. Svendsen, "Bridge over Troubled Water? Migration and Social Capital," *Journal of Ethnic and Migration Studies* 34, no. 4 (2008): 607–31.

42 A. Alesina and E. La Ferrara, "Who Trusts Others?," *Journal of Public Economics* 85, no. 2 (2002): 207–34; Dietland Stolle, S. Soroka, and R. Johnston, "How Diversity Affects Attitudinal Social Capital. A US–Canada Comparison," Paper presented at the Workshop for Preliminary Presentations of Findings from the Citizenship, Involvement, Democracy (CID) survey project, Georgetown University, December 12, 2005; Robert D. Putnam, "*E Pluribus Unum*: Diversity and Community in the Twenty-First Century." The 2006 Johan Skytte Prize Lecture. *Scandinavian Political Studies* 30, no. 2 (2007): 137–74.

43 Stolle *et al.*, "How Diversity Affects Attitudinal Social Capital. A US–Canada Comparison."

44 Alesina and La Ferrara, "Who Trusts Others?"

45 Richard Wilkinson and Kate Pickett, *The Spirit Level: Why More Equal Societies Almost Always Do Better* (London: Penguin, 2010).

46   East-West Philosophers' Conference, "The Chinese Mind: Essentials of Chinese Philosophy and Culture" (Honolulu, HI: East-West Center Press, 1967), 3.

47   A proverb of Confucius.

48   Arthur Waley, trans., *The Way and Its Power: A Study of the Tao Te Ching and Its Place in Chinese Thought* (New York: Grove Press/Atlantic Monthly Press, 1994).

49   陈荣捷 Chan Wing-Tsit, "Chinese Theory and Practice, with Special Reference to Humanism," in *The Chinese Mind: Essentials of Chinese Philosophy and Culture* (Honolulu, HI: East-West Center Press, 1967), 13–14.

50   East-West Philosophers' Conference, "The Chinese Mind: Essentials of Chinese Philosophy and Culture," 5.

51   Angus C. Graham, "The Place of Reason in the Chinese Philosophical Tradition," in *The Legacy of China* (Oxford: Clarendon Press, 1964), 28.

52   Chan Wing-Tsit, "Chinese Theory and Practice, with Special Reference to Humanism," 14.

53   刘殿爵 D. C. Lau, trans., *Mencius* 孟子, Penguin Classics (Harmondsworth: Penguin, 1970), 15.

54   *New Oxford American Dictionary.*

55   今人乍见孺子将入于井⊠皆有怵惕恻隐之心.

56   D. C. Lau, *Mencius* 孟子, 18.

57   Adam Smith, *The Theory of Moral Sentiments* (London: Penguin Classics, 2010).

58   信广来 Shun Kwong-loi, "Mencius," in *The Stanford Encyclopedia of Philosophy*, ed. Edward N. Zalta, 2010, http://plato.stanford.edu/archives/win2010/entries/mencius/.

59   Aristotle, *The Ethics of Aristotle: The Nicomachean Ethics*, trans. J. A. K. (James Alexander Kerr) Thomson, revised edn with notes and appendices by Hugh Tredennick. Penguin Classics (Harmondsworth and New York: Penguin, 1976), 1155a.

60   *Nicomachean Ethics* 30.

61   Jonathan Haidt, *The Happiness Hypothesis: Putting Ancient Wisdom to the Test of Modern Science* (London: William Heinemann, 2006).

62   Richard Kraut, "Aristotle's Ethics," in *The Stanford Encyclopedia of Philosophy*, ed. Edward N. Zalta, Winter 2012, http://plato.stanford.edu/archives/win2012/entries/aristotle-ethics/.

63   Aristotle, *The Nicomachean Ethics*, ed. Lesley Brown, trans. David Ross, revised ed. (Oxford: Oxford University Press, 2009).

64   Smith, *The Theory of Moral Sentiments.*

65   Charles Darwin, *The Descent of Man and Selection in Relation to Sex*, The Essential Darwin (London: Folio Society, 1990).

66   Jeremy Rifkin, *The Empathic Civilization: The Race to Global Consciousness in a World in Crisis* (Cambridge: Polity Press, 2010), 9.

67   John Bowlby, *Maternal Care and Mental Health* (Geneva: World Health Organization, 1951).

68   E. H. Erikson, *Childhood and Society*, new edn. (New York: Vintage, 1995).

69   John Bowlby, *Loss, Sadness and Depression*, vol. 3 of *Attachment and Loss* (New York: Basic Books, 1980), 442.

70   Bruce Bueno de Mesquita, *Principles of International Politics* (Washington, DC: CQ Press, 2013).

71   Graham Allison and Philip Zelikow, *Essence of Decision: Explaining the Cuban Missile Crisis*, 2nd edn. (New York: Longman, 1999).

72   Non-rational behavior is not the same as irrational behavior, which suggests a lack of touch with reality.

73 A. J. P. Taylor, *The First World War: An Illustrated History*. (London: Hamish Hamilton, 1963), 13.
74 John George Stoessinger, *Why Nations Go to War*, 8th edn. (Boston, MA: Bedford/ St. Martin's Press, 2001).
75 J. William Fulbright, *The Arrogance of Power*, Pelican Books (Harmondsworth: Penguin, 1970), 17.
76 Ibid., 17.
77 Konrad Lorenz, *On Aggression*, 2nd edn. (London: Routledge, 2002).
78 Konrad Lorenz, *King Solomon's Ring: New Light on Animal Ways*, trans. Marjorie Kerr Wilson (London: Methuen, 1952).
79 Robert Ardrey, *African Genesis*, reprint (London: Readers Union, 1963); Desmond Morris, *The Naked Ape Trilogy* (London: Cape, 1994).
80 Thomas Hobbes, *Leviathan*, ed. J. C. A. Gaskin, reissue, Oxford Paperbacks (Oxford: Oxford University Press, 2008).
81 Sigmund Freud, *Civilization and Its Discontents*, ed. James Strachey, trans. Joan Riviere (London: Hogarth Press and the Institute of Psychoanalysis, 1963), Ch. 3; Herbert Marcuse, *Eros and Civilization: A Philosophical Inquiry into Freud*, (London: Sphere, 1969), Ch. 4.
82 Erich Fromm, *The Anatomy of Human Destructiveness*, Penguin 1982 (Singapore: Penguin, 1973), 2.
83 Ibid., 305.
84 Ole R. Holsti, "Crisis Decision Making," *Behavior, Society, and Nuclear War* 1 (1989): 8–84.
85 Rose McDermott, *Political Psychology in International Relations*, Analytical Perspectives on Politics (Ann Arbor: University of Michigan Press, 2004), 153.
86 Jonathan Mercer and Barry O'Neill, "Emotion and International Politics: Trust in Identity," Paper presented to the American Political Science Association Conference, San Francisco, CA, 2001.
87 Carroll E. Izard, *Human Emotions* (Berlin and New York: Springer, 1977).
88 Dan Cassino and Milton Lodge, "The Primacy of Affect in Political Evaluations," in George E. Marcus, W. Russell Neuman, Michael MacKuen, and Ann N. Crigler, eds., *The Affect Effect: Dynamics of Emotion in Political Thinking and Behavior* (Chicago, IL: University of Chicago Press, 2007), 101–23.
89 James Gilligan, *Violence: Reflections on a National Epidemic* (New York: Vintage Books, 1997).
90 Jonathan Mercer, "Approaching Emotion in International Politics," Paper presented to the International Studies Association Conference, San Diego, California, vol. 25, 1996, 1.
91 Mercer and O'Neill, "Emotion and International Politics: Trust in Identity."
92 Charles E. Osgood, *An Alternative to War or Surrender* (Urbana: University of Illinois Press, 1962).
93 Mike Patton, "The Growth Of Government: 1980 To 2012," *Forbes*, January 24, 2013, www.forbes.com/sites/mikepatton/2013/01/24/the-growth-of-the-federal-gov ernment-1980-to-2012/.
94 Allison and Zelikow, *Essence of Decision*.
95 Franz Oppenheimer, *The State: Its History and Development Viewed Sociologically*, trans. John M. Gitterman (London: George Allen & Unwin, 1923).
96 Edward L. Bernays, *Propaganda* (Port Washington, NY: Kennikat Press, 1928); Adam Curtis, *Century of Self* (BBC, 2002).
97 Martha L. Cottam, *Introduction to Political Psychology*, 2nd edn. (New York and Hove: Psychology Press, 2010), 163.
98 Robert F. Kennedy, *Thirteen Days: A Memoir of the Cuban Missile Crisis*, 1st edn. (New York: W. W. Norton, 1969).

99   Frank Bruni, *Ambling into History: The Unlikely Odyssey of George W. Bush* (New York: HarperCollins, 2003), 28; Zakaria Fareed, "Colin Powell's Humiliation: Bush Should Clearly Support His Secretary of State – Otherwise He Should Get a New One," *Newsweek Magazine*, April 29, 2002.

100 Irving L. Janis, *Groupthink: Psychological Studies of Policy Decisions and Fiascoes* (Boston, MA: Houghton Mifflin, 1982); Irving L. Janis, *Victims of Groupthink* (Boston, MA: Houghton, Mifflin, 1972).

101 Jerrold M. Post, "Saddam Hussein of Iraq: A Political Psychology Profile," *Political Psychology* 12, no. 2 (1991): 279–89; Raymond Birt, "Personality and Foreign Policy: The Case of Stalin," *Political Psychology*, 1993, 607–25; Colin Campbell and Bert A. Rockman, *The Clinton Presidency: First Appraisals* (Cambridge: Cambridge University Press, 1996); Stoessinger, *Why Nations Go to War*.

102 Ralph Waldo Emerson, *The Essays of Ralph Waldo Emerson*, ed. Edward F. O'Day (San Francisco, CA: J. H. Nash for the Limited Editions Club, 1974).

103 Richard E. Neustadt, *Presidential Power and the Modern Presidents: The Politics of Leadership from Roosevelt to Reagan*, revised edition (New York: The Free Press, 1991).

104 Thomas Preston, *The President and His Inner Circle: Leadership Style and the Advisory Process in Foreign Affairs* (New York: Columbia University Press, 2001); Allison and Zelikow, *Essence of Decision*.

105 Cottam, *Introduction to Political Psychology*, 293.

106 Robert Jervis, *Perception and Misperception in International Politics* (Princeton, NJ: Princeton University Press, 1976).

107 Errol Morris, *The Fog Of War: Eleven Lessons from the Life of Robert McNamara*, DVD (Sony Pictures Home Entertainment, 2004).

108 Stoessinger, *Why Nations Go to War*.

109 Robert Gifford and Donald W. Hine, "'I'm Cooperative, But You're Greedy': Some Cognitive Tendencies in a Commons Dilemma," *Canadian Journal of Behavioural Science* 29, no. 4 (1997): 257–65.

110 Kathleen A Kennedy and Emily Pronin, "When Disagreement Gets Ugly: Perceptions of Bias and the Escalation of Conflict," *Personality and Social Psychology Bulletin* 34, no. 6 (2008): 833–48.

111 Robert S. McNamara and James G. Blight, *Wilson's Ghost: Reducing the Risk of Conflict, Killing, and Catastrophe in the 21st Century* (New York: Public Affairs, 2001).

112 Chris Fraser, "Mohism," in *The Stanford Encyclopedia of Philosophy*, ed. Edward N. Zalta, Fall 2012, http://plato.stanford.edu/archives/fall2012/entries/mohism/.

113 D. E. Stokes, "Party Loyalty and the Likelihood of Deviating Elections," *The Journal of Politics* 24, no. 4 (1962): 689–702; G. A. Almond and S. Verba, *The Civic Culture: Political Attitudes and Democracy in Five Nations* (Boston, MA: Little, Brown, 1963).

114 Anarchy means a society without government and individuals enjoy complete freedom of action. Many IR theorists see the world as an anarchic society where states enjoy freedom of action.

115 Ken Booth, Timothy Dunne, and Michael Cox, eds., *How Might We Live? Global Ethics in a New Century* (Cambridge: Cambridge University Press, 2001), 5.

116 Timothy Dunne, Michael Cox, and Ken Booth, eds., *The Eighty Years' Crisis: International Relations 1919–1999* (Cambridge: Cambridge University Press, 1998), xvi.

117 Kennedy and Pronin, "When Disagreement Gets Ugly: Perceptions of Bias and the Escalation of Conflict."

118   Booth et al., *How Might We Live?*, 5.
119   Alexander Wendt, *Social Theory of International Politics*, Cambridge Studies in International Relations (Cambridge: Cambridge University Press, 1999); Maja Zehfuss, *Constructivism in International Relations: The Politics of Reality*, Cambridge Studies in International Relations (Cambridge: Cambridge University Press, 2002).
120   Alexander Wendt, "Anarchy Is What States Make of It: The Social Construction of Power Politics," *International Organization* 46, no. 2 (1992): 391–425.
121   Wendt, *Social Theory of International Politics*.
122   Hardin, "Concepts and Explanations of Trust."
123   The Motolov–Ribbentrop Pact divided Poland between Germany and the Soviet Union in 1939. The German Army invaded on 1 September 1939 while the Soviet Army crossed into Poland on 17 September 1939.
124   Charles Kupchan, *How Enemies Become Friends: The Sources of Stable Peace*, Princeton Studies in International History and Politics (Princeton, NJ: Princeton University Press, 2010), ch. 5.
125   Nick Hopkins and Luke Harding, "GCHQ Accused of Selling Its Services after Revelations of Funding by NSA," *The Guardian*, August 2, 2013, www.theguardian.com/uk-news/2013/aug/02/gchq-accused-selling-services-nsa; James Ball, Julian Borger, and Glenn Greenwald, "Revealed: How US and UK Spy Agencies Defeat Internet Privacy and Security," *Guardian*, September 5, 2013, www.theguardian.com/world/2013/sep/05/nsa-gchq-encryption-codes-security.
126   Stephen C. Schlesinger and Stephen Kinzer, *Bitter Fruit: The Untold Story of the American Coup in Guatemala*, reprint (New York: Anchor Books, 1990).
127   Hardin, *Trust*.
128   Michael Mann, *The Sources of Social Power* (Cambridge: Cambridge University Press, 1986), 22–30.
129   知己知彼︎百战百胜
130   Kupchan, *How Enemies Become Friends*, 6.
131   Ibid., 1.
132   Guangyuan Yu, Stevine I. Levine, and Ezra F. Vogel, *Deng Xiaoping Shakes the World: An Eyewitness Account of China's Party Work Conference and the Third Plenum (November–December 1978)* (New York: EastBridge, 2004).
133   Allison Jackson, "Island Dispute Disrupts Sino-Japanese Trade," *The Financialist*, January 30, 2013, www.thefinancialist.com/territorial-dispute-disrupts-sino-japanese-trade/.
134   Chas Freeman, "China's Challenge to American Hegemony," January 20, 2012, www.mepc.org/articles-commentary/speeches/chinas-challenge-american-hegemony.
135   Minxin Pei, "The U.S.-China Reset,"*New York Times*, November 13, 2012, Opinion, www.nytimes.com/2012/11/14/opinion/the-us-china-reset.html.

Bibliography

Alesina, A., and E. La Ferrara. "Who Trusts Others?" *Journal of Public Economics* 85, no. 2(2002): 207–234.
Allison, Graham, and Philip Zelikow. *Essence of Decision: Explaining the Cuban Missile Crisis*. 2nd edn. New York: Longman, 1999.
Almond, G. A., and S. Verba. *The Civic Culture: Political Attitudes and Democracy in Five Nations*. Boston, MA: Little, Brown and Company, 1963.
Ardrey, Robert. *African Genesis*. Reprint. London: Readers Union, 1963.

Aristotle. *The Ethics of Aristotle: The Nicomachean Ethics.* Translated by J. A. K. (James Alexander Kerr) Thomson. Revised edn. Revised with notes and appendices by Hugh Tredennick. Penguin Classics. Harmondsworth and New York: Penguin, 1976.

Aristotle. *The Nicomachean Ethics.* Edited by Lesley Brown. Translated by David Ross. Revised edn. Oxford: Oxford University Press, 2009.

Bahry, D., M. Kosolapov, P. Kozyreva, and R. K. Wilson. "Ethnicity and Trust: Evidence from Russia." *American Political Science Review* 99, no. 4(2005): 521–532.

Ball, James, Julian Borger, and Glenn Greenwald. "Revealed: How US and UK Spy Agencies Defeat Internet Privacy and Security." *The Guardian*, September 5, 2013. www.theguardian.com/world/2013/sep/05/nsa-gchq-encryption-codes-security.

Berg, Joyce, John Dickhaut, and Kevin McCabe. "Trust, Reciprocity, and Social History." *Games and Economic Behavior* 10, no. 1(July 1995): 122–142. doi:10.1006/game.1995.1027.

Bernays, Edward L. *Propaganda.* Port Washington, NY: Kennikat Press, 1928.

Birt, Raymond. "Personality and Foreign Policy: The Case of Stalin." *Political Psychology*, 1993, 607–625.

Bohnet, I., and R. Zeckhauser. "Trust, Risk and Betrayal." *Journal of Economic Behavior and Organization* 55, no. 4(2004): 467–484.

Booth, Ken, Timothy Dunne, and Michael Cox, eds, *How Might We Live?: Global Ethics in a New Century.* Cambridge: Cambridge University Press, 2001.

Bowlby, John. *Loss, Sadness and Depression, Vol. 3 of Attachment and Loss.* New York: Basic Books, 1980.

Bowlby, John. *Maternal Care and Mental Health.* Geneva: World Health Organization, 1951.

Bruni, Frank. *Ambling into History: The Unlikely Odyssey of George W. Bush.* 1st Perennial. New York: HarperCollins, 2003.

Bueno de Mesquita, Bruce. *Principles of International Politics.* Washington, DC: CQ Press, 2013.

Campbell, Colin, and Bert A. Rockman. *The Clinton Presidency: First Appraisals.* Cambridge: Cambridge University Press, 1996.

Cassino, Dan, and Milton Lodge. "The Primacy of Affect in Political Evaluations," in George E. Marcus, W. Russell Neuman, Michael MacKuen, and Ann N. Crigler, eds, *The Affect Effect: Dynamics of Emotion in Political Thinking and Behavior*, 101–123. Chicago, IL: University of Chicago Press, 2007.

Chan Wing-Tsit, 陈荣捷. "Chinese Theory and Practice, with Special Reference to Humanism." In *The Chinese Mind: Essentials of Chinese Philosophy and Culture*, 11–30. Honolulu, HI: East-West Center Press, 1967.

Cottam, Martha L. *Introduction to Political Psychology.* 2nd edn. New York and Hove: Psychology Press, 2010.

Cummins, Robert. *Representations, Targets and Attitudes.* Cambridge, MA: MIT Press, 1996.

Curtis, Adam.*Century of Self.* BBC, 2002.

Darwin, Charles. *The Descent of Man and Selection in Relation to Sex.* The Essential Darwin. London: Folio Society, 1990.

D. C. Lau, 刘殿爵, trans. *Mencius* 孟子. Penguin Classics. Harmondsworth: Penguin, 1970.

De las Casas, Bartolomé. *A Short Account of the Destruction of the Indies.* Edited by Nigel Griffin. Penguin Classics. London: Penguin Books, 1992.

De las Casas, Bartolomé. *Historia de Las Indias.* Edited by Lewis Hanke. Biblioteca Americana. Serie de Cronistas de Indias, 15–17. Mexico: Fondo de Cultura Económica, 1951.

Delhey, J., and K. Newton. "Predicting Cross-National Levels of Social Trust: Global Pattern or Nordic Exceptionalism?" *European Sociological Review* 21, no. 4(2005): 311–327.

Delhey, J., and K. Newton. "Who Trusts? The Origins of Social Trust in Seven Societies." *European Societies* 5, no. 2(2003): 93–137.

Dunne, Timothy, Michael Cox, and Ken Booth, eds, *The Eighty Years' Crisis: International Relations 1919–1999.* Cambridge: Cambridge University Press, 1998.

East-West Philosophers' Conference. *The Chinese Mind: Essentials of Chinese Philosophy and Culture.* Honolulu, HI: East-West Center Press, 1967.

Emerson, Ralph Waldo. *The Essays of Ralph Waldo Emerson.* Edited by Edward F. O'Day. San Francisco, CA: J. H. Nash for the Limited Editions Club, 1974.

Erikson, E. H. *Childhood and Society.* New edn. New York: Vintage, 1995.

Fareed, Zakaria. "Colin Powell's Humiliation: Bush Should Clearly Support His Secretary of State – Otherwise He Should Get a New One." *Newsweek Magazine,* April 29, 2002.

Farrell, Henry, and J. Knight. "Trust, Institutions and Institutional Change." *Politics and Society* 4(2003): 357–366.

Fraser, Chris. "Mohism." In *The Stanford Encyclopedia of Philosophy,* edited by Edward N. Zalta, Fall 2012. http://plato.stanford.edu/archives/fall2012/entries/mohism/.

Freeman, Chas. "China's Challenge to American Hegemony." January 20, 2012. www.mepc.org/articles-commentary/speeches/chinas-challenge-american-hegemony.

Freud, Sigmund. *Civilization and Its Discontents.* Edited by James Strachey. Translated by Joan Riviere. London: Hogarth Press and the Institute of Psychoanalysis, 1963.

Fromm, Erich. *The Anatomy of Human Destructiveness.* Penguin 1982. Singapore: Penguin, 1973.

Fukuyama, Francis. *Trust: The Social Virtues and the Creation of Prosperity.* London: Hamish Hamilton, 1995.

Fulbright, J. William. *The Arrogance of Power.* Pelican Books. Harmondsworth: Penguin, 1970.

Gifford, Robert, and Donald W. Hine. "'I'm Cooperative, But You're Greedy': Some Cognitive Tendencies in a Commons Dilemma." *Canadian Journal of Behavioural Science* 29, no. 4(1997): 257–265.

Gilligan, James. *Violence: Reflections on a National Epidemic.* New York: Vintage Books, 1997.

Graham, Angus C. "The Place of Reason in the Chinese Philosophical Tradition." In *The Legacy of China,* 28–56. Oxford: Clarendon Press, 1964.

Haidt, Jonathan. *The Happiness Hypothesis: Putting Ancient Wisdom to the Test of Modern Science.* London: William Heinemann, 2006.

Hardin, Russell. *Trust.* Key Concepts in the Social Sciences. Cambridge, MA: Polity Press, 2006.

Hardin, Russell. "Gaming Trust." In *Trust and Reciprocity,* 80–101. New York: Russell Sage Foundation, 2003.

Hardin, Russell. "Concepts and Explanations of Trust." In *Trust in Society,* 3–39. New York: Russell Sage Foundation, 2001.

Hexmoor, Henry, Cristiano Castelfranchi, and Rino Falcone. *Agent Autonomy*. Berlin/ New York: Springer, 2003.

Hobbes, Thomas. *Leviathan*. Edited by J. C. A. Gaskin. Reissue. Oxford Paperbacks. Oxford: Oxford University Press, 2008.

Holsti, Ole R. "Crisis Decision Making." *Behavior, Society, and Nuclear War* 1(1989): 8–84.

Hopkins, Nick, and Luke Harding. "GCHQ Accused of Selling Its Services after Revelations of Funding by NSA." *The Guardian*, August 2, 2013. www.theguardian. com/uk-news/2013/aug/02/gchq-accused-selling-services-nsa.

Izard, Carroll E. *Human Emotions*. Berlin and New York: Springer, 1977.

Jackson, Allison. "Island Dispute Disrupts Sino-Japanese Trade." *The Financialist*, January 30, 2013. www.thefinancialist.com/territorial-dispute-disrupts-sino-japanese -trade/.

Jackson, Allison. *Victims of Groupthink*. Boston, MA: Houghton Mifflin, 1972.

Janis, Irving L. *Groupthink: Psychological Studies of Policy Decisions and Fiascoes*. Boston, MA: Houghton Mifflin, 1982.

Jervis, Robert. *Perception and Misperception in International Politics*. Princeton, NJ: Princeton University Press, 1976.

Jones, Karen. "Trust as an Affective Attitude." *Ethics* 107, no. 1(1996): 4–25.

Kennedy, Kathleen A., and Emily Pronin. "When Disagreement Gets Ugly: Perceptions of Bias and the Escalation of Conflict." *Personality and Social Psychology Bulletin* 34, no. 6(2008): 833–848.

Kennedy, Robert F. *Thirteen Days: A Memoir of the Cuban Missile Crisis*. 1st. edn. New York: W. W. Norton, 1969.

Knight, J. "Social Norms and the Rule of Law: Fostering Trust in a Socially Diverse Society." *Trust in Society* 2(2001): 354–373.

Koch, Cardinal Kurt. "Trust as the Basic Attitude in a Culture of Humanity." Speech, Woolf Institute, Cambridge, February 26, 2013.

Kosfeld, Michael, Markus Heinrichs, Paul J. Zak, Urs Fischbacher, and Ernst Fehr. "Oxytocin Increases Trust in Humans." *Nature* 435, no. 7042 (June 2, 2005): 673– 676. doi:10.1038/nature03701.

Kraut, Richard. "Aristotle's Ethics." In *The Stanford Encyclopedia of Philosophy*, edited by Edward N. Zalta, Winter 2012. http://plato.stanford.edu/archives/win2012/ entries/aristotle-ethics/.

Kupchan, Charles. *How Enemies Become Friends: The Sources of Stable Peace*. Princeton Studies in International History and Politics. Princeton, NJ: Princeton University Press, 2010.

Kurzban, R. "Biological Foundations of Reciprocity." In Elinor Ostrom and James Walker, eds, *Trust and Reciprocity: Interdisciplinary Lessons from Experimental Research*, 105–127. New York: Russell Sage Foundation, 2003.

Levi, Margaret. "The Transformation of a Skeptic: What Non-Experimentalists Can Learn from Ex-Experimentalists." In Elinor Ostrom and James Walker, eds, *Trust and Reciprocity*, 373–380. New York: Russell Sage Foundation, 2003.

Levi, Margaret. "State of Trust." In M. Levi and V. Braithwaite, eds, *Trust and Governance*, 77–101. New York: Russell Sage Foundation, 1998.

Levi, Margaret. "Social and Unsocial Capital: A Review Essay of Robert Putnam's Making Democracy Work." *Politics and Society* 24, no. 1(1996): 45–55.

Levi, Margaret, and L. Stoker. "Political Trust and Trustworthiness." *Annual Review of Political Science* 3, no. 1(2000): 475–507.

Lorenz, Konrad. *On Aggression*. 2nd edn. London: Routledge, 2002.

Lorenz, Konrad. *King Solomon's Ring: New Light on Animal Ways*. Translated by Marjorie Kerr Wilson. London: Methuen, 1952.

Mann, Michael. *The Sources of Social Power*. Cambridge: Cambridge University Press, 1986.

Marcuse, Herbert. *Eros and Civilization: A Philosophical Inquiry into Freud*. London: Sphere, 1969.

McDermott, Rose. *Political Psychology in International Relations*. Analytical Perspectives on Politics. Ann Arbor: University of Michigan Press, 2004.

McNamara, Robert S., and James G. Blight. *Wilson's Ghost: Reducing the Risk of Conflict, Killing, and Catastrophe in the 21st Century*. New York: Public Affairs, 2001.

Mercer, Jonathan. "Approaching Emotion in International Politics." Paper presented to the International Studies Association Conference, San Diego, California, January 25, 1996.

Mercer, Jonathan, and Barry O'Neill. "Emotion and International Politics: Trust in Identity." Paper presented to the American Political Science Association Conference, San Francisco, California, 2001.

Miller, Jessica. "Trust: The Moral Importance of an Emotional Attitude." *Practical Philosophy* 3, no. 3(2000): 38–49.

Morris, Desmond. *The Naked Ape Trilogy*. London: Cape, 1994.

Morris, Errol. *The Fog of War: Eleven Lessons from the Life of Robert McNamara*. DVD. Sony Pictures Home Entertainment, 2004.

Nannestad, Peter. "What Have We Learned About Generalized Trust, if Anything?" *Annual Review of Political Science* 11, no. 1(2008): 413–436.

Nannestad, P., G. L. H. Svendsen, and G.T. Svendsen. "Bridge over Troubled Water? Migration and Social Capital." *Journal of Ethnic and Migration Studies* 34, no. 4 (2008): 607–631.

Neustadt, Richard E. *Presidential Power and the Modern Presidents: The Politics of Leadership from Roosevelt to Reagan*. Revised edn. New York: Free Press, 1991.

Oppenheimer, Franz. *The State: Its History and Development Viewed Sociologically*. Translated by John M. Gitterman. London: George Allen & Unwin, 1923.

Osgood, Charles E. *An Alternative to War or Surrender*. Urbana: University of Illinois Press, 1962.

Patton, Mike. "The Growth of Government: 1980 to 2012." *Forbes*, January 24, 2013. www.forbes.com/sites/mikepatton/2013/01/24/the-growth-of-the-federal-government-1980-to-2012/.

Pei, Minxin. "The U.S.-China Reset." *New York Times*, November 13, 2012, Opinion section. www.nytimes.com/2012/11/14/opinion/the-us-china-reset.html.

Post, Jerrold M. "Saddam Hussein of Iraq: A Political Psychology Profile." *Political Psychology* 12, no. 2(1991): 279–289.

Preston, Thomas. *The President and His Inner Circle: Leadership Style and the Advisory Process in Foreign Affairs*. New York: Columbia University Press, 2001.

Putnam, Robert D. "*E Pluribus Unum*: Diversity and Community in the Twenty-First Century." The 2006Johan Skytte Prize Lecture. *Scandinavian Political Studies* 30, no. 2(2007): 137–174.

Putnam, Robert D. *Bowling Alone: The Collapse and Revival of American Community*. New York: Simon & Schuster, 2000.

Putnam, Robert D., Robert Leonardi, and Raffaella Y. Nanetti. *Making Democracy Work: Civic Traditions in Modern Italy*. Princeton, NJ: Princeton University Press, 1993.

Rifkin, Jeremy. *The Empathic Civilization: The Race to Global Consciousness in a World in Crisis*. New York and Cambridge: Polity Press, 2010.

Schlesinger, Stephen C., and Stephen Kinzer. *Bitter Fruit: The Untold Story of the American Coup in Guatemala*. Reprint. New York: Anchor Books, 1990.

Shun Kwong-loi, 信广来. "Mencius." In *The Stanford Encyclopedia of Philosophy*, edited by Edward N. Zalta, 2010. http://plato.stanford.edu/archives/win2010/entries/mencius/.

Smith, Adam. *The Theory of Moral Sentiments*. Harmondsworth: Penguin, 2010.

Stoessinger, John George. *Why Nations Go to War*. 8th edn. Boston, MA: Bedford/St. Martin's Press, 2001.

Stokes, D. E. "Party Loyalty and the Likelihood of Deviating Elections." *The Journal of Politics* 24, no. 4(1962): 689–702.

Stolle, Dietland, S. Soroka, and R. Johnston. "How Diversity Affects Attitudinal Social Capital. A US–Canada Comparison." Paper presented at the Workshop for Preliminary Presentations of Findings from the Citizenship, Involvement, Democracy (CID) survey project, Georgetown University, December 12, 2005.

Sztompka, Piotr. *Trust: A Sociological Theory*. Cambridge: Cambridge University Press, 2000.

Sztompka, Piotr. "Trust, Distrust and Two Paradoxes of Democracy." *European Journal of Social Theory* 1, no. 1(1998): 19–32.

Taylor, A. J. P. *The First World War: An Illustrated History*. London: Hamish Hamilton, 1963.

Uslaner, Eric M. "Trust as a Moral Value," in D. Castiglione, J. van Deth, and G. Wolleb, eds, *The Handbook of Social Capital*, 101–121. New York: Routledge, 2008.

Uslaner, Eric M. "Civic Associations: Democratic Elixir or Democratic Illusion?" Paper presented at Joint Sessions of the European Consortium for Political Research. Turin, Italy, 2002a.

Uslaner, Eric M. *The Moral Foundations of Trust*. Cambridge: Cambridge University Press, 2002b.

Waley, Arthur, trans. *The Way and Its Power: A Study of the Tao Te Ching and Its Place in Chinese Thought*. New York: Grove Press/Atlantic Monthly Press, 1994.

Wendt, Alexander. *Social Theory of International Politics*. Cambridge Studies in International Relations. Cambridge: Cambridge University Press, 1999.

Wilkinson, Richard, and Kate Pickett. *The Spirit Level: Why More Equal Societies Almost Always Do Better*. London: Penguin, 2010.

Yamagishi, Toshio. "Trust as a Form of Social Intelligence." In Karen S. Cook, ed., *Trust in Society*, 121–147. New York: Russell Sage Foundation, 2001.

Yu, Guangyuan, Stevine I. Levine, and Ezra F. Vogel. *Deng Xiaoping Shakes the World: An Eyewitness Account of China's Party Work Conference and the Third Plenum (November-December 1978)*. New York: EastBridge, 2004.

Zehfuss, Maja. *Constructivism in International Relations: The Politics of Reality*. Cambridge Studies in International Relations. Cambridge: Cambridge University Press, 2002.

Zinn, Howard. *A People's History of the United States: From 1492 to the Present*. 2nd edn. London: Longman, 1996.

2 Generic trust

It is often said that Britain and America are two nations divided by a common language. If only things were that simple between the US and China. The US is a young nation established by a declaration of independence in 1776, while China is an ancient civilization with a written history as early as 1700 BC. The US has its roots in Europe and the Judaeo-Christian tradition while China rests on a Confucian foundation. Until the clash with Europeans in the nineteenth century, China understood itself to be the world. American missionary David Abeel (1804–1846) wrote: "China, according to their ideas, is the centre, and well nigh the sum of the world; the focus of all intellectual and moral light; not only the glory of the earth, but the counterpart of heaven."[1] John Fairbank warned that Chinese society is very different from America and that US policymakers would fail unless they took the difference into account. "Consequently, one of our worst enemies is wishful thinking, subjectivism and sentiment. Another is plain ignorance."[2] Zeng Guofan (1811–1872), the Confucian statesman, described Americans as "pure minded," of "honest disposition" and loyal to China.[3] A century later Mao Zedong declared that US imperialism was nothing but a paper tiger because it was divorced from the masses and disliked by all, even by the American people, but cautioned to take each battle, each encounter, with it seriously.[4] Yet when the time was ripe, he welcomed reconciliation.

US–China relations is not only the most important bilateral relationship in the twenty-first century but also the most complex. Social psychology tells us that the way we construe the world and ourselves matters.[5] This chapter consists of four sections discussing the manner in which the two nations see themselves and each other. It sets the stage for analyzing trust between the US and China with regard to climate change, financial crisis and international security in Chapters 3, 4 and 5 respectively. No society is monolithic. Although a report of this nature cannot possibly account for the opinion of every segment of society, it does seek to capture salient themes and reflect the diversity of views both in the US and China about each other.

America in her own eyes

> Our Nation's cause has always been larger than our Nation's defense. We fight, as we always fight, for a just peace – a peace that favors liberty. We will defend the peace against the threats from terrorists and tyrants. We will preserve the peace by building good relations among the great powers. And we will extend the peace by encouraging free and open societies on every continent.
>
> G. W. Bush, West Point, NY, June 1, 2002

Ronald Reagan referred to America as the "shining city upon a hill" and George W. Bush declared that America was "chosen by God and commissioned by history to be a model to the world."[6] At the end of the Cold War, Bush asserted that the defeat of totalitarianism left only one "single sustainable mode of national success: freedom, democracy and free enterprise" and that the US would take the opportunity to "spread the benefits of freedom across the globe."[7] According to a Pew Research Survey, 49 percent of Americans believed that: "Our people are not perfect but our culture is superior to others."[8] Americans often see themselves as an exceptional nation with a mission to spread its values around the world. This belief shapes America's foreign policies. William Fulbright observed that "the richer and stronger we are, the more we feel suited to the missionary task, the more indeed we consider it our duty."[9]

History and Identity

As with any nation, the way America sees itself has much to do with its history. America was founded by British settlers arriving in the seventeenth and eighteenth centuries. Samuel Huntington noted that America's origin as an Anglo-Protestant settler society has more than anything else shaped America's culture, institutions, historical development and identity.[10] America's core culture, he argued, has been and still is the culture of the seventeenth- and eighteenth-century settlers who defined themselves first by race, ethnicity, culture and, most importantly, religion. The core of that culture includes the Christian religion, Protestant values and moralism, a work ethic, the English language, British traditions of law, justice, and the limits of government power, and a legacy of European art, literature, philosophy and music. The settlers created a whole new society by defining their institutions with charters, compacts and constitutions. Later as conflict arose with the British, who shared the same race, culture and religion, over issues of trade, taxes, military security and parliamentary representation, the Americans differentiated themselves from the British by political ideology. This ideology embodied in the American Creed consisting of the principles of liberty, equality, democracy, individualism, human rights, the rule of law and private property (except for black slaves and native American Indians) became an important part of the American identity. The marriage of religious passion with political idealism forms the basis of American identity and nationalism.

American identity is strongly influenced by the Puritans. The Puritans felt the English Reformation had not gone far enough in distancing itself from the Catholic Church. Because of their piety, they defined their settlement based on a "covenant with God" to create a "city on the hill" as a model for all the world. They saw themselves as a "chosen people" in the "Promised Land" and America as "the redeemer nation" and "the visionary republic." They did not shy from invoking Old Testament symbolism and theology to justify applying extreme violence to seize the Promised Land. Religion continues to play an important role in America today. The vast majority of Americans profess a religious faith. In a 2003 poll, 92 percent said they believe in God. In another series of polls in 2002–2003, 57 to 65 percent said religion was very important to their lives.[11] A 2006 survey found that 79 percent of college freshmen believed in God, and 69 percent prayed and found "strength, support and guidance in their religious beliefs."[12] Despite separation of church and state, religion plays a key role in politics.

Americans see themselves as masters of their own destiny. Opinion surveys show that Americans believe that success in life depends overwhelmingly on one's own talent and character. According to the 2011 Pew Global Attitudes survey, only 36 percent of Americans believed that "success in life is determined by outside forces" compared to 57 and 72 percent in France and Germany respectively.

But Americans are insular and preoccupied with themselves. With a population of over 310 million, only 30 percent of Americans hold passports, compared to 60 percent in Canada and 75 percent in the UK.[13] Low for an affluent country, the percentage was in the teens until 2007 when it became required for Americans to carry passports to enter Canada and Mexico. Of the 61.5 million trips Americans made abroad in 2009, 50 percent were to Canada or Mexico. It is estimated that in 2009 as few as 3.5 percent of Americans traveled abroad.[14] Many American politicians are proud of their lack of overseas exposure. Vice-presidential candidate Sarah Palin only obtained a passport in 2007, and has only visited US army bases in Germany and Iraq since.

American media

The US media portrays America as the champion of the free world. Films about the conquest of the Wild West (of the John Wayne variety), World War II (*Sands of Iwo Jima, Pearl Harbor, The Battle of the Bulge, Saving Private Ryan*), the Korean War (*M.A.S.H., Take the High Ground*) the Vietnam War (*The Green Berets, Rambo*) and the Middle East wars (*Black Hawk Down, The Kingdom, Green Zone, Charlie Wilson's War*) lionize white Americans. Winning the Second World War and the Cold War confirmed Americans as "the good guys." The news media call America's enemies "terrorists" and "tyrants." And alongside media, education plays a pivotal role in shaping the way Americans see themselves.

American education

Consider the following exam questions:

1   Arrange the following persons or events in historical sequence of the Puritan Revolution and briefly describe the political changes that took place during that period:

(A)   Restoration of the House of Stuart
(B)   Execution of King Charles I
(C)   William and Mary
(D)   King James I

2   "France's defeat in 1815 signified London's triumph over Paris. France lost its superpower status following the years of turmoil from the 1789 Revolution until Napoleon's final downfall in 1815. France became a second rate power, Paris never fully regained her former glory and London became the world's leading center of commerce." This statement primarily:

(A)   describes France's former glory
(B)   gives the reasons why France fell behind England
(C)   shows that France experienced turmoil from 1789 until 1815
(D)   describes England's rise and France's fall

3   The mid-nineteenth century saw large scale migration in Europe and America. From 1846 to 1975 over nine million people left Europe, the majority of whom went to America. The main reason was:

(A)   Plantation owners in the American South needed farm workers
(B)   Fascist genocide broke out in Europe
(C)   European imperialist aggression intensified
(D)   The U.S. government encouraged immigration

4   In classical Greek, *democratia* (democracy) comes from *demos* (the people) + *kratos* (power, rule). This suggests that democracy in ancient Greece emphasized:

(A)   Broad citizen participation coupled with direct rule
(B)   The inviolability of private ownership
(C)   Trial by jury in civil suites
(D)   Democratic rights for all inhabitants

5   Which monarch worked as sailor and carpenter while visiting the West incognito?

(A)   Peter I
(B)   Constantine the Great
(C)   Louis XIV
(D)   The Meiji Emperor

These questions come not from an American college exam but from the history paper of the university entrance examination taken by high school graduates in Shanghai.[15] Other questions in the two-hour exam include:

1   At the recent Summit of the Americas, Venezuelan President Chavez gave President Obama the book *Las Venas Abiertas de America Latina* (The Open Veins of Latin America). The title refers to:

(A)   The outbreak of national wars of independence in Latin America
(B)   Western colonial exploitation of Latin America
(C)   A widespread congenital defect among the indigenous Latin population
(D)   The health care crisis in Latin America

2   A pair of Nike shoes cost less than $10 in Asian emerging markets but $40 in America. This shows that:

(A)   There is inequality in the global division of labor
(B)   The Asia-Pacific Economic Cooperation (APEC) forum works well
(C)   The United States controls the World Trade Organization (WTO)
(D)   Asian businesses receive market information following a time lag

3   The middle class is a continually evolving concept. Its members change over time and include:

1   Medieval city dwellers
2   Modern capitalists who command production resources
3   Medieval monks and nobles
4   Contemporary intellectuals and technology workers

(A)   1, 2 and 3
(B)   2, 3 and 4
(C)   1, 3 and 4
(D)   1, 2 and 4

4   In carrying out the revolution during the first half of the twentieth century, the Chinese Communist Party adopted its own unique strategy consisting of:

(A)   Violent revolution
(B)   The spearheading of worker movements
(C)   The encirclement of cities by villages
(D)   A coalition of nationalists and communists

5   During the Meiji Restoration, Western dress became popular but the *kimono* remained the formal wear of choice; bars proliferated but tea houses contined to be the venue for intellectual discourse; European operas were sung but *noh* and *kabuki* attracted ever larger audiences. This reflects:

(A)   Japan's use of Western culture to widen her citizen's knowledge

(B)   The government's importation of Western culture to consolidate its rule

(C)   The colorful coexistence of indigenous and Western cultures

(D)   The triumph of Western civilization

How does the US history curriculum compare? Education in America is decentralized and school curricula are regulated by individual states. Most states have no standard high school exit exam, and social studies curricula vary widely from state to state, but most American high schoolers only study American history. The topics covered by *American Pageant*, a popular high school history textbook, are shown in Table 2.1.[16]

The topics reflect the nation's insularity. With little exposure to world history and geography, most American high schoolers have never heard of Kiev, Madagascar, Ashoka the Great, the Battle of Hastings or the Opium Wars. Even Ivy League students may have difficulty locating Malaysia on the map.[17]

Racism and violence

Harvard historian Arthur Schlesinger, Jr. affirms that for much of its history, America has been a racist nation.[18] Historically, whites have discriminated against Indians, blacks, Asians and Mexicans, and excluded them from the American community. American racial attitudes are symbolized by one event early in its history. King Philip's War (1675–1676) was a brutal conflict with Indian tribes. Although relations with the Indians started off peacefully with both sides gaining from commerce, tensions soon rose as the settlers encroached on traditional Indian territory. Fearing that coexistence would soon lead to domination, the Indians attacked and pillaged settler towns, driving the settlers back to the coast. In the end, however, the Indians were decimated and their women and children enslaved and shipped to the West Indies. In a battle in 1637 where two Englishmen were killed and twenty others injured, between 400 and 700 Indians, mostly women and children, were massacred.[19] As a result of the war, the Puritans drew sharp boundaries on the land and in their minds between the Indians and themselves, and theorized that God had visited them with war and destruction because they had become too much like the Indians, and concluded that exclusion and extermination was the only way to treat the Indians henceforth. Historian Howard Zinn noted that "there is not a country in the world in which racism has been more important, for so long, as the United States," and the color line still exists.[20] In 1790 the population of the US, excluding Indians, was 3,929,000, of whom 698,000 were slaves and not viewed by others as part of American society. The white population was 80 percent British and 98 percent Protestant. With the exception of its blacks, America was a highly homogeneous society in terms

Table 2.1 History topics covered by *American Pageant*

Chapter	Topic
	Part I: Founding the new nation, c. 33,000 BC–AD 1783
1	New World beginnings, 33,000 BC–1769 AD
2	The planting of English America, 1500–1733
3	Settling the Northern Colonies, 1619–1700
4	American life in the seventeenth century, 1607–1692
5	Colonial society on the eve of revolution, 1700–1775
6	The duel for North America, 1608–1763
7	The road to revolution, 1763–1775
8	America secedes from the Empire, 1775–1783
	Part II: Building the new nation, 1776–1860
9	The Confederation and the Constitution, 1776–1790
10	Launching the new ship of state, 1789–1800
11	The triumphs and travails of Jeffersonian democracy, 1800–1812
12	The Second War for Independence and the upsurge of nationalism, 1812–1824
13	The rise of Jacksonian democracy, 1824–1830
14	Jacksonian democracy at flood tide, 1830–1840
15	Forging the national economy, 1790–1860
	Part III: Testing the new nation, 1820–1877
16	The ferment of reform and culture, 1790–1860
17	The South and the slavery controversy, 1793–1860
18	Manifest destiny and its legacy, 1841–1848
19	Renewing the sectional struggle, 1848–1854
20	Drifting toward disunion, 1854–1861
21	Girding for war: the North and the South, 1861–1865
22	The furnace of Civil War, 1861–1865
	Part IV: Forging an industrial society, 1865–1899
23	The ordeal of Reconstruction, 1865–1877
24	Politics in the gilded age, 1869–1889
25	Industry comes of age, 1865–1900
26	America moves to the city, 1865–1900
	Part V: Struggling for justice at home and abroad, 1899–1945
27	The Great West and the Agricultural Revolution, 1865–1890
28	The revolt of the debtor, 1889–1900
29	The path of empire, 1890–1899
30	America on the world stage, 1899–1909
31	Progressivism and the Republican Roosevelt, 1901–1912
32	Wilsonian progressivism at home and abroad, 1912–1916

Chapter	Topic
33	The war to end war, 1917–1918
34	American life in the roaring twenties, 1919–1929
35	The politics of boom and bust, 1920–1932
	Part VI: Making modern America, 1945–Present
36	The Great Depression and the New Deal, 1933–1938
37	Franklin D. Roosevelt and the shadow of war, 1933–1941
38	America in World War II, 1941–1945
39	The Cold War begins, 1945–1952
40	The Eisenhower era, 1952–1960
41	The stormy sixties, 1960–1968
42	The stalemated seventies, 1968–1980
43	The resurgence of conservatism, 1980–1996
44	The American people face a new century

of race, national origin and religion. Even immigrants from other parts of Europe (Irish, Italian, Slav and Jew) in the late nineteenth century were not considered white by the original Americans of British stock.[21] In order to become white, the arriving "non-whites" had to accept the racial distinctions prevalent in America and embrace the exclusion of Asians and the subordination of blacks.[22] In his 1944 study on race relations in America, Nobel laureate economist Gunnar Myrdal concluded:

> There is no doubt that the overwhelming majority of white Americans desire that there be as few Negroes as possible in America. If the Negroes could be eliminated from America or greatly decreased in numbers, this would meet the whites' approval.
>
> (*An American Dilemma: The Negro Problem and Modern Democracy*
> (New York: Harper, 1944), p. 167)

But most white Americans would not consider themselves racist. Brought up to think of their country as the "land of the free, home of the brave" whose citizens enjoy the right to "life, liberty and the pursuit of happiness," Americans regard their patria as close to perfection as any human society can come.[23] In an interview about the Middle East and China, Hillary Clinton offered help:

> We have figured out (in America) how people from every part of the world, every kind of person you can imagine, can live together, can work together. It wasn't easy. It took a long time, but I think we know a

little bit about how to do it, and we want to offer whatever assistance we can.[24]

Yet on almost every social economic indicator, from infant mortality and life expectancy to employment and home ownership, blacks and Hispanics lag far behind their white counterparts. In corporate boardrooms and elite professions, minorities are grossly underrepresented.[25] The 112th Congress (January 2011–January 2013) had two Hispanics, two Asians, and no black or American Indian members out of 100 senators.

Recounting the "bumps and bruises that the average black person must endure," Barack Obama wrote of how security guards would tail him as he shopped in department stores, white couples would toss him their car keys as he stood outside a restaurant waiting for the valet, and police cars would pull him over for no apparent reason.[26] According to a 2011 report by the New York Civil Liberties Union (NYCLU), young blacks and Hispanics between the ages of 14 and 24 are stopped and frisked by the police in disproportionate numbers.[27] They make up 4.7 percent of the city's population and yet account for 41.6 percent of stops.[28] If all age groups are included, blacks and Hispanics account for 52.9 percent and 33.7 percent of stops respectively. Federal Judge Shira A. Scheindlin found that the New York Police Department resorted to a "policy of indirect racial profiling" and that during police stops, blacks and Hispanics "were more likely to be subjected to the use of force than whites, despite the fact that whites are more likely to be found with weapons or contraband."[29]

Referring to the decision by a Florida court to acquit a white neighborhood watch volunteer who accosted and shot dead Trayvon Martin, an unarmed black teenager, Obama spoke of the frustration of African-Americans and the history of racial disparity in the application of criminal laws in America.[30] The pain that African-Americans felt from the case came from the fact that they viewed it through "a set of experiences and a history that doesn't go away."[31] Since the race riots of the 1960s, whites around the country have largely abandoned the cities for the suburbs. Once America's fourth largest city, Detroit's decline and bankruptcy stemming from that exodus is emblematic of dysfunctional race relations.[32]

Table 2.2 Racial composition of the 112th Congress

	House of representatives	*Senate*
White	361	96
Black	44	0
Hispanic	25	2
Asian	7	2
American Indian	0	0

Source: www.congress.org.

American hegemony

With the disintegration of the Soviet Union and the end of the Cold War, America stood triumphant as the world's sole superpower. *The Economist* noted that "the United States bestrides the globe like a colossus" and that American supremacy extended from the economic and military realm to lifestyle, language and products of mass culture that fascinate even its enemies.[33] In 2007 the 184 North American firms in the FT500 accounted for two-fifths of the total market capitalization of FT500 firms. America accounted for 31 percent of global household wealth and 34 percent of global personal wealth. Two-fifths of the world's leading 1,250 firms ranked by R&D spending are American while 65 percent of the 336 IT firms in the Global 1250 are based in America. America is the brain of capitalist globalization.[34] Its military is unmatched, and the debate at the turn of the century centered on whether America still needed to act in concert with other nations or should use its power unilaterally to pursue its own interests. Pulitzer Prize winner Charles Krauthammer urged his country to "stop playing the docile international citizen" and reassert its freedom of action.[35] Some believe that America's power is so great that its unipolar moment will become a unipolar era.

American decline

Joseph Nye warned, however, that America needed to cooperate with other nations to solve problems like terrorism, nuclear proliferation, environmental degradation and climate change.[36] Former national security advisor Brent Scowcroft believes that America is no longer able to lead the world as it is often seen as being preoccupied with its own narrow interests and seeking to dominate rather than lead.[37] Zbigniew Brzezinski warned of the waning of America and the need to "recapture the admiration of the world and revive its systemic primacy."[38] He expressed concern about the ignorance of the American public about America's changing global circumstances.[39]

Historian Paul Kennedy warned as early as 1987 of "imperial overstretch" i.e. American global interests and obligations had become far larger than its power to defend them all.[40] He pointed to excessive consumption and inadequate savings; persistent trade and current-account deficits; deindustrialization; sluggish economic growth; and chronic budget deficits fueling an ominously rising national debt. Two decades later, the Global Financial Crisis vindicated Kennedy, and the same causes of decline he pointed to are at the center of today's debate about America's economic prospects.[41] In *The Rise and Fall of Great Powers*, Kennedy argued that military power derives from economic strength. Every nation faces a three-way competition for resources for defense, consumption and investment. Investment, however, is the key determinant of long-term national strength. Citing the example of England, he warned that a country that lags behind others in productivity growth of 1 percent for a century could turn from an industrial leader into a second-rate economy. It must balance spending to ensure military security, meet socio-economic needs, and invest to avoid relative economic decline which could jeopardize military and economic security in the future. Every country faces a particular set of circumstances whereby its geography, politics and culture will determine the balance of the three. Without a judicious balance, a great power is unlikely to preserve its status for long.[42]

But power transition can be painful. The greater the distance between reality and who we think we are, the deeper the malaise. Lee Kuan Yew warns:

> For America to be displaced, not in the world, but only in the western Pacific, by an Asian people long despised and dismissed with contempt as decadent, feeble, corrupt, and inept is emotionally very difficult to accept. The sense of cultural supremacy of the Americans will make this adjustment most difficult.[43]

Human behavior is driven by powerful emotions, and how America manages hers in this time of change could mean the difference between war and peace. As America fought in Vietnam, Fulbright wrote of two Americas – one, the America of Lincoln and Adlai Stevenson, and the other, the America of Teddy Roosevelt and the super patriots. "One is generous and humane, the other narrowly egoistical; one is self-critical, the other self-righteous ... one is judicious, and the other arrogant in the use of power."[44] American foreign policy is shaped by two sides of the American character, both of which are distinguished by a kind of moralism – "one is the morality of decent instincts tempered by knowledge of human imperfections and the other is the morality of absolute self-assurance fired by the crusading spirit." Cautioning against "the mischief which the very virtuous do," Fulbright called for a shift of American foreign policy away from the missionary idea of being the world's policeman to the Lincolnian idea of decency and humanity. In the words of John Quincy Adams, America should be "the well wisher to the freedom and independence of all" but "the champion and vindicator only of her own."[45]

If Fulbright's words fell on deaf ears when America was at its crest, will they find resonance when America is at its ebb? America remains the most important actor because it is the center of the global economy and has so much power for good and evil. Because it disposes of great physical power, it must also display great moral power. To critics who say America is a lie because it falls so far short of its ideals, Samuel Huntington bravely answered: "America is not a lie; it is a disappointment. But it can only be a disappointment because it is also a hope."[46]

America's view of China

Those two countries understand each other so little. America speaks all of peace, but bombs China's neighbor. China watches her actions, and ignores her words.

China speaks all of war, but there is not a single Chinese soldier outside China. America listens to her words, and ignores her actions. It is historically determined.

Lord Wayland Kennet speaking to the House of Lords, 10 February 1966

China is a threat

While on the campaign trail, presidential candidate Mitt Romney called China a "cheater" and promised to impose trade restrictions on China if it did not respect intellectual property rights and allow its currency to float freely. "I'll clamp down on the cheaters, and China is the worst example of that," he declared. "If they cheat, there is a price to pay," he added, and threatened to designate China a currency manipulator.[47] Trade disputes are a major source of friction in US–China relations. With unemployment at 9 percent since 2008, US politicians are quick to point the finger at China. They represent a diverse range of constituencies but only few have ever studied China or are knowledgeable about the history of US–China relations. Their antipathy stems from business complaints and ideological assumptions. Many are wary of China's intentions, and believe the Chinese to be sabotaging the American economy through trade, currency policy and cyber theft. Not a few congressmen formed their views of China during the Vietnam War.[48]

Trade is by no means the only source of friction. Hillary Clinton criticized China's "deplorable" human rights record and predicted the fall of the Chinese government: "they are trying to stop history, which is a fool's errand." Her prediction is reminiscent of Reagan's Cold War objective: "My idea of American policy toward the Soviet Union is simple, and some would say simplistic. It is this: We win and they lose."[49] Texas governor Rick Perry predicted that China would "end up in the ash heap of history," while former ambassador Jon Huntsman suggested reaching out to Chinese youth and internet users to "take China down."[50]

Stefan Halper, former deputy assistant secretary of state for political-military affairs, argues that China will challenge America in the realm of ideas. China, he warns, is promoting a brand of authoritarian capitalism as an alternative to Western free markets and liberal democracy.[51] John Mearsheimer argues that states always seek to maximize their power, and according to his theory of "offensive realism," fear one another and cannot possibly cooperate.[52] American leaders believe China is trying to displace the US, and is building military capabilities to constrict US activities in the Western Pacific. They distrust China because its future is "indeterminate."[53] They believe that Chinese leaders, fearful of domestic instability, will use nationalism and external crises to secure stability at home. Authoritarian political systems, they reason, are less transparent and therefore less trustworthy. The lack of transparency deepens fears about Chinese strategic intentions. Some compare the US and

China to Sparta and Athens, and say that war may be imminent.[54] The US thus tries to counterbalance China.[55] Some argue, however, that the US should work with China rather than contain it but the "panda huggers" are dismissed as naive pacifists.[56]

The media

The Anglo-American media paint China as a threat. Books like *America's Coming War with China*; *A Contest for Supremacy: When China Rules the World*; and *The Writing on the Wall* feed the public imagination. *The Coming China Wars* blames China for everything from nuclear proliferation, genocide in Sudan and Japan's remilitarization to drug trade, human trafficking and AIDS,[57] while *Death by China* calls for global action to confront the dragon.[58] Jung Chang's *Wild Swans,* which sold over 10 million copies, made the Cultural Revolution synonymous with China. It has since been adapted as a play in London and Boston. Her biography of Mao also became a bestseller.[59] Samuel Huntington's *Clash of Civilizations* identifies Muslims and Chinese as America's most likely enemies. Taken together, these books reinforce terrifying stereotypes of the Chinese.

Lou Dobb claimed on Fox News that China steals American industrial and military secrets, and that China's economy is progressing by leaps and bounds thanks to the knowledge transfer.[60] Referring to Chinese investments overseas, Ariel Cohen of the Heritage Foundation warned that the "sword will follow the yuan."[61] The Shanghai Cooperation Organization (SCO), which consists of China, Russia and four central Asian republics, "bristles with anti-Western sentiments."[62] The *Financial Times* prints a regular stream of disparaging stories. In a piece lampooning the Chinese restaurant menu, Patti Waldmeir writes:

> The average workaday menu is so poetic as to be almost incomprehensible. "Husband and wife lung slice" and "chicken without a sex life" are all wonderfully evocative as names, but Beijing recently recognized, in a moment of utilitarian clarity, that foreigners might prefer to call a spring chicken a spring chicken.
>
> And naming isn't the only problem: sometimes a duck is not a duck and a fish is not a fish. This isn't a case of beef burgers surreptitiously laced with Black Beauty. It's all legitimate: vegetarian restaurants create dishes that look for all the world like a duck or a fish but are actually tofu. And everyone applauds the artifice.
>
> But even when Chinese food isn't imitating art, literature is never far away. At Yangzhou's newest steamed bun restaurant – where a traditional savory *huaiyang* breakfast can be had for pennies – a patron spontaneously pens a hymn of praise to the humble Yangzhou breakfast bun. Now, did that ever happen to an Egg McMuffin?

For good measure, the article includes a cartoon alleging hacking by the PLA.[63] In another article, she mocks the Chinese for turning to cosmetic surgery to improve their chances in life: "Personally, I'd advise her to lose the dirty high-top shoes before she starts adding body parts ... Speaking as someone who occasionally hires young staff in China, I think she lacks more in the way of charisma than eye-folds."[64]

The New York Times is not far behind. An article entitled "China Takes Aim at Western Ideas" describes Xi Jinping as a hardliner hostile to Western ideas such as constitutional democracy, universal values of human rights, media independence and civic participation.[65] It opens with a grim report of communist party cadres filling meeting halls around China to hear "a somber, secretive warning issued by senior leaders." The story, which carries a picture of Xi flanked by an honor guard, suggests that Xi fears the party is "vulnerable to an economic slowdown, public anger about corruption and challenges from liberals impatient for political change." The party, it suggests, fears "Western forces hostile to China and dissidents within the country ... constantly infiltrating the ideological sphere." The party's concern, to be fair, is not entirely groundless given the West's record of fomenting political unrest and regime change.[66] The newspaper accuses the party of corruption and power abuse but when it moves to tackle those ills, its efforts are roundly dismissed as "political theater" with "kangaroo courts."[67] Ambassador Winston Lord warned that the media should keep things in perspective,[68] but it is rare to read anything positive about the Chinese in the Anglo-American press. The Chinese, it seems, can do no right.

Racism

America's attitude toward China may be informed by racist instincts. A sense of civilizational superiority supported by technological power accompanied Europeans wherever they went. A Chinese engineer recalls his return to China with his Belgian wife and son in 1913:

> In Shanghai it was agony, for there it was only too plain that in my own country I was nothing but an inferior, despised being. There were parks and restaurants and hotels I could not enter, although she could. I had no rights on the soil of a Chinese city which did not belong to the Chinese; she had rights by reason of something called skin.
>
> We boarded the English steamer from Shanghai to Hankow; the first class was for Europeans only, and there was no other steamer. Marguerite leaned her arms on the railings and stared at the river. She was in first class, with our son. I went second class. I had insisted it should be so. "It is too hot for you here below." [69]

Although less high-handed in China than the British and French, the Americans shared their sentiments. This was nowhere more clearly to be seen than at home in America. The Chinese, who first arrived as laborers in the nineteenth century, suffered discrimination from the very start. They achieved economic and professional success but no political power. In the words of historian Alexander Saxton, they were the "indispensable enemy" – a people needed but feared at the same time. They were often seen as the "Yellow Peril," a reference to their skin color and the belief that hordes of Asians would eventually wipe out Western civilization and values. They were sometimes portrayed as rats, vermin and roaches that would contaminate America.

Throughout history, American society used the Chinese but resisted accepting them as fellow Americans.[70] White America viewed them as perpetual foreigners. In the nineteenth century, white laborers killed Chinese competitors during periods of excess labor supply and lobbied politicians to pass the Chinese Exclusion Act (1882) which barred Chinese immigration for the next eighty years. During the Cold War, research labs recruited Chinese scientists and engineers to strengthen American defense, only to suspect them later of passing secrets on to China. Whenever they excelled, whether as scholars, businessmen or laborers, their efforts were seen as a threat. Generations of American-born Chinese suffer a sense of alienation in their own country and of having to live up to higher standards than the rest of the population. The fate of the Chinese in America is often linked to international relations. When relations between the US and China were good, they played the role of goodwill ambassadors but when relations soured, they were often vilified as enemies or accused of spying.

Western representations of the East are often crude and reductionist.[71] As Edward Said pointed out, imperialism did not go away with colonialism, and there is still an intense need to justify dominance in cultural terms.[72] The mass media dehumanizes Asians by painting them as a servile class to be exploited or a force to be destroyed. Chinese are snail-eating, buck-toothed, pigtailed caricatures with slanted eyes and long fingernails. Hollywood depicts them as bowing sycophants, spies or crime bosses and their women as sex toys or prostitutes.[73] American pop culture portrays Asians not as real people but an abstraction. Scott Kurashige, professor of American history and culture, argues further that the biggest problem is not the stereotypes of Asians on the screen but their invisibility, which taught that if they wanted to succeed in certain areas of life, they had to be white.[74] Sadly, Asians often internalize those stereotypes, and live out the identity constructed by the mainstream.

Presidential candidate John McCain, who served as a bomber pilot in the Vietnam War, still refers to Vietnamese as "gooks."[75] William Fulbright wrote:

> To most Americans China is a strange, distant, and dangerous nation, not a society made up of … individual human beings but a kind of menacing abstraction. When Chinese soldiers are described, for example, as "hordes of Chinese coolies," it is clear that they are being thought of

not as people but as something terrifying and abstract, or as something inanimate, like the flow of lava from a volcano.[76]

In short, America looks at China through racial as well as ideological lenses.

China is not a threat

But not all Americans see China as a threat. Starting from the early 1920s writers like Pearl S. Buck, John Lossing Buck, William H. Hinton, Walter H. Mallory, Edgar Snow and John K. Fairbank have written sympathetically about China and her struggles. Admiral Mike Mullen believes that relations with China are "too important to manage through blind suspicion and mistrust."[77] America, he urges, should not let narrow interests and suspicion define the relationship but should "work toward more transparency, more pragmatic expectations of each other, and more focus on common challenges" in order to build strategic trust. Alastair Johnston believes China will not challenge the status quo.[78] Zbigniew Brzezinski agrees.[79] Veteran diplomat Chas Freeman argues that analogies to other rising powers with shorter histories – France, the United States, Germany, Japan, the USSR – are not helpful in predicting the consequences of China's rise.[80] Freeman points out that

> China has no messianic ideology to export; no doctrine of 'manifest destiny' to advance; no belief in social Darwinism or imperative of territorial expansion to act upon; no cult of the warrior to animate militarism or glorify war; no exclusion from contemporary global governance to overcome; no satellite states to garrison; no overseas colonies or ideological dependencies.[81]

He points out that the Chinese Communist Party has delivered prosperity to ordinary Chinese and 86 percent of Chinese think their country is on the right track. Freeman sees China taking its place alongside the US and others at the head of multilateral system of global governance where it will enjoy prestige but no monopoly of power. The US will remain the only military power with global reach for years to come, Freeman contends.

Others like Dan Griswold and Edward Steinfeld have argued that Americans have benefited from globalization and trade with China.[82] By integrating itself into the Western economic order, China is playing by Western rules, and reinforcing the dominance of Western companies and regulatory institutions. China has in many ways outsourced the remaking of its economy and institutions to foreign companies and foreign rule-making authorities. America's share of global manufacturing value has actually increased since 1990, meaning that American companies are capturing a greater share of the wealth even as the products are "made in China." R&D centers built by Western companies in China harness the country's talent to global, rather than indigenous Chinese, innovation efforts. The global production system benefits both Chinese and American society but the social and resource pressures on China are intense. Participation in the global supply chain means complying to foreign rules, and Walmartization is not something that Chinese manufacturing power is doing to America, but rather it is how America is transforming China, argues Steinfeld.

Susan Shirk, deputy assistant secretary of state in the Clinton administration, sees China as a fragile superpower and believes the US has more to fear from China's weakness than its strength.[83] Chinese leaders face huge challenges at home such as income disparity, corruption, and the environment, and rather than challenge the US, would like to "keep the neighborhood quiet" so that they can deal with these problems. David Shambaugh dismisses fears of a China model or "Beijing Consensus."[84] China's political and economic models are hybrids adapted to China's own conditions and are not easily transferable, he reasons.

On balance

China's rise at a time when the US is facing difficulties makes Americans ever more sensitive to Chinese aspirations. Although President Obama has repeatedly said America welcomes a strong and prosperous China, many Americans hold more complicated views. As the gap between China and the United States narrows, the US faces three strategy options.[85] The first option assumes China does not want to change the current international order, and therefore, the United States should engage China and bring her into the international system as a responsible stakeholder. The second option holds that power transition is never peaceful and conflict is inevitable. China's rise will shake the world order, and the United States should contain China and prevent it from becoming the dominant power in East Asia. The third option holds that peace cannot be taken for granted but conflict can be avoided with wise diplomacy and policies, and the US should apply a mix of engagement and containment. Christoper Layne cautions that the United States will run into endless trouble if it chooses to maintain its hegemony.[86] The two countries, however, lack an overarching concept for interaction. Such a framework is not a simple matter, as it requires each side to subordinate national aspirations to a vision of a global order, but neither side has a blueprint for such a task.[87]

China in her own eyes

> From this day onward, we renounce class struggle and instead take up economic development as our central focus.
>
> Third Plenum of the 11th Party Congress, 1978[88]

Perhaps no other nation is as conscious of its history and culture as China. Chinese civilization has enjoyed continuity since antiquity, and China today must be understood in the context of its long history.[89] The country is undergoing unprecedented social and economic change but the reforms of the last three decades, significant as they are, represent but a brief moment in China's history. The Global Financial Crisis casts doubt on Western theories, and there are signs that the Chinese are turning back to their own intellectual resources.[90] To appreciate how the Chinese see themselves and their place in the world, it is necessary to look at classical Chinese thought and China's quest for modernity.

Chinese political theory

According to classical Chinese thought, effective political leadership is the key to national power, but political leadership must be undergirded by morality. While economic and military strength are important elements of national power, they are secondary to moral leadership, an idea with important implications for the modern world order.[91] Benevolence (*ren*) forms the core of Confucian teaching, which holds that rule by moral example is far more efficacious than rule by law or coercion. *Badao* (霸道) refers to the rule of might rather than *wangdao* (王道) or benevolent rule. Contrasting the two types of rule, Mencius wrote: "The people turn to a humane ruler as water flows downward or wild beasts take to the wilderness. Win the people's hearts, and the Mandate of Heaven (天命) will be yours."[92] There were also competing schools of thought. Han Fei (280–233 BC) advocated the use of force to unite the country, and his philosophy became the ideological foundation of the Qin Dynasty (221–206 BC). The harsh Qin rule, however, lasted a mere fifteen years before being overthrown by the people.

Mencius and other Confucianists held that benevolent rule (仁政) was the only legitimate form of government.[93] They advocated morality (德) over law (法), a principle that shaped China's foreign policy. Throughout their long history, the Chinese focused on defending borders rather than conquering neighbors. The Great Wall is emblematic of this defensive posture. The emperors were preoccupied with threats from the north.[94] China was conquered by the Mongols in the thirteenth century and the Manchus in the seventeenth century, while the Japanese tried to invade in the sixteenth century. China ruled northern Vietnam for a thousand years until AD 938 but made no attempt to expand its control beyond it. Unlike the maritime cultures of Greece and Rome, the Chinese possessed a continental mindset.[95] It had a strong sense of its own centrality, an order it conceptualized as cultural and philosophical rather than political and power oriented.[96] Chinese civilization enjoyed strong prestige, and peace was maintained through trade, tribute and cultural diplomacy, often through alliances sealed by marriage.[97] In 604, for instance, Songtsän Gampo, the ruler of Tibet, married Princess Wencheng, the niece of Emperor Taizong, as part of a peace treaty.[98] China's most well known maritime expeditions, the voyages of Zheng

He (1371–1433), neither brought back slaves nor established colonies.[99] Sun Yat-sen asserted: "Oriental civilization is the rule of Right; Occidental civilization is the rule of Might. The rule of Right respects benevolence and virtue, while the rule of Might only respects force and utilitarianism."[100] Peter Nolan observes that while Western philosophy is more strongly oriented toward individual rights and freedom, Eastern ideology is more inclined towards common interests and a harmonious society.[101]

Socialism

For two millennia, China was the world's largest economy, producing three-quarters of the world's output at the beginning of the first century AD.[102] In 1820 it commanded 32.9 percent of world GDP (compared to America's 1.8 percent) but contact with European powers shattered its confidence.[103] It experienced repeated defeat at the hands of the colonial powers, which led to a long quest for national salvation.[104] Having lost faith in its own resources, it looked outward. There were many competing ideologies but in the end it embraced socialism.[105] Marxian socialism meant public ownership of the means of production, including natural resources and capital. Explaining the party's goal, Lin Biao said:

> Actually we could have picked a different name, such as the Chinese People's Party, the Revolutionary Party, the Liberation Party – any of these would have been OK. But no matter what, our intention remains to resolve the "property" issue. What are we fighting for? What is our goal all about? Getting "property" – not private property, but public property. For everybody to get rich, for everybody to lead a good life. That's why there has to be a revolution.[106]

China took the socialist road, and in the first years of the people's republic enjoyed success in stabilizing the economy after years of turmoil. But in 1958 Mao launched the "Great Leap Forward", a five-year plan aimed at transforming China into a modern state through accelerated industrialization and farm collectivization. Mao pushed to raise not only grain but also steel production using backyard furnaces. Farmers were organized into communes of thousands of households but the restructuring and poor weather in 1959 and 1960 sharply reduced farm output and led to famine, killing millions (estimates range from 18 to 45 million people). Mao accepted responsibility for the disaster and took a back seat, but later reasserted himself through the Cultural Revolution, a ten-year mass campaign beginning in 1966 that resulted in "the most severe setback and the heaviest losses suffered by the party and the people since the founding of the People's Republic."[107] The revolution only came to an end upon Mao's death in 1976.

Market reform

During the decades of power struggle and socio-economic experimentation, China's neighbors forged ahead in the economic, political and social spheres. China's living standard lagged far behind, and in 1978 the party renounced class struggle in favor of economic development. With the Mao era behind them, the Chinese began a new chapter. Deng Xiaoping was determined to lift the country from poverty and isolation. He skillfully built a coalition of the party, the revolutionary elders, regional governors, and the army.[108] He invented *socialism with Chinese characteristics* to free the country from the strictures of socialist orthodoxy by arguing that "revolution sets productive forces free." He famously declared that it doesn't matter whether the cat is black or white as long as it catches the mouse. Rebuking theoretical purists, he warned that "we should talk less and do more." In his Southern Tour of special economic zones in 1992, he urged reform to set free productive forces (解放生产力) by warning that "unless we uphold socialism, reform and open up, develop the economy, and improve the lives of the people, we have no future."[109] The reforms were in practice a rejection of the planned economy and full public ownership of resources.[110]

Global integration

The market reform took place within the context of a globalizing world and a worldwide technological revolution. Chinese leaders watched closely the clash between globalization and anti-globalization forces in the wake of the Asian financial crisis. They saw globalization proceeding from an unjust international order where developing countries often suffer loss rather than gain, but which optimizes the allocation of resources, and produces benefits through the spread of technology. After careful deliberation, China took its reform to new heights by joining the WTO. Foreign trade now represents 75 percent of GDP, and despite plans to make the economy more reliant on domestic demand, China's integration into the global economy has passed the point of no return. Exports and imports in 2011 grew by 20.3 percent and 24.9 percent respectively.[111] Inward foreign direct investment totaled $116 billion, while non-financial outward direct investment reached $60.1 billion. International and regional economic cooperation continues to grow. While choosing deeper integration with the global economy, however, China guards its independence and sovereignty, a vigilance that stems from history and is today directed mainly toward America.

Peaceful development

China's primary source of tension is the United States, which it has repeatedly sought to reassure. For continued economic growth, China needs peace, not war. Speaking at the Brookings Institution in 2005, Zheng Bijian pointed out that more than two decades of reform showed that China's development was not a threat but an opportunity.[112] Far from wanting to challenge America, China is preoccupied with its own development. It faces major challenges in energy, environment and economic and social development, and unless it succeeds in managing these problems, peaceful development will be at risk. Zheng assured his audience that China would not follow the American model of high energy consumption (US annual per capita consumption of oil is 25 barrels compared to China's less than 1.5 barrel), European colonization (over 60 million Europeans migrated and established colonies around the world) nor the Soviet arms race.[113] According to Feng Chenyu, president of Sinopec, China does not seek to overturn the world order but to participate, reinforce and even profit from it.[114]

How socialist is China?

After confronting the mistakes of the Cultural Revolution, Chinese leaders had to think hard about what socialism meant. China's experience seemed to suggest incompatibility between socialism and economic efficiency. Free markets and private enterprise promised higher productivity but also labor exploitation and wealth disparity. Socialism, on the other hand, made everyone equal but also equally poor (共同贫穷). Deng concluded that development had to come before equality. Indeed, Marx himself posited that socialism emerges after a phase of wild capitalism. Deng urged party cadres to "liberate the mind" (解放思想), and to "seek truth from facts" (实事求是). At the 12th Party Congress in 1982, he declared that China would forge its own path (走自己的道路) and build its own brand of socialism.[115]

After thirty years of socialism with Chinese characteristics, China achieved an impressive rise in living standards. According to the World Bank, the number of Chinese living on less than $1 a day, fell from 490 to 88 million between 1981 and 2003, representing poverty eradication on a scale unknown in history. During this period China accounted for three-quarters of the population lifted out of extreme poverty worldwide. It made huge improvement in reducing child malnutrition and reducing the death rate of children under the age of five. It overtook the US in car sales in 2009, and mobile phone usage (over 900 million mobile phone users in 2011).[116] It will surpass Japan as the top consumer of high-end goods by 2015, even as millions of Chinese travel abroad (Chinese tourists made 47 million trips overseas in 2009).[117]

With economic success, the Chinese have regained confidence. Not since before the Opium Wars have they felt more optimistic. According to the 2012 Pew Global Survey, 70 percent of Chinese say they are better off financially than they were five years ago, and 92 percent say their standard of living is better than their parents' at a similar age.[118] At the same time, half say corrupt officials are a problem. The state promotes capital accumulation (money making) and the enrichment of a new bourgeoisie. The concentration of wealth and capital has increased. According to the 2010 Blue Book of China's

Society (社会蓝皮书) published by the Chinese Academy of Social Sciences (CASS), China had a Gini coefficient of 0.5, surpassing the warning threshold of 0.4.[119] (The US Gini coefficient was 0.45 in 2011.[120]) Economist Wu Jinglian sees rent-seeking as the root cause of income inequality, and urges the party to punish those who prosper through bureaucratic power.[121] Education and health care that were once free have been marketized (产业化) threatening to wipe out two of the Chinese revolution's proudest achievements. Farm de-collectivization eliminated the clinics and "barefoot doctors" that provided basic health care. Since 1990 infant mortality has declined at a slower rate than India and middle-income countries with a slower increase in income. Despite a government pledged since 1993 to increase spending on education to 4 percent of GDP, education spending (3.33 percent of GDP in 2008), remains well below the 4.1 percent average for developing countries.[122]

There is intense debate within the Party, and leaders past and present such as Hu Yaobang, Zhao Ziyang and Wen Jiabao have urged greater openness and accountability.[123] In 2000, party elder Ren Zhongyi wrote in a newspaper article:

> Absolute power corrupts absolutely. The Communist Party is no exception to that rule. The Communist Party supervising itself is like having the left hand supervise the right hand. That just won't do. The Party needs to be supervised not just by the Party but by the people, the democratic party groupings and by independent persons. Not only must it be subject to the supervision of society and public opinion, it must be constrained by law as well.[124]

On the eve of the 18th Party Congress in 2012, the *People's Daily* lamented that as awareness increased of the right to know and the rule of law, democracy in China had yet to meet people's expectations.[125] In his first speech as president, Xi Jinping promised to address the public's grievances and root out corruption.[126] Unless the Party acted, he warned, it would lose its roots, lifeblood and strength.[127]

China's vision

Does China have a vision of the future and if so, what does it look like? Where does its own path lead to? Since the founding of the People's Republic, China has all along sought an alternative modernity, one different from the Soviet and capitalist models, and despite its departure from orthodox communism, the Party has not abandoned the constitutional commitment to the working class. Socialism with Chinese characteristics seeks to attain broad prosperity (小康社会) but the reforms instituted in 1978 took a neoliberal turn after Tiananmen, bringing in deregulation and the marketization of political power (权利产业化). Yan Xuetong of Tsinghua University believes that China should shift its priority from economic development to building a harmonious society free of huge gaps between rich and poor. It should replace money worship with traditional morality and stamp out political corruption in favor of social justice and fairness.[128]

Even as it reassures America that it is not a threat, China is conscious of its growing role on the world stage. Yan warns that China should not follow the US practice of saying one thing and doing another, such as proclaiming that all states are equal but in practice always trying to dominate.[129] According to classical Chinese thought, international leadership endures only when it is based on moral authority rather than power. The Global Financial Crisis brought into sharp focus the contradictions of global capitalism.[130] If humankind is to survive the twenty-first century, it must tame global capitalism. The time for keeping a low profile (韬光养晦) may be over. China's quest for an equitable modernity must include the interests of all human beings, and the Party may need to look beyond its own existence to the survival of the species.[131]

China's view of America

> Like it or not, America is a country we need to face.
>
> Bai Yansong[132]

Two hundred years ago the Chinese gave America the name *meiguo* or "beautiful country." Two hundred years later they still admire America's economy and technology, but following China's rapid rise, do the Chinese still think of America as that beautiful land?

Crisis of capitalism

China sees a crisis in America. Quoting US research, Wang Jing of the Chinese Academy of Social Sciences writes about the failure of American democracy:

> Capitalist society is a dictatorship of the capitalist class and the US government machinery is a tool of violence at the service of the capitalist class. America uses the global media to portray itself as the model of freedom, human rights, democracy and "universal values" but figures from the US Center for Responsive Politics in 2009 show that 46 percent of US congressmen are millionaires (Capitol Hill is full of fat cats). Instead of acting as checks and balances, the three branches of government work together to serve the capitalist oligarchs. American presidents, vice-presidents, secretaries of state and treasury secretaries all enjoy close ties to the arms, oil and financial industries.[133]

Wang points to the privileges of the right and the suppression of the left by a government and media that promote the interests of a wealthy minority:

A Time magazine survey showed that 54 percent of the public supports Occupy Wall Street and only 27 percent supports the Tea Party movement but the media at first tried to ignore or ridicule the Occupy Wall Street movement. The authorities suppress the Occupy movement but not the Tea Party because the Tea Party is a rightwing movement of the capitalist class whereas Occupy is a leftwing movement against the capitalist class. The Tea Party receives generous coverage from mainstream media such as Fox News and backing from the political and financial elite.

She describes the glaring injustices in the world's most prosperous nation where millions live in poverty and without health insurance while their elected government extends largesse to the banks and the military:

> According to a Brookings study (3 November 2011),[134] 46.2 million Americans live in poverty, including 20.5 million in extreme poverty.[135] In 2010 over 49.9 million Americans had no health insurance and two-thirds of American university students graduate with debts averaging $80,000 each. Warren Buffet's income is taxed at 17.4 percent while twenty of his office colleagues pay 36 percent. In 2008 the US government allocated $700 billion to bail out the banks. In just over two months it paid out $350 billion to the banks, and by the end of 2010 the top five US banks had a combined market worth of $800 billion or 5 percent of the GDP. US military spending in 2010 totaled almost $700 billion, an 81% increase from 2001. America's defense budget represents over 40 percent of world total military spending.

Trade and investment

The Chinese see a hostile America that politicizes trade and investment.[136] Vice-Premier Wang Qishan warned that the politicization of economic and trade issues distorts US–China relations.[137] In a newspaper commentary commemorating the 40th anniversary of Richard Nixon's visit to China, a group of professors from Peking University and Tsinghua University noted that no other bilateral economic and trade relationship in modern history has been so poisoned by politics.[138] They pointed out that US–China trade is the world's most complementary. Bilateral trade between 1979 and 2011 increased 118-fold from $2.37 billion to $446.7 billion. US exports to China between 2000 and 2010 grew by 468 percent while its exports to other countries grew by only 55 percent in the same period. Bilateral trade between the two countries is expected to reach $700 billion in 2015 and imports from the US are expected to double. Chinese exports meet the demands of US consumers while US electronic, aerospace, medical, and agricultural products and services support China's development.

Foreign direct investment (FDI), however, is quite a different story. Chinese FDI to the US totals 2.6 percent of total Chinese outbound FDI, and US FDI to China totals only 1 percent of US outbound FDI.[139] US politicians and interests groups reject Chinese investment on purported national security grounds.[140] Congress blocked bids by CNOOC, Huawei and Chinalco to purchase US assets, and compared to $70 billion of US investments into China, the Chinese have only managed to make direct investments into the US worth $4.8 billion.

Double standards

Chinese officials voice frustration at US "congagement" (engagement + containment) and double standards.[141] Admiral Mike Mullen warned his Chinese counterpart General Chen Bingde against resolving disputes by "coercing smaller nations."[142] Given the American use of force in Vietnam, Iraq, Afghanistan and Latin America, not to mention the wholesale suppression of native American Indians, McMullen's words strike the Chinese as breathtaking hypocrisy. The Chinese are wary of Western "universal values." Song Luzheng, vice-president of the Chinese Students Association in France, writes:

> In 1840 the Western powers forced China open with gunboats and opium, and for more than a hundred years dominated and plundered China. China was an ally of the West during the First and Second World Wars and counted among the victors but that did not stop the West from betraying her interests. At the Paris Peace Conference, they transferred Germany's concessions in Shandong to Japan. After the Second World War, Britain and America sold out China's interests in Manchuria (China's northeast provinces) to the Soviet Union while Britain refused to return Hong Kong. Considering their self-serving policies and lack of integrity, how are the Chinese to believe that Western "universal values" are good for them? Even if the West were to lay down the butcher's knife and become saints, the bitter past makes it hard to trust them.[143]

Song's stinging critique of the British and Americans is conveyed in the following paragraphs. The British, he writes, are especially devious.[144] Britain made no attempt to build democratic institutions in Hong Kong for over a 150 years until the time came to hand the colony back to China. Why didn't the West require Britain to grant Hong Kong democracy during those long years of colonial rule? From three centuries of Western democracy, the Chinese discern no plausible link between democracy and equality. England had the first constitutional government but that did not always mean freedom and equality for its citizens. Arbitrary measures such as enclosures deprived the peasantry of the commons and allowed landlords to amass land and capital. Deprived of their livelihood, peasants could not even turn to begging because it was forbidden by law. Those who lost their land became urban workers who, without laws to protect them, worked 12–18 hours a day for meager wages. This class of people had neither the right to vote nor to stand for election. When famine broke out in Ireland (1845–1852), a virtual English colony, the English sent no aid but continued to ship Irish food stocks to England.

For 200 years, the British lower class was at risk. But Britain enriched itself through colonial plunder and slave trade, and the increase in national wealth together with the resistance of the lower class finally persuaded the government to build social welfare and expand the franchise to workers. Women only won the right to vote through hunger strikes, suicides and their contribution in the First World War. Even the French Revolution did not deliver the equality, liberty and fraternity it promised as the gentry became the new privileged and exploited the poor. As in Britain, it took an increase in national wealth and violent struggle by workers to bring about the welfare state.

American history

Chinese who read American history quickly become cynical about universal values.[145] America became independent declaring that all men are equal, and yet many of the founding fathers, including George Washington, kept slaves. The Civil War was billed as a fight to free slaves but Lincoln's wife came from a prominent slave-owning family, and General Ulysses Grant kept slaves too. Seats in the House of Representatives were allocated according to population but while slaves were included in the census, every five slaves were worth only three. After independence from the British, America industrialized and reenacted the repression of workers that took place earlier in England and France.[146] The eight-hour working day was bought with the blood of Chicago workers. Racial segregation in America continued even after the Second World War and the Holocaust. Even churches and cemeteries remain segregated. It was only after a ten-year-long civil rights struggle that African Americans finally won citizenship and the right to vote in 1965. Women were only allowed into White House press conferences during John Kennedy's administration. In brief, the past 300 years show that democracy does not guarantee freedom, equality and human rights. Why, the Chinese ask, does the West continue to misrepresent democracy? Doesn't forcing "universal values" on others violate democracy?

American imperialism

US imperialism disabuses the Chinese of any notion of American moral virtue.[147] In 1898 the US waged war on Mexico and seized the Philippines. President William McKinley declared:

We have no choice but to put down the uprising. This piece of land belongs to us. We shall bring them civilization. Our flag is not the flag of imperialism nor the symbol of oppression but the banner of freedom, hope and civilization.

An American general wrote home saying: "We may have to kill off half the Filipinos so that the remaining half may enjoy a better life." If war in the Philippines lies in the distant past, the Iraq War is more recent. When it failed to win a UN mandate, America led a handful of allies ("the coalition of the willing") to invade Iraq on trumped up charges.[148] The invasion turned a country with the highest education levels, the most advanced health care and the best infrastructure in the Middle East into one of the world's most dangerous and corrupt places. Trust is eroded when the Chinese see America applying double standards. Tibet, Taiwan, Chechnya, and Kosovo are condemned as human rights violations but not the Spanish crackdown on the Basques, Turkish bombing of the Kurds, or the British shooting of Irish protestors. The narrative depends almost entirely on whether you are America's ally or enemy.

Ambivalence

But China remains ambivalent about America. Despite geopolitics, the Chinese public still thinks of America as meiguo, the beautiful land. Many see it as a land of prosperity and opportunity. The USA remains the "dream" destination for the Chinese. Despite having to fill out visa forms in English and stand in line for hours, Chinese visitors to the US went from 400,000 in 2007 to a million in 2010.[149] Only Mexico has more visa applicants to the US. There are 300 million Chinese learning English compared to 200,000 Americans learning Chinese.[150] The elite send their children there, and a stint at Harvard opens doors in China. President Xi Jinping's daughter was among 220,000 Chinese studying in America, where they constitute by far the largest group of foreign students.[151] After graduation many find employment in America, where the top science and engineering labs are replete with Asian talent.[152]

Brands like Apple, Coca Cola, Walmart, McDonald's and Starbucks are popular in China. Indeed, US companies are firmly embedded in China.[153] China is Coca-Cola's fastest growing market. Since 1979, the company has invested $5 billion in China, where it operates forty-one bottling plants employing 48,000 workers. Pepsi-Cola has twenty-seven bottling plants and 20,000 employees. Yum!, which owns Kentucky Fried Chicken, Pizza Hut and Taco Bell, operates almost 4,000 restaurants. With 1,300 outlets, McDonald's is the second largest fast-food restaurant in China. Walmart employed over 95,000 people in China in 2010 while Nike employed 176,000. Apple sales in Greater China topped $8.8 billion in the first three quarters of 2011. American science and technology is admired in China where IBM, Boeing,

Caterpillar and General Motors are household names. Otis controls 25 percent of the Chinese elevator market while Carrier controls a fifth of the air-conditioning market. Dow Chemical has twenty manufacturing sites in China and sales totaling $3.7 billion in 2010, while General Electric's revenues totaled nearly $4 billion. In 2010 General Motors sold more vehicles in China (2.4 million) than in the USA. Caterpillar has ninety dealerships employing several thousand workers.

The influence of American cinema, music and fashion is everywhere to be seen. American pop culture is unstoppable. Chinese pop or "C-pop" mirrors American pop, and despite efforts by the Ministry of Culture to halt undue Western influence, Lady Gaga, Beyoncé and Jay-Z are well known icons as hip-hop, rock and rap (说唱) put their stamp on youth culture in China and across Asia.[154] *Mission Impossible; Kungfu Panda; Men in Black; Titanic;* and *The Avengers* are box office hits. *Harry Potter and the Goblet of Fire* was the top box office hit in 2005 while *Star Wars Episode III* and *Mr. and Mrs. Smith* drew huge crowds. *Avatar* was the top-selling Hollywood film until *Iron Man 3* broke the record in 2013.[155] Paramount Pictures plans to produce *Transformers 4* in China.[156] Between 2000 and 2004, China imported 4,332 films of which 40–50 percent were made in Hollywood. Of the eighty-eight most popular foreign films during that period, seventy were American.[157] *Saving Private Ryan*, the tale of an infantry squad sent to save the sole surviving son of a widowed mother, moved Chinese audiences. China's Oscar – the Huabiao Awards and the Golden Rooster Awards – gave prizes to *Saving Private Ryan, Pearl Harbor*, and *Forrest Gump*. American tastes, lifestyle and values are synonymous with modernity. Western visitors are treated with honor, and luxury goods advertised with Caucasian faces. Starbucks coffee, which costs twice as much in Beijing as in San Francisco, is a sign of sophistication[158] while *Elle, Vogue*, and *Cosmopolitan* are changing middle-class tastes.[159]

Americans enjoy plenty of goodwill in China, an asset which they often fail to appreciate. Even though America did not enter the Pacific War in order to save China, the Chinese remember its pivotal role in defeating Japan. Despite the Korean and Vietnam wars, Mao welcomed Nixon's overtures, and China today has stronger economic and cultural ties with the US than any other country. On balance, the Chinese are more disposed to be friends than enemies of America.

Notes

1   David Abeel, *Journal of a Residence in China and the Neighbouring Countries from 1830 to 1833* (London: J. Nisbet and Co., 1835), 120.
2   John K Fairbank, *The United States and China* (Cambridge, MA: Harvard University Press, 1948), 310.
3   Warren I. Cohen, *America's Response to China: A History of Sino-American Relations*, 4th edn. (New York: Columbia University Press, 2000), 27.

4   Mao Zedong, "U.S. Imperialism Is a Paper Tiger," (Speech, July 14, 1956), www. marxists.org/reference/archive/mao/selected-works/volume-5/mswv5_52.htm.

5   David G. Myers, *Social Psychology*, 11th edn. (New York: McGraw-Hill, 2013), 6.

6   Charles M. Blow, "Decline of American Exceptionalism," *New York Times*, November 18, 2011, Opinion. www.nytimes.com/2011/11/19/opinion/blow-decli ne-of-american-exceptionalism.html?nl=todaysheadlines&emc=tha212.

7   *National Security Strategy*, September 2002.

8   "Superiority Complex," *New York Times*, November 19, 2011, www.nytimes. com/imagepages/2011/11/19/opinion/19blow-ch.html?ref=opinion.

9   J. William Fulbright, *The Arrogance of Power* (London: Cape, 1967), 12.

10 Samuel P. Huntington, *Who Are We?: America's Great Debate*, New edition (Free Press, 2005), 39.

11 Ibid., 86–90.

12 John I. Jenkins and Thomas Burish, "Reason and Faith at Harvard," *Washington Post*, October 23, 2006, Opinions. www.washingtonpost.com/wp-dyn/con tent/article/2006/10/22/AR2006102200714.html.

13 Natalie Avon, "Why More Americans Don't Travel Abroad," *CNN Travel*, February 4, 2011, http://articles.cnn.com/2011-02-04/travel/americans.travel.dom estically_1_western-hemisphere-travel-initiative-passports-tourism-industries?_s= PM:TRAVEL.

14 William D. Chalmers, "The Great American Passport Myth: Why Just 3.5% of Us Travel Overseas!," *Huffington Post*, September 29, 2012, www.huffingtonpost. com/william-d-chalmers/the-great-american-passpo_b_1920287.html.

15 2009 年普通高等学校招生全国统一考试(上海卷), 2009 Shanghai history *gaokao*.

16 David Kennedy, *The American Pageant, International Edition*, 14th revised edn. (New York: Wadsworth, 2009).

17 The writer's classmates at Cornell did not know if Malaysia was in Asia or Africa.

18 Arthur Schlesinger, *The Disuniting of America: Reflections on a Multicultural Society*, 3rd revised edn. (New York: W. W. Norton & Co., 1999).

19 Patrice L. R. Higonnet, *Attendent Cruelties: Nation and Nationalism in American History* (New York: Other Press, 2007), 11.

20 Howard Zinn, *A People's History of the United States: From 1492 to the Present*, 2nd edn. (London: Longman, 1996), 23.

21 Richard Sennett and Jonathan Cobb, *The Hidden Injuries of Class* (New York: Vintage Books, 1973), 14–15.

22 *Who Are We?*, 300.

23 Gore Vidal, *Perpetual War for Perpetual Peace: How We Got to Be so Hated – Causes of Conflict in the Last Empire* (Forest Row: Clairview Books, 2002), x.

24 Jeffrey Goldberg, "Hillary Clinton: Chinese System Is Doomed, Leaders on a 'Fool's Errand,'" *The Atlantic*, May 10, 2011, www.theatlantic.com/internationa l/archive/2011/05/hillary-clinton-chinese-system-is-doomed-leaders-on-a-fools-err and/238591/.

25 Nelson D. Schwartz and Michael Cooper, "Black Professionals' Progress Stalls,"*New York Times*, May 27, 2013, U.S.. www.nytimes.com/2013/05/28/us/ texas-firm-highlights-struggle-for-black-professionals.html.

26 Barack Obama, *The Audacity of Hope: Thoughts on Reclaiming the American Dream* (Edinburgh: Canongate, 2007), 232–33.

27 *Stop and Frisk 2011: NYCLU Briefing* (New York: New York Civil Liberties Union, May 9, 2012), www.nyclu.org/files/publications/NYCLU_2011_Stop -and-Frisk_Report.pdf.

28 "Injustices of Stop and Frisk," *New York Times*, May 13, 2012, Opinion. www. nytimes.com/2012/05/14/opinion/injustices-of-stop-and-frisk.html.

29   Joseph Goldstein, "Judge Rejects New York's Stop-and-Frisk Policy," *New York Times*, August 12, 2013, N.Y./Region. www.nytimes.com/2013/08/13/nyregion/stop-and-frisk-practice-violated-rights-judge-rules.html.

30   "Transcript: Obama Speaks of Verdict Through the Prism of African-American Experience," *New York Times*, July 19, 2013, U.S./Politics. www.nytimes.com/2013/07/20/us/politics/transcript-obama-speaks-of-verdict-through-the-prism-of-african-american-experience.html.

31   "Protests in US at Zimmerman Verdict," *BBC News*, July 20, 2013, US and Canada. www.bbc.co.uk/news/world-us-canada-23390975.

32   Marilyn Salenger, "'White Flight' and Detroit's Decline," *Washington Post*, July 21, 2013, Opinions. www.washingtonpost.com/opinions/marilyn-salenger-white-flight-and-detroits-decline/2013/07/21/7903e888-f24a-11e2-bdae-0d1f78989e8a_story.html?wpisrc=nl_opinions.

33   "America's World," *The Economist*, October 21, 1999, www.economist.com/node/250970.

34   Peter Nolan, *Crossroads* (London: Marshall Cavendish, 2009), 104–5.

35   Joseph S. Nye, *The Paradox of American Power: Why the World's Only Superpower Can't Go It Alone* (Oxford: Oxford University Press, 2003), 2.

36   Nye, *The Paradox of American Power*.

37   Brent Scowcroft, "A World in Transformation," *The National Interest*, April 25, 2012, http://nationalinterest.org/article/world-transformation-6794?page=1.

38   Zbigniew Brzezinski, *Strategic Vision: America and the Crisis of Global Power* (New York: Basic Books, 2012), 37.

39   Ibid., 121–2.

40   Paul M. Kennedy, *The Rise and Fall of the Great Powers: Economic Change and Military Conflict from 1500 to 2000* (New York: Vintage Books, 1989).

41   Immanuel Maurice Wallerstein, *The Decline of American Power: The U.S. in a Chaotic World* (New York: New Press, 2003).

42   Kennedy, *The Rise and Fall of the Great Powers*, 446.

43   Graham Allison, Robert D. Blackwill, and Ali Wyne, *Lee Kuan Yew: The Grand Master's Insights on China, the United States, and the World* (Cambridge, MA: MIT Press, 2013), ch. 3.

44   Fulbright, *The Arrogance of Power*, 245.

45   John Quincy Adams quoted in ibid., 258.

46   Samuel Huntington quoted in Edward Luce, *Time To Start Thinking: America and the Spectre of Decline* (Boston, MA: Little, Brown, 2012), 280.

47   Annalyn Censky, "Romney Talks Tough on China," *CNNMoney*, October 19, 2011, http://money.cnn.com/2011/09/06/news/economy/romney_china/index.htm.

48   Kenneth Lieberthal and Jisi Wang, "Addressing U.S.–China Strategic Distrust," accessed April 8, 2012, www.brookings.edu/papers/2012/0330_us_china_liebertha l.aspx.

49   Jeffrey Goldberg, "Hillary Clinton: Chinese System Is Doomed, Leaders on a 'Fool's Errand'" *The Atlantic*, May 10, 2011, www.theatlantic.com/international/archive/2011/05/hillary-clinton-chinese-system-is-doomed-leaders-on-a-fools-err and/238591/.

50   *US Ambassador Urges Reaching Out to Chinese Youth and Internet Users to Take China Down*, 2011, www.youtube.com/watch?v=N6O20dcJONQ&feature=youtube_gdata_player.

51   Stefan Halper, *The Beijing Consensus* (New York: Basic Books, 2010).

52   John J. Mearsheimer, *The Tragedy of Great Power Politics* (New York: W. W. Norton & Company, 2003).

53   Lieberthal and Wang, "Addressing U.S.–China Strategic Distrust."

54 Graham Allison, "Thucydides's Trap Has Been Sprung in the Pacific," *Financial Times*, August 21, 2012, www.ft.com/cms/s/0/5d695b5a-ead3-11e1-984b-00144fea b49a.html#axzz24Ft4mczq.

55 Joseph S. Nye, "Work With China, Don't Contain It," *New York Times*, January 25, 2013, Opinion. www.nytimes.com/2013/01/26/opinion/work-with-china-dont-contain-it.html.

56 Jeffrey Bader, "The Current Sino–US Relation: Not That Tense," *International and Strategic Studies* no. 66 (April 24, 2012).

57 Peter Navarro, *The Coming China Wars: Where They Will Be Fought and How They Can Be Won* (London and Englewood Cliffs, NJ: Financial Times/Prentice Hall, 2006).

58 Peter Navarro and Greg Autry, *Death by China: Confronting the Dragon – a Global Call to Action* (Englewood Cliffs, NJ: Prentice Hall, 2011).

59 Jung Chang, *Mao: The Unknown Story* (London: Vintage, 2007).

60 *China Buying Batteries and Aircraft in Latest Takeovers of US Companies – Lou Dobbs – Megyn Kelly*, 2012, www.youtube.com/watch?v=37wSwB7w7QI&fea ture=youtube_gdata_player.

61 *Ariel Cohen: The Sword Will Follow the Yuan*, 2010, www.youtube.com/watch? v=pWftSCjzCBI&feature=youtube_gdata_player.

62 Ariel Cohen, "Mr. Erdogan Goes to Shanghai," *The National Interest*, February 18, 2013, http://nationalinterest.org/commentary/mr-erdogan-goes-shangh ai-8113.

63 Patti Waldmeir, "China's New Rich Revive Eating as Art," *Financial Times*, February 19, 2013, www.ft.com/cms/s/0/7d2ef942-79e2-11e2-9dad-00144feabdc0. html#axzz2LLJDJIka.

64 Patti Waldmeir, "When One Pair of Eyelids Isn't Enough," *Financial Times*, July 23, 2013, www.ft.com/cms/s/0/f3e12b58-e7ee-11e2-babb-00144feabdc0.html#a xzz2Zx9ptMgG.

65 Chris Buckley, "China Takes Aim at Western Ideas," *New York Times*, August 19, 2013, World/Asia Pacific. www.nytimes.com/2013/08/20/world/asia/chinas-ne w-leadership-takes-hard-line-in-secret-memo.html.

66 Malcolm Byrne, ed., "CIA Confirms Role in 1953 Iran Coup" (The National Security Archive, August 19, 2013), http://www2.gwu.edu/~nsarchiv/NSAEBB/ NSAEBB435/; "BBC Admits Role in 1953 Iranian Coup," accessed August 22, 2013, www.presstv.ir/detail/195008.html.

67 Edward Wong and Jonathan Ansfield, "Political Staging in Trial of Fallen China Official," *New York Times*, August 25, 2013, World/Asia Pacific. www.nytimes. com/2013/08/26/world/asia/prosecutors-say-chinese-official-bypassed-protocol. html; Zhang Qiang, "Microblogging the Trial: Transparency or Theatre?," *BBC News*, August 23, 2013, China. www.bbc.co.uk/news/world-asia-china-23806657; Jamil Anderlini, "Bo Xilai 'tiger' Trial Goes off Script for China's Leaders: Children of the Revolution Have Been Forced to Eat Each Other," *Financial Times*, August 22, 2013, www.ft.com/cms/s/0/71ede0b6-0b46-11e3-aeab-00144fea bdc0.html?ftcamp=crm/email/2013823/nbe/ChinaBusiness/product&siteedition= uk#axzz2cPDu41Yf.

68 *Current State of Sino-American Relations* (US-China Insitute, USC, 2010), www. youtube.com/watch?v=sbtf6eLTsCU&feature=youtube_gdata_player.

69 Suyin Han, *The Crippled Tree; China: Biography, History, Autobiography* (London: Cape, 1965), 280.

70 Iris Chang, *The Chinese in America: A Narrative History* (New York: Viking, 2003), xi.

71 Edward W. Said, *Orientalism: Western Conceptions of the Orient*, Reprinted with a new preface (Harmondsworth: Penguin, 1985).

72 Edward W. Said, *Culture and Imperialism* (London: Chatto & Windus, 1993).

73   *The Manchurian Candidate*, 1962; *The Sand Pebbles*, 1966.

74   *Professor Kurashige Discusses His Memory of Images of Asians in the U.S. Media in His Childhood*, 2011, www.youtube.com/watch?v=-spwN5CIdfg.

75   Irwin A. Tang, *Gook: John McCain's Racism and Why It Matters* (New York: Paul Revere Books, 2008).

76   Fulbright, *The Arrogance of Power*, 164.

77   Mike Mullen, "A Step Toward Trust With China," *New York Times*, July 25, 2011, Opinion. www.nytimes.com/2011/07/26/opinion/26Mullen.html?nl=toda ysheadlines&emc=tha212.

78   Alastair I. Johnston, "Is China a Status Quo Power?," *International Security* 27, no. 4 (Spring 2003): 5–56.

79   Brzezinski, *Strategic Vision*, 75.

80   With a Harvard law degree, Freeman accompanied Nixon to China as his interpreter.

81   Chas Freeman, "China's Challenge to American Hegemony," January 20, 2012, www. mepc.org/articles-commentary/speeches/chinas-challenge-american-hegemony.

82   Daniel T. Griswold, *Mad About Trade: Why Main Street America Should Embrace Globalization* (Washington, DC: Cato Institute, 2009); Edward S. Steinfeld, *Playing Our Game: Why China's Rise Doesn't Threaten the West* (New York: Oxford University Press, 2010).

83   Susan L. Shirk, *China: Fragile Superpower: How China's Internal Politics Could Derail Its Peaceful Rise* (New York: Oxford University Press, 2008).

84   David Shambaugh, "Is There a Chinese Model?," accessed September 18, 2010, www.chinadaily.net/china/2010-03/01/content_9515478.htm.

85   Robert J. Art, *A Grand Strategy for America* (Ithaca, NY: Cornell University Press, 2013); Wang Tian, "Ambassador: China–US Relations Not Zero-Sum Game," *People's Daily Online* 人民网, October 27, 2011, http://english.people. com.cn/90780/7628565.html.

86   Christopher Layne, "China's Challenge to US Hegemony," *Current History*, January 2008; Christopher Layne, "The Global Power Shift from West to East," *The National Interest*, April 28, 2012, http://nationalinterest.org/article/the-globa l-power-shift-west-east-6796?page=1.

87   Henry Kissinger, "Avoiding a U.S.–China Cold War," *Washington Post*, January 14, 2011, www.washingtonpost.com/wp-dyn/content/article/2011/01/13/AR20110 11304832.html?wpisrc=nl_opinions.

88   Guangyuan Yu, Stevine I. Levine, and Ezra F. Vogel, *Deng Xiaoping Shakes the World: An Eyewitness Account of China's Party Work Conference and the Third Plenum (November-December 1978)* (New York: EastBridge, 2004).

89   C. P. Fitzgerald, *The Chinese View of Their Place in the World*. (London/New York: Oxford University Press, 1964), 6.

90   Nele Noesselt, "Is There a 'Chinese School'of IR?," GIGA Working Papers, Power, Norms and Governance in International Relations (German Institute of Global and Regional Studies, March 2012).

91   阎学通 Yan Xuetong, *Ancient Chinese Thought, Modern Chinese Power*, ed. Daniel Bell and Zhe Sun, trans. Edmund Ryden, Princeton-China Series (Princeton, NJ: Princeton University Press, 2011).

92   Mencius as quoted in David Shambaugh, *Beautiful Imperialist: China Perceives America, 1972–1990* (Princeton, NJ: Princeton University Press, 1991), 82.

93   以不忍人之心，行不忍人之政(用怜悯体恤别人的心情，实行怜悯体恤百姓的政治)，rule with compassion.

94   C. P. Fitzgerald, *The Southern Expansion of the Chinese People: Southern Fields and Southern Ocean* (London: Barrie and Jenkins, 1972), xvi.

95 Gungwu Wang, *The Chinese Overseas: From Earthbound China to the Quest for Autonomy*, The Edwin O. Reischauer Lectures, 1997 (Cambridge, MA: Harvard University Press, 2000), 4–7.

96 Michael D. Swaine, "The Policy Analyst and Historical Perspectives: Notes of a Practitioner," in *Past and Present in China's Foreign Policy* (Portland, ME: MerwinAsia, n.d.), 1–2.

97 David Kang, *East Asia Before the West: Five Centuries of Trade and Tribute* (New York: Columbia University Press, 2012).

98 One of greatest emperors in Chinese history, Taizong (599–649) was the standard by which later emperors were measured. His reign was a golden age and required study by future crown princes.

99 Fitzgerald, *The Southern Expansion of the Chinese People*, 91–99.

100 孙中山 Sun Yat-sen, "Pan Asianism, 大亚细亚主义," November 28, 1924.

101 Peter Nolan, *A New Peloponnesian War: China, the West and the South China Seas* (Cambridge: Cambridge University Press, 2012).

102 Angus Maddison and Organization for Economic Co-operation and Development, *The World Economy: A Millennial Perspective* (Paris: OECD), 2001).

103 Angus Maddison, *Chinese Economic Performance in the Long Run: 960–2030 AD*, 2nd ed. (Paris: OECD, 2007), Chs 1 and 2.

104 William A. Callahan, "National Insecurities: Humiliation, Salvation, and Chinese Nationalism," *Alternatives: Global, Local, Political* 29, no. 2 (2004): 199–218.

105 M. Schoenhals, "Political Movements, Change and Stability: The Chinese Communist Party in Power," *The China Quarterly* 159, no. 1 (1999): 595–605.

106 Lin Biao's remarks to the Seventh National Congress of the CCP on 22 May 1945.

107 David S. G. Goodman, "The Sixth Plenum of the 11th Central Committee of the CCP: Look Back in Anger?," *The China Quarterly*, no. 87 (1981): 518–27.

108 Michael E. Marti, China and the Legacy of Deng Xiaoping: From Communist Revolution to Capitalist Evolution (Washington, DC: Brassey's US, 2002).

109 邓小平 Deng Xiaoping, "在武昌、深圳、珠海、上海等地的谈话要点, Key Points of Speeches at Wuchang, Shenzhen, Zhuhai and Shanghai," *Xinhua News*, January 18, 1992, http://news.xinhuanet.com/ziliao/2005-02/17/content_2586970.htm.

110 赵紫阳 Zhao Ziyang, *Prisoner of the State* (London: Simon & Schuster, 2009), 205.

111 "Full Text: Report on the Work of the Government," *English.xinhuanet.com*, March 15, 2012, http://news.xinhuanet.com/english/china/2012-03/15/c_13146970 3.htm.

112 郑必坚 Zheng Bijian, 关于历史机遇和中国特色社会主义的战略道路, *On historic opportunity and the strategic road of socialism with Chinese characteristics* (Shanghai: Renmin Publishing, 2005), 1361.

113 Ibid., 1365.

114 Feng Chenyu, president of Sinopec, as quoted in Shirk, *Fragile Superpower.*

115 Zheng Bijian, 关于历史机遇和中国特色社会主义的战略道路 *On Historic Opportunity and the Strategic Road of Socialism with Chinese Characteristics*, 1255.

116 工业和信息化部关于电信服务质量的通告*2011 Report on Telecommunications Service Quality* (Ministry of Industry and Information Technology, 2011), www.miit.gov.cn/n11293472/n11293832/n11293907/n11368223/13719816.html.

117 "China to Be a Top Consumer of High-End Products by 2015," *China Daily*, March 8, 2011, www.chinadaily.com.cn/bizchina/2011-03/08/content_12133649.htm.

118 "Growing Concerns in China about Inequality, Corruption," Pew Global Attitudes Project, October 16, 2012, www.pewglobal.org/2012/10/16/growing-concerns-in-china-about-inequality-corruption/.

119   Zou Le, "Income Gap Growing to Alarming Level: CASS Report," *People's Daily Online* 人民网, December 16, 2010, http://english.people.com.cn/90001/90776/90882/7232826.html.

120   Max Fisher, "U.S. Ranks Near Bottom on Income Inequality," *The Atlantic*, September 19, 2011, www.theatlantic.com/international/archive/2011/09/map-us-ranks-near-bottom-on-income-inequality/245315/.

121   吴敬琏 Wu Jinglian, "贫富差距巨大根源在权力寻租, Rent-Seeking: The Root Cause of Income Inequality," 腾讯财经 *Tengxun Finance and Economics*, November 29, 2012, http://finance.qq.com/a/20121129/006629.htm.

122   "Government to Increase Spending on Education," accessed April 8, 2012, www.chinadaily.com.cn/china/2010-03/01/content_9515384.htm.

123   Jamil Anderlini, "China Wrestles over Democratic Reform," *Financial Times*, November 7, 2012, www.ft.com/cms/s/0/5e952fee-2873-11e2-afd2-00144feabdc0.html#axzz2BW9MvE93.

124   任仲夷 Ren Zhongyi, "The Four Cardinal Principles Reconsidered," 南方周末, *Southern Weekend*, May 5, 2000.

125   Anderlini, "China Wrestles over Democratic Reform."

126   Kathrin Hille, "Xi Presents New Face of China's Socialism," *Financial Times*, November 15, 2012, www.ft.com/cms/s/0/66d399ae-2f24-11e2-b88b-00144feabdc0.html#axzz2CD7LW2fk.

127   Andrew Jacobs, "Xi Jinping Imposes Austerity Measures on China's Elite," *New York Times*, March 27, 2013, World/Asia Pacific. www.nytimes.com/2013/03/28/world/asia/xi-jinping-imposes-austerity-measures-on-chinas-elite.html.

128   阎学通 Yan Xuetong, "How China Can Defeat America," *New York Times*, November 20, 2011, Opinion. www.nytimes.com/2011/11/21/opinion/how-china-can-defeat-america.html&sq=how%20china%20can%20defeat%20the%20US&st=cse&scp=1.

129   Yan Xuetong, *Ancient Chinese Thought, Modern Chinese Power*, 219.

130   Nolan, *Crossroads*.

131   Ross Garnaut, Ligang Song, and Wing Thye Woo, *China's New Place in a World in Crisis: Economic, Geopolitical and Environmental Dimensions* (Canberra, ACT, Australia: ANU E Press, 2009).

132   Bai Yansong (白岩松) is a popular host and news commentator on the Central China Television (CCTV) network.

133   王静 Wang Jing, "'占领华尔街'运动与美国资本主义的危机, The Occupy Wall Street Movement and the Crisis of American Capitalism," *Qiushi*, February 9, 2012, www.qstheory.cn/zywz/201202/t20120209_137842.htm.

134   E. Kneebone, C. Nadeau, and A. Berube, *The Re-Emergence of Concentrated Poverty* (Washington, DC: Brookings Institution Center on Metropolitan Policy, 2011), http://community-wealth.com/_pdfs/news/recent-articles/01-12/paper-kneebone-nadeau-berube.pdf.

135   The poverty line in America is defined as a household of four with annual household income below $22,300. Extreme poverty is defined as a household of four with annual income below $11,157.

136   "中美贸易投资摩擦频生 商务部称美指责言论'很搞笑' Trade and Investment Friction: Chinese Ministry of Commerce Says US Allegations 'Ludicrous,'" *Xinhua Online* 新华网, October 20, 2012, http://news.xinhuanet.com/fortune/2012-10/20/c_123847386.htm.

137   Vice-premier Wang Qishan's remarks at meeting with Governor Chris Gregoire of Washington State on 19 October 2011.

138   钱颖一 Qian Yingyi, Wang Jisi, Wang Min, Bai Chongen, and Jia Qingguo, "New Foundations for Sino-US Cooperation," *Chinadaily.com.cn*, February 14, 2012, http://europe.chinadaily.com.cn/opinion/2012-02/14/content_14598449.htm.

139 Lee Branstetter and C. Fritz Foley, *Facts and Fallacies about US FDI in China*, NBER Working paper (Cambridge, MA: National Bureau of Economic Research, October 2007), www.nber.org/chapters/c10471.pdf; "[经济发展新动力] 中美经贸关系, 推进合作 减少摩擦, US-China Trade Relations: Foster Cooperation, Reduce Tension," *Xinhua Online* 新华网, September 10, 2012, http:// news.xinhuanet.com/yzyd/fortune/20120910/c_113020631.htm.

140 David Barboza, "China Backs Away from Unocal Bid," *New York Times*, August 3, 2005, www.nytimes.com/2005/08/02/business/worldbusiness/02iht-u nocal.html?_r=0; Stephanie Kirchgaessner, "Senator Raises US Food Security Fears in Smithfield Deal," *Financial Times*, July 10, 2013, www.ft.com/cms/s/0/ f8aca252-e96f-11e2-bf03-00144feabdc0.html?ftcamp=crm/email/2013710/nbe/ AsiaMorningHeadlines/product#axzz2YIVs7UF8; "Huawei Tells U.S. to Shut up," *People's Daily Online*, July 22, 2013, http://english.people.com.cn/90778/ 8336661.html.

141 赵启正 Zhao Qizheng, *America and Americans through Chinese Eyes* (五洲传播 出版社 China Intercontinental Press, 2005).

142 Mullen, "A Step Toward Trust With China."

143 宋鲁郑 Song Luzheng, "中国为什么要怀疑西方的'普世价值,' Why China Should Beware of Western 'Universal Values,'" *Qiushi* 求是, June 22, 2009, www. qstheory.cn/yw/200906/t20090622_1953.htm.

144 Ibid.

145 Ibid.

146 Zinn, *A People's History of the United States*, 206–246.

147 Song Luzheng, "中国为什么要怀疑西方的'普世价值,' Why China Should Beware of Western 'Universal Values.'"

148 Steve Schifferes, "US Names 'Coalition of the Willing,'" *BBC News*, March 18, 2003, Americas. http://news.bbc.co.uk/1/hi/world/americas/2862343.stm.

149 Xin Dingding, Zheng Yangpeng, and Shi Yingying, "Simpler Visa Procedures Are Passport to Success," *China Daily*, February 10, 2012, European edition, http://europe.chinadaily.com.cn/epaper/2012-02/10/content_14578679.htm.

150 David Shambaugh, *China Goes Global: The Partial Power* (New York: Oxford University Press, 2013).

151 Raisa Belyavina, *US Students in China: Meeting the Goals of the 100,000 Strong Initiative* (International Institute of Education, January 2013), www.iie.org/ ~/media/Files/Corporate/Publications/US-Students-in-China.ashx.

152 "78.8%受访者认为人情关系复杂阻碍优秀人才回国, Survey Shows Complex Social Relations Keeps Talent from Returning Home to China," *Xinhua Online* 新华网, September 6, 2013, http://news.xinhuanet.com/hr/2013-09/06/c_ 125335728.htm.

153 Peter Nolan, *Is China Buying the World?* (Cambridge: Polity Press, 2012).

154 James C. McKinley Jr., "China Says Lady Gaga, Beyoncé and Other Pop Stars Are a Threat," *New York Times*, August 26, 2011, http://artsbeat.blogs.nytimes. com/2011/08/26/china-says-lady-gaga-beyonce-and-other-pop-stars-are-a-threat/.

155 "'Iron Man 3' Breaks China's Box Office Record," *China.org.cn*, May 2, 2013, www.china.org.cn/arts/2013-05/02/content_28714797.htm.

156 "'Transformers 4' to Be Produced in China," *Financial Times*, April 3, 2013, www.ft.com/cms/s/0/6631b490-9bf3-11e2-8485-00144feabdc0.html#a xzz2PJLUuTbj.

157 "Hollywood Movies Dominate Chinese Movie Market as China Increasingly Opens," *People's Daily Online* 人民网, December 8, 2005, http://english.peop ledaily.com.cn/200512/08/eng20051208_226455.html.

158 Amy Li, "Is Starbucks Overcharging Chinese Coffee Drinkers?" *South China Morning Post*, January 30, 2013, www.scmp.com/comment/blogs/article/1078478/ starbucks-overcharging-chinese-coffee-drinkers-ask?page=all.

159   Y. Feng and K. Frith, "The Growth of International Women's Magazines in China and the Role of Transnational Advertising," *Journal of Magazine and New Media Research* 10, no. 1 (2008): 1.

Bibliography

"78.8%受访者认为人情关系复杂阻碍优秀人才回国, Survey Shows Complex Social Relations Keeps Talent from Returning Home to China." *Xinhua Online* 新华网, September 6, 2013. http://news.xinhuanet.com/hr/2013-09/06/c_125335728.htm.

Allison, Graham. "Thucydides's Trap Has Been Sprung in the Pacific." *Financial Times*, August 21, 2012. www.ft.com/cms/s/0/5d695b5a-ead3-11e1-984b-00144fea b49a.html#axzz24Ft4mczq.

Allison, Graham, Robert D. Blackwill, and Ali Wyne. *Lee Kuan Yew: The Grand Master's Insights on China, the United States, and the World*. Cambridge, MA: MIT Press, 2013.

"America's World." *The Economist*, October 21, 1999. www.economist.com/node/ 250970.

Anderlini, Jamil. "Bo Xilai 'Tiger' Trial Goes off Script for China's Leaders: Children of the Revolution Have Been Forced to Eat Each Other." *Financial Times*, August 22, 2013. www.ft.com/cms/s/0/71ede0b6-0b46-11e3-aeab-00144feabdc0.html?ftcamp=cr m/email/2013823/nbe/ChinaBusiness/product&siteedition=uk#axzz2cPDu41Yf.

Anderlini, Jamil. "China Wrestles over Democratic Reform." *Financial Times*, November 7, 2012. www.ft.com/cms/s/0/5e952fee-2873-11e2-afd2-00144feabdc0.htm l#axzz2BW9MvE93.

Ariel Cohen: The Sword Will Follow the Yuan, 2010. www.youtube.com/watch?v=p WftSCjzCBI&feature=youtube_gdata_player.

Art, Robert J. *A Grand Strategy for America*. Ithaca, NY: Cornell University Press, 2013.

Avon, Natalie. "Why More Americans Don't Travel Abroad." *CNN Travel*, February 4, 2011. http://articles.cnn.com/2011-02-04/travel/americans.travel.domestically_1_ western-hemisphere-travel-initiative-passports-tourism-industries?_s=PM:TRAVEL.

Bader, Jeffrey. "The Current Sino-US Relation: Not That Tense." *International and Strategic Studies*, no. 66 (April 24, 2012).

Barboza, David. "China Backs Away from Unocal Bid." *New York Times*, August 3, 2005. www.nytimes.com/2005/08/02/business/worldbusiness/02iht-unocal.html?_r=0.

"BBC Admits Role in 1953 Iranian Coup." Accessed August 22, 2013. www.presstv.ir/ detail/195008.html.

Belyavina, Raisa. "US Students in China: Meeting the Goals of the 100,000 Strong Initiative." International Institute of Education, January 2013. www.iie.org/~/media/ Files/Corporate/Publications/US-Students-in-China.ashx.

Blow, Charles M. "Decline of American Exceptionalism." *New York Times*, November 18, 2011, Opinion. www.nytimes.com/2011/11/19/opinion/blow-decline-of-am erican-exceptionalism.html?nl=todaysheadlines&emc=tha212.

Branstetter, Lee, and C. Fritz Foley. "Facts and Fallacies about US FDI in China." NBER Working Paper. Cambridge, MA: National Bureau of Economic Research, October 2007. www.nber.org/chapters/c10471.pdf.

Brzezinski, Zbigniew. *Strategic Vision: America and the Crisis of Global Power*. New York: Basic Books, 2012.

Buckley, Chris. "China Takes Aim at Western Ideas." *New York Times*, August 19, 2013, World/Asia Pacific. www.nytimes.com/2013/08/20/world/asia/chinas-new-lea dership-takes-hard-line-in-secret-memo.html.

Byrne, Malcolm, ed. "CIA Confirms Role in 1953 Iran Coup." The National Security Archive, August 19, 2013. http://www2.gwu.edu/~nsarchiv/NSAEBB/NSAEBB435/.

Callahan, William A. "National Insecurities: Humiliation, Salvation, and Chinese Nationalism." *Alternatives: Global, Local, Political* 29, no. 2(2004): 199–218.

Censky, Annalyn. "Romney Talks Tough on China." *CNNMoney*, October 19, 2011. http://money.cnn.com/2011/09/06/news/economy/romney_china/index.htm.

Chalmers, William D. "The Great American Passport Myth: Why Just 3.5% Of Us Travel Overseas!" *Huffington Post*, September 29, 2012. www.huffingtonpost.com/ william-d-chalmers/the-great-american-passpo_b_1920287.html.

Chang, Iris. *The Chinese in America: A Narrative History*. New York: Viking, 2003.

Chang, Jung. *Mao: The Unknown Story*. London: Vintage, 2007.

China Buying Batteries and Aircraft in Latest Takeovers of US Companies – Lou Dobbs – Megyn Kelly, 2012. www.youtube.com/watch?v=37wSwB7w7QI&feature= youtube_gdata_player.

"China to Be as Top Consumer of High-End Products by 2015." *China Daily*, March 8, 2011. www.chinadaily.com.cn/bizchina/2011-03/08/content_12133649.htm.

Cohen, Ariel. "Mr. Erdogan Goes to Shanghai." *The National Interest*, February 18, 2013. http://nationalinterest.org/commentary/mr-erdogan-goes-shanghai-8113.

Cohen, Warren I. *America's Response to China: A History of Sino-American Relations*. 4th edn. New York: Columbia University Press, 2000.

Current State of Sino-American Relations. US-China Insitute, USC, 2010. www.you tube.com/watch?v=sbtf6eLTsCU&feature=youtube_gdata_player.

Deng Xiaoping, 邓小平. "在武昌、深圳、珠海、上海等地的谈话要点, Key Points of Speeches at Wuchang, Shenzhen, Zhuhai and Shanghai." *Xinhua News*, January 18, 1992. http://news.xinhuanet.com/ziliao/2005-02/17/content_2586970.htm.

Fairbank, John K. *The United States and China*. Cambridge, MA: Harvard University Press, 1948.

Feng, Y., and K. Frith. "The Growth of International Women's Magazines in China and the Role of Transnational Advertising." *Journal of Magazine and New Media Research* 10, no. 1(2008): 1.

Fisher, Max. "U.S. Ranks Near Bottom on Income Inequality." *The Atlantic*, Sep- tember 19, 2011. www.theatlantic.com/international/archive/2011/09/map-us-ra nks-near-bottom-on-income-inequality/245315/.

Fitzgerald, C. P. *The Southern Expansion of the Chinese People: Southern Fields and Southern Ocean*. London: Barrie and Jenkins, 1972.

Fitzgerald, C. P. *The Chinese View of Their Place in the World*. London and New York: Oxford University Press, 1964.

Freeman, Chas. "China's Challenge to American Hegemony." January 20, 2012. www. mepc.org/articles-commentary/speeches/chinas-challenge-american-hegemony.

Fulbright, J. William. *The Arrogance of Power*. London: Cape, 1967.

"Full Text: Report on the Work of the Government." *English.xinhuanet.com*, March 15, 2012. http://news.xinhuanet.com/english/china/2012-03/15/c_131469703.htm.

Garnaut, Ross, Ligang Song, and Wing Thye Woo. *China's New Place in a World in Crisis: Economic, Geopolitical and Environmental Dimensions*. Canberra, ACT, Australia: ANU E Press, 2009.

Goldberg, Jeffrey. "Hillary Clinton: Chinese System Is Doomed, Leaders on a 'Fool's Errand'." *The Atlantic*, May 10, 2011. www.theatlantic.com/international/archive/2011/05/hillary-clinton-chinese-system-is-doomed-leaders-on-a-fools-errand/238591/.

Goldstein, Joseph. "Judge Rejects New York's Stop-and-Frisk Policy." *New York Times*, August 12, 2013, N.Y./Region. www.nytimes.com/2013/08/13/nyregion/stop-and-frisk-practice-violated-rights-judge-rules.html.

Goodman, David S. G. "The Sixth Plenum of the 11th Central Committee of the CCP: Look Back in Anger?" *The China Quarterly*, no. 87(1981): 518–527.

"Government to Increase Spending on Education." Accessed April 8, 2012. www.chinadaily.com.cn/china/2010-03/01/content_9515384.htm.

Griswold, Daniel T. *Mad About Trade: Why Main Street America Should Embrace Globalization*. Washington, DC: Cato Institute, 2009.

"Growing Concerns in China about Inequality, Corruption." Pew Global Attitudes Project. October 16, 2012. www.pewglobal.org/2012/10/16/growing-concerns-in-china-about-inequality-corruption/.

Halper, Stefan. *The Beijing Consensus*. New York: Basic Books, 2010.

Han, Suyin. *The Crippled Tree; China: Biography, History, Autobiography*. London: Cape, 1965.

Higonnet, Patrice L. R. *Attendent Cruelties: Nation and Nationalism in American History*. New York: Other Press, 2007.

Hille, Kathrin. "Xi Presents New Face of China's Socialism." *Financial Times*, November 15, 2012. www.ft.com/cms/s/0/66d399ae-2f24-11e2-b88b-00144feabdc0.html#axzz2CD7LW2fk.

"Hollywood Movies Dominate Chinese Movie Market as China Increasingly Opens." *People's Daily Online*, 人民网, December 8, 2005. http://english.peopledaily.com.cn/200512/08/eng20051208_226455.html.

"Huawei Tells U.S. to Shut up." *People's Daily Online*, July 22, 2013. http://english.people.com.cn/90778/8336661.html.

Huntington, Samuel P. *Who Are We?: America's Great Debate*. New edition. New York: Free Press, 2005.

"Injustices of Stop and Frisk." *New York Times*, May 13, 2012, Opinion. www.nytimes.com/2012/05/14/opinion/injustices-of-stop-and-frisk.html.

"'Iron Man 3' Breaks China's Box Office Record." *China.org.cn*, May 2, 2013. www.china.org.cn/arts/2013-05/02/content_28714797.htm.

Jacobs, Andrew. "Xi Jinping Imposes Austerity Measures on China's Elite." *New York Times*, March 27, 2013, World/Asia Pacific www.nytimes.com/2013/03/28/world/asia/xi-jinping-imposes-austerity-measures-on-chinas-elite.html.

Jenkins, John I., and Thomas Burish. "Reason and Faith at Harvard." *Washington Post*, October 23, 2006, Opinion. www.washingtonpost.com/wp-dyn/content/article/2006/10/22/AR2006102200714.html.

Johnston, Alastair I. "Is China a Status Quo Power?" *International Security* 27, no. 4 (Spring 2003): 5–56.

Kang, David. *East Asia Before the West: Five Centuries of Trade and Tribute*. New York: Columbia University Press, 2012.

Kennedy, David. *The American Pageant, International Edition*. 14th revised edition. New York: Wadsworth, 2009.

Kennedy, Paul M. *The Rise and Fall of the Great Powers: Economic Change and Military Conflict from 1500 to 2000*. New York: Vintage Books, 1989.

Kirchgaessner, Stephanie. "Senator Raises US Food Security Fears in Smithfield Deal." *Financial Times*, July 10, 2013. www.ft.com/cms/s/0/f8aca252-e96f-11e2-bf03-00144 feabdc0.html?ftcamp=crm/email/2013710/nbe/AsiaMorningHeadlines/product#axzz 2YIVs7UF8.

Kissinger, Henry. "Avoiding a U.S.-China Cold War." *Washington Post*, January 14, 2011. www.washingtonpost.com/wp-dyn/content/article/2011/01/13/AR20110113048 32.html?wpisrc=nl_opinions.

Kneebone, E., C.Nadeau, and A. Berube. *The Re-Emergence of Concentrated Poverty.* Washington, DC: The Brookings Institution Center on Metropolitan Policy, 2011. http://community-wealth.com/_pdfs/news/recent-articles/01-12/paper-kneebone-na deau-berube.pdf.

Layne, Christopher. "The Global Power Shift from West to East." *The National Interest*, April 28, 2012. http://nationalinterest.org/article/the-global-power-shift-west-east-6796?page=1.

Layne, Christopher. "China's Challenge to US Hegemony." *Current History*, January 2008.

Li, Amy. "Is Starbucks Overcharging Chinese Coffee Drinkers?" *South China Morning Post*, January 30, 2013. www.scmp.com/comment/blogs/article/1078478/starbucks-o vercharging-chinese-coffee-drinkers-ask?page=all.

Lieberthal, Kenneth, and Jisi Wang. "Addressing U.S.-China Strategic Distrust." Accessed April 8, 2012. www.brookings.edu/papers/2012/0330_us_china_lieberthal. aspx.

Luce, Edward. *Time To Start Thinking: America and the Spectre of Decline.* Boston, MA: Little, Brown, 2012.

Maddison, Angus. *Chinese Economic Performance in the Long Run: 960–2030 AD.* 2nd edn. Paris: OECD, 2007.

Maddison, Angus, and Organization for Economic Co-operation and Development. *The World Economy: A Millennial Perspective.* Paris: OECD, 2001.

Mao Zedong."U.S. Imperialism Is a Paper Tiger." Speech, July 14, 1956. www.ma rxists.org/reference/archive/mao/selected-works/volume-5/mswv5_52.htm.

Marti, Michael E. *China and the Legacy of Deng Xiaoping: From Communist Revolution to Capitalist Evolution.* Washington, DC: Brassey's US, 2002.

McKinley Jr., James C. "China Says Lady Gaga, Beyoncé and Other Pop Stars Are a Threat." *New York Times*, August 26, 2011. http://artsbeat.blogs.nytimes.com/2011/ 08/26/china-says-lady-gaga-beyonce-and-other-pop-stars-are-a-threat/.

Mearsheimer, John J. *The Tragedy of Great Power Politics.* New York: W. W. Norton, 2003.

Mullen, Mike. "A Step Toward Trust With China." *New York Times*, July 25, 2011, Opinion. www.nytimes.com/2011/07/26/opinion/26Mullen.html?nl=todaysheadlines &emc=tha212.

Myers, David G. *Social Psychology.* 11th edn. New York: McGraw-Hill, 2013.

Navarro, Peter, and Greg Autry. *Death by China: Confronting the Dragon – a Global Call to Action.* Englewood Cliffs, NJ: Prentice Hall, 2011.

Navarro, Peter. *The Coming China Wars: Where They Will Be Fought and How They Can Be Won.* London and Englewood Cliffs, NJ: Financial Times/Prentice Hall, 2006.

Noesselt, Nele. "Is There a 'Chinese School'of IR?" GIGA Working Papers. Power, Norms and Governance in International Relations. Hamburg: German Institute of Global and Regional Studies, March 2012.

Nolan, Peter. *A New Peloponnesian War: China, the West and the South China Seas.* Cambridge: Cambridge University Press, 2012.

Nolan, Peter. *Crossroads.* London: Marshall Cavendish, 2009.

Nolan, Peter. *Is China Buying the World?.* Cambridge: Polity Press, 2012.

Nye, Joseph S. *The Paradox of American Power: Why the World's Only Superpower Can't Go It Alone.* Oxford: Oxford University Press, 2003.

Nye, Joseph S. "Work With China, Don't Contain It." *New York Times,* January 25, 2013, Opinion. http://www.nytimes.com/2013/01/26/opinion/work-with-china-dont-contain-it.html.

Obama, Barack. *The Audacity of Hope: Thoughts on Reclaiming the American Dream.* Edinburgh: Canongate, 2007.

Professor Kurashige Discusses His Memory of Images of Asians in the U.S. Media in His Childhood, 2011. www.youtube.com/watch?v=-spwN5CIdfg.

"Protests in US at Zimmerman Verdict." *BBC News,* July 20, 2013, US and Canada. www.bbc.co.uk/news/world-us-canada-23390975.

QianYingyi, 钱颖一, 王缉思WangJisi, Wang Min, 白重恩BaiChongen, and 贾庆国 JiaQingguo."New Foundations for Sino-US Cooperation." *Chinadaily.com.cn,* February 14, 2012. http://europe.chinadaily.com.cn/opinion/2012-02/14/content_14598449.htm.

RenZhongyi, 任仲夷. "The Four Cardinal Principles Reconsidered." 南方周末,*Southern Weekend,* May 5, 2000.

Said, Edward W. *Culture and Imperialism.* London: Chatto & Windus, 1993.

Said, Edward W. *Orientalism: Western Conceptions of the Orient.* Reprinted with a new preface. Harmondsworth: Penguin, 1985.

Salenger, Marilyn. "'White Flight' and Detroit's Decline." *Washington Post,* July 21, 2013, Opinions. www.washingtonpost.com/opinions/marilyn-salenger-white-flight-and-detroits-decline/2013/07/21/7903e888-f24a-11e2-bdae-0d1f78989e8a_story.html?wpisrc=nl_opinions.

Schifferes, Steve. "US Names 'Coalition of the Willing.'" *BBC News,* March 18, 2003, Americas. http://news.bbc.co.uk/1/hi/world/americas/2862343.stm.

Schlesinger, Arthur. *The Disuniting of America: Reflections on a Multicultural Society.* 3rd revised edition. New York: W. W. Norton & Co., 1999.

Schoenhals, M. "Political Movements, Change and Stability: The Chinese Communist Party in Power." *China Quarterly* 159, no. 1(1999): 595–605.

Schwartz, Nelson D., and Michael Cooper. "Black Professionals' Progress Stalls." *New York Times,* May 27, 2013, U.S.. www.nytimes.com/2013/05/28/us/texas-firm-highlights-struggle-for-black-professionals.html.

Scowcroft, Brent. "A World in Transformation." *The National Interest,* April 25, 2012. http://nationalinterest.org/article/world-transformation-6794?page=1.

Sennett, Richard, and Jonathan Cobb. *The Hidden Injuries of Class.* New York: Vintage Books, 1973.

Shambaugh, David. *Beautiful Imperialist: China Perceives America, 1972–1990.* Princeton, NJ: Princeton University Press, 1991.

Shambaugh, David. *China Goes Global: The Partial Power.* New York: Oxford University Press, 2013.

Shambaugh, David. "Is There a Chinese Model?" *China Daily.* Accessed September 18, 2010. www.chinadaily.net/china/2010-03/01/content_9515478.htm.

Shirk, Susan L. *China: Fragile Superpower: How China's Internal Politics Could Derail Its Peaceful Rise.* New York: Oxford University Press, 2008.

Song Luzheng, 宋鲁郑. "中国为什么要怀疑西方的'普世价值, Why China Should Beware of Western 'Universal Values.'" *Qiushi,* 求是, June 22, 2009. www.qstheory. cn/yw/200906/t20090622_1953.htm.

Steinfeld, Edward S. *Playing Our Game: Why China's Rise Doesn't Threaten the West.* New York: Oxford University Press, 2010.

Stop and Frisk 2011: NYCLU Briefing. New York: New York Civil Liberties Union, May 9, 2012. www.nyclu.org/files/publications/NYCLU_2011_Stop-and-Frisk_Rep ort.pdf.

SunYat-sen, 孙中山. "Pan Asianism (大亚细亚主义)." Speech, Kobe, Japan, November 28, 1924.

"Superiority Complex." *New York Times,* November 19, 2011. www.nytimes.com/ima gepages/2011/11/19/opinion/19blow-ch.html?ref=opinion.

Swaine, Michael D. "The Policy Analyst and Historical Perspectives: Notes of a Practitioner." In *Past and Present in China's Foreign Policy,* 1–12. Portland, ME: MerwinAsia, n.d.

Tang, Irwin A. *Gook: John McCain's Racism and Why It Matters.* New York: Paul Revere Books, 2008.

The Manchurian Candidate (Film), John Frankenheimer, 1962, US.

The Sand Pebbles (Film), Robert Wise, 1966, US.

"Transcript: Obama Speaks of Verdict Through the Prism of African-American Experience." *New York Times,* July 19, 2013, U.S./Politics. www.nytimes.com/2013/07/20/ us/politics/transcript-obama-speaks-of-verdict-through-the-prism-of-african-america n-experience.html.

"'Transformers 4' To Be Produced in China." *Financial Times,* April 3, 2013. www.ft. com/cms/s/0/6631b490-9bf3-11e2-8485-00144feabdc0.html#axzz2PJLUuTbj.

US Ambassador Urges Reaching out to Chinese Youth and Internet Users to Take China down, 2011. www.youtube.com/watch?v=N6O20dcJONQ&feature=youtube_ gdata_player.

Vidal, Gore. *Perpetual War for Perpetual Peace: How We Got to Be so Hated – Causes of Conflict in the Last Empire.* Forest Row: Clairview Books, 2002.

Waldmeir, Patti. "China's New Rich Revive Eating as Art." *Financial Times,* February 19, 2013. www.ft.com/cms/s/0/7d2ef942-79e2-11e2-9dad-00144feabdc0.html#axzz2L LJDJIka.

Waldmeir, Patti. "When One Pair of Eyelids Isn't Enough." *Financial Times,* July 23, 2013. www.ft.com/cms/s/0/f3e12b58-e7ee-11e2-babb-00144feabdc0.html#axzz2Zx9p tMgG.

Wallerstein, Immanuel Maurice. *The Decline of American Power: The U.S. in a Chaotic World.* New York: New Press, 2003.

Wang, Gungwu. *The Chinese Overseas: From Earthbound China to the Quest for Autonomy.* The Edwin O. Reischauer Lectures 1997. Cambridge, MA: Harvard University Press, 2000.

Wang Tian. "Ambassador: China-US Relations Not Zero-Sum Game." *People's Daily Online,* 人民网, October 27, 2011. http://english.people.com.cn/90780/7628565.html.

Wong, Edward, and Jonathan Ansfield. "Political Staging in Trial of Fallen China Official." *New York Times,* August 25, 2013, World/Asia Pacific. www.nytimes.com/ 2013/08/26/world/asia/prosecutors-say-chinese-official-bypassed-protocol.html.

Wu Jinglian, 吴敬琏. "贫富差距巨大根源在权力寻租. Rent-Seeking: The Root Cause of Income Inequality." 腾讯财经, *Tengxun Finance and Economics,* November 29, 2012. http://finance.qq.com/a/20121129/006629.htm.

Xin Dingding, Zheng Yangpeng, and Shi Yingying. "Simpler Visa Procedures Are Passport to Success." *China Daily*, February 10, 2012, European edition. http://europe.chinadaily.com.cn/epaper/2012-02/10/content_14578679.htm.

Yan Xuetong, 阎学通. *Ancient Chinese Thought, Modern Chinese Power*. Edited by Daniel Bell and Zhe Sun. Translated by Edmund Ryden. Princeton-China Series. Princeton, NJ: Princeton University Press, 2011.

Yan Xuetong, 阎学通. "How China Can Defeat America." *New York Times*, November 20, 2011, Opinion. www.nytimes.com/2011/11/21/opinion/how-china-can-defeat-america.html&sq=how%20china%20can%20defeat%20the%20US&st=cse&scp=1.

Yu, Guangyuan, Stevine I. Levine, and Ezra F. Vogel. *Deng Xiaoping Shakes the World: An Eyewitness Account of China's Party Work Conference and the Third Plenum (November-December 1978)*. New York: EastBridge, 2004.

Zhang Qiang. "Microblogging the Trial: Transparency or Theatre?" *BBC News*, August 23, 2013, China. www.bbc.co.uk/news/world-asia-china-23806657.

Zhao Qizheng, 赵启正. 五洲传播出版社. *America and Americans through Chinese Eyes*. Beijing: China Intercontinental Press, 2005.

Zhao Ziyang, 赵紫阳. *Prisoner of the State*. London: Simon & Schuster, 2009.

Zheng Bijian, 郑必坚. 关于历史机遇和中国特色社会主义的战略道路. *On historic Opportunity and the Strategic Road of Socialism with Chinese Characteristics*. Shanghai: Renmin Publishing, 2005.

Zinn, Howard. *A People's History of the United States: From 1492 to the Present*. 2nd edn. London: Longman, 1996.

Zou Le. "Income Gap Growing to Alarming Level: CASS Report." *People's Daily Online* 人民网, December 16, 2010. http://english.people.com.cn/90001/90776/90882/7232826.html.

"中美贸易投资摩擦频生 商务部称美指责言论'很搞笑', Trade and Investment Friction: Chinese Ministry of Commerce Says US Allegations 'Ludicrous.'" *Xinhua Online* 新华网, October 20, 2012. http://news.xinhuanet.com/fortune/2012-10/20/c_123847386.htm.

工业和信息化部关于电信服务质量的通告 *2011 Report on Telecommunications Service Quality*. Ministry of Industry and Information Technology, 2011. www.miit.gov.cn/n11293472/n11293832/n11293907/n11368223/13719816.html.

"[经济发展新动力]中美经贸关系:推进合作 减少摩擦 US-China Trade Relations: Foster Cooperation, Reduce Tension." *Xinhua Online* 新华网, September 10, 2012. http://news.xinhuanet.com/yzyd/fortune/20120910/c_113020631.htm.

3   Climate change

Like the Norns in Wagner's Der Ring des Nibelungen, we are at the end of our tether, and the rope, whose weave defines our fate, is about to break.

James Lovelock, *The Revenge of Gaia*[1]

On the morning of October 21, 2009 President Hu Jintao spoke on the phone with President Barack Obama about climate change and the upcoming Copenhagen Conference.[2] He said there were many unresolved issues but if both sides were to work hard, there was hope that the Copenhagen Conference would bear fruit. Both sides faced common challenges but shared common interests too. Bilateral cooperation, he said, would not only benefit the international community but also carry great significance for US–China relations. President Obama said the US was ready to work with all parties to produce good results at the conference. He added that the US and China should work together to take concrete steps to make the conference a success. The Copenhagen conference ended, however, in "blood, sweat and recrimination."[3] More than 100 heads of state turned up but failed to get any agreement to stop rising temperatures. President Obama failed to bring legislation to limit greenhouse gases in the US, while the Chinese declined to have their emissions measured. Both sides accused the other of not making clear promises to cut carbon.

The US and China are the world's largest emitters of carbon dioxide. Together they account for over 40 percent of the carbon emitted each year and the level of cooperation between the two countries may determine the future of global warming. During the last 100 years the US emitted more greenhouse gases than any other country (CO_2 remains trapped in the atmosphere for about 100 years), but in 2007 China surpassed the US in terms of current CO_2 emission.[4] In 2009 it also overtook the US as the world's largest energy consumer. The United States is the world's leading oil consumer, using more than twice as much as China, while China leads in coal, consuming more than twice as much as the US. Both countries rely on coal for over 50 percent of their energy needs, and it is imperative that they switch to cleaner energy.

This chapter uses the HISE framework to analyze the state of trust between the US and China with regard to global warming. It discusses the imperative for climate action, and the US and Chinese perspectives. The climate change debate brings national interests and structures such as urbanization, Big Oil, and shale gas into focus. The chapter discusses industrial concentration and the role of US firms in China's quest for a sustainable future. Will strong central authority and the latecomer advantage give the Chinese a leg up? Despite much talk, collective action is rare.[5] This chapter concludes that Cold War thinking hampers trust. Nonetheless, both sides have taken unilateral climate measures, although these may not be adequate to counter the drive to increase economic output and the consequent use of fossil fuel.[6]

Climate change

UN secretary-general Ban Ki-Moon calls global warming "the major, overriding environmental issue of our time," and "a growing crisis with economic, health and safety, food production, security, and other dimensions." Greenhouse gases in the atmosphere trap the sun's heat and cause global warming. Since the Industrial Revolution, we have been emitting greenhouse gases faster than the earth can absorb, especially in the second half of the twentieth century. Continuing current practices, the earth's atmosphere is expected to rise to 3°C above the pre-industrial temperature some time between 2030 and 2060. Such an increase is far outside the experience of human civilization, and will disrupt the climate and lead to large scale migration, hardship and conflict. The danger from global warming lies not only in the heat; most of the damage comes from storms, droughts and floods. For more than 600,000 years, carbon dioxide concentration in the atmosphere remained below 300 parts per million (ppm) but in the last century it climbed to about 385 ppm and is growing by a 2 ppm per year. The Intergovernmental Panel on Climate Change (IPCC) predicts that droughts and heavy rains will increase, storms intensify, rainfall patterns shift and the health of millions will be affected. The humanitarian organization DARA estimates that 100 million will die between 2012 and 2030, with 90 percent of the deaths occurring in developing countries, if world fails to act on climate.[7]

The current greenhouse gas (GHG) level is 430 ppm of carbon dioxide equivalent (CO2e)[8] and rising by 2 ppm each year, but the worst climate effects can be avoided if levels are kept between 450 ppm and 550 ppm CO_2e.[9] Stabilizing in this range will involve cutting emissions to 25 percent below current levels by 2050, but ultimately to more than 80 percent below current levels. Emissions can be cut through increased energy efficiency, reduced demand, and the use of clean energy and transport technologies. To stabilize at or below 550ppm CO_2e, power generation around the world would have to be 60 percent decarbonized by 2050. But deep cuts in the transport sector, and non-energy emissions from deforestation, agriculture and industrial processes will also be needed.

Without action, the stock of greenhouse gases in the atmosphere could double its pre-industrial level as early as 2035, resulting a global temperature rise of over 2°C over the pre-industrial level.[10] In the longer term, there is a 50 percent chance that the temperature rise could exceed 5°C, or equivalent to the temperature spread between the last ice age and today.[11] Such a rise in the average global temperature would bring drastic change to how and where people live. All countries will be affected but the poorest will suffer earliest and most, even though they have contributed least to global warming. Because it is no longer possible to prevent the change that is already on the way, adaptation will be necessary.

Global climate is a "public good" and climate change the ultimate "externality." Climate change calls for a collective international response based on a framework of action. Key elements include emissions trading, technological cooperation, reducing deforestation, and adaptation to the effects of climate change. The Stern Review warns that without remedial action, climate change will cost us the equivalent of 5 percent of world GDP each year, now and forever, and if wider risks are taken into account, the damage could rise to 20 percent of GDP or more.[12] In contrast, the costs of action could be kept to around 1 percent of GDP each year. But are we too late?

Racing against the clock

In 2011 the International Energy Agency (IEA) warned that without a bold change in policy direction, the world would lock itself into an insecure, inefficient and high-carbon energy system.[13] "There is still time to act but the window of opportunity is closing." Growth, prosperity and population growth will continue to drive energy needs but the world can no longer rely on environmentally unsustainable uses of energy, the report cautioned. The Fukushima disaster, unrest in the Middle East and a steep rise in energy demand in 2010 pushed CO_2 emissions to a record high, and the IEA urged governments to encourage investments in low-carbon technologies.

Primary energy[14] demand is expected to grow by one-third between 2010 and 2035, with 90 percent of the growth coming from non-OECD countries.[15] By 2035 China will consume 70 percent more energy than the US but most of the energy will still come from fossil fuel. Fossil fuel use will fall from 81 percent to 75 percent while the share of renewables will increase from 13 percent today to 18 percent in 2035. According to one scenario, 80 percent of the energy-related CO_2 emissions allowed (in order to limit temperature rise to 2°C above the pre-industrial level) are already locked in by the existing capital stock including buildings, power stations and factories. Without further action by 2017, the energy-related infrastructure then in place would generate all the CO_2 emissions allowed up to 2035.

Global warming is all about energy, and energy lies at the foundation of the economy. Moving to a low carbon growth path will involve real economic and political costs. A successful response to climate change will require the most radical transformation of the energy system since the Industrial Revolution, and a redesign of the economy and the power relations that underpin it.[16] There have been calls to transition to renewable energy, but energy systems and infrastructure take a long time to change.[17] Renewables such as solar, wind, and biofuel present enormous challenges and require fossil fuel backup. To deflect the sun's heat, there have even been suggestions to launch space-mounted sunshades or floating nuclei generators that put white reflecting clouds across the ocean surface but nuclear energy may be the only feasible solution at the moment.

Scientist James Lovelock believes, however, that we may already be too late, as positive feedback pushes the global temperature past the point of no return.[18] His fears are echoed by the UNEP 2012 Emissions Gap Report, which warned that even if nations adhered to their current reduction goals, emissions will not be reduced in time to stop runaway global warming. It is now unlikely that the average global temperature rise will be kept to within 2°C. The gap between current emissions and the needed reductions is not only wide, but widening.[19] Now that a 2°C rise is no longer avoidable we are facing the risk of a 4°C rise, but a World Bank report warned that even with current commitments fully implemented, there is a 20 percent chance of exceeding a 4°C rise by 2100.[20] If the commitments are not met, the 4°C warming could come as early as 2060. Instead of searching for new sources of energy, we may need to consume less. As Vaclav Smil points out, the shaping of future energy use is primarily a moral issue, not a technical or economic one.[21]

The US perspective on climate change

In October 1997 Lee Raymond, CEO of Exxon, told the audience at the 15th World Petroleum Congress in Beijing that only 4 percent of the CO_2 entering the atmosphere was due to human activity, and that 96 percent came from nature.[22] He urged China and other industrializing countries to block any agreement on the Kyoto Protocol that would result in "lower economic growth, lost jobs, and a profound and unpleasant impact on the way we live." He argued that:

> The most pressing environmental problems of the developing nations are related to poverty, not global climate change. Addressing these problems will require economic growth, and that will necessitate increasing, not curtailing, the use of fossil fuels.

At Raymond's urging, the American Petroleum Institute (API) poured money into independent think tanks and advocacy groups to undermine the Kyoto Protocol. An API document showed that the oil industry association planned to repeat the tactics of the tobacco industry, which between the 1960s and 1980s spent millions of dollars to fund scientists and think tanks willing to challenge scientific evidence about smoking's danger. The document called for up to $7.9 million in spending to sow doubt about climate science through the media and argue that the Kyoto treaty was out of touch with reality. It recommended recruiting and training a team of scientists to "add their voices to those recognized scientists who are already vocal." Through layers of disguise and subterfuge, the industry funded "grassroots" programs and purpose-built think tanks as finger-print free as possible to manufacture confusion and perpetual controversy.[23] A long-time friend of Dick Cheney, Raymond enjoyed easy access to the White House, and influenced the Bush administration's energy policy and stance on Kyoto.[24] ExxonMobil spends more lobbying than any other company,[25] and former government officials often serve as advisors to oil companies.[26] The company seeking to build the Keystone pipeline has hired lobbyists with close links to Barack Obama, Hillary Clinton and John Kerry.[27] The government itself is the biggest beneficiary of the oil industry. Federal and state gasoline taxes add up to 19 percent of the retail price, and between 1977 and 2005 totaled twice the combined profits of the major oil companies ($1.4 trillion versus $700 billion).[28]

National interests

Concerned that America was adrift and lacking strategic focus, a commission which included Graham Allison, Robert Blackwill, Paul Krugman, Condoleeza Rice, Sam Nunn and Brent Scowcroft was formed in 2000 to identify America's key national interests.[29] The commission's report called *America's National Interests* identified the global environment as a vital national interest (other concerns include weapons of mass destruction, terrorism, transnational crime and drugs, international trade and investment, cyberspace and information technology). The report called for the preservation of a physical environment in which current and future generations of Americans could survive and thrive. It noted that America had a vital interest in preventing major changes in the natural environment that would degrade the physical health or economic well-being of American citizens. It warned that global warming could shift crop and disease zones, increase storminess, and raise the sea level. Evidence that burning fossil fuels contributed to global warming had become "persuasive" and could present serious long-term risks to American society, the commission reported. The US, it declared, should exercise leadership in slowing the rate of worldwide carbon emissions into the atmosphere.

The military too became concerned about climate change and published a report on climate change and its implications for American national security.[30] The report warned that abrupt changes in the climate evinced by increased droughts, floods and storms could lead to violence and political instability related to poverty, food, water and energy shortages, and a flow of refugees. In a separate report, eleven retired generals and admirals warned that climate change introduced the threat of catastrophic, non-linear change, and had become a "force multiplier for instability in some of the most volatile regions of the world."[31]

But concern for global warming has fluctuated. President George W. Bush ignored the commission's warning, and did little to join international efforts to fight global warming; but calls for the government to take stronger measures increased as the public became more aware of the dangers posed by climate change. When the Democrats won control of both houses of Congress in 2006, environmental legislative action increased. Toward the end of his term, Bush softened his position, and in his 2007 State of the Union message acknowledged for the first time the serious challenge posed by global warming and its link to fossil fuels. The Obama administration moved away from Bush's hard-line unilateralism and declared America's willingness to lead the fight against global warming. Obama supported "cap-and-trade" and proposed cutting greenhouse gas emissions back to the 1990 level by 2020, and 80 percent below the 1990 level by 2050, matching European Union commitments.[32]

Al Gore's film *An Inconvenient Truth* made a powerful impact, and an MIT survey found a sharp increase in climate change awareness between 2005 and 2006. Media coverage peaked in 2006, and attitudes began to change among opponents of measures to reduce carbon emissions. Business and unions began to show understanding and support for compulsory emissions targets. But media coverage dropped as public attention turned to the recession in the wake of the Global Financial Crisis.

State and local action

Much is happening at the state and local level to combat climate change through carbon cap, renewable energy and energy efficiency.[33] In 2008 ten states in the northeast including Connecticut, Maine, Maryland, Delaware, Massachusetts, New York and New Jersey instituted the first mandatory cap-and-trade program. The program caps carbon dioxide emissions from power plants in participating states by 2014 and requires a 10 percent reduction by 2018. Companies subject to the program bought $38.5 million in carbon permits at an auction in 2008. California launched its own cap-and-trade for greenhouse gases while six Midwestern states (together with the Canadian province of Manitoba) formed a regional carbon cap-and-trade program. Seven Western and Southwestern states have followed suit. State governments have been promoting the use of renewal energy too. Thirty states and the District of Columbia require electric utilities to use a minimum percentage of renewal energy while twelve states require a mix of bio-fuels with motor fuel. California requires a 10 percent reduction in carbon intensity by 2020 for fuel sold in the state, which can only be met by supplementing with renewable fuels. States are also actively promoting energy efficiency. California's "de-coupling" utility regulation has made the state one of the most energy efficient in the US. Twenty-three states levy "public benefits charges" on electricity bills to fund energy efficiency programs (similar to a tobacco tax to fund anti-smoking campaigns). A growing number of states are implementing time-of-day pricing for electricity and net metering which allows commercial users to generate their own electricity and sell it back to the grid.

Local governments have taken strong action to fight global warming too. More than 800 mayors from all 50 states have pledged their cities to meet or even exceed the Kyoto targets. They have taken measures to reduce urban sprawl and create compact urban communities, promote the use of bicycle trails, car pooling and public transit, and improve energy efficiency through building codes and retrofitting city facilities with energy-efficient lighting. These measures have yielded impressive results in some areas. Houston has cut energy use by 6 percent in 5 years even as its population grew by 10 percent. Seattle has reduced carbon emissions by 8 percent below 1990 levels, exceeding its own goal of meeting the Kyoto targets. Salt Lake City has cut emissions from its buildings and municipal vehicle fleet by over 30 percent since 2001, while San Diego has prevented over 700,000 tons of CO_2 equivalent by capturing the methane released by landfills. Things move faster at the state and local level, and these initiatives demonstrate the commitment by sections of the country to mitigate climate change. Action at the federal level would be more effective in terms of establishing national goals, regulations and international cooperation, but given the size of the states' territory and population (bigger than many countries), their contribution is significant.

Federal action

When Obama became president, he gave climate change and clean energy top priority but Republicans blocked large scale legislative action.[34] Nevertheless, he managed to enact new fuel economy standards for cars and light trucks of 54.5 mpg by 2025. The transportation sector accounts for 35 percent of US greenhouse gas emissions, and the standards represent the single biggest step by the US government to cut emissions. In the building sector, which accounts for 40 percent of US emissions, improved appliance standards are expected to decrease CO_2 emissions by 2.4 percent (instead of a 53 percent increase) by 2030. In the power sector, the EPA introduced CO_2 regulations for new power plants that would require the capture and sequestration of CO_2. The US has almost doubled the electricity generated by wind, solar and geothermal energy since 2008 and launched R&D efforts bringing together researchers in academia, business and government. CO_2 emissions have fallen 7.7 percent since 2006, which is the largest reduction of any country during the same period (2006–2012), and are today 14 percent lower than in 2005 (although some of the decline is due to the economic slowdown). Meanwhile, shale gas extraction using hydraulic fracturing promises to change the game.

The shale gas revolution

Hydraulic fracturing or "fracking" is a process of natural gas extraction used in deep gas well drilling. Once the well is drilled, millions of gallons of water, sand and chemicals are pumped at high pressure into wells of up to 8,000 feet deep to break up layers of shale (soft, finely stratified sedimentary rock) to release natural gas trapped within the shale. Developed by major oil companies including ExxonMobil, Chevron, Texaco, Shell, BP and their drilling contractors such as Schlumberger and Halliburton, the method led to the "unconventional-natural-gas revolution." Conventional gas refers to gas in porous reservoirs which have interconnected spaces that allow the gas to flow freely, whereas unconventional gas refers to gas trapped in impermeable shale which can only be released using a process such as fracking. Fracking opened up vast natural gas resources in North America. In 2000, shale gas accounted for only 1 percent of America's natural gas supply; today it is about 25 percent and could increase to 50 percent in the next twenty years. Estimates of total natural gas reserves including shale gas could be as high as 2,500 trillion cubic feet with another 500 trillion cubic feet in Canada – enough gas for industrial and household use for the next 100 years.[35] China has proven shale gas reserves of 600 billion cubic meters and exploitable reserves of 200 billion cubic meters.[36] Giant new fields have been discovered in the Mediterranean off Israel's shores and in the Atlantic near Brazil. There are also extensive deposits of shale gas in Europe, particularly in Poland. Meanwhile, the recent reduction in the cost of gas liquefaction and the increased size of LNG tankers mean that LNG can now be transported like oil to consumers on any continent and delivered at increasingly affordable prices. Natural gas supplies have surged and prices have fallen by half over the last three years.

The *Golden Age of Gas* promises to change the entire energy landscape in the US and around the world. The IEA sees a bright future for natural gas over the next five years.[37] According to its 2012 Medium-Term Gas Market Report, China will become a major gas importer and double its consumption of natural gas over the next five years; gas will generate as much electricity as coal in the US by 2017 and global gas trade will expand by 35 percent after 2015. Natural gas is a cleaner fuel and emits 43 percent less carbon than coal and 30 percent less than petroleum while producing only a third as much nitrogen oxide as coal.[38] In 1970 natural gas supplied 18 percent of global commercial energy but by 2010 it rose to 24 percent, while the worldwide crude oil share fell from 46 percent to 34 percent. The discovery of large new fields, the spread of shale gas production, the expansion of LNG exports, the high prices of crude oil and the unrivaled efficiency of gas converters together suggest that natural gas may soon become the dominant source of energy.[39] Demand for oil is expected to fall in the age of gas,[40] and shale gas could push oil prices down by 40 percent and boost the world economy by as much as $2.7 trillion by 2035.[41]

There are, however, serious concerns about its impact on the environment (air and water) during extraction, processing and transportation, as documented in the award-winning film *Gasland*.[42] For each frack, between 80 and 300 tons of chemicals, including volatile organic compounds (VOCs) such as benzene, toluene, ethylbenzene and xylene, are injected, together with 1–8 million gallons of water. A well may be fracked up to eighteen times. Waste water from fracking can be highly toxic, but only 30–50 percent is recovered;

the rest stays in the ground and could seep into aquifers that supply drinking water. The VOCs evaporated from the waste water combine with diesel exhaust from trucks and generators on the ground, sending ozone into the atmosphere. To address environmental and social risks, the IEA proposed seven "Golden Rules for the Golden Age of Gas," principles governing disclosure of environmental and drilling data, choice of drilling location, prevention of leaks, waste water treatment, ventilation of greenhouse gases, and production economies of scale.[43] The successful legislation and enforcement of such guidelines remains to be seen, however, in a powerful industry skilled at lobbying.

How the US views the Kyoto Protocol

Intended to bring the world together to combat global warming, the Kyoto Protocol has turned out to be an article of heated debate between the US and China. The protocol was adopted in Kyoto in 1997, but due to a complex ratification process only entered into force in 2005. It operationalizes the United Nations Framework Convention on Climate Change (UNFCCC) and commits industrialized countries to stabilize greenhouse gas emissions based on the principles of the convention. The convention itself is non-binding but the protocol sets binding emission reduction targets for thirty-seven industrialized countries in its first commitment period. The protocol recognizes that developed countries are largely responsible for the current store of greenhouse gases in the atmosphere, which are the consequence of 150 years of industrial activity.[44] Under the principle of "common but differentiated responsibility," the industrialized countries are obliged to cut emissions by 5 percent compared to 1990 levels over the five-year period 2008–2012.

Americans argue, however, that emissions reduction by the US will be more than offset by emissions in China, and the Byrd-Hagel resolution passed by Congress in July 1997 forbids the president from signing any climate agreement unless it requires specific commitments to limit or reduce greenhouse gas emissions by developing countries.[45] In 2001 the Bush administration withdrew from the Kyoto Protocol, complaining of the lack of obligations by developing countries such as China and India. Americans contend that efforts to control emissions will raise energy costs and cause manufacturers to move jobs overseas to countries with looser emissions standards such as China.[46] Resistance comes from management as well as the unions. American Electric Power (AEP), a major electricity company, and the International Brotherhood of Electric Workers (IBEW) proposed that legislation to control greenhouse gases must require the president to determine if major trading partners have comparable regulations. Otherwise, the legislation requires importers of energy intensive goods from that country to purchase US carbon credits. Although illegal under the WTO, a version of the proposal was incorporated into the Boxer-Lieberman-Warner cap-and-trade bill in 2008.

In a similar vein, Todd Stern, Obama's special envoy for climate change, stressed that it would be wrong to focus only on developed countries when developing countries already "account for around 55% of global emissions from fossil fuels and will account for 65% by 2030." Pointing to differences among developing countries in terms of size and stage of development, he said that China should not be treated like Chad since China was "the world's second largest economy, largest emitter, second largest historic emitter, will be twice the size of the US in emissions in a few years and has even caught up to the EU in per capita emissions."[47] Todd Stern's claims typify US complaints against the protocol, and he stressed that developed and developing countries alike need to commit to action even though the actions need not be the same. Reflecting persistent US reluctance to binding commitments, he argued that the key to reducing emissions was national rather than international action.

In her statement to the US–China Economic and Security Review Commission (USCESRC) in 2008, Joanna Lewis, an expert on US–China energy and environmental politics, testified that the Chinese leadership was concerned about climate change but even more concerned about sustaining economic growth and enhancing energy security. China is already doing much to reduce emissions with aggressive policies, but implementation has been challenging because it is difficult for the central government to establish the right incentives to ensure implementation at the local level, she explained. China is unlikely to commit to absolute emissions targets for technical reasons too. Chinese data collection and emissions monitoring are often unreliable, and Joseph Aldy, director of the Harvard Project on International Climate Agreements, suggested that China should focus on lowering carbon intensity rather than negotiate a quantitative cap on emission. Only after further economic growth and institutional development would it be feasible to consider an emissions cap.[48] China has more experience in fiscal policy measures than in the cap-and-trade favored by the US, and Aldy urged China to reduce energy subsidies and implement a carbon tax to motivate households and firms to adopt more energy-efficient technologies.[49] China has in fact moved from energy subsidies to a system of prices linked to world markets. The IEA estimates that after thirty years of gradual cuts, China's total energy consumption subsidies (including coal, electricity, natural gas and oil products) in 2006 amounted to around $11 billion, a drop of 58 percent from the previous year.[50] The rise in energy prices has added to the urgency to cut energy intensity.

Distrusting the Chinese

National security and economic calculations hamstring US nuclear technology assistance to China. Sino–American nuclear collaboration is a far cry from the friendly US partnership with India.[51] Nuclear power is one of the chief means for China to decarbonize but it supplies only 2 percent of China's energy compared to an average of 16 percent in developed countries. China wants to double reliance on nuclear power to 4 percent by 2020. The US and China signed an agreement concerning the use of nuclear energy as early as

1985, but implementation has been slow.[52] In 1997 Jiang Zemin and Bill Clinton signed the Agreement of Intent on Cooperation Concerning Peaceful Uses of Nuclear Technology but it was only six years later that Westinghouse sold its first advanced pressurized light-water reactor, the AP1000, to China. Also, nothing has taken place under the Kyoto Clean Development Mechanism (CDM) for technology transfer. The CDM allows developed countries to earn emission credits by helping developing countries build green infrastructure. Developed countries can use the emission credits to offset their own emission obligations. China is the most active CDM participant, registering over 700 CDM projects by 2010, but only with Europe and Japan.[53]

Americans increasingly perceive China as a major threat to the global environment.[54] Jared Diamond paints a nightmare vision of China's rise.[55] In a new version of the "Yellow Peril," Diamond warns that if China achieves First World living standards, it will double the entire world's resource use and environmental impact. By virtue of its huge population, China's environmental problems will "spill over to the rest of the world." If current trends continue, China will account for 40 percent of the world's total CO_2 emissions by the year 2050, he writes. Diamond warns that

> [p]ropelled eastwards by winds, the pollutant-dust, sand, and soil originating from China's deserts, degraded pastures, and fallow farmland gets blown to Korea, Japan, the Pacific Islands, and across the Pacific within a week to America and Canada. Those aerial particles are the result of China's coal-burning, deforestation, overgrazing, erosion, and destructive agricultural methods.

China is conserving its forest by exporting deforestation to other countries, "several of which have already reached or are on the road to catastrophic deforestation." Insects from China have wiped out numerous North American tree populations, and the Chinese grass carp competes with native fish species in forty-five states, causing large changes in aquatic communities, Diamond reports. But there is a more fearsome menace:

> Still another species of which China has an abundant population, which has large ecological and economic impacts, and which China is now exporting in increasing numbers is *Homo sapiens* ... China has now moved into third place as a source of illegal immigration into Australia, and significant numbers of illegal as well as legal immigrants crossing the Pacific reach even the United States.

Chinese perspective on climate change

In the past environmental protection occupied a marginal place on China's political agenda, and the 9th and 10th five-year plans paid little attention to climate change.[56] Climate change first received attention at the 17th Party Congress when President Hu Jintao warned that managing environmental resources was the main challenge to China's development and proposed building an "ecological civilization." The National Climate Change Program (NCCP) released in June 2007 detailed China's stance on climate change, and a task force headed by the premier was formed.[57] Hu declared: "Climate change respects no national borders, and no country is immune. Meeting this challenge requires the wholehearted cooperation and coordinated actions of the international community."[58] The Chinese government committed to cut carbon emissions "by a notable margin" by 2020 from the 2005 level, and there is now more discussion of sustainable development by top leaders in China than in almost any Western country.[59] The 12th Five-Year Plan reflects the party's determination to tackle global warming and build a sustainable economy.

The 12th Five-Year Plan

The 12th Five-Year Plan adopted in March 2011 calls for sweeping measures to reduce fossil fuel consumption, promote low-carbon energy sources, and restructure China's economy.[60] Xu Huaqing, director of the Energy Research Institute, sees the plan as crucial to attaining China's emissions targets.[61] Along with the gradual establishment of a carbon trade market, it calls for a 16 percent reduction in energy intensity by 2015 (from 2010 levels); increasing non-fossil energy to 11.4 percent of total energy use (up from 8.3 percent in 2010); and a 17 percent reduction in carbon intensity (carbon emissions per unit of GDP).[62] British economist Nicholas Stern calls the plan a "remarkable document" that will transform China's economy and give it an edge over the US and Europe.[63] The white paper on China's Policy and Actions in Responding to Climate Change released in November 2011 outlined priorities across eleven major areas including legal and strategic planning, economic restructuring to promote low carbon industries, development of clean energy sources and support to other developing countries.

In its quest for modernity, China faces daunting challenges. A continent-sized country with a massive population, it is short of water and for energy relies heavily on coal, the most polluting of fuels. Air pollution in its cities is among the worst seen anywhere. The only resource it possesses in abundance – its people – also brings enormous pressures through demand for jobs, housing and transportation. The Chinese are building in 50 years what took the West, with its vast colonial resources, 500 years. In the process, they face the triple challenges of modernization (with poverty eradication), transition (from command to market economy), and globalization (with intense competition) in a Western world order. So far the best technologies in elevators, air-conditioning, automobile and aircraft engines, illumination, power generation, and smart grids are owned by a handful of Western firms. The next sections will discuss the contradictions of development, energy and emissions.

Will the Chinese follow in the footsteps of the West or will they strike a path that eschews wasteful consumption?

Water shortage

China has 20 percent of the world's population but only 7 percent of its water resources. Water is a key resource for life, and the conservation of water resources is vital to climate change adaptation. Water has been indispensable in sustaining fast economic expansion but the growth is pushing the country toward a water crisis. The geographical distribution of water resources in China is very uneven, with more in the south and less in the north. Water scarcity has worsened severely in the north even as demand keeps rising everywhere. The North China Plain is an economic powerhouse with more than 200 million people, but has low rainfall and depends on groundwater for 60 percent of its supply. Scientists say aquifers below the North China Plain may be drained within thirty years.[64] Depending on the product, industry in China uses 3–10 times more water per dollar of output than industries in developed nations. Water usage has risen five-fold since 1949, and Chinese leaders face difficult choices as cities, industry and farming compete for a finite water supply. The 12th Five-Year Plan will invest 1.8 trillion yuan ($285.7 billion) in water conservation, with 800 billion yuan from the central government and 1 trillion yuan from local governments. By 2020, investment in water resources is expected to reach 4 trillion yuan ($634.8 billion).[65]

Pollution

China's leaders face myriad environmental concerns but the most immediate are water and air quality. Polluted water and air cause major health problems and inadequate usable water is affecting production. Some environmentalists consider the water problem more pressing than global warming. Severe water pollution affects three-quarters of China's rivers and lakes and 90 percent of its groundwater. According to a 2007 OECD study, hundreds of millions of Chinese drink water contaminated by fluoride, arsenic, fertilizers, pesticides and untreated waste water.[66] These concerns compete against pressures to build infrastructure and housing and promote exports to stimulate economic growth. Like other developing countries, China opted to "pollute now, pay later."[67] But its environmental crisis can be seen in historical context. Contamination of air, water, soil, and foodstuffs have accompanied industrialization around the world. China's level of pollution is reminiscent of the West's earlier on. Until their reduction beginning in the late 1970s, US per capita SO_2 emissions were more than ten times as high as the recent Chinese mean, and the absolute level then was higher than China's today. Atmospheric concentrations of particulate matter and SO_2 were as high in London in the early 1950s as they were in Beijing in the 1990s. A rarely appreciated fact is that the Chinese spend more on environmental protection than Western nations or

Japan at a comparable stage of development.[68] In a major policy move, the State Council has announced sweeping air pollution control measures to stop heavy pollutants within ten years.[69]

Population growth

Population growth adds enormous pressures. In one decade (the 1990s), the Chinese population grew by 125 million, or the size of Japan; in two decades, it grew by the size of the US, presenting a staggering challenge even to countries with far more natural resources. Large population increases require the channeling of a major part of GDP into feeding, clothing, sheltering and educating new citizens.[70] The population is growing despite the strict one-child policy, and the country also faces massive urbanization.[71] Over the past thirty years, the urban population grew by 500 million, and will swell by another 300 million by 2030. The share of urban residents in the total population rose from 36.2 percent in 2000 to 51.3 percent in 2011.[72] The current pace of migration of 15 million people moving into cities each year will continue for the next 15–20 years, which means China needs to build infrastructure and create jobs for 1.25 million people every month. Meeting this demand is essential to social stability, and the authorities are forced to balance this imperative against that of urgent climate control. Without the one-child policy, China would have an additional 530 million people[73] today, with important implications for energy use, Peter Nolan points out.

Energy

Most of the industries related to urbanization and infrastructure such as steel, cement, petrochemicals and aluminum also happen to be energy-intensive and important sources of greenhouse gases. China produces about 35 percent of the world's steel and 28 percent of its aluminum compared to 12 percent and 8 percent respectively a decade ago.[74] Increases in energy-related emissions in recent years have been driven primarily by industrial energy use, exacerbated by a higher percentage of coal in the overall energy mix. China's factories, which supply much of the world, consume about 70 percent of the country's energy.

China has made great strides in improving energy efficiency and increasing the use of renewables. Although GDP quadrupled between 1980 and 2000, it only doubled the amount of energy it consumed, marking an improvement in energy intensity unmatched by any country at a similar stage of industrialization. Without the improvement, China would have used more than three times the energy during this period. The 11th Five-Year Plan (2006–2010) reduced energy intensity by 20 percent, cutting carbon emissions by roughly 1 billion tons. Government planners envisage the use of renewables (hydro, solar, wind) for 15 percent of total energy consumption by 2020. According to Qi Ye, director of the Beijing Climate Policy Research Center, the government will spend 1.8 trillion yuan ($300 billion) over the next ten years on renewable energy development.[75]

China has become the world's largest producer of solar panels and the world leader by far in installed solar power capacity. Solar power capacity totaled 300,000 kW in 2010 while wind power went from 1.26 million kW in 2005 to 10 million kW in 2010. Hydropower rose from 117 million kW in 2005 to 190 million kW in 2010, meeting 6.8 percent of the country's energy needs.[76] China gets only about 2 percent of its electricity from thirteen nuclear reactors, but it plans to sharply increase nuclear power generation. It is now building twenty-seven new reactors, or about 40 percent of the total number being built around the world.[77] By 2030 China will operate 13 percent of the world's nuclear energy capacity.

Coal dependence

Coal remains China's most important source of energy. It provides nearly 70 percent of the country's energy (compared to the world average of 27.8 percent) and 80 percent of its electricity. China became the world's largest coal user in 1986, and in 2007 accounted for 41 percent of world consumption. In five years (2004–2009), China built the equivalent of America's entire coal power capacity. There are more coal power plants in China than in the US and India combined. Chinese coal power use is expected to more than double by 2030, representing an additional carbon commitment of 86 billion tons.[78]

Despite efforts to reduce dependence on coal since the 1980s, the share of coal in the total commercial energy source has stayed above 60 percent. About half of the coal is used to produce electricity but coal emits more CO_2 (61 percent) than oil or natural gas (36 percent). China's quest for lower carbon emission per unit of energy is constrained by its mix of energy resources and the lack of technology. Government support for advanced coal technology is still not enough to influence the kind of technology adopted by power utilities.[79] China has huge reserves of shale gas which may allow it to shift to natural gas for a major share of energy. Natural gas emits half as much CO_2 as coal, and Beijing, promising policy support and subsidies for drilling, wants to produce 60 billion cubic meters of shale gas by 2020.[80] But the shale gas is located in the western regions were there is a shortage of water, a resource needed in abundance for fracking.[81] China does not possess fracking technology, and questions over foreign investment and technology have yet to be addressed,[82] but if domestic production fails to materialize, it can turn to overseas sources. Russia has agreed to supply 38 billion cubic meters of gas per year,[83] and Burma is pumping gas through a pipeline from the Indian Ocean port of Kyaukpyu to Kunming, bypassing the Straits of Malacca.[84] A 1,800-kilometer pipeline delivers 40 billion cubic meters of gas a year from Turkmenistan to western China.[85]

Buildings

Despite impressive gains in industrial efficiency, much remains to be done at the residential level. Missing are energy consumption meters conveniently located in the kitchen which would enable residents to see the effect of turning off unnecessary appliances. Energy efficiency standards for home appliances have been introduced, and the average refrigerator in 2030 will be 32 percent more energy efficient that a 2005 model while the average air conditioner is expected to be 35 percent more efficient.[86] But few of China's residential buildings are centrally cooled or heated; they rely instead on less efficient individual air-conditioner units fixed to the outside of the buildings. The use of air-conditioners grew from less than 1 per 100 households in the early 1990s to over 100 per 100 in 2008, and usage will increase as income levels rise and homes get bigger, adding to the growing demand for energy. Most Chinese homes lack double-glazed windows and wall or ceiling insulation, and few have individual temperature controls. Fiberglass and thermostats in millions of new buildings would bring energy savings for decades to come but China's building codes will not match those of the OECD until 2030, by which time its residential construction boom will be almost complete, and China may be locked for decades in energy-inefficient buildings.[87]

Transportation

China has less than 30 vehicles per 1,000 people compared to over 800 in the USA, over 600 in the Eurozone and almost 600 in Japan. Despite the modest per capita car ownership, China by virtue of its population overtook the USA to become the world's largest automobile market in 2009. The government has taken steps to combat pollution through tighter fuel economy standards, a progressive tax based on engine displacement and curbs on ownership in big cities, but in a land where cars are a status symbol, car sales will likely grow as incomes rise. China has the world's fastest growing aviation market, and its stock of commercial aircraft more than tripled from 330 planes in 1995 to 1,155 planes in 2008. Its demand for aviation fuel grew by 12 percent annually from 1990 to 2005. The IEA expects Chinese consumption of aviation fuel to quadruple from 2005 to 2030, and its share of global consumption to increase from 6 to 12 percent.[88] Meanwhile, it is aggressively expanding its rail network, and plans to build 30,000 kilometers of high speed track by 2015. The Beijing–Guangzhou line, inaugurated on New Year's Day 2013, marked an important milestone. A train running at 275 km/hr uses only a third as much energy as airline flights, and can be powered by non-polluting wind and nuclear power.[89] The high-speed rail network may slow the growth of aviation traffic and carbon emissions. Just five years after it opened, China's high-speed rail network carries twice as many passengers each month as the country's domestic airlines, and is expected to surpass the passenger load of US domestic flights by early 2014.[90] The nation, according to Premier Li Keqiang, plans to spend $100 billion a year on its rail system for years to come, mainly on high-speed rail.

Central authority

Whereas the most important efforts in the US have come from state and local authorities, Chinese initiatives proceed from the center. China's top-down administrative system allows the country to build large-scale infrastructure such as rail and airports much quicker than the West (the US and the UK have yet to build a single high-speed rail line). The Chinese Communist Party is deeply embedded in the country's economic and financial system, giving it control over key resources. But green initiatives are sometimes blunted by the conflicting local interests. The chief impediment lies in the incentive structure whereby officials are rewarded according to the amount built, not the energy efficiency of the projects.[91] But there are signs that this is beginning to change as President Xi Jinping seeks a more balanced approach to development. On the eve of the 92nd anniversary of the founding of the Party, Xi said officials should not be judged solely on their record of boosting GDP but instead on achievements in improving people's livelihood, social development and environmental quality.[92] William Overholt saw in Xi's words the "forward-looking recognition that obsessive emphasis on economic growth targets is obsolete and must now be balanced against vital environmental and social concerns."[93]

How China views the Kyoto Protocol

Global warming is the consequence of greenhouse gases emitted by developed nations since the Industrial Revolution. According to the World Resources Institute, developed countries produced between 70 percent and 80 percent of the stock of carbon in the atmosphere. The historical CO_2 emissions per capita figure for the UK and the US is 1,100 tons compared to 66 tons for China and 23 tons for India.[94] A cornerstone of China's climate change program is the principle of "common but differentiated responsibilities" agreed at the 1992 Earth Summit. According to the principle, developed countries should take the lead in reducing greenhouse gas emissions as well as provide financial and technical support to developing countries, while developing countries focus on sustainable development and poverty eradication. Since China has much lower per capita emissions, it is unreasonable to expect it to reduce emissions in step with developed countries.[95] Its efforts to curb CO_2 not only involve doing so at a much lower per capita emissions but also deliver handsome profits to firms from high-income countries (which command the key energy saving technologies). Moreover, a significant share of Chinese CO_2 is produced in the manufacture of consumer goods for high-income countries. Some see in this a triple injustice.[96]

Distrusting the Americans

The Chinese suspect the Americans of using global warming as a pretext to restrain their growth. No one, they reason, can possibly expect China in its current stage of development to commit to greenhouse gas reduction targets. They are disappointed that the US, wealthy as it is and more responsible than anyone for the CO_2 in the atmosphere, rejects the Kyoto Protocol. Its infrastructure has long been built, and it is now largely a service economy but refuses to take on carbon commitments. It is the most technologically advanced country, and yet is unsympathetic to the needs of developing countries. Deng Yingtao of the Chinese Academy of Social Sciences warned:

> We cannot count on developed countries to offer genuine, generous aid. Leaving aside ideological, political and economic factors, there is tacit agreement among them to maintain and reinforce the unjust world order representing their common interests. This is the best way to perpetuate their dominance; no matter how fierce the quarrel among themselves, they will always unite to make war on the developing world. It is wholly naïve to expect them, except a small number of politicians, to help developing countries grow.[97]

The US promises to ease Cold War restrictions on hi-tech exports to China, but as minister of commerce Chen Deming puts it: "The stairs creak but no one comes down."[98] In fact, the restrictions have become tighter: between 2001 and 2011 hi-tech products fell from 16.67 percent to 6.26 percent of total imports from the US.

Zou Ji, director of the Program of Energy and Climate Economics (PECE) at Renmin University, sees the carbon tax proposed by Congress under the Clean Energy Bill as a way to squeeze Chinese exporters.[99] The tax is levied on products based on carbon emission, and those with the highest emission happen to be major Chinese exports such as raw materials, minerals, cement, steel and non-ferrous metals. Zou sees the tax as a stick to force China to accept carbon commitments but by inducing cost-push inflation, the tax ultimately hurts American consumers. Only interests groups such as US steel makers stand to gain, he argues.

Development model

The Chinese leadership, according to Nicholas Stern, who has worked off and on in China for the last twenty-five years, regards the current model as untenable, and is very concerned about climate change and global pollution.[100] The Chinese economy is expected to grow at least tenfold between now and 2050.[101] Its annual emissions stand at over 5 tons of CO_2 per capita, and it wants to cut emissions by half by 2050. If total emissions are to halve as the economy grows by a factor of ten, then emissions per unit of output must fall by a factor of twenty. This means a 95 percent reduction of emissions per unit of output, radically decarbonizing the economy. Historically, however, there is a correlation between per capita energy consumption, CO_2 emission and GDP. No country has ever attained high per capita GDP with low per capita energy consumption. To catch up with industrialized countries, China will necessarily consume more energy and emit more CO_2 per capita unless it adopts a different economic model.

China does not want to be trapped in the high-polluting and least profitable segment of the global value chain, and is looking to move out of low-end, labor-intensive manufacturing. But there is still growth in energy-intensive sectors such as aluminum, cement, steel and automobiles. It produces 35 percent of the world's steel and 28 percent of its aluminum.[102] Power generation continues to increase as energy demand rises.[103] It wants to shift from exporting to domestic consumption but that may take time because of high savings (53 percent of GDP in 2007, surpassing Japan and South Korea), the bulk of which is in the business (profits retained in large state-owned enterprises) rather than household sector.[104] The Chinese aspire to Western living standards but until they redefine prosperity, it is hard to see what sustainable development will look like. China, indeed the world, is at a crossroads, and must find an alternative to free market fundamentalism.[105]

Industrial concentration and latecomer advantage

Capitalism has led to a high degree of industry consolidation, a development Marx foresaw. Concentration in market share is matched by concentration in technology.[106] Key innovations are owned by a handful of firms based in high-income countries. The UK Department of Business Enterprise and Regulatory Reform (BERR) ranks the top 1,400 firms worldwide in terms of R&D spending. In 2007 the G1400 spent US$545 billion, a significant part of it on technology that directly or indirectly improves energy efficiency. The spending is driven by fierce competition – profitable companies can afford to spend more but less profitable ones cannot afford to spend less.[107] The top fifty firms account for 45 percent of total R&D investment. About 100 firms sit at the center of global R&D activity, but firms from the US, Japan, Germany, France and the UK make up 80 percent of the G1400. Even small countries like Denmark, Finland, Sweden, Switzerland and the Netherlands with a total population of 42 million boast 132 firms in the G1400, compared to only thirty-four firms from the BRIC countries which have a combined population of 2.6 billion. The low and middle-income countries as a whole, with 84 percent of the world's population, have only thirty-seven firms in the G1400. This asymmetry is a source of distrust between high- and low-income countries.

The giant oligopolistic firms are a boon and a bane. They are at the root of carbon emission but also create the technologies needed to address the problem. They command vital sectors like power generation and transmission, transport equipment, building construction and household appliances. China is central to their long-term growth and many have built facilities in China. The stock of FDI into China increased from $21 billion in 1990 to $378 billion in 2009, making a significant contribution to technical progress. These firms account for two-thirds of Chinese hi-tech output and 90 percent of hi-tech exports.[108] Their products contain global standards, allowing China to reap the benefits of a latecomer. They are part of the story of its quest for sustainable growth, and the gap between the best available technologies worldwide and what exists in China is narrowing. Advanced energy technology is increasingly available and in many cases developed indigenously. China's best ultra supercritical coal-fired power plants are now more efficient than the best coal-fired power plants in the US, converting 44 percent of coal energy into electricity compared to the US maximum of 40 percent. China has also become self-sufficient in nuclear reactor design, while economies of scale are driving down fabrication costs.

Can the US and China cooperate?

Zhang Haibin, professor of international environmental politics at Peking University, describes Sino–American climate cooperation as "wide but shallow, a lot of thunder but few raindrops."[109] When President Obama took office, expectations were high that a new treaty would be concluded in Copenhagen but hopes were dashed. There is a huge gap between the two sides on the question of responsibility, and relations are poisoned by Cold War thinking. Refusing to "feed the dragon,"[110] the US grants no aid to the Chinese.[111] The US holds the technology needed to improve energy efficiency, while the Chinese have become very efficient at producing solar panels, wind turbines and high-speed rail. Nuclear power is a cornerstone of the Chinese push toward a green future, but the US is unwilling to transfer advanced nuclear technology. China wants to purchase technology under concessionary terms of the Kyoto Protocol but the US will only sell on commercial conditions. Japan, by contrast, shares many viewpoints with China on global warming, and has been quick to act.[112] Because sulfur dioxide from China brings acid rain down on Japanese forests, the Japanese are keen to help, and instead of a "take charge" attitude, they try to accommodate their neighbor's policies.[113]

Will China lead the way?

When first elected, President Obama announced plans for "green path" infrastructure that will create "green collar" jobs.[114] The US possesses advanced technology and unrivaled capacity for research and innovation but uncertainty over long-term climate policy has made companies reluctant to invest in green technology development. The US political system has a short-term bias, and despite bold measures by a number of cities, states and corporations, the federal government cannot summon the will to act. Even extreme weather events that inflict unprecedented damage on American forests and agriculture have failed to galvanize action. Meanwhile, the shale gas revolution may soothe the urgency to act.

China enjoys certain advantages. Much of its infrastructure remains to be constructed, giving it the chance to build green transport systems, buildings and power plants, and, as a latecomer, to leapfrog older technologies. More importantly, Chinese leaders appear keen to adopt a new development model.[115] Senior party theorist Zheng Bijian stressed China's intention to transcend the old model of industrialization characterized by bitter rivalry over resources:

> Were China to follow this path it would harm both others and itself. China is determined to forge a new path of industrialization based on technology, economic efficiency, low consumption of natural resources relative to population size, low environmental pollution, and optimal human resource allocation. The Chinese government is trying to reduce the percentage of the country's imported energy resources and to rely more on China's own. The objective is to build a "society of thrift."[116]

The country's top-down political system allows it to implement long range plans swiftly. To accelerate change, the 12th Five-Year Plan will spend US $1.6 trillion in strategic industries and make China the global leader in energy-efficient buildings, smart grids, and solar and wind energy.[117] It is building low-carbon pilot zones (green cities) and experimenting with low-carbon development policies encompassing over 300 million people.[118] Instead of merely reducing carbon intensity, the economic planning authority (发改委), in a sharp departure from its previous position, is considering an outright cap on emissions in the 13th Five-Year Plan (2016–2020).[119] To prepare for the cap, it launched its first carbon trading scheme in Shenzhen in June 2013, and plans to roll out seven pilot schemes by 2014.[120] If things proceed according to plan, China may surpass the US and Europe in greening its infrastructure.

Conclusion

Climate is a public good, shared by all, belonging to none. As with all public goods, there is the risk of free-riding.[121] When nations are called to make sacrifices, zero-sum thinking sets in. Caught in a prisoner's dilemma, people tend to choose in ways that produce the worst joint outcome. All countries share in the responsibility to protect the climate but the urgency is not always well appreciated in high-income countries which do not suffer the worst effects.[122] They do not always feel morally responsible for global warming, while developing countries sense a double injustice when asked to tackle a problem they did not create and to reduce emissions before they escape poverty.[123] Injustice breeds distrust.

Many Americans fail to appreciate the challenges the Chinese face. China's per capita income is smaller than Cuba's and only a tenth that of the US.[124] It is only now in the process of building its infrastructure and is heavily dependent on coal. Even with increased nuclear power capacity and the use of natural gas, coal will remain its main energy source.[125] Its pollution is reminiscent of the levels seen during the industrialization of the West; countries whose main advantage is low cost often have no choice but to pollute first and clean up later. Nevertheless, the Chinese made remarkable improvements in carbon intensity and energy efficiency in the 11th Five-Year Plan, and expect further gains in the 12th Five-Year Plan.

US businesses contribute to and benefit from China. The technology China needs to build a sustainable future is concentrated in a small number of Western firms, and the demand for their products and services is growing.[126] Indeed, technology and commerce are central to US–China relations.[127] China is the third biggest buyer of US products, and US exports to China jumped 542 percent between 2000 and 2011 compared to 80 percent to the rest of the world.[128] Forty years after the Shanghai Communiqué, bilateral trade is approaching $500 billion (a 200-fold increase from $2.5 billion).[129] Despite interdependence and mutual benefit, however, Cold War thinking and other factors are hindering trust.

Climate change is all about energy. Humanity has consumed ten times more energy since 1900 than in the previous 1,000 years.[130] Both the US and China have taken strong measures to cut emissions but these may not be enough to halt global warming given the obsession with GDP growth.[131] Global warming can only be stopped by moving to a zero-carbon economy but a successful response requires the redesign of the world economic system and the interests and structures that underpin it. The Chinese are rethinking development.[132] They enjoy latecomer advantages and seem determined to invent a wiser mode of economic life.

Notes

1 James Lovelock, *The Revenge of Gaia: Why the Earth Is Fighting Back – and How We Can Still Save Humanity* (London: Allen Lane, 2006), 6.
2 "中美领导人就共同应对气候变化通电话 – 努力推进中美合作伙伴关系建设 US and Chinese Leaders Talk on Phone about Climate Change," 求是理论网 *Qiushi*, October 22, 2009, www.qstheory.cn/dd/dd2012/zmgx/201203/t20120315_145853.htm.
3 "Copenhagen Summit Ends in Blood, Sweat and Recrimination," *Telegraph.co.uk*, December 20, 2009, copenhagen-climate-change-confe, www.telegraph.co.uk/earth/copenhagen-climate-change-confe/6845892/Copenhagen-summit-ends-in-blood-sweat-and-recrimination.html.
4 "China Overtakes U.S. in Greenhouse Gas Emissions," *New York Times*, June 20, 2007, www.nytimes.com/2007/06/20/business/worldbusiness/20iht-emit.1.6227564.html?_r=0.
5 Anna Fifield, "China and US Agree Non-Binding Climate Plan," *Financial Times*, July 10, 2013, www.ft.com/cms/s/0/32336fe8-e98d-11e2-9f11-00144feabdc0.html#axzz2YIVs7UF8.
6 Tim Jackson, *Prosperity without Growth: Economics for a Finite Planet* (London: Earthscan, 2009).
7 Nina Chestney, "100 Million Will Die by 2030 If World Fails to Act on Climate," *Reuters*, September 25, 2012, www.reuters.com/article/2012/09/25/us-climate-inaction-idUSBRE88O1HG20120925.

8   "What Are CO2e and Global Warming Potential (GWP)?," *Guardian*, April 27, 2011, www.theguardian.com/environment/2011/apr/27/co2e-global-warming-potential.

9   Nicholas Stern, *The Economics of Climate Change: The Stern Review* (Cambridge: Cambridge University Press, 2007).

10 Ibid.

11 Alex Kirby, "Ex-IPCC Head: Prepare for 5°C Warmer World," *Climate News Network*, February 14, 2013, www.climatenewsnetwork.net/2013/02/ex-ipcc-head-prepare-for-5c-warmer-world/.

12 *The Economics of Climate Change*, xv.

13 "The World Is Locking Itself into an Unsustainable Energy Future Which Would Have Far-reaching Consequences, IEA Warns in Its Latest World Energy Outlook," *International Energy Agency*, November 9, 2011, www.iea.org/newsroomandevents/pressreleases/2011/november/name,20318,en.html.

14 Primary energy refers to energy that exists in a naturally occurring form, such as coal and natural gas, before being converted into end-use form.

15 "World Energy Outlook 2011," *International Energy Agency*, November 9, 2011, www.worldenergyoutlook.org/media/weowebsite/2011/executive_summary.pdf.

16 John Ashton, "Climate Change and the Race for Growth" (Speech presented at the Asahi World Environmental Forum, Tokyo, October 16, 2012), www.e3g.org/programmes/climate-articles/john-ashton-speaks-at-asahi-world-environmental-forum-tokyo1.

17 Vaclav Smil, *Energy Myths and Realities: Bringing Science to the Energy Policy Debate* (Cambridge, MA: AEI Press, 2010).

18 James Lovelock, *The Vanishing Face of Gaia: A Final Warning* (London: Penguin, 2010).

19 *The Emissions Gap Report 2012: UNEP Synthesis Report* (New York: United Nations Environment Programme, n.d.), accessed January 22, 2013.

20 World Bank, *Turn down the Heat: Why a 4°C Warmer World Must Be Avoided* (Washington, DC: World Bank Publications, November 2012).

21 Vaclav Smil, *Energy at the Crossroads: Global Perspectives and Uncertainties* (Cambridge, MA: MIT Press, 2005), 370.

22 Steve Coll, *Private Empire: ExxonMobil and American Power* (London: Allen Lane, 2012), 82.

23 Ibid., 86.

24 Ibid., 70.

25 Steve Coll, *Private Empire: ExxonMobil and American Power* (London: Allen Lane, 2012).

26 Conor Friedersdorf, "Remembering Why Americans Loathe Dick Cheney," *The Atlantic*, August 30, 2011, www.theatlantic.com/politics/archive/2011/08/remembering-why-americans-loathe-dick-cheney/244306/.

27 Anna Fifield, "Who's Who of Obama Lobbyists Pushes Keystone Pipeline," *Financial Times*, May 30, 2013, www.ft.com/cms/s/0/91300bf0-c80e-11e2-be27-00144feab7de.html#axzz2UQTUsz3u.

28 Vaclav Smil, *Oil: A Beginner's Guide* (London: Oneworld Publications, 2008), 22.

29 Graham Allison and Robert Blackwill, "America's National Interests: A Report from The Commission on America's National Interests, 2000," July 2000, http://belfercenter.ksg.harvard.edu/publication/2058/americas_national_interests.html.

30 Peter Schwartz and Doug Randall, *An Abrupt Climate Change Scenario and Its Implications for the United States National Security* (Jet Propulsion Lab, October 2003), http://oai.dtic.mil/oai/oai?verb=getRecord&metadataPrefix=html&identifier=ADA528610.

31 Gordon R. Sullivan, F. Bowman and L. P. Farrell, Jr., *National Security and the Threat of Climate Change* (The CNA Corporation, 2007), www.npr.org/documents/2007/apr/security_climate.pdf.

32   Joseph Romm, "The United States Needs a Tougher Greenhouse Gas Emissions Reduction Target for 2020," *Center for American Progress*, January 13, 2009, www.americanprogress.org/issues/green/report/2009/01/13/5472/the-united-states-needs-a-tougher-greenhouse-gas-emissions-reduction-target-for-2020/.

33   Johannes Urpelainen, "Explaining the Schwarzenegger Phenomenon: Local Frontrunners in Climate Policy," *Global Environmental Politics* 9, no. 3 (2009): 82–105.

34   Jeff Zeleny, "G.O.P. Captures House, but Not Senate," *New York Times*, November 2, 2010, U.S./Politics, www.nytimes.com/2010/11/03/us/politics/03elect.html.

35   Daniel Yergin, "Stepping on the Gas," *Wall Street Journal*, April 2, 2011, The Saturday Essay, http://online.wsj.com/article/SB100014240527487037125045762 32582990089002.html.

36   Wang Xiaocong, "Uncertainty Clouds Development of Shale Gas Sector," *Caixin Online* 英文频道, August 28, 2012, http://english.caixin.com/2012-08-28/ 100429442.html.

37   "IEA Report Sees Bright Future for Natural Gas over next 5 Years," *International Energy Agency*, June 5, 2012, www.iea.org/newsroomandevents/pressrelea ses/2012/june/name,27383,en.html.

38   Melanie J. Martin, "Is Natural Gas Cleaner Than Petroleum and Coal?," *National Geographic*, accessed September 4, 2012, http://greenliving.nationalgeo graphic.com/natural-gas-cleaner-petroleum-coal-20485.html.

39   Vaclav Smil, "Placing the American Gas Boom in Perspective," *The American (Journal of the American Enterprise Institute)*, May 3, 2012, www.vaclavsmil. com/wp-content/uploads/smil-article0the-american-20120503.pdf.

40   Seth Kleinman, "Oil Demand Is Set to Fall in the Age of Gas," *Financial Times*, April 1, 2013, www.ft.com/cms/s/0/70bacdb0-987a-11e2-867f-00144feabdc0.htm l#axzz2PJLUuTbj.

41   "Shale Oil 'to Boost World Economy,'" *BBCNews*, February 14, 2013, Business, www.bbc.co.uk/news/business-21453393.

42   Josh Fox, *Gasland: A Film by Josh Fox*, accessed September 4, 2012, www.gasla ndthemovie.com/whats-fracking.

43   Fatih Birol, *WEO2012 Golden Rules Report: Special Report on Unconventional Gas* (International Energy Agency, 2012), www.worldenergyoutlook.org/media/ weowebsite/2012/goldenrules/WEO2012_GoldenRulesReport.pdf.

44   "Kyoto Protocol Introduction," *United Nations Framework Convention of Climate Change*, accessed August 18, 2012, http://unfccc.int/essential_background/ kyoto_protocol/items/6034.php.

45   "Byrd-Hagel Resolution (S. Res. 98) Expressing the Sense of the Senate Regarding Conditions for the U.S. Signing the Global Climate Change Treaty," July 25, 1997, www.nationalcenter.org/KyotoSenate.html.

46   Analysis shows that energy cost is not the key determinant of plant location. Other factors such as labor cost are more important except in industries such as aluminum, steel, cement, glass and paper where energy costs make up the bulk of production costs.

47   Todd Stern, "Remarks at Dartmouth College," *U.S. Department of State*, August 2, 2012, www.state.gov/e/oes/rls/remarks/2012/196004.htm.

48   Joseph. E. Aldy, *Hearing on China's Energy Policies and Environmental Impact: Testimony of Joseph E. Aldy* (Washington, DC, 2008), www.uscc.gov/hearings/ 2008hearings/written_testimonies/08_08_13_wrts/08_08_13_aldy_statement.php.

49   Chinese energy subsidies totaled $11 billion in 2006 and may become higher as energy prices increase.

50   *World Energy Outlook 2007* (Paris: IEA, 2007), 280.

51 张海滨 Zhang Haibin, "China and the US: Moving Forward on Climate (Part Two)," *Chinadialogue* 中外对话, January 29, 2008, www.chinadialogue.net/article/show/single/en/1668-China-and-the-US-moving-forward-on-climate-part-two-.

52 *Agreement between the United States and the People's Republic of China Concerning the Peaceful Uses of Nuclear Energy* (1985).

53 杨宏伟 Yang Hongwei, 2012碳减排交易不终结 CDM will not end in 2012, April 8, 2010, http://finance.ifeng.com/news/people/20100408/2654017.shtml.

54 Peter Nolan, *Crossroads* (London: Marshall Cavendish, 2009), 158–59.

55 Jared M. Diamond, *Collapse: How Societies Choose to Fail or Succeed* (London: Penguin Books, 2006), ch. 12.

56 邓英淘 Deng Yingtao, 新发展方式与中国的未来 *A New Development Model and China's Future*, 2nd ed. (Hong Kong: Strong Wind Press, 香港大风出版社, 2012).

57 "China's National Climate Change Program" (发改委 National Development and Reform Commission, June 2007), http://works.bepress.com/shi_ling_hsu/14/.

58 "Hu Jintao's Speech on Climate Change," September 2009, www.cfr.org/china/hu-jintaos-speech-climate-change-september-2009/p20262.

59 Judith Shapiro, *China's Environmental Challenges* (Cambridge: Polity Press, 2012), 100.

60 Joanna Lewis, "Energy and Climate Goals of China's 12th Five-Year Plan," *Pew Center on Global Climate*, 2011, www.pewclimate.org/docUploads/energy-climate-goals-china-twelfth-five-year-plan.pdf.

61 徐华清 Xu Huaqing, "十二五是实现温室气体排放目标关键期 12th Five-Year Plan Is Critical to Achieving Emission Targets," 中国新能源网 *China New Energy*, February 21, 2011, www.newenergy.org.cn/html/0112/2211138806.html.

62 "Chinese Government: 12th Five-Year Plan and Climate Change White Paper," *Post Carbon Pathways*, accessed September 10, 2012, www.postcarbonpathways.net.au/transition-strategies/chinese-government-12th-five-year-plan-and-climate-change-white-paper/.

63 Ben Sills, "Stern Says China Takes Lead on Clean Energy Neglected by West," *Bloomberg*, June 13, 2011, www.bloomberg.com/news/2011-06-13/stern-says-china-takes-lead-on-clean-energy-neglected-by-west.html.

64 Jim Yardley, "Beneath Booming Cities, China's Future Is Drying Up," *New York Times*, September 28, 2007, International / Asia Pacific, www.nytimes.com/2007/09/28/world/asia/28water.html.

65 "China to Invest 4 Trln Yuan in Water Resources," *China.org.cn*, April 25, 2012, www.china.org.cn/environment/2012-04/25/content_25236790.htm.

66 Shapiro, *China's Environmental Challenges*, 8.

67 先污染, 后治理 pollute now, clean up later.

68 Vaclav Smil, "China's Environment and Security: Simple Myths and Complex Realities," *SAIS Review* 17, no. 1 (1997): 107–26, doi:10.1353/sais.1997.0015.

69 "国务院加强大气污染防治 力争十年消除重污染 State Council Tightens Air Pollution Control to End Heavy Pollutants within 10 Years," *Tencent News* 腾讯新闻, September 12, 2013, http://news.qq.com/a/20130912/008241.htm; FT reporters, "China Seeks Cut in Coal Usage to Boost Air Quality," *Financial Times*, September 12, 2013, www.ft.com/cms/s/0/f758cce0-1b84-11e3-b678-00144feab7de.html?ftcamp=crm/email/2013913/nbe/ChinaBusiness/product&siteedition=uk#axzz2efJoYZzz.

70 Vaclav Smil, *China's Environmental Crisis: An Inquiry into the Limits of National Development* (Armonk, NY: M. E. Sharpe, 1993).

71 Tom Miller, *China's Urban Billion: The Story Behind the Biggest Migration in Human History* (London: Zed Books Ltd, 2012).

72 周小川 Zhou Xiaochuan, "新世纪以来中国货币政策主要特点 China's Mone-tary Policy since the Turn of the Century," *Tencent News* 腾讯新闻, November 26, 2012, http://finance.qq.com/a/20121126/003553.htm.
73 Simon Rabinovitch, "New Data Reveal Scale of China Abortions," *Financial Times*, March 15, 2013, www.ft.com/cms/s/2/6724580a-8d64-11e2-82d2-00144feabdc0.html?ftcamp=crm/email/2013315/nbe/BreakingNews1/product#axzz2Nb9kYSu3.
74 Joanna Lewis, "China's Energy Policies and Their Environmental Impacts" (Washington, DC, 2008), www.uscc.gov/hearings/2008hearings/written_testimonies/08_08_13_wrts/08_08_13_lewis_statement.php.
75 齐晔 Qi Ye's interview with the Fung Global Institute about China's energy policy, April 2013.
76 Kenneth Lieberthal and David Sandalow, "Overcoming Obstacles to U.S.-China Cooperation on Climate Change," *The Brookings Institution*, 25, accessed August 19, 2012, www.brookings.edu/research/reports/2009/01/climate-change-lieberthal-sandalow.
77 "China Suspends Nuclear Building," *BBC News*, March 17, 2011, Asia-Pacific, www.bbc.co.uk/news/world-asia-pacific-12769392.
78 Lewis, *China's Energy Policies and Their Environmental Impacts*.
79 Sun Guodong, *Coal in China: Resources, Uses, and Advanced Technologies*, Coal Initiative Report (Kennedy School of Government, Harvard University, March 2010), www.c2es.org/docUploads/coal-in-china-resources-uses-technologies.pdf.
80 Leslie Hook, "Chinese Groups Flock to Shale Gas Projects," *Financial Times*, October 25, 2012, www.ft.com/cms/s/0/23ff8d52-1e8c-11e2-bebc-00144feabdc0.html?ftcamp=published_links%2Frss%2Fhome_asia%2Ffeed%2F%2Fproduct&ftcamp=crm/email/20121025/nbe/AsiaMorningHeadlines/product#axzz2A4NUUPrW.
81 Jaeah Lee, "China Planning 'Huge Fracking Industry,'" *Guardian*, November 27, 2012, www.guardian.co.uk/environment/2012/nov/27/china-planning-huge-fracking-industry.
82 Wang Xiaocong, "Uncertainty Clouds Development of Shale Gas Sector."
83 路炳阳 Lu Bingyang, "中俄能源谈判取得进展 东线年供气380亿立方米 Russia to Supply China 38 Billion Cubic Meters of Gas per Year," *Caixin Online*, February 26, 2013, http://companies.caixin.com/2013-02-26/100494434.html.
84 Leslie Hook, "China Starts Importing Natural Gas from Myanmar," *Financial Times*, July 29, 2013, www.ft.com/cms/s/0/870f632c-f83e-11e2-92f0-00144feabdc0.html#axzz2aNmtQyZ2.
85 "Turkmenistan-China Gas Link Opens," *BBC News*, December 14, 2009, Asia-Pacific, http://news.bbc.co.uk/1/hi/world/asia-pacific/8411204.stm.
86 International Energy Agency, *World Energy Outlook 2007: China and India Insights* (Paris: IEA, 2007).
87 Peter Nolan, *China's Energy and Climate Change: A Long Term Perspective* (Shanghai: n.p., 2010).
88 International Energy Agency, *World Energy Outlook 2007*.
89 Alec Broers, *The Triumph of Technology* (Cambridge: Cambridge University Press, 2005), 87–8.
90 Keith Bradsher, "Speedy Trains Transform China," *New York Times*, September 23, 2013, Business Day / International Business, www.nytimes.com/2013/09/24/business/global/high-speed-train-system-is-huge-success-for-china.html.
91 Robin Banerji and Patrick Jackson, "China's Ghost Towns and Phantom Malls," *BBC News*, August 13, 2012, Magazine, www.bbc.co.uk/news/magazine-19049254.
92 Jun Luo and Kevin Hamlin, "Xi Says GDP Not Officials' Sole Focus in Signal on Growth," *Bloomberg*, June 30, 2013, www.bloomberg.com/news/2013-06-30/xi-says-gdp-not-officials-sole-focus-in-signal-on-growth.html.

93 Ibid.
94 胡鞍钢 Hu Angang and 管清友 Guan Qingyou, "Fighting Climate Change: China's Contribution (part One)," *Chinadialogue* 中外对话, October 10, 2008, www.chinadialogue.net/article/show/single/en/2459-Fighting-climate-change-China-s-contribution-part-one-.
95 Zhang Haibin, "China and the US: Moving Forward on Climate (Part Two)."
96 Peter Nolan, *Chinese Firms, Global Firms: Industrial Policy in the Era of Globalization* (Cambridge: Cambridge University Press, 2013), Ch. 5.
97 Deng Yingtao, 新发展方式与中国的未来 *A New Development Model and China's Future.*
98 "美'放松管制'不能总玩口头承诺 Easing US Export Restrictions: Empty Promises," *Xinhua Online* 新华网, December 21, 2012, http://news.xinhuanet.com/world/2012-12/21/c_114103730.htm.
99 邹骥 Zou Ji, "碳关税阻碍全球气候进程 Carbon Tax Hinders Global Climate Progress," 通商汇, August 12, 2009, www.gotohui.com/show.php?contentid=1187.
100 Pilita Clark, "China Looks at Reducing Pollution Faster in next Five-Year Plan," *Financial Times*, September 24, 2013, www.ft.com/cms/s/0/425868ce-2529-11e3-9b22-00144feab7de.html?ftcamp=crm/email/2013925/nbe/ChinaBusiness/product&siteedition=uk#axzz2fnEvaviV.
101 An economy growing at 7 percent a year doubles every ten years. China has been growing at more than 7 percent in the last three decades. Four decades of doubling each decade will give a factor of 16, i.e. $2^4=16$. A growth factor of 10 between now and 2050 is therefore a conservative estimate.
102 Lewis, *China's Energy Policies and Their Environmental Impacts.*
103 Lewis, "Energy and Climate Goals of China's 12th Five-Year Plan."
104 D. T. Yang, J. Zhang, and S. Zhou, *Why Are Saving Rates so High in China?* (Chicago, IL: University of Chicago Press, 2011), 1, www.nber.org/chapters/c12068.pdf.
105 Peter Nolan, "China at the Crossroads," *Journal of Chinese Economic and Business Studies* 3, no. 1 (2005): 1–22.
106 Nolan, *China's Energy and Climate Change: A Long Term Perspective.*
107 *2008 R&D Scoreboard* (British Enterprise and Regulatory Reform (BERR), 2008), http://webarchive.nationalarchives.gov.uk/20101208170217/http://www.innovation.gov.uk/rd_scoreboard/downloads/2008_RD_Scoreboard_analysis.pdf.
108 Nolan, *China's Energy and Climate Change: A Long Term Perspective.*
109 张海滨 Zhang Haibin, "Tackling Climate Change: Can the US and China Cooperate?" 中国国际战略论坛 *China International Strategy Review*, 2008.
110 *Feeding the Dragon: Reevaluating U.S. Development Assistance to China: Hearing Before the Subcommittee on Asia and the Pacific of the Committee on Foreign Affairs, House of Representatives, 112th Congress, First Session, November 15, 2011* (Washington, DC: U.S. Government Printing Office, 2011).
111 In 2011, the US gave $4 million to NGOs to develop green energy and fight wildlife trafficking.
112 张海滨 Zhang Haibin, "Tackling Climate Change: Why Sino-US Cooperation Lags behind Sino-Japanese Cooperation," 中国国际战略论坛 *China International Strategy Review*, 2009.
113 Michiyo Nakamoto and Ben McLannahan, "Japanese on Alert over China's Toxic Smog," *Financial Times*, February 27, 2013, www.ft.com/cms/s/0/f4cbd10a-80bd-11e2-9fae-00144feabdc0.html#axzz2M3dVFnjN.
114 Lorraine Woellert, "Obama Embraces 'Green Path' in Economic Stimulus Plan (Update1)," *Bloomberg*, December 2, 2008, www.bloomberg.com/apps/news?pid=newsarchive&sid=aGZs6vevDXyg.
115 Deng Yingtao, 新发展方式与中国的未来 *A New Development Model and China's Future.*

116   郑必坚 Zheng Bijian, "China's 'Peaceful Rise' to Great-Power Status," *Foreign Affairs* 84, no. 5 (2005).
117   Xu Huaqing, "十二五是实现温室气体排放目标关键期 12th Five-Year Plan Is Critical to Achieving Emission Targets."
118   John Ashton, "Climate Change and the Race for Growth" (Speech presented at the Asahi World Environmental Forum, Tokyo, October 16, 2012), www.e3g.org/p rogrammes/climate-articles/john-ashton-speaks-at-asahi-world-environmental-forum-tokyo1.
119   Leslie Hook and Pilita Clark, "China Eyes Cap on Carbon Emissions by 2016," *Financial Times*, May 27, 2013, www.ft.com/cms/s/0/61cd4ec6-c6b1-11e2-a 861-00144feab7de.html#axzz2UQTUsz3u.
120   Leslie Hook, "China Reveals Details of First Carbon Trading Scheme," *Financial Times*, May 21, 2013, www.ft.com/cms/s/0/9221daf4-c221-11e2-ab66-00144fea b7de.html?ftcamp=published_links%2Frss%2Fworld_asia-pacific_china%2Ffeed %2F%2Fproduct&ftcamp=crm/email/2013522/nbe/ChinaBusiness/product#axzz 2TumrMKHo.
121   Garrett Hardin, "The Tragedy of the Commons," *Science*, NS, 162, no. 3859 (Dec. 13, 1968): 1243–48.).
122   Chestney, "100 Million Will Die by 2030 if World Fails to Act on Climate."
123   T. Banuri, K. Göran-Mäler, M. Grubb, H. K. Jacobson, and F. Yamin, "Equity and Social Considerations," *Climate Change*, 1995, 79–124.
124   "United Nations Statistics Division – National Accounts," accessed April 15, 2013, http://unstats.un.org/unsd/snaama/selbasicFast.asp.
125   Keith Bradsher, "China Outpaces U.S. in Cleaner Coal-Fired Plants," *New York Times*, May 11, 2009, International / Asia Pacific, www.nytimes.com/2009/05/11/ world/asia/11coal.html.
126   Peter Nolan, "New Technology Development and Green Growth," Paper presented to China Development Forum 2012, Beijing, March 17–19.
127   "[经济发展新动力]中美经贸关系]推进合作 减少摩擦 US-China Trade Relations: Foster Cooperation, Reduce Tension," *Xinhua Online* 新华网, September 10, 2012, http://news.xinhuanet.com/yzyd/fortune/20120910/c_113020631.htm.
128   John Frisbie, "Best Way to Deal with China Is to Heal Ourselves," *The Columbus Dispatch*, October 17, 2012, www.dispatch.com/content/stories/editorials/ 2012/10/17/best-way-to-deal-with-china-is-to-heal-ourselves.html.
129   "美国总统奥巴马会见王岐山 President Obama Meets with Wang Qishan," *Xinhua Online* 新华网, December 21, 2012, http://news.xinhuanet.com/world/ 2012-12/21/c_114112579.htm.
130   John Robert McNeill, *Something New under the Sun: An Environmental History of the Twentieth-Century World* (New York: W.W. Norton & Co., 2001).
131   Tim Jackson, *Prosperity Without Growth: Economics for a Finite Planet* (London: Earthscan, 2009).
132   "习近平:不能照搬发达国家现代化模式 Xi Jinping: China Should Not Follow Developed Countries' Modernization Model," *Tencent News* 腾讯新闻, July 22, 2013, http://news.qq.com/a/20130722/012112.htm.

Bibliography

2008 R&D Scoreboard. British Enterprise and Regulatory Reform (BERR), 2008. http://webarchive.nationalarchives.gov.uk/20101208170217/ www.innovation.gov.uk/ rd_scoreboard/downloads/2008_RD_Scoreboard_analysis.pdf.
Aldy, Joseph. E. Hearing on China's Energy Policies and Environmental Impact: Testimony of Joseph E. Aldy. Washington, D.C, 2008. www.uscc.gov/hearings/2008hea rings/written_testimonies/08_08_13_wrts/08_08_13_aldy_statement.php.

Allison, Graham, and Robert Blackwill. *America's National Interests: A Report from The Commission on America's National Interests, 2000*, July 2000. http://belfercen ter.ksg.harvard.edu/publication/2058/americas_national_interests.html.

Ashton, John. "Climate Change and the Race for Growth." Speech presented at the Asahi World Environmental Forum, Tokyo, October 16, 2012. www.e3g.org/p rogrammes/climate-articles/john-ashton-speaks-at-asahi-world-environmental-forum -tokyo1.

Banerji, Robin, and Patrick Jackson. "China's Ghost Towns and Phantom Malls." *BBC News*, August 13, 2012, Magazine. www.bbc.co.uk/news/magazine-19049254.

Banuri, T., K. Göran-Mäler, M. Grubb, H. K. Jacobson, and F. Yamin. "Equity and Social Considerations." *Climate Change*, 1995, 79–124.

Birol, Fatih. *WEO2012 Golden Rules Report: Special Report on Unconventional Gas.* International Energy Agency, 2012. www.worldenergyoutlook.org/media/weo website/2012/goldenrules/WEO2012_GoldenRulesReport.pdf.

Bradsher, Keith. "Speedy Trains Transform China." *New York Times*, September 23, 2013, Business Day/International Business. www.nytimes.com/2013/09/24/business/ global/high-speed-train-system-is-huge-success-for-china.html.

Bradsher, Keith. "China Outpaces U.S. in Cleaner Coal-Fired Plants." *New York Times*, May 11, 2009, International/Asia Pacific. www.nytimes.com/2009/05/11/ world/asia/11coal.html.

Broers, Alec. *The Triumph of Technology.* Cambridge: Cambridge University Press, 2005.

"Byrd-Hagel Resolution (S. Res. 98) Expressing the Sense of the Senate Regarding Conditions for the U.S. Signing the Global Climate Change Treaty," July 25, 1997. www.nationalcenter.org/KyotoSenate.html.

Chestney, Nina. "100 Million Will Die by 2030 If World Fails to Act on Climate." *Reuters.* September 25, 2012. www.reuters.com/article/2012/09/25/us-climate-ina ction-idUSBRE88O1HG20120925.

"China Overtakes U.S. in Greenhouse Gas Emissions."*New York Times*, June 20, 2007. www.nytimes.com/2007/06/20/business/worldbusiness/20iht-emit.1.6227564.ht ml?_r=0.

"China Suspends Nuclear Building." *BBC News*, March 17, 2011, Asia-Pacific. www. bbc.co.uk/news/world-asia-pacific-12769392.

"China to Invest 4 Trln Yuan in Water Resources." *China.org.cn*, April 25, 2012. www. china.org.cn/environment/2012-04/25/content_25236790.htm.

"China's National Climate Change Program." 发改委 National Development and Reform Commission,June 2007. http://works.bepress.com/shi_ling_hsu/14/.

"Chinese Government: 12th Five-Year Plan and Climate Change White Paper." *Post Carbon Pathways.* Accessed September 10, 2012.www.postcarbonpathways.net.au/ transition-strategies/chinese-government-12th-five-year-plan-and-climate-change-wh ite-paper/.

Clark, Pilita. "China Looks at Reducing Pollution Faster in next Five-Year Plan." *Financial Times*, September 24, 2013. www.ft.com/cms/s/0/425868ce-2529-11e3-9b22 -00144feab7de.html?ftcamp=crm/email/2013925/nbe/ChinaBusiness/product&siteedi tion=uk#axzz2fnEvaviV.

Coll, Steve. *Private Empire: ExxonMobil and American Power.* London: Allen Lane, 2012.

"Copenhagen Summit Ends in Blood, Sweat and Recrimination." *Telegraph.co.uk*, December 20, 2009. www.telegraph.co.uk/earth/copenhagen-climate-change-confe/ 6845892/Copenhagen-summit-ends-in-blood-sweat-and-recrimination.html.

Deng Yingtao, 邓英淘. 新发展方式与中国的未来, *A New Development Model and China's Future*. 2nd edn. Hong Kong: Strong Wind Press 香港大风出版社, 2012.

Diamond, Jared M. *Collapse: How Societies Choose to Fail or Succeed*. London: Penguin Books, 2006.

Feeding the Dragon: Reevaluating U.S. Development Assistance to China: Hearing Before the Subcommittee on Asia and the Pacific of the Committee on Foreign Affairs, House of Representatives, 112th Congress, First Session, November 15, 2011. Washington, DC: U.S. Government Printing Office, 2011.

Fifield, Anna. "Who's Who of Obama Lobbyists Pushes Keystone Pipeline." *Financial Times*, May 30, 2013. www.ft.com/cms/s/0/91300bf0-c80e-11e2-be27-00144feab7de. html#axzz2UQTUsz3u.

Fifield, Anna. "China and US Agree Non-Binding Climate Plan." *Financial Times*, July 10, 2013. www.ft.com/cms/s/0/32336fe8-e98d-11e2-9f11-00144feabdc0.html#a xzz2YIVs7UF8.

Fox, Josh. *Gasland: A Film by Josh Fox*. Accessed September 4, 2012. www.gasla ndthemovie.com/whats-fracking.

Friedersdorf, Conor. "Remembering Why Americans Loathe Dick Cheney." *The Atlantic*, August 30, 2011. www.theatlantic.com/politics/archive/2011/08/remember ing-why-americans-loathe-dick-cheney/244306/.

Frisbie, John. "Best Way to Deal with China Is to Heal Ourselves." *Columbus Dis-patch*, October 17, 2012. www.dispatch.com/content/stories/editorials/2012/10/17/ best-way-to-deal-with-china-is-to-heal-ourselves.html.

FT reporters. "China Seeks Cut in Coal Usage to Boost Air Quality." *Financial Times*, September 12, 2013. www.ft.com/cms/s/0/f758cce0-1b84-11e3-b678-00144feab7de. html?ftcamp=crm/email/2013913/nbe/ChinaBusiness/product&siteedition=uk#axzz 2efJoYZzz.

Hardin, Garrett. "The Tragedy of the Commons.," *Science, NS*, 162, no. 3859 (December 13, 1968): 1243–1248.

Hook, Leslie. "China Starts Importing Natural Gas from Myanmar." *Financial Times*, July 29, 2013. www.ft.com/cms/s/0/870f632c-f83e-11e2-92f0-00144feabdc0.html#a xzz2aNmtQyZ2.

Hook, Leslie. "China Reveals Details of First Carbon Trading Scheme." *Financial Times*, May 21, 2013. www.ft.com/cms/s/0/9221daf4-c221-11e2-ab66-00144feab7de.h tml?ftcamp=published_links%2Frss%2Fworld_asia-pacific_china%2Ffeed%2F%2Fp roduct&ftcamp=crm/email/2013522/nbe/ChinaBusiness/product#axzz2TumrMKHo.

Hook, Leslie. "Chinese Groups Flock to Shale Gas Projects." *Financial Times*, Octo-ber 25, 2012. www.ft.com/cms/s/0/23ff8d52-1e8c-11e2-bebc-00144feabdc0.html? ftcamp=published_links%2Frss%2Fhome_asia%2Ffeed%2F%2Fproduct&ftcamp= crm/email/20121025/nbe/AsiaMorningHeadlines/product#axzz2A4NUUPrW.

Hook, Leslie, and Pilita Clark. "China Eyes Cap on Carbon Emissions by 2016." *Financial Times*, May 27, 2013. www.ft.com/cms/s/0/61cd4ec6-c6b1-11e2-a861-0014 4feab7de.html#axzz2UQTUsz3u.

HuAngang,胡鞍钢, and 管清友 GuanQingyou."Fighting Climate Change: China's Contribution (part One)." *Chinadialogue* 中外对话, October 10, 2008. www.china dialogue.net/article/show/single/en/2459-Fighting-climate-change-China-s-contributi on-part-one-.

"Hu Jintao's Speech on Climate Change,"September 2009. www.cfr.org/china/hu-jinta os-speech-climate-change-september-2009/p20262.

"IEA Report Sees Bright Future for Natural Gas over next 5 Years." International Energy Agency, June 5, 2012. www.iea.org/newsroomandevents/pressreleases/2012/june/name,27383,en.html.

International Energy Agency. *World Energy Outlook 2007: China and India Insights.* Paris: IEA, 2007.

Jackson, Tim. *Prosperity without Growth: Economics for a Finite Planet.* London: Earthscan, 2009.

Kirby, Alex. "Ex-IPCC Head: Prepare for 5°C Warmer World." *Climate News Network*, February 14, 2013. www.climatenewsnetwork.net/2013/02/ex-ipcc-head-prepare-for-5c-warmer-world/.

Kleinman, Seth. "Oil Demand Is Set to Fall in the Age of Gas." *Financial Times*, April 1, 2013. www.ft.com/cms/s/0/70bacdb0-987a-11e2-867f-00144feabdc0.html#axzz2PJLUuTbj.

"Kyoto Protocol Introduction." United Nations Framework Convention of Climate Change. Accessed August 18, 2012. http://unfccc.int/essential_background/kyoto_protocol/items/6034.php.

Lee, Jaeah. "China Planning 'Huge Fracking Industry.'" *The Guardian*, November 27, 2012. www.guardian.co.uk/environment/2012/nov/27/china-planning-huge-fracking-industry.

Lewis, Joanna. "Energy and Climate Goals of China's 12th Five-Year Plan." Pew Center on Global Climate, 2011. www.pewclimate.org/docUploads/energy-climate-goals-china-twelfth-five-year-plan.pdf.

Lewis, Joanna. "China's Energy Policies and Their Environmental Impacts." Washington, DC, 2008. www.uscc.gov/hearings/2008hearings/written_testimonies/08_08_13_wrts/08_08_13_lewis_statement.php.

Lieberthal, Kenneth, and David Sandalow. *Overcoming Obstacles to U.S.-China Cooperation on Climate Change.* Washington, DC: Brookings Institution. Accessed August 19, 2012. www.brookings.edu/research/reports/2009/01/climate-change-lieberthal-sandalow.

Lovelock, James. *The Vanishing Face of Gaia: A Final Warning.* London: Penguin, 2010.

Lovelock, James. *The Revenge of Gaia: Why the Earth Is Fighting Back – and How We Can Still Save Humanity.* London: Allen Lane, 2006.

Lu Bingyang, 路炳阳. "中俄能源谈判取得进展 东线年供气380亿立方米, Russia to Supply China 38 Billion Cubic Meters of Gas per Year." *Caixin Online*, February 26, 2013. http://companies.caixin.com/2013-02-26/100494434.html.

Luo, Jun, and Kevin Hamlin. "Xi Says GDP Not Officials' Sole Focus in Signal on Growth." *Bloomberg*, June 30, 2013. www.bloomberg.com/news/2013-06-30/xi-says-gdp-not-officials-sole-focus-in-signal-on-growth.html.

Martin, Melanie J. "Is Natural Gas Cleaner Than Petroleum & Coal?" *National Geographic*. Accessed September 4, 2012. http://greenliving.nationalgeographic.com/natural-gas-cleaner-petroleum-coal-20485.html.

McNeill, John Robert. *Something New under the Sun: An Environmental History of the Twentieth-Century World.* New York: W.W. Norton & Co., 2001.

Miller, Tom. *China's Urban Billion: The Story Behind the Biggest Migration in Human History.* New York: Zed Books, 2012.

Nakamoto, Michiyo, and Ben McLannahan. "Japanese on Alert over China's Toxic Smog." *Financial Times*, February 27, 2013. www.ft.com/cms/s/0/f4cbd10a-80bd-11e2-9fae-00144feabdc0.html#axzz2M3dVFnjN.

Nolan, Peter. *Chinese Firms, Global Firms: Industrial Policy in the Era of Globalization.* Cambridge:Cambridge University Press, 2013.

Nolan, Peter. "New Technology Development and Green Growth." Paper presented to the China Development Forum 2012, Beijing, March 17–19.

Nolan, Peter. *China's Energy and Climate Change: A Long Term Perspective.* Shanghai, n.p., 2010.

Nolan, Peter. *China at the Crossroads.* London: Marshall Cavendish, 2009.

Nolan, Peter. "China at the Crossroads." *Journal of Chinese Economic and Business Studies* 3, no. 1(2005): 1–22.

Rabinovitch, Simon. "New Data Reveal Scale of China Abortions." *Financial Times,* March 15, 2013. www.ft.com/cms/s/2/6724580a-8d64-11e2-82d2-00144feabdc0.html?ftcamp=crm/email/2013315/nbe/BreakingNews1/product#axzz2Nb9kYSu3.

Romm, Joseph. *The United States Needs a Tougher Greenhouse Gas Emissions Reduction Target for 2020.* Center for American Progress, January 13, 2009. www.americanprogress.org/issues/green/report/2009/01/13/5472/the-united-states-needs-a-tougher-greenhouse-gas-emissions-reduction-target-for-2020/.

Schwartz, Peter, and Doug Randall. *An Abrupt Climate Change Scenario and Its Implications for the United States National Security.* Jet Propulsion Lab, October 2003. http://oai.dtic.mil/oai/oai?verb=getRecord&metadataPrefix=html&identifier=ADA528610.

"Shale Oil 'to Boost World Economy.'" *BBC News,* February 14, 2013, Business. www.bbc.co.uk/news/business-21453393.

Shapiro, Judith. *China's Environmental Challenges.* Cambridge: Polity Press, 2012.

Sills, Ben. "Stern Says China Takes Lead on Clean Energy Neglected by West." Bloomberg, June 13, 2011. www.bloomberg.com/news/2011-06-13/stern-says-china-takes-lead-on-clean-energy-neglected-by-west.html.

Smil, Vaclav. "Placing the American Gas Boom in Perspective." *The American (Journal of the American Enterprise Institute),* May 3, 2012. www.vaclavsmil.com/wp-content/uploads/smil-article0the-american-20120503.pdf.

Smil, Vaclav. *Energy Myths and Realities: Bringing Science to the Energy Policy Debate.* Cambridge, MA: AEI Press, 2010.

Smil, Vaclav. *Oil: A Beginner's Guide.* London: Oneworld Publications, 2008.

Smil, Vaclav. *Energy at the Crossroads: Global Perspectives and Uncertainties.* Cambridge, MA: MIT Press, 2005.

Smil, Vaclav. "China's Environment and Security: Simple Myths and Complex Realities." *SAIS Review* 17, no. 1(1997): 107–126. doi:10.1353/sais.1997.0015.

Smil, Vaclav. *China's Environmental Crisis: An Inquiry into the Limits of National Development.* Armonk, NY: M. E. Sharpe, 1993.

Stern, Todd. "Remarks at Dartmouth College." U.S. Department of State, August 2, 2012. www.state.gov/e/oes/rls/remarks/2012/196004.htm.

Sullivan, Gordon R., Frank Bowman, Lawrence P. Farrell Jr., Paul G. Gaffney, Paul J. Kern, Joseph Lopez, Donald L. Pilling, *et al. National Security and the Threat of Climate Change.* The CNA Corporation, 2007. www.npr.org/documents/2007/apr/security_climate.pdf.

Stern, Nicholas. *The Economics of Climate Change: The Stern Review.* Cambridge: Cambridge University Press, 2007.

SunGuodong. *Coal in China: Resources, Uses, and Advanced Technologies.* Coal Initiative Report. Kennedy School of Government, Harvard University, March 2010. www.c2es.org/docUploads/coal-in-china-resources-uses-technologies.pdf.

The Emissions Gap Report 2012: UNEP Synthesis Report. United Nations Environment Programme, n.d. Accessed January 22, 2013.

"Turkmenistan-China Gas Link Opens." *BBC News*, December 14, 2009, Asia-Pacific. http://news.bbc.co.uk/1/hi/world/asia-pacific/8411204.stm.

Turn down the Heat: Why a 4°C Warmer World Must Be Avoided. Washington, DC: World Bank Publications, November 2012.

"United Nations Statistics Division – National Accounts." Accessed April 15, 2013. http://unstats.un.org/unsd/snaama/selbasicFast.asp.

Urpelainen, Johannes. "Explaining the Schwarzenegger Phenomenon: Local Frontrunners in Climate Policy." *Global Environmental Politics* 9, no. 3(2009): 82–105.

Wang Xiaocong. "Uncertainty Clouds Development of Shale Gas Sector." *Caixin Online* 英文频道, August 28, 2012. http://english.caixin.com/2012-08-28/100429442.html.

"What Are CO2e and Global Warming Potential (GWP)?" *Guardian*, April 27, 2011. www.theguardian.com/environment/2011/apr/27/co2e-global-warming-potential.

Woellert, Lorraine. "Obama Embraces 'Green Path' in Economic Stimulus Plan (Update1)." *Bloomberg*, December 2, 2008. www.bloomberg.com/apps/news?pid=newsarchive&sid=aGZs6vevDXyg.

World Energy Outlook 2011. International Energy Agency, November 9, 2011. www.worldenergyoutlook.org/media/weowebsite/2011/executive_summary.pdf.

World Energy Outlook 2007. Paris: IEA, 2007.

Xu Huaqing, 徐华清. "十二五是实现温室气体排放目标关键期, 12th Five-Year Plan Is Critical to Achieving Emission Targets." 中国新能源网 *China New Energy*, February 21, 2011. www.newenergy.org.cn/html/0112/2211138806.html.

Yang, D. T., J. Zhang, and S. Zhou. *Why Are Saving Rates so High in China?* Chicago, IL: University of Chicago Press, 2011. www.nber.org/chapters/c12068.pdf.

Yang Hongwei, 杨宏伟. "2012碳减排交易不终结 CDM will not end in 2012," April 8, 2010. http://finance.ifeng.com/news/people/20100408/2654017.shtml.

Yardley, Jim. "Beneath Booming Cities, China's Future Is Drying Up." *New York Times*, September 28, 2007, International / Asia Pacific. www.nytimes.com/2007/09/28/world/asia/28water.html.

Yergin, Daniel. "Stepping on the Gas." *Wall Street Journal*, April 2, 2011, The Saturday Essay. http://online.wsj.com/article/SB10001424052748703712504576232582990089002.html.

Zeleny, Jeff. "G.O.P. Captures House, but Not Senate." *New York Times*, November 2, 2010, U.S./Politics. www.nytimes.com/2010/11/03/us/politics/03elect.html.

Zhang Haibin, 张海滨. "Tackling Climate Change: Comparative Study of Sino–Japanese versus Sino–American Cooperation 应对气候变化: 中日合作与中美合作比较研究." World Economics and Politics 世界经济与政治, no. 1(2009). http://xueshu.baidu.com/s?tn=SE_baiduxueshu_c1gjeupa&wd=%E5%BC%A0%E6%B5%B7%E6%BB%A8%20%E5%BA%94%E5%AF%B9%E6%B0%94%E5%80%99%E5%8F%98%E5%8C%96%20%E4%B8%AD%E7%BE%8E%E5%90%88%E4%BD%9C&ie=utf-8

Zhang Haibin, 张海滨. "US–China Cooperation in Tackling Climate Change: Challenges and Opportunities 中美应对气候变化合作 : 挑战与机遇." International Economic Forum 国际经济论坛, no. 6(2007). http://xueshu.baidu.com/s?tn=SE_baiduxueshu_c1gjeupa&wd=%E5%BC%A0%E6%B5%B7%E6%BB%A8%20%E5%BA%94%E5%AF%B9%E6%B0%94%E5%80%99%E5%8F%98%E5%8C%96%20%E4%B8%AD%E7%BE%8E%E5%90%88%E4%BD%9C&ie=utf-8

Zhang Haibin, 张海滨. "China and the US: Moving Forward on Climate (part Two)." *Chinadialogue* 中外对话, January 29, 2008. www.chinadialogue.net/article/show/single/en/1668-China-and-the-US-moving-forward-on-climate-part-two-.

Zou Ji, 邹骥. "碳关税阻碍全球气候进程, Carbon Tax Hinders Global Climate Progress." 通商汇, August 12, 2009. www.gotohui.com/show.php?contentid=1187.

Zhou Xiaochuan, 周小川. "新世纪以来中国货币政策主要特点, China's Monetary Policy since the Turn of the Century." *Tencent News* 腾讯新闻, November 26, 2012. http://finance.qq.com/a/20121126/003553.htm.

"中美领导人就共同应对气候变化通电话_努力推进中美合作伙伴关系建设, US and Chinese Leaders Talk on Phone about Climate Change." 求是理论网 *Qiushi*, October 22, 2009. www.qstheory.cn/dd/dd2012/zmgx/201203/t20120315_145853.htm.

"习近平:不能照搬发达国家现代化模式, Xi Jinping: China Should Not Follow Developed Countries' Modernization Model." *Tencent News* 腾讯新闻, July 22, 2013. http://news.qq.com/a/20130722/012112.htm.

"国务院加强大气污染防治 力争十年消除重污染, State Council Tightens Air Pollution Control to End Heavy Pollutants within 10 Years." *Tencent News* 腾讯新闻, September 12, 2013. http://news.qq.com/a/20130912/008241.htm.

"[经济发展新动力]中美经贸关系:推进合作 减少摩擦, US-China Trade Relations: Foster Cooperation, Reduce Tension." *Xinhua Online* 新华网, September 10, 2012. http://news.xinhuanet.com/yzyd/fortune/20120910/c_113020631.htm.

"美国总统奥巴马会见王岐山, President Obama Meets with Wang Qishan." *Xinhua Online* 新华网, December 21, 2012. http://news.xinhuanet.com/world/2012-12/21/c_114112579.htm.

"美'放松管制'不能总玩口头承诺, Easing US Export Restrictions: Empty Promises." *Xinhua Online* 新华网, December 21, 2012. http://news.xinhuanet.com/world/2012-12/21/c_114103730.htm.

4   Financial crisis

> There are some economic lessons that are never learned. One is the need for the most profound suspicion of innovation in matters concerning money and more generally the field of finance ... Ingenious monetary and financial designs, without known exception, turn out to be, if not innocuous, then frauds on the public or, frequently, on their perpetrators themselves.
>
> John Kenneth Galbraith, *A History of Economics* [1]

Introduction

John Galbraith's words proved true. The subprime crisis started to unwind in the summer of 2007.[2] In August, as housing prices tumbled, the Fed and the European Central Bank injected $300 billion into the interbank markets to shore up liquidity. In September the Bank of England intervened to rescue Northern Rock, the first British bank run in 189 years, by guaranteeing all bank deposits. In March 2008, Bear Stearns, the fifth largest US investment bank, was taken over by J. P. Morgan for $2 a share (instead of $170 a year before).[3] In July the US Treasury stepped in to rescue Fannie Mae and Freddie Mac, the government sponsored corporations that together held $5 trillion of mortgages. The oil price shot up to $147 per barrel. By September, the Treasury had nationalized Fannie Mae and Freddie Mac, and the Bank of America bought Merrill Lynch. Lehman Brothers folded immediately after with over $613 billion in debt, and AIG, the world's largest insurer, received a $182 billion bailout.[4] On September 17 the Treasury had to intervene to save money market funds worth $3.4 trillion. Finally, on September 20, treasury secretary Henry Paulson announced a $700 billion rescue package to buy up assets nobody wanted. The global financial system seized up, triggering the worst recession in seventy years.

This chapter uses the HISE framework to analyze the state of trust between the US and China with respect to finance. It compares the views of American and Chinese economists on the causes of the Global Financial Crisis (GFC), and shows that economists on both sides agree on many of the causes but the two countries manage their economies differently. While the US practices free market fundamentalism, the Chinese adopt a non-ideological pragmatism.

The GFC served as a warning to the Chinese of the hazards of financial liberalization. This chapter also discusses the global financial industry, and the implications for trust in US–China relations. It concludes that Sino–American distrust is deepening, financial reform in limbo, and the next crisis inevitable.

Chinese perspectives on the Global Financial Crisis

Chinese economists

Many top Chinese economists are US-trained.[5] World Bank chief economist Justin Lin earned his Ph.D. from the University of Chicago; Qian Yingyi of Tsinghua University obtained master's degrees from Yale and Columbia, and his Ph.D. from Harvard; Bai Chongen, professor of economics at Tsinghua, received a Ph.D. in mathematics from the University of California–San Diego and a Ph.D. in economics from Harvard; Zhu Min, deputy managing director of the IMF and former deputy governor of the People's Bank of China (China's central bank), obtained a master's degree from Princeton and his Ph.D. from Johns Hopkins. The Chinese have a deep respect for Western science, and the government sends large numbers of academics each year as visiting scholars to Western universities. But although there are over 6,000 Chinese economists, only around a hundred publish in international journals. Because leading journals print in English, writers outside the Anglo-sphere are disadvantaged. Their views rarely carried in the international press, Chinese economists wield limited influence.[6] Although knowledgeable about Marx, most are fluent in neoclassical economics and the workings of Keynesian and monetary policies. Rather than adhere to dogma, however, Chinese economists follow Deng Xiaoping's advice to use the cat, be it black or white, as long as it catches the mice.[7] As C. P. Fitzgerald observed, the Chinese have traditionally preferred behavior over theory, and content over form.[8] The GFC discredited many Western theories, and some see this as the moment to put forth new theories on the role of markets and government,[9] but no distinctively Chinese theory of financial crises has yet emerged.

Monetary policy

Like many Chinese economists, Wu Jinglian of the Development Research Center (DRC) traces the GFC to Alan Greenspan's loose monetary policy.[10] Following the dot.com bust and 9/11, Greenspan lowered interest rates, encouraged the development of derivatives, and relaxed prudential regulations. These measures, taken to stimulate the economy, led to excessive liquidity, which enabled banks to leverage up their operations and chase higher profits. Between 2001 and 2007, US repossession and refinancing volume doubled from $9.6 to $17 trillion.[11] The sharp growth in the monetary base supported an increase in securitization and derivatives, which inflated asset bubbles. Others who concur with this diagnosis include Justin Lin,

Xu Xiaonian of the China Europe International Business School (CEIBS), Cao Yuanzheng, chief economist of the Bank of China, and Jiang Jianqing, chairman of the Industrial and Commercial Bank of China (ICBC).

Lax regulation

Others, including the China Banking and Regulatory Commission (CBRC), trace the financial crisis to loopholes and shortcomings in financial regulations.[12] As a banking regulator, the CBRC was quick to spot the implications of deregulation. It blamed the crisis on the removal of firewalls between banking and capital markets, over-reliance on financial innovation, and misplaced confidence in the ability of financial markets to self-regulate. The lack of oversight on bankers' compensation led to aggressive leveraging to expand trading volume and boost bonuses.[13] In the wake of the 1997 Asian Financial Crisis, the IMF and World Bank had developed financial sector assessment programs (FSAP) to gauge financial stability and review regulations. Since 1999 more than three-quarters of IMF and World Bank members have completed or requested FSAPs. The US was, and is, not one of them.[14]

Fiat currency and the Triffin dilemma

Governor of the People's Bank of China Zhou Xiaochuan sees the Triffin dilemma as the root cause of the Global Financial Crisis.[15] Together with DRC director Xia Bin, Zhou argues it was the unrestrained supply of dollars that caused the subprime crisis.[16] With the demise of the Bretton Woods gold standard, the dollar became the *de facto* world currency. Between 40 and 60 percent of international transactions are denominated in dollars[17] and over 60 percent of the world's foreign exchange reserves are held in dollars.[18] Robert Triffin posited in the 1960s that the country whose currency other countries wanted to hold must be prepared to issue an extra supply of the currency to meet international demand. But this sets up a tension in the country's current account as well as a conflict between domestic monetary goals and the monetary needs of the global economy. Since the issuing country is not able to take into consideration all external factors when formulating its monetary policy, global financial volatility is the natural consequence.[19]

The adoption of a fiat currency as the international reserve, a recent innovation in the history of finance, presents peculiar challenges. In theory, there should be clear issuing guidelines for the reserve currency. The issuer must be able to regulate the supply promptly, flexibly, and independently of the interests of any single country. But because the dollar is no longer anchored to any physical commodity, there is no objective constraint on its issuance, and the current international monetary system has no control over the supply of dollars. Zhou argues that the failure after the Second World War to adopt the *bancor* proposed by Keynes was a mistake, a view shared by Brad DeLong of U. C. Berkeley. No single currency, Zhou contends, should serve as the reserve currency, and he has proposed adopting the IMF special drawing rights (SDR), as a supranational currency like the *bancor*, instead.[20]

Virtual economy

There is deep concern in China about the virtual economy (financial sector). Many see it as a root cause of the GFC. The combination of vast amounts of capital, computer technology and the internet has made the virtual economy more powerful than the real economy.[21] At the 2012 National Financial Work Conference, Premier Wen Jiabao stressed the need for the financial sector to serve the real economy rather than speculation.[22] He warned against the hollowing out of the real economy and the expansion of the virtual economy.[23] In 2006, just before the GFC, the US financial sector accounted for an astounding 40 percent of US corporate profits. At the same time, there was a growing mismatch between the market value of companies and their contribution to the real economy. Many raised concerns about the rise of "casino capitalism"[24] and the disconnect between stock price and company performance.[25] The giant investment funds which own 60 percent of all stocks and bonds rarely select stocks based on company accounts or factory visits. Factors beyond management control affect 70–80 percent of stock price movements. Stock investing has become stock trading which is based mainly on price movements; investors "buy low and sell high" regardless of the performance of the company. As long as the stock price rises, there will be buyers, and as long as there are buyers, the price will rise. This suggests that financial institutions can and do inflate bubbles.

Global imbalances

Many blame "global imbalances" or a "global savings glut" for the crisis. Federal Reserve chairman Ben Bernanke declared that the flow of savings from emerging economies fueled consumption in the US. He argued that East Asian economies, chastened by the Asian Financial Crisis, increased savings which flowed into the US and funded consumption. But Zhou dismissed the notion arguing that "imbalance is a state of normalcy and balance is only a relative concept."[26] He pointed out that there are no data on the flow of global savings and that China's current account surplus in 2007 while large, was in fact smaller than Japan's and even smaller than the oil exporting countries together as a whole.[27] A study by the WTO and the OECD revising the way trade statistics are calculated showed that the 2009 US trade deficit against China was 25 percent smaller ($131 billion instead of $176 billion) than previously held.[28] The study took into account the fact that many goods "made in China" in fact contain high-value components from elsewhere such as South Korea, Japan and Taiwan.

In a 2012 World Bank paper, Justin Lin refuted the charge that deliberate policies by East Asian countries led to global imbalance.[29] He argued instead that the imbalances resulted from excess US demand due to the Afghanistan and Iraq wars, tax cuts and excessive consumption supported by the wealth effect from the housing bubble. The housing bubble itself was caused by the Fed's low interest rate policy following the dot.com bust in 2001, the lack of financial regulation, and government policy supporting home ownership by low-income households. Andy Xie, former IMF economist, suggested that had Alan Greenspan not expanded the money supply and American households not borrowed, the "savings glut" would not have flowed to the US.[30] The US posts by far the largest current account deficit, which it has managed to maintain for so long because of the position of the dollar as the reserve currency. Meanwhile, China's trade surplus grew because of the relocation of labor-intensive manufacturing from other East Asian countries (e.g. Japan, South Korea, Taiwan). Furthermore, the amount of US debt held by China is often exaggerated. Total US government debt in 2011 was $14.3 trillion but the bulk ($9.8 trillion) was held by the American public and institutions.[31] China held $1.2 trillion or around 8 percent. The US Treasury market is wide and deep, with a trading volume of half a trillion dollars per day; China's holding represents only two to three days' worth of trading.

Former deputy treasury secretary and CEO of Bankers Trust, Frank Newman, calls the global savings glut a myth.[32] Because the Chinese capital account is not convertible, renminbi savings do not "flow" to the US; they can only be used domestically to purchase Chinese goods, services or assets. Neither do dollars earned by Chinese exporters flow to China. The dollars remain in the US bank accounts (of Chinese exporters, banks and the PBOC), and can be used to purchase American goods, services and assets. Rather than leave them in banks earning low interest (and not guaranteed by the government over $250,000), the Chinese like everyone else park them in bonds. In 2008, on the eve of the GFC, the Chinese held nearly $600 billion in US Treasury securities and more than $470 billion in Freddie Mac and Fannie Mae bonds.[33] But these holdings have no effect on the US money supply; the quantity of money circulating in the US economy can only expand through Fed monetary policy or when financial institutions make loans.

Table 4.1 Holdings of US government debt in 2011

Total US debt	*$14.3 trillion*
Social Security Trust Fund	$3 trillion
Federal Reserve	$2 trillion
China	$1.2 trillion
Japan	$912 billion
United Kingdom	$347 billion
Brazil	$211 billion
Taiwan	$153 billion
Hong Kong	$122 billion

Source: US government.

Structural shift and consumption binge

Other Chinese economists, including Chen Zhiwu, finance professor at Yale, and Cao Yuanzheng, BOC chief economist, identify important structural shifts in the US economy brought about by globalization and innovation. With globalization, the US economy quietly shifted away from steel, automobiles and property, the three traditional pillars of the economy, to the "new economy" and from manufacturing to services. Furthermore, technological innovation lifted productivity to such a level that growth was no longer constrained by production or investment, as is normally the case, but by consumption.[34] To overcome the consumption bottleneck, households had to save less and spend more. Here, credit and insurance played a pivotal role. Consumer, housing and education loans together with health and retirement insurance set people free from the need to save and enabled them to spend.

Then, in the wake of the dot.com bubble and 9/11, the US government saw deregulation and financial innovation as extra ways of spurring the economy, and very soon, the securitization of mortgages was born. Financial innovation allowed American households to spend using credit borrowed on their assets, and home equity loans (HEL) soon became a major source of household income.[35] Credit allowed Americans to spend beyond their means even as real income declined. The real wages of 60–70 percent of Americans had fallen since the 1980s, and 20 percent of households depended on credit to maintain their living standards. Although consumption had already become the largest part of the economy by the 1980s, securitization further boosted household spending, and by 2007 consumption shot past 70 percent of GDP.[36] Household consumption accounted for a full 80 percent of GDP growth between 2000 and 2007.[37] The consumption-led growth model was never sustainable, but securitization obscured the risks. At the same time, the opposite trend emerged in China, where consumption fell from 70 percent of GDP in 1970 to below 50 percent in 2007.

Washington Consensus

There is deep skepticism in China about the Washington Consensus and free market fundamentalism. Yu Yongding, a member of the People's Bank of China's (PBOC) Monetary Policy Committee and director of the Institute of World Economics and Politics (IWEP), believes that the GFC was not a business cycle or a short-term crisis like the LTCM debacle of 1998 but a crisis of the Washington Consensus, "Anglo-Saxon capitalist mode of production."[38] The US blamed the Asian Financial Crisis on "crony capitalism," weak capital markets, inadequate regulation, and an overly large banking sector. It considered the Anglo-Saxon model superior and promoted it around the world as part of a system of universal values. But that model led to overconsumption. Yu is skeptical about its ability to regulate markets, and believes there are valuable lessons to learn from the GFC: Unrestrained borrowing will lead to financial crisis; capital markets must be carefully regulated; investment banking kept separate from commercial banking, debt securitization restrained and complex derivatives banned. Yu recalls:

> The US financial system was regarded as a model, and we tried our best to copy whatever we could. Suddenly, we find that our teacher is not that excellent, so the next time .. we will use our own head more."[39]

US perspectives on the Global Financial Crisis

We shall now turn to the US views of the causes of the GFC, and consider opinions from officialdom, think tanks and academia. While few foresaw the crisis or questioned the Washington Consensus, the GFC stimulated intense debate and sparked populist movements such as the Tea Party and Occupy Wall Street. There was sober reflection but also obfuscation and scapegoating.

Financial Crisis Inquiry Commission

In the aftermath of the GFC, a bipartisan commission called the Financial Crisis Inquiry Commission (FCIC) spent more than a year examining the crisis. Hailing it as "the most comprehensive indictment of the American financial failure" and "the definitive history of this period," the commission concluded that the crisis was avoidable.[40] It was the result of human actions, inactions, and misjudgments. Warnings were ignored: "The greatest tragedy would be to accept the refrain that no one could have seen this coming and thus nothing could have been done. If we accept this notion, it will happen again."[41] Published in January 2011, the report noted that

> more than 30 years of deregulation and reliance on self-regulation by financial institutions, championed by former Federal Reserve chairman Alan Greenspan and others, supported by successive administrations and Congresses, and actively pushed by the powerful financial industry at every turn, had stripped away key safeguards, which could have helped avoid catastrophe.

Deregulation opened up gaps in the supervision of critical areas with trillions of dollars at risk, such as the shadow banking system and the derivatives market. Furthermore, the government allowed financial firms to choose their preferred regulators in what became "a race to the weakest supervisor."

The commission cited failures of corporate governance and risk management, excessive borrowing, risky investments, lack of transparency, systematic breakdowns in accountability and ethics, the collapse of mortgage lending standards and the rise of mortgage securitization as causes of the crisis. For every $40 in assets, the nation's five largest investment banks had only $1 in capital to cover losses, meaning that a 3 percent drop in asset values would have wiped out the banks. The banks hid their excessive leverage using derivatives, off-balance-sheet entities and other devices, the report revealed. The speculative binge was abetted by a giant shadow banking system in which the banks relied heavily on short-term debt. Over-the counter (OTC) derivatives too played a part while the government's inconsistent response to the crisis (rescuing Bear Stearns but letting Lehman fall) added to uncertainty and panic in the financial market. The report found fault with Alan Greenspan who led the central bank as the housing bubble expanded, and his successor Ben Bernanke, who did not foresee the crisis. It criticized Greenspan for advocating deregulation and cited a "pivotal failure to stem the flow of toxic mortgages" under his leadership as a prime example of negligence. The report noted that like Bernanke, treasury secretary Henry Paulson too claimed that the subprime collapse would be contained.

Taking aim at the influence of Wall Street, the report said the financial industry spent $2.7 billion on lobbying from 1999 to 2008, while individuals and committees affiliated with it made more than $1 billion in campaign contributions. The Securities and Exchange Commission failed to require big banks to hold more capital to cushion potential losses and halt risky practices, and the Federal Reserve "neglected its mission." Regulators "lacked the political will" to scrutinize and hold accountable the institutions they were supposed to oversee. "The crisis was the result of human action and inaction, not of Mother Nature or computer models gone haywire," the report concluded.

> The captains of finance and the public stewards of our financial system ignored warnings and failed to question, understand and manage evolving risks within a system essential to the well-being of the American public. Theirs was a big miss, not a stumble.

The report called the credit-rating agencies "cogs in the wheel of financial destruction" and compared the banks that bought, created, packaged and sold trillions of dollars in mortgage-related securities to Icarus: "Like Icarus, they never feared flying ever closer to the sun."

US–China Economic and Security Review Commission

Some quarters, however, blame China for the GFC. The US–China Economic and Security Review Commission (USCESRC) which reports to Congress on the national security implications of the economic relationship with China, wrote in a section of its 2009 report entitled *China's Role in the Origins of the Global Financial Crisis and China's Response* that the GFC had its roots in massive global economic imbalances, and placed responsibility for the imbalances partly on the US as the world's biggest spender and borrower, but also on China as the world's biggest saver and lender. It charged that China pursued policies that increased Chinese savings, restrained consumption and kept the renminbi undervalued.[42] These policies generated a huge flow of liquidity into US markets and created "perverse incentives that encouraged banks to make risky loans to US households," which in turn grew ever more indebted. High US demand for imports allowed China to save even more, creating a vicious cycle and laying the foundation for the crisis. China's export boom helped China accumulate the world's largest foreign exchange reserves, valued at over $2.27 trillion by the end of September 2009, most of which is invested in US Treasury bonds and other dollar assets. The report claimed further that China's industrial policy harms US companies and workers. Its low labor cost, high-tech industrial parks and government sub-sidies induce US companies to invest in China. China "provides subsidized land, energy, and water to many foreign manufacturers who relocate their operations in China." The report lamented the "near record levels of trade surplus" against the US despite a drop of 17.6 percent in the first eight months of 2009 compared with the same period in 2008 due to the global economic slowdown. The report deemed the renminbi "significantly undervalued" despite a 21 percent rise against the dollar since July 2005.[43]

Economists, however, are divided over the currency allegation, with some (e.g. Paul Krugman, Edwin Truman) supporting it and others (e.g. Stephen Roach, Martin Feldstein and Alan Greenspan) dismissing it.[44] Krugman charged that China has the "most distortionary exchange rate policy any major nation has ever followed" and suggested a 25 percent countervailing tariff on Chinese imports.[45] Roach points out, however, that the problem consisted not in a US bilateral trade deficit with China but a US multilateral trade deficit with a hundred countries.[46] Importing less from China would not reduce the trade deficit since the US would switch to buying from other potentially more expensive producers, he explained. America's trade problem is a savings problem. Lacking in savings, the US "must import surplus savings from abroad in order to grow, and run massive current account and multi-lateral trade deficits to attract the capital." Although the FCIC found no fault with China, the USCESRC view is more popular in Congress and in the media.

Think tanks

Think tanks represent a diverse range of views depending on political orien-tation and funding source. Washington-based think tanks exercise a powerful influence on policymakers and the public through their publications, lectures and discussions on radio and television. The Brookings Institution, the Cato Institute, the American Enterprise Institute (AEI) and the Peterson Institute are among the most well known. A Brookings paper blamed everyone – Wall Street, the government, and the wider society.[47] The authors Elliot and Baily held that institutions as well as individuals had become blasé about risk-taking and leverage, creating a bubble across a wide range of investments. The authors argue that well-designed regulations would fix the problems. Edwin

Truman of the Peterson Institute considered failures in macroeconomic policies (in the US and the rest of the developed world) and financial supervision as major causes of the GFC but also blamed exchange rate and the policies of China and some oil-exporting countries.[48] Economist Anna Schwartz of the National Bureau of Economic Research (NBER) pointed to expansionary monetary policy, flawed financial innovation and the collapse of trading for some financial instruments[49] while Peter Wallison of the AEI suggested that the crisis was caused by the government's affordable-housing policies rather than market forces. Fannie Mae was the cause of the loose mortgage underwriting standards that brought down the whole system, he wrote.[50]

Federal Reserve Board

Testifying before the FCIC, Fed chairman Ben Bernanke distinguished between "triggers" (particular events or factors that touched off the crisis) and "vulnerabilities" (weaknesses in the financial system and in regulation and supervision).[51] He argued that a number of developments helped trigger the crisis but the most prominent was the prospect of huge losses on subprime mortgage loans. The over $1 trillion in subprime loans, Bernanke suggested, was by itself not large enough in relation to the global financial market to explain the magnitude of the crisis (forgetting that derivatives based on the loans were a few orders of magnitude larger). He maintained that vulnerabilities in the financial system together with the government's crisis response (allowing Lehman to go bust), transformed a decline in housing prices "which by itself was no more severe than the dot-com stock crisis" into a very severe crisis.[52] He blamed excessive borrowing by the private sector, the banks' inability to monitor their own risks (failure to self-regulate), excessive reliance on short-term funding, and increased use of exotic financial instruments like credit default swaps. He pointed to gaps in the regulatory structure where important firms and markets did not have adequate oversight, and even where there was adequate oversight, supervisors and regulators sometimes failed to do a good job. Regulators failed to get banks to do a better job of monitoring and managing risks. Individual regulators looked at different parts of the system but not at the stability of the system as a whole. While acknowledging that domestic factors were responsible for the housing boom and bust, Bernanke blamed the "global savings glut" for keeping interest rates low and contributing to the excessive risk-taking and borrowing behind the housing bubble.[53]

Alan Greenspan, who along with Robert Rubin and Larry Summers championed the financial deregulation (especially of the multi-trillion-dollar derivatives market) widely blamed for the GFC, later admitted at a congressional hearing that he "made a mistake in presuming" that financial markets were self-regulating.[54] But in a paper published two years later, he denied that monetary policy caused the bubble and blamed "a worldwide decline in real long-term interest rates after the Cold War" that produced housing bubbles in several countries, and the securitization of subprime mortgages. To reform the financial system, he suggested increasing capital, liquidity and collateral requirements for banks and shadow banks to safeguard against financial contagion.[55] After leaving the Fed, Greenspan joined Pimco, the world's largest bond investor.

Academics

There is a wide range of opinion among American academics on the causes of the Global Financial Crisis. John Cochrane of the University of Chicago dismisses global imbalances, the Fed's low interest rates, a housing bubble, subprime mortgages and complex derivatives as causes of the crisis. Instead, he blames moral hazard, excessive risk-taking, "too big to fail," inconsistent government response to failing banks and the subsequent panic. Like Bernanke, he argues that had panic not occurred, the contraction following the housing bust would have been no worse than the mild recession that followed the dot.com bust.[56] Stiglitz traces the crisis to the dot.com bubble, the notion that markets are self-regulating, and the lack of regulation to counter the agency problem and externalities.[57] He criticizes the economic doctrine behind deregulation but also blames weak global demand. Aggregate demand shrank as many countries saved for the rainy day with half a trillion dollars or more set aside as reserves each year before the GFC. Rather than turn to the IMF, developing countries built up billions in reserves to protect against global volatility.

Kenneth Rogoff and Carmen Reinhardt trace the subprime crisis to excessive public and private sector debt.[58] In 1945 consumer credit in the US totaled $5.7 billion but within ten years it had grown eightfold to $43 billion. By July 2008, just before the Wall Street collapse, it had reached $2.6 trillion or over $8,000 for every man, woman and child in the country.[59] By 2012, it had reached $30,000 per man, woman and child.[60] Living beyond one's means was no longer considered reckless but the mark of a good American.[61] Jeffrey Sachs sees "the decline in civic virtue among America's political and economic elite" as the root of the crisis.[62] He cited corporate governance failure (CEO pay surged from 40 to 400 times the salary of the average worker), rising income disparity (from 1980 to 2010 the top 1 percent's share of household income rose from 10 percent to over 20 percent), control of politics by the rich, tax cuts and deregulation as the most likely causes.[63] Krugman points to irrational exuberance, the inflow of cheap money from China, moral hazard, "regulatory imprudence," and most of all, free-market fundamentalism that supported deregulation and the proliferation of derivatives.[64] Raghuram Rajan sees social fault lines such deepening income inequality, and financial sector compensation that encouraged excessive risk-taking as root causes of the GFC, while Simon Johnson draws attention to regulatory capture and the corrupt links between Wall Street, academics and politicians.[65] Nobel laureate Robert Solow blames the shift from relationship banking to debt securitization,[66] while Henry Kaufman sees deregulation and financial industry concentration as the problem.[67]

Some identify a seismic shift in the US economy.[68] Increases in farm productivity in the 1920s meant that only a small percentage of the population could produce all the food the nation could consume. This prompted a shift into manufacturing but subsequent increases in industrial productivity meant that only a small percentage of the population was needed to produce all the goods American consumers could buy. The economy then shifted into services. Globalization, by allowing the outsourcing of manufacturing to developing countries, sped up the shift, particularly into finance. As a result, financial sector profits doubled from 20 percent of total corporate profits in the 1990s to 40 percent in 2006. After a dip during the GFC, they rebounded to 29 percent in 2011.[69] Finance, once the life blood of the economy, had become the heart as well. Even as the size of the financial sector became a concern, demographic challenges emerged too. Just when the country ought to be saving for the retirement of the baby-boomers, it is living beyond its means, and as it sinks deeper into debt, foreign lenders may lose confidence in its ability to repay.[70]

How different are US and Chinese perspectives on the GFC?

The preceding survey summarized in Table 4.2 below suggests that Chinese and American economists share many views about the crisis, and identify causes such as low interest rates, the federal home ownership program, regulatory failure, and the securitization of subprime mortgages.[71] They disagree, however, about global imbalances and currency manipulation. The Chinese say they cannot be held responsible for American profligacy and deny manipulating the renminbi. They are wary of credit-fueled consumption and free market fundamentalism, two key insights they draw from the GFC. In this regard, many American economists such as Paul Krugman, Nouriel Roubini and Joseph Stiglitz are in agreement with the Chinese. Despite the public outcry against the excesses of Wall Street and the privileged "one percent," however, the political elite remains committed to that ideology. Free market fundamentalism undergirds American financial interests and structures, and is the substance of a good deal of mistrust between the US and China.

Vested interests

Perhaps the most disturbing feature from the Chinese perspective is the power of Wall Street. The American political process is compromised by campaign contribution and other forms of lobbying. The banking and securities industry is one of the top contributors to campaign financing but its most important source of influence lies elsewhere. Former IMF chief economist Simon Johnson has argued that the American financial industry gained political

Table 4.2 US versus Chinese views on causes of the GFC

	Causes of the GFC	China	USA
1	Monetary policy/role of the FED/low interest rates	Wu Jinglian 吴敬琏 Justin Lin 林毅夫 Jiang Jianqing 姜建清 Xu Xiaonian 许小年 Cao Yuanzheng 曹远征 Li Daokui 李稻葵 Zhang Weiying 张维迎	Anna Schwartz Joseph Stiglitz
2	Consumption-led growth	Chen Zhiwu 陈志武 Yu Yongding 余永定	
3	Deregulation/regulatory failure	Liu Mingkang 刘明康 CBRC Justin Lin	FCIC Joseph Stiglitz Jeffrey Sachs Henry Kaufman Simon Johnson Nouriel Roubini Raghuram Rajan Edwin Truman Ben Bernanke
4	Triffin dilemma/role of dollar as international reserve currency	Zhou Xiaochuan 周小川 Xia Bin 夏斌 Stephen Cheung 张五常	Alan Greenspan Brad DeLong
5	Casino capitalism	Zhou Xiaochuan 周小川 Wen Jiabao 温家宝	Nouriel Roubini
6	Global imbalance/global savings glut		Ben Bernanke Paul Krugman Joseph Stiglitz Paul Volcker
7	Renminbi exchange rate/current account deficit		Paul Krugman Edwin Truman USCESRC
8	Seismic shift	Cao Yuanzheng 曹远征	Joseph Stiglitz
9	Washington Consensus/free market fundamentalism	Yu Yongding 余永定	Joseph Stiglitz Paul Krugman Nouriel Roubini
10	Irrational exuberance		Alan Greenspan Robert Shiller
11	Moral hazard/too big to fail		John Cochrane Paul Krugman
12	Regulatory capture		Simon Johnson FCIC
13	Federal housing policy		Peter Wallison Raghuram Rajan

	Causes of the GFC	China	USA
14	Excessive debt	Chen Zhiwu 陈志武 Yu Yongding 余永定	Ben Bernanke Kenneth Rogoff Carmen Reinhardt Paul Krugman Henry Kaufman Sheldon Garon Simon Johnson
15	Bank bonuses	CBRC Liu Mingkang 刘明康	Nouriel Roubini Raghuram Rajan
16	Rating agencies		Nouriel Roubini FCIC
17	Debt securitization	Chen Zhiwu 陈志武	Henry Kaufman Nouriel Roubini Robert Solow Paul Volcker FCIC
18	Moral crisis (behavioral and ethical shortcomings)		Jeffrey Sachs Henry Kaufman
19	Rising income inequality		Raghuram Rajan
20	Greed and hubris		Paul Volcker

power through cultural capital and the belief that what was good for Wall Street was good for Main Street.[72] Many Washington insiders believed that large financial institutions and free-flowing capital markets were advantageous to America's position in the world.[73] The Congressional Oversight Panel reviewing the TARP bailout concluded that the regulatory failure that gave rise to the financial crisis was "one of philosophy more than structure." Over the past thirty years, the economics profession has become compromised by conflicts of interests and functions virtually as a support group for financial services and other industries whose profits depend heavily on government policies. The careers of Martin Feldstein, Glenn Hubbard, Frederic Mishkin, Laura Tyson, Richard Portes and Larry Summers among others illustrate a three-way nexus between academic economics, Wall Street and political power.[74] Summers championed financial deregulation both as Harvard professor and Treasury official, while enjoying handsome fees from Wall Street giants.[75]

Another source of influence is the revolving door between Wall Street and Washington. Robert Rubin, former co-chairman of Goldman Sachs, served as treasury secretary under Bill Clinton. Henry Paulson, former CEO of Goldman Sachs, served as treasury secretary under George W. Bush. John Snow, Paulson's predecessor left to work for Cerberus Capital Management, a large private-equity firm where Dan Quayle also worked. After leaving the Federal Reserve, Greenspan joined Pimco, a large bond trader. While they have deep knowledge of the practices of the financial industry, Wall Street executives do not always appreciate the systemic implications and impact of policies on the broader economy. Contrary to his campaign promise to check lobbying, Barack Obama has been soft on Wall Street. Treasury secretary Timothy F. Geithner opposed nationalizing ailing banks while director of the National Economic Council, Gene Sperling, and his predecessor, Larry Summers, both worked at investment firms before joining the Obama administration. Three of Obama's White House chiefs-of-staff have worked in the financial industry: Rahm Emanuel (Wasserstein Perella), William M. Daley (JPMorgan Chase), and Jacob Lew (Citigroup). Two private equity executives, Richard D. Parsons[76] and Mark T. Gallogly,[77] sit on the President's Council on Jobs and Competitiveness.[78]

Meanwhile, bankers' compensation has only grown more generous since the GFC. According to the *Financial Times*, the big international banks are slashing dividends and paying staff bigger bonuses. Figures from thirteen major banks show that 81 percent of profits now go to the staff, up from 58 percent before the crisis.[79] Obama vowed to end "too big to fail," but America's largest banks have only gotten bigger. JPMorgan Chase, Bank of America, Citigroup, Wells Fargo and Goldman Sachs together held $8.5 trillion in assets at the end of 2011, which is equal to 56 percent of the US economy, up from 43 percent before the GFC. The "Big Five" are twice as big as a decade ago relative to GDP. Simon Johnson blames a "lack of leadership at Treasury and the White House" for the lack of reform.[80] Putting it more bluntly, Stiglitz concludes that those who designed the bank bailout are "either in the pocket of the banks or they're incompetent."[81]

In the wake of the crisis, Congress passed the Dodd-Frank Financial Regulatory Reform Bill to protect consumers, restrain Wall Street and prevent another financial crisis. To shield borrowers against abusive lending practices, the bill establishes watchdog agencies to monitor banking policies and oversee troubled financial institutions. But so far it has had scant effect.[82] The act has been kept in limbo by Republican congressmen who repeatedly block nominees to head the agencies.[83] Without strong leaders in key agencies, financial reform has no chance. Greenspan attacked the Dodd-Frank reforms, warning they could create the "largest regulatory-induced market distortion" since the imposition of wage and price controls in 1971.[84] The reforms, he claimed, would be "impossible to implement, distortive to markets and a possible threat to US living standards." Chinese observers see little hope of reforming Wall Street and the global financial system.

Global banks

In the era of globalization, the financial sector has become increasingly concentrated. Mergers and acquisitions since 1980s have created giant global

Table 4.3 Bank mergers since the 1980s

Bank	Constituent firms
Citibank	Travelers Group Salomon Smith Barney Schroders Banamex Bank Handlowy
JPMorgan Chase	JP Morgan Chase Manhattan Robert Fleming
HSBC	HSBC Holdings Midland Bank Republic Bank of New York Crédit Commercial de France Banque Hervet Bital
Deutsche Bank	Deutsche Bank Morgan Grenfell Bankers Trust
Bank of America (BoA)	Bank of America Bank of Boston Fleet Boston MBNA Nations Bank
UBS	United Bank of Switzerland (UBS) Swiss Bank Corporation Phillips & Drew Dillon Read S. G. Warburg O'Conner Associates Paine Webber
Crédit Agricole	Crédit Agricole Banque Indosuez Crédit Lyonnais
BNP Paribas	BNP Paribas Compagnie Bancaire

banks. Between 1997 and 2006, the top 25 banks increased their share of the total assets of the top 100 banks from 28 percent to 41 percent.[85] Another round of mergers since the GFC boosted the share of total assets to 45 percent.[86] In 2010 the top five banks accounted for 52 percent of foreign exchange traded each day while the top ten banks accounted for 77.3 percent.[87] In 2012–2013, the top ten banks accounted for 53 percent of investment banking revenues, while the top twenty banks accounted for 66 percent. The top five investment banks were American, and the top twenty were all from high-income countries. In the same year, the 500 largest asset managers

Table 4.4 Bank mergers since the Global Financial Crisis

Bank	Firms acquired
JPMorgan	Bear Stearns Washington Mutual
Wells Fargo	Wachovia
Bank of America	Merrill Lynch
BNP Paribas	Fortis
Santander	ABN Amro (Latin America) Abbey National
Nomura	Lehman Brothers (Asia and Europe)
Barclays	Lehman Brothers (USA)
Commerzbank	Dresdner Bank

had $64 trillion under management. The top fifty firms accounted for 61 percent of the total funds under management.[88] At the end of 2012, the top firm, BlackRock, alone managed over $3.792 trillion, surpassing the entire Chinese foreign exchange reserves, as well as the French or German GDP.[89]

The Washington Consensus institutions (the World Bank and the IMF) have played a critical role in shaping thinking about financial institutions. Since their inception in the 1940s they have been controlled by OECD states. Just before the GFC, the OECD, which represents only 16 percent of the world's population, held 61 percent of the votes in the IMF, and by an unspoken rule, the president of the IMF is always a European, and the head of the World Bank always an American. Not surprisingly, both institutions have worked tirelessly to promote the interests of American and European banks, on whose behalf they pry open new markets by claiming that the Western banks bring better prudential, accounting and disclosure standards, higher quality services, and economic growth through more efficient allocation of financial resources.[90] The World Bank asserts that by bringing competition, foreign entrants improve efficiency.[91] Transition economies "more willing to cede majority control of their banks to foreign interests" enjoyed higher growth rates.[92] The benefits of entry by foreign banks outweigh the risks associated with foreign ownership, and foreign banks are rarely dominant nor do they undermine the domestic banking system, it assured.[93] But in fact, liberalization led to rapid growth in market share for the global banks. By 2001, foreign banks controlled 49 percent of bank assets in Brazil, 59 percent in Venezuela, 61 percent in Argentina and Peru, and 62 percent in Chile.[94] Between 2000 and 2002 global banks acquired four of Mexico's five largest banks, and gained control of 80 percent of Mexican bank assets. The global giants swept through Eastern Europe in the 1990s, and by 2001 controlled 99 percent of bank assets in Estonia, 90 percent in the Czech Republic, 89 percent in Croatia and Hungary, 86 percent in Slovakia, 78 percent in

Table 4.5 Percentage of bank assets owned by foreign banks in 2002

Country	Percentage
Brazil	49
Venezuela	59
Argentina	61
Peru	61
Chile	62
Mexico	80
Estonia	99
Czech Republic	90
Croatia	89
Hungary	89
Slovakia	86
Lithuania	78
Bulgaria	75
Bosnia-Herzegovina	73
Poland	75

Lithuania, 75 percent in Bulgaria, 73 percent in Bosnia-Herzegovina, and 75 percent in Poland. By 2004, foreign banks owned over 75 percent of East European bank assets.[95]

Chinese banks

According to Chinese folklore, the world's first banks originated in thirteenth-century China amid the prosperity of the Yuan dynasty. By the dawn of the twenty-first century, however, Chinese banks were in dire straits. They were too frail to compete on the global "level playing field." Unsophisticated internal processes, poorly trained staff and backward technology were the order of the day. The government ordered banks to make "policy loans" to support state-owned enterprises even if these were making losses. Corporate governance was weak and fraud involving bank managers and regulators was commonplace.[96] So too were non-performing loans (NPL) of up to 40 percent of assets.[97] Too big to fail, the state-owned banks suffered from moral hazard, knowing that the state would bail them out no matter how poorly they performed. In 2003, Citigroup urged China to "tear apart the big four banks into relatively small units in order to switch on the process of bank reform," warning of certain bankruptcy otherwise.[98] The break-up, said to be the "only way out," would promote competition and spur reform. In 2001 China joined the WTO, exposing itself to powerful competitors such as Citigroup, JPMorgan Chase, and Bank of America. Citigroup spans 140 countries, with 16,000 offices and 260,000 employees.[99] At the turn of century, Peter Nolan likened China's integration into the international financial system to a boat setting out to sea.[100] What are the prospects for the weather? How strong is the boat?

As pressure intensified, the Chinese banks made surprising progress. The first National Financial Work Conference ordered the cleaning up of NPLs; the banks were to become commercially driven businesses and were encouraged to list on stock markets.[101] In one decade, they transformed themselves from basket cases into some of the most profitable banks. China now has four of the top ten banks by market value, and some of the fattest loan books. The NPL ratio at the Industrial and Commercial Bank of China (ICBC) fell from 48 percent in 2000 to 10 percent within six years. It has since become the world's largest bank by market capitalization[102] and also the most profitable.[103] In 2013 it became the top bank by tier 1 capital, a respectable measure of capital adequacy.[104] Despite the global economic slowdown, Chinese banks offer higher earnings yields (16 percent) than foreign banks.[105] The Agricultural Bank of China broke the world IPO record by raising $22.1 billion.[106] The combined assets of the Big Four totaled $6.3 trillion in 2010, roughly the size of the Chinese GDP.[107] The banks have become more sophisticated and moved into investment banking. BOC's investment bank underwrote a $2.55 billion flotation in 2010. The Chinese banks' meteoric rise stunned market watchers but they remain a largely domestic affair with little international exposure.[108] Compared to their Western colleagues, Chinese bankers are paid modestly. ICBC chairman, Jiang Jianqing, earns $185,000, or less than 1 percent of the compensation received by Goldman Sachs CEO Lloyd Blankfein.[109]

Conclusion

On close examination, the GFC was seen to have deep ideological roots. Free market fundamentalism provided the intellectual basis for financial deregulation. Markets, it was argued, were self-regulating, and bankers should be left to their own devices. Deregulation, which came about through Wall Street's influence in Washington, opened the way for debt securitization, allowing mortgage risks to be passed on to investors around the world. The nature of banking changed, and credit appraisal standards declined.[110] The rating agencies, in tacit collusion with their clients, underestimated the risk of the bonds.[111] The crisis was due as much to malfeasance as to institutional failure.[112] The GFC has been dubbed the biggest bank heist in history and an "inside job."[113] Yet no senior bank or government official has been indicted,[114] and much needed reforms continue to face dogged resistance.[115]

The global economic and financial crisis shook the consensus on how to run macroeconomic policy. Joseph Stiglitz sees the current economic trauma as a big opportunity to revolutionize the flawed economic models and "exit from an interminable cycle of crises."[116] But after five years of "rethinking," the IMF had only the following to offer:

Table 4.6 The top 10 Banks in 2012 (ranked according to Tier 1 capital)

Rank	Bank	Country	$million tier 1 capital	$million assets
1	Bank of America	US	159,232.00	2,136,577.91
2	JPMorgan Chase	US	150,384.00	2,265,792.00
3	ICBC	China	140,027.62	2,456,294.82
4	HSBC Holdings	UK	139,590.00	2,555,579.00
5	Citigroup	US	131,874.00	1,873,878.00
6	China Construction Bank Corporation	China	119,135.36	1,949,219.00
7	Mitsubishi UFJ Financial Group	Japan	117,017.65	2,664,170.61
8	Wells Fargo & Co	US	113,952.00	1,313,867.00
9	Bank of China	China	111,172.53	1,877,520.04
10	Agricultural Bank of China	China	96,413.05	1,853,318.89

Source: The Banker Database.

Note: The ranking is based on Tier 1 capital, the core measure of a bank's strength from a regulator's point of view. Unlike the accounting net worth (equity) of a company, tier 1 capital is the core capital of a company and consists of retained earnings and common stock held by the company.

> Macro-prudential tools may provide a new policy lever to curb danger-ous booms and contain imbalances. But evidence about their effective-ness is mixed and we are a long way from knowing how to use them reliably. Their relation with other policies is not yet fully understood; they are fraught with complicated political economy issues; and there is little consensus on how to organize their governance.[117]

At a conference in April 2013 billed as "first steps and early lessons" of the financial crisis, IMF chief economist Olivier Blanchard conceded that "we are still navigating by sight," and that he had "no clue where we will end." The conference produced no radical redesign of the financial system. David Romer warned against the notion that large financial shocks are rare, and concluded that the modest changes discussed at the conference were unlikely to prevent future shocks from inflicting serious harm.[118] A circumspect Martin Wolf would only say that "we have a reasonable idea of what went wrong but don't know how to fix it." None were prepared to acknowledge the powerful vested interests and structures which stand in the way of reasoned remedies.

Meanwhile, the global economic landscape is shifting. In 2011 China became the top manufacturing country (with 19.8 percent of world manu-facturing output) ending America's 110-year run as the premier goods pro-ducer.[119] Historian Robert Allen notes that China's reversion to the top position marked the closing of a 500-year cycle in economic history.[120] In

2012, developing countries attracted for the first time more FDI than the developed countries.[121] From 1990 to 2006, the former's share of world GDP rose from 15.9 to 25 percent, contributing 30 percent to GDP growth or 50 percent in PPP terms, and the Chinese are calling for reform of the existing financial order which, in their view, represents the interests of high-income countries against those of developing countries. What the reforms will look like requires further dialog, but they "must end the marginalization of the developing world," declared the *People's Daily*.[122] Globalization is a double-edged sword, which does not guarantee the healthy development of the global economy, and reform requires "new ideas and new methods," and a bigger voice in the IMF, World Bank and the WTO for the developing world in order to create an "equitable, inclusive and orderly global financial system." At the St. Petersburg G20 Summit, Xi Jinping called for the reform of the IMF and the SDR representation to reflect the GDP of member states.[123]

If reform fails to come from the center, it may emerge from the periphery. In 2009 and 2010 China made more loans ($110 billion) to developing countries than the World Bank.[124] Meanwhile, the renminbi trade circle is expanding, and the share of China's external trade settled in renminbi is expected to exceed 20 percent or 4 trillion yuan ($653 billion) in 2013.[125] Since China overtook the US as Japan's biggest trading partner in 2007, Japan has a heightened incentive to settle in renminbi. In addition to Japan, Southeast Asian and African countries have also started to settle bilateral trade in renminbi, and a third of China's cross-border trade is expected to use the currency by 2015, according to an HSBC forecast. Since 2009, overseas sales of renminbi-denominated bonds have surged elevenfold to 174 billion yuan ($28.4 billion), and trading in the currency in London more than tripled.[126] China has signed currency swaps with eighteen countries, totaling 2.4 trillion yuan ($392 billion) since 2008. While the currency still accounts for less than 1 percent of global payments, compared to 85 percent combined for the dollar, euro, pound and yen, John McCormick, chairman of the Royal Bank of Scotland, predicts it will become a global currency by 2015.[127] Philippe Lintern, head of wholesale banking for Europe at Standard Chartered, calls it "a revolution of financial markets."[128] Zhou Xiaochuan has proposed using the SDR as the international reserve currency, a key move that could open the way for other reforms.

Before the GFC, the Chinese had looked to the US for banking know-how. Shang Fulin, chairman of the China Banking Regulatory Commission, likened Chinese financial firms to high school athletes and American firms to NBA players.[129] The GFC changed all that. It exposed profound intellectual and institutional flaws, and undermined Beijing's trust in US governance. But to make matters worse, the Americans blamed the Chinese for their own profligacy, and, by implication, for the Wall Street collapse. The Chinese were speechless. They saw in the "savings glut" theory (that Americans spent so much only because the Chinese saved so much) an attempt to absolve speculators and regulators, and protect Western vested interests and power structures.[130] Making scapegoats of the Chinese betrayed a deep-seated antipathy that precludes trust.

Notes

1   John Kenneth Galbraith, *A History of Economics: The Past as the Present* (London: Hamish Hamilton, 1987), 99.
2   Andrew Sheng, *From Asian to Global Financial Crisis: An Asian Regulator's View of Unfettered Finance in the 1990s and 2000s* (Cambridge: Cambridge University Press, 2009), 5–6.
3   Matthew Goldstein, "JPMorgan Buys Bear on the Cheap," *Businessweek.com*, March 16, 2008, www.businessweek.com/stories/2008-03-16/jpmorgan-buys-bear-on-the-cheapbusinessweek-business-news-stock-market-and-financial-advice.
4   William Greider, "The AIG Bailout Scandal," *The Nation*, August 6, 2010, www.thenation.com/article/153929/aig-bailout-scandal#.
5   "China's Top Economists Meet Press," *China.org.cn*, accessed April 20, 2013, www.china.org.cn/china/NPC_CPPCC_2013/2013-03/07/content_28162711.htm.
6   "Wall Street Wire Unveils 'Top 10 Chinese Economists,'" *People's Daily Online*, February 25, 2006, http://english.peopledaily.com.cn/200602/25/eng2006 0225_245921.html.
7   邓小平黑猫白猫轮:不管黑猫白猫, 抓到老鼠就是好猫
8   C. P. Fitzgerald, *The Chinese View of Their Place in the World* (London and New York: Oxford University Press, 1964), 46.
9   刘明康 Liu Mingkang, "全球金融危机带给中国巨大机遇 Global Financial Crisis Brings Opportunities to China," 基金网, February 17, 2012, http://fund. cnfol.com/120217/105,1485,11779055,00.shtml.
10 DRC: Development Research Center of the State Council.
11 姜建清 Jiang Jianqing, "在危机下重塑金融新秩序 Creating a New Financial Order," *Global Entrepreneur* 环球企业家, November 17, 2008, www.gemag.com. cn/html/2008/hotmoney_1117/9410.html.
12 *CBRC Annual Report 2008* (Beijing: 中国银监会 China Banking Regulatory Commission), accessed July 18, 2012, http://zhuanti.cbrc.gov.cn/subject/subject/ nianbao2008/english/zwqb.pdf.
13 Justin Lin and Volker Treichel, "The Unexpected Global Financial Crisis: Researching Its Root Cause," *World Bank Policy Research Working Paper 5937* (2012), http://papers.ssrn.com/sol3/papers.cfm?abstract_id=1982446.
14 Sheng, *From Asian to Global Financial Crisis*, 352.
15 周小川 Zhou Xiaochuan, "Reform the International Monetary System," Beijing: People's Bank of China, March 23 (2009), http://portfolioconstruction. com.au/obj/articles_BRIC/Zhou_Xiaochuan_Reform_the_International_Moneta ry_System_90323.pdf.
16 王宇 Wang Yu, "从周小川文章看金融危机的真实根源和化解之道 Understanding the Root of the Financial Crisis and Its Resolution from Zhou Xiaochuan's Essay," *Xinhua Online* 新华网, March 25, 2009, http://news.xinhuanet. com/fortune/2009-03/26/content_11073108.htm.
17 L. Goldberg, "Is the International Role of the Dollar Changing?," *Current Issues in Economics and Finance* 16, no. 1, January 2010, http://papers.ssrn.com/ soL3/papers.cfm?abstract_id=1550192.
18 Anchalee Worrachate and John Detrixhe, "IMF May Classify Aussie, Canada Dollar as Reserve Currencies," *Bloomberg*, accessed April 20, 2013, www. bloomberg.com/news/2012-11-19/imf-may-classify-aussie-canadian-dollars-as-res erve-currencies.html.

19 "Reserve Accumulation and International Monetary Stability" (International Monetary Fund, April 13, 2010), www.imf.org/external/np/pp/eng/2010/041310.pdf.

20 The Special Drawing Rights (SDR), the IMF's unit of accounting, is a notional currency based on the US dollar, the euro, the British pound and the Japanese yen.

21 周小川 Zhou Xiaochuan, "金融业脱离实体经济诱发本次国际金融危机 Disconnect between Financial Industry and the Real Economy Sparked the Financial Crisis," 财经_凤凰网 *Phoenix Online*, June 29, 2012, http://finance.ifeng.com/news/special/lujiazui2012/20120629/6680487.shtml.

22 The National Financial Work Conference meets every five years to review major financial reforms.

23 "全国金融工作会议在京召开 温家宝讲话 李克强出席 National Financial Work Conference Opens in Beijing: Wen Jiabao Speaks, Li Keqiang Attends," 新华网 *Xinhua News*, January 7, 2012, http://news.xinhuanet.com/fortune/2012-01/07/c_111392011.htm.

24 Susan Strange, *Casino Capitalism*, New edition (Manchester: Manchester University Press, 1997); Sheng, *From Asian to Global Financial Crisis*, 356.

25 王小强 Wang Xiaoqiang, 投机赌博新经济 (Hong Kong: Strong Wind Press, 2007), 15–7.

26 周小川 Zhou Xiaochuan, "Issues Related to the Global Financial Crisis," Speech at Global Think-tank Summit (Beijing, July 3, 2009), www.bis.org/review/r090710b.pdf?frames=0.

27 Most of China's consists of corporate savings (retained earnings). In 2007 household savings accounted for 20 percent of GDP while government savings accounted for 8 percent of GDP.

28 Chris Giles and Claire Jones, "Research Rewrites Global Trade Data," *Financial Times*, January 16, 2013, www.ft.com/cms/s/0/346568c2-6001-11e2-b657-00144feab49a.html#axzz2Hzc2QWQ9.

29 Lin and Treichel, "The Unexpected Global Financial Crisis."

30 谢国忠 Xie, Andy, "格林斯潘应该为金融危机负责 Greenspan Should Be Held Responsible for the Financial Crisis," 财经_腾讯网, February 18, 2009, http://finance.qq.com/a/20090218/002588.htm.

31 Tom Murse, "How Much U.S. Debt Does China Really Own?," *About.com US Government Info*, accessed April 20, 2013, http://usgovinfo.about.com/od/moneymatters/ss/How-Much-US-Debt-Does-China-Own.htm.

32 Frank N. Newman, *Six Myths That Hold Back America: And What America Can Learn from the Growth of China's Economy*, Kindle edition (New York: Diversion Books, 2011), Ch. 1.

33 夏斌 Xia Bin, "全球金融危机对我国的影响及中国对策(上) Impact of the Global Financial Crisis on China and China's Response," Development Research Center of the State Council, December 2008, www.drcnet.com.cn/DRCNet.Channel.Web/gylt/20081210/gylt_29.htm.

34 陈志武 Chen Zhiwu, "美国金融危机根源与教训 The Root of the US Financial Crisis and Its Lessons," 理财师博客_大渝网_腾讯网, September 23, 2008, http://cq.qq.com/a/20080923/000698_1.htm.

35 Cao Yuanzheng, "美国金融危机及其影响 The US Financial Crisis and Its Impact."

36 "Personal Consumption as a Percentage of U.S. GDP, 1970–2008," *Blended Purple*, August 11, 2007, http://blendedpurple.blogspot.co.uk/2007/08/personal-consumption-as-percentage-of.html.

37 曹远征 Cao Yuanzheng, "美国金融危机及其影响 US Financial Crisis and Its Impact," 国际战略研究简报 *International and Strategic Studies Report* no. 24 (October 27, 2008).

38 余永定 Yu Yongding, 美国次贷危机: 背景, 原因与发展 *US Subprime Crisis: Background, Causes and Development* (CASS Research Center for International

126   *Financial crisis*

Finance, October 8, 2008), http://course.lixin.edu.cn/course_center/files_upload/699ebe8f-3ef7-4792-a764-4b6dd93749a4/content/f6417374-81b9-428e-afc7-397eb21ac541/COLUMN_7/rdjj09.pdf.

39   Zhao Yidi and Kevin Hamlin, "China Shuns Paulson's Free Market Push as Meltdown Burns U.S.," *Bloomberg*, September 23, 2008, www.bloomberg.com/apps/news?pid=newsarchive&sid=aCl7bFUJzWRk.

40   *The New York Review of Books*.

41   The Financial Crisis Inquiry Commission website http://fcic.law.stanford.edu/.

42   Executive Summary of USCESRC 2009 Report to Congress (US–China Economic and Security Review Commission, 2009), www.uscc.gov/annual_report/2009/executive_summary.pdf.

43   Ibid., 2–3.

44   Newman, *Six Myths That Hold Back America*.

45   Paul Krugman, "Taking On China," *New York Times*, March 15, 2010, Opinion section, www.nytimes.com/2010/03/15/opinion/15krugman.html.

46   Stephen Roach, Nicholas Lardy, and Robert Cassidy, "China's Role in the Origins of and Response to the Global Recession" (Washington, DC, 2009), https://mail-attachment.googleusercontent.com/attachment/?ui=2&ik=925828fbf3&view=att&th=138321a476a8e753&attid=0.1&disp=safe&realattid=f_godonnqr0&zw&saduie=AG9B_P8M-pEX1ScT_7aJrn_zjECe&sadet=1340870412563&sads=dMjylKYcX9MAclLYZk2yTJ2yZBM&sadssc=1.

47   Douglas J. Elliot and Martin Neil Baily, "Telling the Narrative of the Housing Bubble" (Washington, DC: Brookings Institution, November 23, 2009), www.brookings.edu/~/media/research/files/papers/2009/11/23%20narrative%20elliott%20baily/1123_narrative_elliott_baily.

48   Edwin M. Truman, "Speech: The Global Financial Crisis: Lessons Learned and Challenges for Developing Countries," Peterson Institute of International Economics, June 16, 2009, www.piie.com/publications/papers/paper.cfm?ResearchID=1240.

49   A. J. Schwartz, "Origins of the Financial Market Crisis of 2008," *Cato Journal* 29, no. 1 (2009): 19–23.

50   Peter Wallison, "Government-Sponsored Meltdown," Wall Street Journal, July 12, 2011, Opinion section, http://online.wsj.com/article/SB10001424052702304760604576423670655568418.html.

51   "Causes of the Financial Crisis: Testimony before the Financial Crisis Inquiry Commission," *Federal Reserve Board*, September 2, 2010, www.federalreserve.gov/newsevents/testimony/bernanke20100902a.htm.

52   Ben Bernanke, "The Federal Reserve's Response to the Financial Crisis," Lecture to George Washington University Business School, March 27, 2012, www.federalreserve.gov/newsevents/files/chairman-bernanke-lecture3-20120327.pdf.

53   B. Bernanke, C. C. Bertaut, L. DeMarco and S. B. Kamin., "International Capital Flows and the Return to Safe Assets in the United States, 2003–2007," *FRB International Finance Discussion Paper* no. 1014, 2011, http://papers.ssrn.com/sol3/papers.cfm?abstract_id=1837780.

54   Robert Neate, "Financial Crisis: 25 People at the Heart of the Meltdown – Where Are They Now?," *The Guardian*, August 6, 2010, www.guardian.co.uk/business/2012/aug/06/financial-crisis-25-people-heart-meltdown.

55   Alan Greenspan, "The Crisis," *Brookings Papers on Economic Activity*, Spring 2010, www.freepatentsonline.com/article/Brookings-Papers-Economic-Activity/237453501.html.

56   J. H. Cochrane, "Lessons from the Financial Crisis," *Regulation* 32, no. 4 (2009): 34–37.

57   Joseph Stiglitz, *Freefall: Free Markets and the Sinking of the Global Economy* (London and New York: Allen Lane, 2010), 3–18.

58 Kenneth S. Rogoff and Carmen M. Reinhart, *This Time Is Different: Eight Centuries of Financial Folly* (Princeton, NJ: Princeton University Press, 2009).

59 Philip Coggan, *Paper Promises: Money, Debt and the New World Order* (London: Allen Lane, 2011), 185.

60 Simon Johnson and James Kwak, *White House Burning: The Founding Fathers, Our National Debt, and Why It Matters to You*, 1st edn. (New York: Pantheon Books, 2012).

61 Sheldon M. Garon, *Beyond Our Means: Why America Spends While the World Saves* (Princeton, NJ: Princeton University Press, 2012), 355.

62 Jeffrey Sachs, *The Price of Civilization: Economics and Ethics After the Fall* (London: Bodley Head, 2011).

63 Jeffrey Sachs on the US Economy: "It's Been an Amazing Ride for the Rich" – Video, *The Guardian*, April 12, 2012, www.guardian.co.uk/business/video/2012/apr/12/jeffrey-sachs-us-economy-video.

64 Paul Krugman, "An Irish Mirror," *New York Times*, March 8, 2010, Opinion section, www.nytimes.com/2010/03/08/opinion/08krugman.html?th&emc=th.

65 Raghuram Rajan, *Fault Lines: How Hidden Fractures Still Threaten the World Economy* (Princeton, NJ: Princeton University Press, 2010).

66 Robert Solow, "Robert M. Solow on the Global Economic Crisis," Video, MIT School of Humanities, Arts and Social Sciences, November 2009, http://shass.mit.edu/multimedia/video-2010-robert-m-solow-global-economic-crisis.

67 Henry Kaufman, "Big Banks Are Not the Future," Wall Street Journal, June 5, 2012, Opinion section, http://online.wsj.com/article/SB10001424052702304707604577427941294873400.html.

68 Stiglitz, *Freefall*, 24.

69 Maxwell Strachan, "Financial Sector Back To Accounting For Nearly One-Third Of U.S. Profits," March 30, 2011, www.huffingtonpost.com/2011/03/30/financial-profits-percentage_n_841716.html.

70 Stiglitz, *Freefall*, 25.

71 王君 Wang Jun, 国际金融危机与我国应对政策 *Global Financial Crisis and China's Policy Response* (中共中央党校出版社 Beijing: Central Party School Publishing House, 2009).

72 Simon Johnson, "The Quiet Coup," *The Atlantic*, May 2009, www.theatlantic.com/magazine/archive/2009/05/the-quiet-coup/7364/.

73 Ibid.

74 David Kocieniewski, "Academics Who Defend Wall St. Reap Reward," *New York Times*, December 27, 2013, Business Day section, www.nytimes.com/2013/12/28/business/academics-who-defend-wall-st-reap-reward.html; Charles Ferguson, *Inside Job: The Financiers Who Pulled Off the Heist of the Century* (London: Oneworld Publications, 2012).

75 Charles Ferguson, "Larry Summers and the Subversion of Economics," *Chronicle of Higher Education*, October 3, 2010, http://chronicle.com/article/Larry-Summersthe/124790/; John D. McKinnon and T. W. Farnam, "Hedge Fund Paid Summers $5.2 Million in Past Year," *Wall Street Journal*, April 5, 2009, http://online.wsj.com/article/SB123879462053487927.html.

76 Richard Parsons is a former chairman of Citigroup and senior adviser to Providence Equity Partners.

77 Mark Gallogly is a founder of Centerbridge Partners and a top Obama donor.

78 Nicholas Confessore, "Bain Strategy Against Romney May Have Pitfalls for Obama," *New York Times*, May 23, 2012, U.S./Politics section, www.nytimes.com/2012/05/24/us/politics/bain-strategy-against-romney-may-have-pitfalls-for-obama.html.

79   Patrick Jenkins and Patrick Mathurin, "Bank Staff Costs Take Bigger Share of Pot," *Financial Times*, June 5, 2012, www.ft.com/cms/s/0/d4fe3186-ac0d-11e1-a8a0-00144feabdc0.html#axzz1xURvIi4R.

80   David J. Lynch, "Banks Seen Dangerous Defying Obama's Too-Big-to-Fail Move," *Bloomberg*, accessed June 11, 2012, www.bloomberg.com/news/2012-04-16/obama-bid-to-end-too-big-to-fail-undercut-as-banks-grow.html.

81   Michael McKee and Matthew Benjamin, "Stiglitz Says Ties to Wall Street Doom Bank Rescue," *Bloomberg*, April 17, 2009, www.bloomberg.com/apps/news?pid=newsarchive&sid=afYsmJyngAXQ&refer=home.

82   Jessica Silver-Greenberg and Peter Eavis, "JPMorgan Discloses $2 Billion in Trading Losses," *DealBook*, accessed May 11, 2012, http://dealbook.nytimes.com/2012/05/10/jpmorgan-discloses-significant-losses-in-trading-group/.

83   "Dodd-Frank in Limbo," *New York Times*, May 27, 2011, Opinion section, www.nytimes.com/2011/05/28/opinion/28sat3.html?_r=1&nl=todaysheadlines&emc=tha211.

84   Tom Braithwaite, "Greenspan Warns Dodd-Frank Reforms Risk 'market Distortion,'" *FT Chinese*, March 30, 2011, www.ftchinese.com/story/001037805/en.

85   *The Banker*, July 2006.

86   *The Banker*, July 2010.

87   *Euromoney*, 2011.

88   Peter Nolan, *The West and China: Globalization and Competition in Banking* (Cambridge: Cambridge University Press, 2013).

89   "Who Is BlackRock?," *BlackRock*, 2013, http://www2.blackrock.com/global/home/AboutUs/index.htm.

90   Nolan, *The West and China: Globalization and Competition in Banking*.

91   World Bank, *World Development Report 1999/2000: Entering the 21st Century* (New York and Oxford: Oxford University Press, 2000), 96.

92   World Bank, *World Development Report 2002: Building Institutions for Markets* (Oxford: Oxford University Press for the World Bank, 2002), 86.

93   World Bank, *World Development Report 1999/2000*, 36.

94   Song Chang, *Consolidation and Internationalization in the Global Banking Industry since the 1980s, and the Implication for Chinese Banking Reform* (Cambridge: Cambridge University Press, 2005).

95   Ibid.

96   Elisabeth Rosenthal, "Chinese Monetary Official Dies in Fall From 7th-Story Window," *New York Times*, May 13, 2000, http://partners.nytimes.com/library/world/asia/051300china-official.html.

97   "会见索罗斯时的谈话 2001年9月17日 Discussion with George Soros on 17 September 2001," in 朱镕基讲话实录 *Zhu Rongji's Speeches* (Beijing: People's Press 人民出版社, 2011), 240.

98   Nolan, *The West and China: Globalization and Competition in Banking*.

99   According to the *Fortune Global 500: The World's Biggest Companies* (2011).

100   Peter Nolan, *China at the Crossroads* (Cambridge: Polity Press, 2004), 46, www.loc.gov/catdir/toc/ecip042/2003007751.html.

101   戴相龙 Dai Xianglong, "回顾1997年全国金融工作会议 Revisiting the 1997 National Financial Work Conference," 中国金融 *China Finance*, October 21, 2010, www.cnfinance.cn/magzi/2010-10/21-10813.html.

102   ICBC was China's largest bank at the end of 2011 with assets worth $2.5 trillion, and 71 percent owned by the government.

103   Cai Muyuan, "ICBC Is World's Most Profitable Bank," *China Daily*, July 4, 2011, www.chinadaily.com.cn/business/2011-07/04/content_12830891.htm.

104   "ICBC Tops Banking List," Caixin Online, July 3, 2013, http://english.caixin.com/2013-07-03/100551087.html; "Top 1000 World Banks," *The Banker*, 2013, www.thebanker.com/Top-1000-World-Banks.

105 "Chinese Banks – Business as Usual," *Financial Times*, October 29, 2012, www. ft.com/cms/s/3/bc1984be-2196-11e2-b5d2-00144feabdc0.html#axzz2GFc989e8.

106 Jamil Anderlini, "AgBank IPO Officially the World's Biggest," *Financial Times*, August 13, 2010, www.ft.com/cms/s/0/ff7d528c-a6bc-11df-8d1e-00144feabdc0. html#axzz237a7xeWS.

107 "Chinese Banks Turning into Modern Global Financial Giants," *China Post*, July 20, 2010, www.chinapost.com.tw/business/asia-china/2010/07/20/265352/Chi nese-banks.htm.

108 Peter Nolan, Zhang Jing, and Liu Chunhang, "Globalization and China's Large Firms," in Nolan, *Chinese Firms, Global Firms* (Abingdon: Routledge, 2014), 64–80.

109 Simon Rabinovitch, "China's Bosses Criticised over High Pay," *Financial Times*, April 28, 2013, www.ft.com/cms/s/0/be2fdcdc-afc4-11e2-acf9-00144feabdc0.htm l#axzz2RnQPSkPF.

110 Robert Solow, "Robert M. Solow on the Global Economic Crisis."

111 Adam Palin, "Rating Agencies Compromised by Payment Model," *Financial Times*, accessed September 3, 2013, www.ft.com/cms/s/2/2c03e6ba-7ce2-11e2-a fb6-00144feabdc0.html#axzz2dpBWxFYo; Cynthia Clark and Sue Newell, "Institutional Work and Complicit Decoupling Across the US Capital Markets: The Work of Rating Agencies," *Business Ethics Quarterly*, 2012.

112 Sewell Chan, "Financial Crisis Was Avoidable, Inquiry Concludes," *New York Times*, January 25, 2011, Business Day/Economy section, www.nytimes.com/ 2011/01/26/business/economy/26inquiry.html?_r=1&nl=todaysheadlines&adxnnl =1&emc=tha2&adxnnlx=1296047225-PXCiZoc8EEpqOwetRxl60A; FCICR, *Financial Crisis Inquiry Commission Report* (Washington, DC: US Government Printing Office, 2011).

113 *The Biggest Bank Heist Ever!*, 2012, www.youtube.com/watch?v=Buyr BRUsu9A&feature=youtube_gdata_player; Ferguson, Inside Job.

114 Ben Protess and Susanne Craig, "Inside the End of the U.S. Bid to Punish Lehman Executives," *New York Times/Dealbook*, September 8, 2013, http://dea lbook.nytimes.com/2013/09/08/inside-the-end-of-the-u-s-bid-to-punish-lehman-ex ecutives/.

115 "Dodd-Frank in Limbo."

116 Joseph Stiglitz, "The Lessons of the North Atlantic Crisis for Economic Theory and Policy," *iMFdirect – The IMF Blog*, May 3, 2013, http://blog-imfdirect.imf. org/2013/05/03/the-lessons-of-the-north-atlantic-crisis-for-economic-theory-and-p olicy/.

117 Olivier J. Blanchard, Giovanni Dell'Ariccia, and Paolo Mauro, *Rethinking Macro Policy II: Getting Granular* (Washington, DC: International Monetary Fund, April 15, 2013), http://books.google.com/books?hl=en&lr=&id=sxEIE_ oDKW0C&oi=fnd&pg=PT6&dq=%222008%E2%80%9309+global+economic+ and+financial+crisis+shook+the+consensus+on+how+to%22+%22has+been+m ade,+both+theoretical+and+empirical.+This+paper+updates+the+status+of%2 2+&ots=xmyJzuj1sp&sig=NsHTlax2zixnvaKPhgil5wjbyDo.

118 David Romer, "Preventing The Next Catastrophe: Where Do We Stand?," *iMFdirect – The IMF Blog*, May 3, 2013, http://blog-imfdirect.imf.org/2013/05/ 03/preventing-the-next-catastrophe-where-do-we-stand/.

119 "[经济发展新动力]中美经贸关系: 推进合作 减少摩擦 US-China Trade Rela- tions: Foster Cooperation, Reduce Tension," *Xinhua Online* 新华网, September 10, 2012, http://news.xinhuanet.com/yzyd/fortune/20120910/c_113020631.htm.

120 Peter Marsh, "China Noses Ahead as Top Goods Producer," *Financial Times*, March 13, 2011, www.ft.com/cms/s/0/002fd8f0-4d96-11e0-85e4-00144feab49a. html#axzz2ePX1Aywj.

121   李盛明 Li Shengming, "发展中国家2012年全球直接投资流入量首次超过发达国家 Developing Countries Attract More FDI than Developed Countries for the First Time," *People's Daily* 人民日报, June 28, 2013, http://world.people.com.cn/n/2013/0628/c157278-22001582.html.

122   国纪平 Guo Jiping, "呼唤公平合理的国际金融新秩序 A Call for an Equitable and Rational New Global Financial Order," *People's Daily Online* 人民网, November 6, 2008, http://world.people.com.cn/GB/1030/8291119.html.

123   "习近平出席二十国集团领导人第八次峰会并发表重要讲话 Xi Jiniping's Speech at Eighth G20 Summit," People's Daily 人民日报, September 6, 2013.

124   Geoff Dyer, Jamil Anderlini, and Henny Sender, "China's Lending Hits New Heights," *Financial Times*, January 17, 2011, www.ft.com/cms/s/0/488c60f4-2281-11e0-b6a2-00144feab49a.html#axzz1BEtk4jFy.

125   "比美元结算划算 亚非国家爱用 人民币贸易圈快速形成 Renminbi Trade Circle Swiftly Takes Shape," *Nanyang* 南洋商报, August 17, 2013, www.nanyang.com.my/node/556959?tid=643.

126   Maria Levitov, Ye Xie, and Lyubov Pronina, "London Gains First-Mover Advantage in EU's Yuan Race," *Bloomberg*, March 13, 2013, www.bloomberg.com/news/2013-03-12/london-gains-first-mover-advantage-in-eu-s-yuan-race-currencies.html.

127   John McCormick, "Why RMB Will Be a Global Currency by 2015," *Royal Bank of Scotland*, February 5, 2013, http://insight.rbs.com/articles/why-rmb-will-be-a-global-currency-by-2015.html.

128   Levitov *et al.*, "London Gains First-Mover Advantage in EU's Yuan Race."

129   Rick Rothhacker, "WikiLeaks: China, Paulson at Odds over Threat from Subprime Crisis," *McClatchy*, September 4, 2011, www.mcclatchydc.com/2011/09/04/122986/wikileaks-china-paulson-at-odds.html.

130   Guo Jiping, "呼唤公平合理的国际金融新秩序 A Call for an Equitable and Rational New Global Financial Order."

Bibliography

Anderlini, Jamil. "AgBank IPO Officially the World's Biggest." *Financial Times,* August 13, 2010. www.ft.com/cms/s/0/ff7d528c-a6bc-11df-8d1e-00144feabdc0.html#axzz237a7xeWS.

Bernanke, Ben. "The Federal Reserve's Response to the Financial Crisis." Lecture, George Washington University Business School, March 27, 2012. www.federalreserve.gov/newsevents/files/chairman-bernanke-lecture3-20120327.pdf.

Bernanke, B., C. BertautL. DeMarco, and S. Kamin. "International Capital Flows and the Return to Safe Assets in the United States, 2003–2007." FRB International Finance Discussion Paper no. 1014, 2011. http://papers.ssrn.com/sol3/papers.cfm?abstract_id=1837780.

Blanchard, Olivier J., Giovanni Dell'Ariccia, and Paolo Mauro. *Rethinking Macro Policy II: Getting Granular.* Washington, DC: International Monetary Fund, April 15, 2013. http://books.google.com/books?hl=en&lr=&id=sxEIE_oDKW0C&oi=fnd&pg=PT6&dq=%222008%E2%80%9309+global+economic+and+financial+crisis+shook+the+consensus+on+how+to%22+%22has+been+made,+both+theoretical+and+empirical.+This+paper+updates+the+status+of%22+&ots=xmyJzuj1sp&sig=NsHTlax2zixnvaKPhgil5wjbyDo.

Braithwaite, Tom. "Greenspan Warns Dodd-Frank Reforms Risk 'Market Distortion.'" *FT Chinese*, March 30, 2011. www.ftchinese.com/story/001037805/en.

Cai Muyuan."ICBC Is World's Most Profitable Bank." *China Daily*, July 4, 2011. www.chinadaily.com.cn/business/2011-07/04/content_12830891.htm.

"Causes of the Financial Crisis: Testimony before the Financial Crisis Inquiry Commission." *Federal Reserve Board*, September 2, 2010. www.federalreserve.gov/newse vents/testimony/bernanke20100902a.htm.

CBRC Annual Report 2008. Beijing: 中国银监会 China Banking Regulatory Commission. Accessed July 18, 2012. http://zhuanti.cbrc.gov.cn/subject/subject/nianba o2008/english/zwqb.pdf.

Chang, Song. *Consolidation and Internationalization in the Global Banking Industry since the 1980s, and the Implication for Chinese Banking Reform*. Cambridge: Cambridge University Press, 2005.

Chan, Sewell."Financial Crisis Was Avoidable, Inquiry Concludes." *New York Times*, January 25, 2011, Business Day/Economy section. www.nytimes.com/2011/ 01/26/business/economy/26inquiry.html?_r=1&nl=todaysheadlines&adxnnl=1&emc =tha2&adxnnlx=1296047225-PXCiZoc8EEpqOwetRxl60A.

"China's Top Economists Meet Press." *China.org.cn*. Accessed April 20, 2013. www. china.org.cn/china/NPC_CPPCC_2013/2013-03/07/content_28162711.htm.

"Chinese Banks – Business as Usual." *Financial Times*, October 29, 2012. www.ft.com/ cms/s/3/bc1984be-2196-11e2-b5d2-00144feabdc0.html#axzz2GFc989e8.

"Chinese Banks Turning into Modern Global Financial Giants." *www.ChinaPost.com. tw*, July 20, 2010. www.chinapost.com.tw/business/asia-china/2010/07/20/265352/ Chinese-banks.htm.

Clark, Cynthia, and Sue Newell. "Institutional Work and Complicit Decoupling Across the US Capital Markets: The Work of Rating Agencies." *Business Ethics Quarterly* 23, no. 1(2013, February): 1–29.

Cochrane, J. H. "Lessons from the Financial Crisis." *Regulation* 32, no. 4(2009): 34–37.

Coggan, Philip. *Paper Promises: Money, Debt and the New World Order*. London: Allen Lane, 2011.

Confessore, Nicholas. "Bain Strategy Against Romney May Have Pitfalls for Obama." *New York Times,*May 23, 2012, U.S./Politics section. www.nytimes.com/2012/05/24/ us/politics/bain-strategy-against-romney-may-have-pitfalls-for-obama.html.

Dai Xianglong, 戴相龙. "回顾1997年全国金融工作会议 Revisiting the 1997 National Financial Work Conference." 中国金融 *China Finance*, October 21, 2010. www. cnfinance.cn/magzi/2010-10/21-10813.html.

"Dodd-Frank in Limbo." *New York Times*, May 27, 2011, Opinion section. www.nytim es.com/2011/05/28/opinion/28sat3.html?_r=1&nl=todaysheadlines&emc=tha211.

Dyer, Geoff, Jamil Anderlini, and Henny Sender. "China's Lending Hits New Heights." *Financial Times*, January 17, 2011. www.ft.com/cms/s/0/488c60f4-2281-11e0-b6a 2-00144feab49a.html#axzz1BEtk4jFy.

Elliot, Douglas J., and Martin Neil Baily. "Telling the Narrative of the Housing Bubble." Brookings Institution, November 23, 2009. www.brookings.edu/~/media/research/ files/papers/2009/11/23%20narrative%20elliott%20baily/1123_narrative_elliott_baily.

Executive Summary of USCESRC 2009 Report to Congress. US–China Economic and Security Review Commission, 2009. www.uscc.gov/annual_report/2009/executive_ summary.pdf.

Ferguson, Charles. *Inside Job: The Financiers Who Pulled Off the Heist of the Century*. London: Oneworld Publications, 2012.

Ferguson, Charles. "Larry Summers and the Subversion of Economics." *Chronicle of Higher Education*, October 3, 2010, The Chronicle Review section. http://chronicle.com/article/Larry-Summersthe/124790/.

"Final Consumption Expenditure, etc. (% of GDP) in China." *Trading Economics*. Accessed April 22, 2013. www.tradingeconomics.com/china/final-consumption-expenditure-etc-percent-of-gdp-wb-data.html.

Financial Crisis Inquiry Commission Report. Washington, DC: US Government Printing Office, 2011.

Fitzgerald, C. P. *The Chinese View of Their Place in the World*. London/New York: Oxford University Press, 1964.

Galbraith, John Kenneth. *A History of Economics: The Past as the Present*. London: Hamish Hamilton, 1987.

Garon, Sheldon M. *Beyond Our Means: Why America Spends While the World Saves*. Princeton, NJ: Princeton University Press, 2012.

Giles, Chris, and Claire Jones. "Research Rewrites Global Trade Data." *Financial Times*, January 16, 2013. www.ft.com/cms/s/0/346568c2-6001-11e2-b657-00144feab49a.html#axzz2Hzc2QWQ9.

Goldberg, L. "Is the International Role of the Dollar Changing?" *Current Issues in Economics and Finance* 16, no. 1(2010). http://papers.ssrn.com/soL3/papers.cfm?abstract_id=1550192.

Goldstein, Matthew. "JPMorgan Buys Bear on the Cheap." *Businessweek.com*, March 16, 2008. www.businessweek.com/stories/2008-03-16/jpmorgan-buys-bear-on-the-cheap businessweek-business-news-stock-market-and-financial-advice.

Greenspan, Alan. "The Crisis." Brookings Papers on Economic Activity, Spring2010. www.freepatentsonline.com/article/Brookings-Papers-Economic-Activity/237453501.html.

Greider, William. "The AIG Bailout Scandal." *The Nation*, August 6, 2010. www.thenation.com/article/153929/aig-bailout-scandal#.

Guo Jiping, 国纪平. "呼唤公平合理的国际金融新秩序 A Call for an Equitable and Rational New Global Financial Order." *People's Daily Online* 人民网, November 6, 2008. http://world.people.com.cn/GB/1030/8291119.html.

"ICBC Tops Banking List." *Caixin Online*, July 3, 2013. http://english.caixin.com/2013-07-03/100551087.html.

Jeffrey Sachs on the US Economy: "It's Been an Amazing Ride for the Rich." Video, 2012. www.guardian.co.uk/business/video/2012/apr/12/jeffrey-sachs-us-economy-video.

Jenkins, Patrick, and Patrick Mathurin. "Bank Staff Costs Take Bigger Share of Pot." *Financial Times*, June 5, 2012. www.ft.com/cms/s/0/d4fe3186-ac0d-11e1-a8a0-00144feabdc0.html#axzz1xURvIi4R.

Jiang Jianqing, 姜建清. "在危机下重塑金融新秩序 Creating a New Financial Order." *Global Entrepreneur* 环球企业家, November 17, 2008. www.gemag.com.cn/html/2008/hotmoney_1117/9410.html.

Johnson, Simon. "The Quiet Coup." *The Atlantic*, May 2009. www.theatlantic.com/magazine/archive/2009/05/the-quiet-coup/7364/.

Johnson, Simon, and James Kwak. *White House Burning: The Founding Fathers, Our National Debt, and Why It Matters to You*. 1st edn. New York: Pantheon Books, 2012.

Kaufman, Henry. "Big Banks Are Not the Future." *Wall Street Journal*, June 5, 2012, Opinion section. http://online.wsj.com/article/SB10001424052702304707604577427941294873400.html.

Kocieniewski, David. "Academics Who Defend Wall St. Reap Reward." *New York Times,* December 27, 2013, Business Day section. www.nytimes.com/2013/12/28/business/academics-who-defend-wall-st-reap-reward.html.

Krugman, Paul. "Taking On China." *New York Times*, March 15, 2010, Opinion section. www.nytimes.com/2010/03/15/opinion/15krugman.html.

Krugman, Paul. "An Irish Mirror." *New York Times*, March 8, 2010, Opinion section. www.nytimes.com/2010/03/08/opinion/08krugman.html?th&emc=th.

Levitov, Maria, YeXie, and Lyubov Pronina. "London Gains First-Mover Advantage in EU's Yuan Race." *Bloomberg*, March 13, 2013. www.bloomberg.com/news/2013-03-12/london-gains-first-mover-advantage-in-eu-s-yuan-race-currencies.html.

Li Shengming, 李盛明. "发展中国家2012年全球直接投资流入量首次超过发达国家 Developing Countries Attract More FDI than Developed Countries for the First Time." *People's Daily* 人民日报. June 28, 2013. http://world.people.com.cn/n/2013/0628/c157278-22001582.html.

Lin, Justin, and Volker Treichel. "The Unexpected Global Financial Crisis: Researching Its Root Cause." World Bank Policy Research Working Paper 5937 (2012). http://papers.ssrn.com/sol3/papers.cfm?abstract_id=1982446.

Liu Mingkang, 刘明康. "全球金融危机带给中国巨大机遇 Global Financial Crisis Brings Opportunities to China." 基金网, February 17, 2012. http://fund.cnfol.com/120217/105,1485,11779055,00.shtml.

Lynch, David J. "Banks Seen Dangerous Defying Obama's Too-Big-to-Fail Move." *Bloomberg*. Accessed June 11, 2012. www.bloomberg.com/news/2012-04-16/obama-bid-to-end-too-big-to-fail-undercut-as-banks-grow.html.

Marsh, Peter. "China Noses Ahead as Top Goods Producer." *Financial Times*, March 13, 2011. www.ft.com/cms/s/0/002fd8f0-4d96-11e0-85e4-00144feab49a.html#axzz2ePX1Aywj.

McCormick, John. "Why RMB Will Be a Global Currency by 2015." Royal Bank of Scotland, February 5, 2013. http://insight.rbs.com/articles/why-rmb-will-be-a-global-currency-by-2015.html.

McKee, Michael, and Matthew Benjamin. "Stiglitz Says Ties to Wall Street Doom Bank Rescue." *Bloomberg*, April 17, 2009. www.bloomberg.com/apps/news?pid=newsarchive&sid=afYsmJyngAXQ&refer=home.

McKinnon, John D., and T.W. Farnam. "Hedge Fund Paid Summers $5.2 Million in Past Year." *Wall Street Journal*, April 5, 2009. http://online.wsj.com/article/SB123879462053487927.html.

Murse, Tom. "How Much U.S. Debt Does China Really Own?" *About.com US Government Info*. Accessed April 20, 2013. http://usgovinfo.about.com/od/moneymatters/ss/How-Much-US-Debt-Does-China-Own.htm.

Neate, Robert. "Financial Crisis: 25 People at the Heart of the Meltdown – Where Are They Now?" *Guardian*, August 6, 2010. www.guardian.co.uk/business/2012/aug/06/financial-crisis-25-people-heart-meltdown.

Newman, Frank N. *Six Myths That Hold Back America: And What America Can Learn from the Growth of China's Economy*. Kindle edn. New York: Diversion Books, 2011.

Nolan, Peter, ZhangJing, and Liu Chunhang. "Globalization and China's Large Firms," in Nolan, *Chinese Firms, Global Firms*, 64–80. Abingdon: Routledge, 2014.

Nolan, Peter. *The West and China: Globalization and Competition in Banking*. Cambridge: Cambridge University Press, 2013.

Nolan, Peter. *China at the Crossroads.* Cambridge: Polity Press, 2004. www.loc.gov/ca tdir/toc/ecip042/2003007751.html.

Palin, Adam. "Rating Agencies Compromised by Payment Model." *Financial Times.* Accessed September 3, 2013. www.ft.com/cms/s/2/2c03e6ba-7ce2-11e2-afb6-00144fe abdc0.html#axzz2dpBWxFYo.

Protess, Ben, and Susanne Craig. "Inside the End of the U.S. Bid to Punish Lehman Executives." *New York Times/Dealbook*, September 8, 2013. http://dealbook.nytim es.com/2013/09/08/inside-the-end-of-the-u-s-bid-to-punish-lehman-executives/.

Rabinovitch, Simon. "China's Bosses Criticised over High Pay." *Financial Times*, April 28, 2013. www.ft.com/cms/s/0/be2fdcdc-afc4-11e2-acf9-00144feabdc0.html#a xzz2RnQPSkPF.

Rajan, Raghuram. *Fault Lines: How Hidden Fractures Still Threaten the World Economy.* Princeton, NJ: Princeton University Press, 2010.

Reserve Accumulation and International Monetary Stability. International Monetary Fund, April 13, 2010. www.imf.org/external/np/pp/eng/2010/041310.pdf.

Roach, Stephen, NicholasLardy, and Robert Cassidy. *China's Role in the Origins of and Response to the Global Recession.* U.S.–China Economic and Security Review Commission, Hearing on China's Role in the Origins of and Response to the Global Recession, Washington, DC, 2009. https://mail-attachment.googleusercontent.com/atta chment/?ui=2&ik=925828fbf3&view=att&th=138321a476a8e753&attid=0.1&disp= safe&realattid=f_godonnqr0&zw&saduie=AG9B_P8M-pEX1ScT_7aJrn_zjECe&sa det=1340870412563&sads=dMjylKYcX9MAclLYZk2yTJ2yZBM&sadssc=1.

Rogoff, Kenneth S., and Carmen M. Reinhart. *This Time Is Different: Eight Centuries of Financial Folly.* Princeton, NJ: Princeton University Press, 2009.

Romer, David. "Preventing The Next Catastrophe: Where Do We Stand?" *iMFdirect – The IMF Blog*, May 3, 2013. http://blog-imfdirect.imf.org/2013/05/03/preventing-th e-next-catastrophe-where-do-we-stand/.

Rosenthal, Elisabeth. "Chinese Monetary Official Dies in Fall From 7th-Story Window." *New York Times*, May 13, 2000. http://partners.nytimes.com/library/ world/asia/051300china-official.html.

Rothhacker, Rick. "WikiLeaks: China, Paulson at Odds over Threat from Subprime Crisis." *McClatchy*, September 4, 2011. www.mcclatchydc.com/2011/09/04/122986/ wikileaks-china-paulson-at-odds.html.

Sachs, Jeffrey. *The Price of Civilization: Economics and Ethics After the Fall.* London/ New York: Bodley Head, 2011.

Schwartz, A. J. "Origins of the Financial Market Crisis of 2008." *Cato Journal* 29, no. 1(2009): 19–23.

Sheng, Andrew. *From Asian to Global Financial Crisis: An Asian Regulator's View of Unfettered Finance in the 1990s and 2000s.* Cambridge: Cambridge University Press, 2009.

Silver-Greenberg, Jessica, and Peter Eavis. "JPMorgan Discloses $2 Billion in Trading Losses." *DealBook.* Accessed May 11, 2012. http://dealbook.nytimes.com/2012/05/ 10/jpmorgan-discloses-significant-losses-in-trading-group/.

Solow, Robert. "Robert M. Solow on the Global Economic Crisis." Video. MIT School of Humanities, Arts and Social Sciences, November2009. http://shass.mit. edu/multimedia/video-2010-robert-m-solow-global-economic-crisis.

Stiglitz, Joseph. "The Lessons of the North Atlantic Crisis for Economic Theory and Policy." *iMFdirect – The IMF Blog,*May 3, 2013. http://blog-imfdirect.imf.org/2013/ 05/03/the-lessons-of-the-north-atlantic-crisis-for-economic-theory-and-policy/.

Stiglitz, Joseph. *Freefall: Free Markets and the Sinking of the Global Economy.* London/New York: Allen Lane, 2010.

Strachan, Maxwell. "Financial Sector Back to Accounting for Nearly One-Third of U. S. Profits," *Huffington Post,* March 30, 2011. www.huffingtonpost.com/2011/03/30/financial-profits-percentage_n_841716.html.

Strange, Susan. *Casino Capitalism.* New ed. Manchester: Manchester University Press, 1997.

The Biggest Bank Heist Ever! Video, 2012. www.youtube.com/watch?v=Buyr BRUsu9A&feature=youtube_gdata_player.

"Top 1000 World Banks." *The Banker*, 2013. www.thebanker.com/Top-1000-World-Banks.

Truman, Edwin M. "Speech: The Global Financial Crisis: Lessons Learned and Challenges for Developing Countries." Peterson Institute of International Economics, June 16, 2009. www.piie.com/publications/papers/paper.cfm?ResearchID=1240.

"Wall Street Wire Unveils 'Top 10 Chinese Economists.'" *People's Daily Online*, February 25, 2006. http://english.peopledaily.com.cn/200602/25/eng20060225_245921.html.

Wallison, Peter. "Government-Sponsored Meltdown." *Wall Street Journal*, July 12, 2011, Opinion section. http://online.wsj.com/article/SB10001424052702304760604576423670655568418.html.

Wang Jun, 王君. 国际金融危机与我国应对政策 *Global Financial Crisis and China's Policy Response.* 中共中央党校出版社 Beijing: Central Party School Publishing House, 2009.

Wang Yu, 王宇. "从周小川文章看金融危机的真实根源和化解之道 Understanding the Root of the Financial Crisis and Its Resolution from Zhou Xiaochuan's Essay." *Xinhua Online*新华网, March 25, 2009. http://news.xinhuanet.com/fortune/2009-03/26/content_11073108.htm.

"Who Is BlackRock?" *BlackRock*, 2013. http://www2.blackrock.com/global/home/AboutUs/index.htm.

World Bank. *World Development Report 2002: Building Institutions for Markets.* Oxford: Oxford University Press for the World Bank, 2002.

World Bank. *World Development Report 1999/2000: Entering the 21st Century.* Oxford: Oxford University Press, 2000.

Worrachate, Anchalee, and John Detrixhe. "IMF May Classify Aussie, Canada Dollar as Reserve Currencies." *Bloomberg.* Accessed April 20, 2013. www.bloomberg.com/news/2012-11-19/imf-may-classify-aussie-canadian-dollars-as-reserve-currencies.html.

Xia Bin, 夏斌. "全球金融危机对我国的影响及中国对策0上0 Impact of the Global Financial Crisis on China and China's Response." *Development Research Center of the State Council*, December2008. www.drcnet.com.cn/DRCNet.Channel.Web/gylt/20081210/gylt_29.htm.

Xie, Andy, 谢国忠. "格林斯潘应该为金融危机负责 Greenspan Should Be Held Responsible for the Financial Crisis." 财经_腾讯网, February 18, 2009. http://finance.qq.com/a/20090218/002588.htm.

Zhao Yidi, and Kevin Hamlin. "China Shuns Paulson's Free Market Push as Meltdown Burns U.S." *Bloomberg*, September 23, 2008. www.bloomberg.com/apps/news?pid=newsarchive&sid=aCl7bFUJzWRk.

Zhou Xiaochuan, 周小川. "金融业脱离实体经济诱发本次国际金融危机 Disconnect between Financial Industry and the Real Economy Sparked the Financial Crisis."

财经_凤凰网 *Phoenix Online,*June 29, 2012. http://finance.ifeng.com/news/special/lujiazui2012/20120629/6680487.shtml.

Zhou Xiaochuan, 周小川. "Issues Related to the Global Financial Crisis." Speech at Global Think-tank Summit, Beijing, July 3, 2009. www.bis.org/review/r090710b.pdf?frames=0.

"习近平出席二十国集团领导人第八次峰会并发表重要讲话 Xi Jiniping's Speech at Eighth G20 Summit." *People's Daily*人民日报, September 6, 2013.

"会见索罗斯时的谈话 2001年9月17日 Discussion with George Soros on 17 September 2001." In 朱镕基讲话实录 *Zhu Rongji's Speeches*, 237–244. Beijing: People's Press 人民出版社, 2011.

余永定 Yu Yongding. 美国次贷危机: 背景, 原因与发展 *US Subprime Crisis: Background, Causes and Development.* CASS Research Center for International Finance, October 8, 2008, http://course.lixin.edu.cn/course_center/files_upload/699ebe8f-3ef7-4792-a764-4b6dd93749a4/content/f6417374-81b9-428e-afc7-397eb21ac541/COLUMN_7/rdjj09.pdf.

"全国金融工作会议在京召开 温家宝讲话 李克强出席 National Financial Work Conference Opens in Beijing: Wen Jiabao Speaks, Li Keqiang Attends." 新华网 *Xinhua News*, January 7, 2012. http://news.xinhuanet.com/fortune/2012-01/07/c_111392011.htm.

"比美元结算划算 亚非国家爱用 人民币贸易圈快速形成 Renminbi Trade Circle Swiftly Takes Shape." *Nanyang* 南洋商报, August 17, 2013. www.nanyang.com.my/node/556959?tid=643.

"[经济发展新动力]中美经贸关系:推进合作 减少摩擦 US–China Trade Relations: Foster Cooperation, Reduce Tension." *Xinhua Online* 新华网, September 10, 2012. http://news.xinhuanet.com/yzyd/fortune/20120910/c_113020631.htm.

5 International security

> In actual history, it is a notorious fact that conquest, enslavement, robbery, murder, in short, force play the greatest part.
>
> Karl Marx, *Capital* Vol. 1

War between the US and China cannot be ruled out. Writing in the *Financial Times*, Harvard political scientist Graham Allison warned of the Thucydides trap.[1] Sparta went to war out of fear that Athens was becoming too strong. The Spartans formed an alliance and attacked Athens but after thirty years of war, both states were destroyed. It was the rapid rise of Athens that provoked Spartan fear. China's fast-paced development too has inspired angst in the US. Its economy went in one generation from smaller than Spain's to become the world's second largest – a feat with no historical parallel. In 11 out of 15 cases in the last 500 years, where a rising power challenged an incumbent great power, the outcome was war.[2] Since the Second World War, the US and its Western allies have crafted a world order with America as the undisputed head, but there are signs of a power shift from West to East.[3] The US share of world GDP declined from 35 percent in 1945 to 20 percent today, losing share mainly to China.[4] Already the IMF predicts that the Chinese economy will surpass the US economy in purchasing power by 2016, much earlier than expected even a few years ago.[5] The role of the dollar as the international reserve currency allowed the US to spend beyond its means but that may end soon. The Global Financial Crisis dealt a body blow to the American economy. The costly bank bailout and the Iraq and Afghanistan wars pushed the national debt to new heights. It is hard to escape comparison with the Soviet collapse brought about by the fiscal strain of an arms race and a long-drawn Afghan war. By August 2012, US federal debt topped $16 trillion, rising by $1 trillion in less than a year.[6] At the same time, China has become a major lender to the US government. National wealth underpins military strength, and a frail economy cannot support a robust foreign policy.

Giacomo Luciani defines national security as the ability to withstand aggression from abroad.[7] Laurence Martin regards it as "the assurance of future well being."[8] Trager and Simonie describe it as "national and international political conditions favorable to the protection or extension of vital national values against existing and potential adversaries."[9] Definitions of national security abound,[10] but at the core it is the survival of the state in the face of military threats. Thus, security has to do with military force, although economic strength has assumed great importance in a globalized world.[11] Can the US and China trust each other and keep the peace? This chapter begins by looking at the military balance. It uses the HISE framework to analyze trust between the two states with respect to security. It contrasts US and Chinese perspectives with special focus on Taiwan, Tibet, Xinjiang, Japan and the South China Sea. It concludes that the Chinese have more to fear. While professing a desire to engage, Washington seeks to contain China. With economic development as its first priority, China needs peace but the US is preparing for war.[12] To prepare the American public for conflict, the media sows ill feelings toward the Chinese.[13] Japan is a key factor in US–China relations but its alliance with the US hinders its ability to play a constructive role.

Military balance

Despite dire warnings about China's military modernization, the disparity in military spending is striking. The US defense budget in 2011 totaled $739.3 billion compared to China's $89.8 billion.[14] Over eight times bigger than China's, the US budget accounts for 45.7 percent of world total compared to China's 5.5 percent. Even NATO spends three times more than China. The US uses 4.91 percent of its GDP on defense compared to China's 1.27 percent. China spends a smaller fraction of GDP on defense than the US, the UK, Russia, India or France.

Moreover, the US defense budget of $739.3 billion does not show the whole picture. When homeland security and veterans' affairs (veterans health care) spending are included, the budget tops $1 trillion.[15] In addition to the official budget, however, the Pentagon is known to keep a "black budget" to fund secret weapons and wars without proper congressional oversight.[16] The

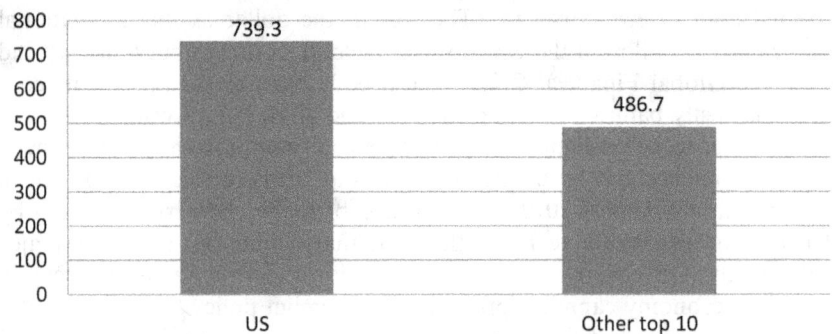

Figure 5.1 US vs other top 10 budgets combined 2011
Source: IISS, *The Military Balance 2012*.

Reagan administration had $36 billion a year available to the president, the secretary of defense, and the director of the CIA, or roughly $100 million a day, outside of the normal channels of accountability. The black budget, according to Tim Weiner, is the

> Pentagon's own term for every program that the secretary of defense, the director of the CIA or the president of the United States wants to keep off the books, deleted from the public budget and kept at a classification of top secret or above. These are the secret weapons and the secret policies for combating the Cold War and World War III and, should it come to that, World War IV.[17]

Leaked documents reveal a black budget of $52.6 billion in fiscal 2013, and spending for intelligence gathering well above the Cold War peak.[18]

The PLA

The People's Liberation Army (PLA) is the world's largest standing army. According to a 2013 Chinese defence white paper, the PLA has 1.48 million

Table 5.1 US defense related budget requests for 2011

Spending category	President's 2011 budget request ($ billions)	
"Base" DOD budget (discretionary only)	548.9	
DOD (mandatory only)	4.3	
DOD war spending	159.1	
DOD total		**712.3**
DOE (defense)[1]	18.8	
Miscellaneous defense-related agencies	7.6	
National defense budget function total		**738.7**
Homeland security (DHS)	43.6	
Veterans affairs (DVA)	122.0	
International affairs	65.3	
Treasury Dept of Military Retirement Payments	25.9	
Interest on DOD Retiree Health Care Fund	5.7	
19% of interest on debt (DOD proportional share)	47.7	
Grand total		**1,048.9**

Source: Winslow Wheeler, "Decoding the Defence Budget."

Note: 1 All defence nuclear facilities fall under the ownership and jurisdiction of the Department of Energy (DOE).

service members.[19] With China's growing affluence, the PLA has embarked on a modernization program commensurate with the country's expanding national interests. The Clinton administration did not consider this modernization to be a threat to the United States and its allies but powerful voices today differ. How strong is the Chinese military and why is it modernizing? During the Cold War, China's biggest threat was the Soviet Union, and the PLA prepared to fight a "people's war" employing the tactics used against the Japanese in the 1930s and 1940s. The military technology deployed in the 1991 Gulf War and the NATO air campaign in Bosnia showed, however, that a revolution in military affairs (RMA) had taken place. The Chinese woke up to a vast technology gap. In response, they developed a doctrine of 'asymmetric warfare' to fight limited wars against technologically superior adversaries. The PLA switched from a labour-intensive to a technology-intensive military.[20] This meant raising the technical competence of troops and the caliber of weaponry, but many factors inhibit the process. First of all, the bulk of the PLA's equipment remains obsolete. The Chinese defence industry is unable to produce modern weaponry, and relies on Russian technology from at best 1970s vintage. Chinese fighter jets fly on Russian engines.[21] The old technology constrains the development of new operational doctrine. Purchases from Russia are far from adequate to build a power projection capability.[22] Information warfare (IW) and other innovations are extremely complicated to produce and deploy without access to Western technology. The PLA will have difficulty closing the gap. Indeed the disparity is growing. But the gap is not in technology alone.

Logistics is another chink in the armour. No amount of weapons and soldiers can fight a battle without supplies. During the devastating snow storms of 2008 the PLA mobilized over two million troops and reservists for rescue work. The same year it rushed another 138,000 troops to aid in the Sichuan earthquake.[23] The difficulty it experienced dispatching soldiers and heavy equipment exposed a serious lack of tactical and long-range transportation capabilities. Designed to support ground forces in positional defensive wars, the PLA logistics system lacks mobility and is plagued by chronic inefficiency, technical backwardness, and inter-service rivalries.[24] It lacks, for instance, the air- and sea-lift capabilities to mount an amphibious invasion of Taiwan. The Chinese navy can carry no more than two infantry divisions across the Taiwan Straits, too few to match the 230,000-strong Taiwanese army.[25]

There are concerns over the PLA's build-up of ballistic and cruise missiles but most analysts estimate that China's military remains at least twenty years out of date. Robert Ross of the Council of Foreign Relations believes the Chinese arms build-up is aimed at confronting Taiwan and Japan rather the US, and that the development of its navy is constrained by a traditional focus on ground forces.[26] Whereas the Indian Navy has operated aircraft carriers since 1961, China has yet to commission a single flat top.[27] Its build-up of submarines, destroyers and frigates has not been matched by an increase in military efficiency and vital command and communication capabilities.[28]

In the long term the importance of education to developing military technology is clear, but spending on education accounts for only 2.2 percent of GDP compared to 22.3 percent for Singapore or 15.9 percent for the Philippines.[29] Legions of Chinese students study abroad but many settle in the West.[30] To draw graduates home the Chinese government is offering better salaries, but institutional barriers remain. Older scientists, many in their seventies, control the research agenda and promotion is often linked to connections. Official figures show that 87 percent of Chinese science and engineering graduates abroad choose to remain overseas.[31]

The strength of an army depends on the quality of its generals too. Professionalism is growing, and since 1992 the PLA top brass has experienced a sweeping turnover and virtually the entire high command consists of new faces. The new commanders no longer consist of soldier-politicians, thus weakening the link between the army and the Party.[32] Many political commissars have been replaced by professionals, but few PLA generals have traveled abroad or experienced the complexity of modern warfare, although many have watched recent wars closely.

The US armed forces

By contrast, the US military is unmatched. Despite the fiscal strain from bank bailout, wars and health care reform, the US military will continue to enjoy by far the most generous defense budget.[33] It enjoys a massive advantage over the PLA both in quantity and quality of equipment.

But even more significant is the location of those assets. The US maintains more than 1,000 military bases outside the continental USA and 320,000 troops in the Pacific region.[34] There are bases in Japan, South Korea, Guam, and Hawaii, and plans to rebuild air bases on Saipan, Wake and the Palau islands.[35] President Obama is moving yet more resources to bottle the Chinese Navy up inside the "first island chain" and there is vigorous debate on how to counter Chinese anti-ship ballistic missiles (ASBM) that could sink US aircraft carriers.[36] The Joint Operational Access Concept (JOAC) outlines the US strategy to overcome 'anti-access/area denial' barriers by synchronizing land, sea, air, space and cyber attacks to blind the adversary and strike deep inside the Chinese defense network.[37] The US military is far more seasoned than the PLA, which last saw action in 1979 in a brief clash with Vietnam where it suffered heavy casualties. To be sure, military superiority alone does not assure victory but it can cause an awful lot of damage.

Equally important are the powerful defense contractors who hold a vested interest in war.[38] During the Cold War the US spent an annual average of $440 billion (in 2011 dollars) on defense but after the Cold War, from 1993 to 2000, the Pentagon still managed to average $392 billion (in 2011 dollars) a year, a dip of only 10 percent.[39] With armaments-related jobs scattered across almost every state of the union, it is virtually incumbent on congressmen to support defense spending.[40] Outsourcing of war-related services has become a

Table 5.2 US and Chinese military capability

Capability	USA	China
ICBM launchers	450	66
Bomber aircraft	155	132
Ballistic missile nuclear-powered submarines	14	3
Modern main battle tanks	6,302	2,800
Modern armored infantry fighting vehicles	6,452	2,390
4th generation tactical aircraft	3,029	747
5th generation tactical aircraft	179	0
Attack helicopters	862	16
Heavy/medium transport helicopters	2,809	294
Aircraft carriers	11	0
Nuclear powered submarines	57	5
Cruisers/destroyers	83	13
Heavy/medium transport aircraft	847	57
Heavy unmanned aerial vehicles	370	unknown
Imagery satellites	10	15
Intelligence satellites	20	11
Navigational satellites	31	10

Source: IISS, The Military Balance 2012.

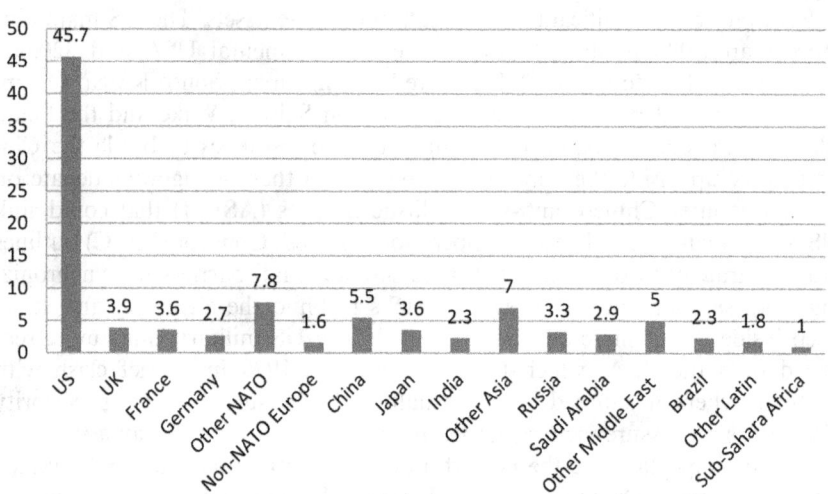

Figure 5.2 Planned defense expenditure by country 2011 (as a percentage of world total)
Source: IISS, *The Military Balance 2012*.

lucrative business too. The US spent over $138 billion on mercenaries, logistics and reconstruction contractors during its ten years in Iraq.[41] Kellog Brown & Root (KBR), a subsidiary of Halliburton once run by Dick Cheney, was awarded over $39.5 billion in contracts for Iraq.[42] Retired generals often serve as consultants to arms contractors, helping them to forge links with the Pentagon and the government.[43] They use the media to influence policy in ways that benefit the war industry.[44] In the 1970s powerful interest groups scuttled detente with the Soviet Union by suppressing intelligence reports and exaggerating the threat posed by Soviet weapons and defenses.[45] A three-year study by the General Accounting Office found that military officers lied in order to preserve weapons programs that the nation did not need.[46] After the demise of the Soviet Union, China became the convenient threat.[47]

Nuclear arsenal

The US has 7,700 active nuclear warheads, 2,000 of which are on hair-trigger alert, meaning they can be launched with 15 minutes' warning.[48] It has never endorsed the "no first use" (NFU) policy, and is prepared to use nuclear weapons – by the decision of one man, the president – against a nuclear or non-nuclear enemy whenever it believes it is in America's interest to do so. The average US nuclear warhead has a destructive power twenty times greater than that of the Hiroshima bomb. An act of Congress is required to declare war but launching a nuclear attack only requires a 20-minute deliberation by the president and two or three of his advisors, a policy that dates back to the Cold War. Since the end of the Cold War, however, the procedure has not been revised to make the president less likely to push the button. Despite appeals from various quarters including former secretary of defense Robert McNamara and former commander of the Strategic Air Command (SAC), General

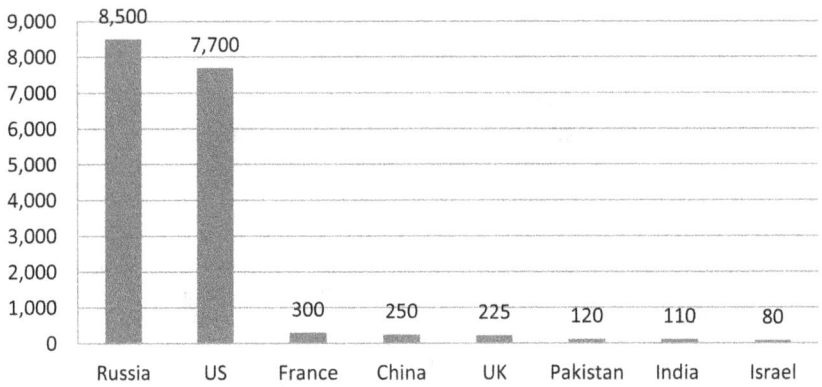

Figure 5.3 Nuclear arsenals in 2013 by country
Source: Stockholm International Peace Research Institute.

George Lee Butler, the missiles remain on hair-trigger alert. China has around 250 nuclear warheads but pledges no first use.[49]

Cyber warfare

Since the secret US–Israeli cyber attack on Iranian nuclear facilities in 2012, cyber weapons have drawn much attention. Part of a wider program called the "Olympic Games" begun under the Bush administration in 2006,[50] the cyber attack constituted an act of war carried out without congressional approval.[51] Like drone strikes, it initiated a new dimension of war and justified its use by other countries, terrorists or hackers. From the beginning of 2013, the US accused the PLA of hacking American corporate, government and military computers.[52] The Chinese denied the allegations. Huang Chengqing, director of the Computer Network Emergency Response Technical Team (CNCERT), retorted with: "We have mountains of data if we wanted to accuse the US, but it's not helpful in solving the problem … the issue can only be settled through communication, not confrontation."[53] Events took a dramatic turn in June 2013 when whistleblower Edward J. Snowden disclosed that the US National Security Agency PRISM and *Xkeyscore* programs allow the agency to search through vast databases containing emails, online chats and the browsing histories of millions of individuals.[54] Such spying capabilities afford unrivaled opportunities for blackmail. He also revealed that the NSA hacked major Chinese telecommunications companies, network backbones at Chinese universities hosting some of the country's most important internet hubs, and the Hong Kong headquarters of Pacnet, which owns one of the most extensive undersea fiber-optic cable networks in the Asia-Pacific.[55] Given America's record of overthrowing governments,[56] Beijing believes Washington is sowing dissent in China to bring down the communist party through "digital diplomacy" on social media.[57]

The US perspective on international security

Barely three years after the collapse of the Soviet Union, the Clinton White House published the National Security Strategy of Engagement and Enlargement calling for the extension of "the community of market democracies while deterring and containing a range of threats" to America and its interests. Instead of reaping a peace dividend, the US sought to maintain a strong military. A year later the Department of Defense produced the *United States Security Strategy for East Asia* (also called the "Nye Report," 1995) reaffirming the US–Japan alliance, and calling for the retention of 100,000 troops in East Asia.[58] In addition to Japan, the US has bilateral security treaties with South Korea, Australia, the Philippines and Thailand.[59] US troops stationed in Japan and South Korea serve to "deter aggression and contribute to political and economic advances in the region." Security, Joseph Nye wrote, is like oxygen (you don't notice it until it's not there), and America is the oxygen for East Asian development. The Nye report described Asia as a region of ethnic, religious and cultural diversity with strong historical animosities, and where the US is a trusted honest broker. Without an American presence in Asia, it warned, the security of Asia would be jeopardized, and there could be war.[60] The US intends to maintain its leadership and military presence in the region to "den[y] political and economic control of the Asia-Pacific region by a rival power." That rival is China. Reviewing his own report six years later, Nye noted with satisfaction that his strategy had largely been implemented.[61] Statements by subsequent administration officials show an increasingly forceful stance toward China.

American exceptionalism

Condoleeza Rice, a proponent of the invasion of Iraq, advocated the unilateral use of force.[62] The United States "has a special role in the world and should not adhere to every international convention and agreement that someone thinks to propose." She attached little importance to winning United Nations support for military action and argued that America should act in its own national interests and not the interests of an "illusory international community."[63] "Great powers do not just mind their own business" but are entitled to play a decisive role in international politics. If America does not lead, there will be chaos or "others who do not share our values will fill the vacuum."[64] Accusing Clinton of "witlessly" cutting military spending, Rice called for increased military spending to maintain America's already huge lead.[65] American values, she proclaimed, are universal values, and American military power must be strong because America is the only guarantor of global peace and security. She saw economic policies as tools of international politics, particularly those that leverage the strengths of the American economy and expand free trade. "An international order that reflects American values is the best guarantee of America's national interest," and America should shape the world order to its advantage.[66]

Rice saw the spread of capitalism as necessary for the promotion of human rights and individual liberty and believed that the contradiction between economic liberalization and political control in China would intensify. China resents the role of the US in the Asia-Pacific and wants to change the balance of power, Rice wrote. China is a strategic competitor, not a strategic partner, and will do what it can to enhance its power, including "stealing nuclear secrets and bullying Taiwan." She accused China of a lack of transparency about its military spending and strategic goals, and believed the US should bring about "internal transition."

Robert Zoellick invoked the notion of evil, saying there were people who hated America and the ideas it stood for. He argued that economic ties alone would not ensure peace,[67] and that the US "must maintain unquestioned military superiority over dangerous regimes." Extolling America's economy, military and ideas, Zoellick declared that the primary task of the US government was to shape the world in order to protect and promote American interests and values.[68] Power, he declared, is the foremost principle, and the US "should not be paralyzed by intellectual penchant for moral relativism." Not all states are equal and given America's responsibilities, "it must retain its freedom to act." International agreements and institutions are "means to achieve ends, not as forms of political therapy." Along with Donald Rumsfeld, Paul Wolfowitz, Richard Perle and William Kristol, Zoellick signed a statement by the *Project for the New American Century* (PNAC) urging President Clinton to go to war with Iraq and remove Saddam Hussein from power. A neoconservative think tank, the PNAC supported a "policy of military strength and moral clarity."[69] It influenced George W. Bush's decision to invade Iraq.

Of China, America must take a realistic, not romantic view, warned Zoellick. China should best be integrated into the Western-sponsored world order but if integration failed, the US must be prepared to "shield against" it. In a speech to the National Committee on US–China Relations in 2005, Zoellick invited China to become a "responsible stakeholder" in the international system. What he left unsaid was that the responsible stakeholder would need to submit to American leadership.

Secretary of state Hillary Clinton called into question the very future of the Chinese government.[70] Like many Americans, she sees her country as the defender of the free world. According to her, the United States seeks not just its own good, but the greater good, which is "what makes American leadership exceptional."[71] Claiming that "the American model of democracy and free entreprise is the most powerful source of prosperity and progress known to mankind," Hillary made clear America's intention to continue its global hegemony in this century as it did in the last.[72] Asia, she said, is "eager for American leadership and business," and called the twenty-first century "America's Pacific Century." She called for China, the rest of Asia and the Pacific islands to be inducted into a "rule-based regional and global order."

Pivot to Asia

The US is moving to establish control throughout Asia over the long run.[73] Despite its Atlantic roots, it is recasting itself as a Pacific nation, and intends to play a leadership role in Asia for decades to come.[74] It seeks leadership of key Asian multilateral institutions and to keep China at bay. To counter the ASEAN–China Free Trade Area (ACFTA), it is promoting a rival bloc, the Transpacific Partnership (TPP), that excludes China.[75] Obama plans to shift 60 percent of US military resources to the Asia-Pacific and station 2,500 marines in Australia.[76] Discussions are underway to fly drones from Cocos Island and expand US naval access to Australian ports.[77] The US plans to station warships in Singapore, boost its military presence in the Philippines, and upgrade military ties with Thailand, Vietnam, Malaysia, Indonesia and Brunei.

"Leadership" is diplomatic jargon for hegemony, and sustaining US global leadership entails preparing for war with China. A report entitled Sustaining US Global Leadership published by the US Department of Defense in January 2012 affirmed the US decision to "rebalance" toward the Asia-Pacific.[78] The *National Security Strategy* published by the White House in 2010 called for the renewal of American leadership to advance American interests in the twenty-first century.[79] In the foreword, Obama declared that America fostered commerce, supported international laws and institutions, and spilled blood in foreign lands "not to build an empire, but to shape a world in which more individuals and nations could determine their own destiny, and live with peace and dignity that they deserve." No nation is better positioned to lead than America, and it calls for the strengthening of alliances to fight a war against a "network of hate and violence." It calls for the US military to maintain conventional superiority and a nuclear deterrent while enhancing its ability to defeat asymmetric threats. In a speech at the US Air Force Academy, Obama told the cadets that the US will be the "one indispensable nation in world affairs."[80] "I see an American century because no other nation seeks the role that we play in global affairs, and no other nation can play the role that we play in global affairs. That includes shaping the global institutions of the 20th century to meet the challenges of the 21st," he said.

Former Australian prime minister Malcolm Fraser warns, however, that the US drive to maintain supremacy could likely lead to war. He sees no evidence that China engages in the kind of imperialism "practiced by Russia or by most European states, and indeed by the US."[81] He cautions that Australia would lose more of its independence in Asia should Cocos Island become a base for drones, and that it is foolish to believe that Australia's security could be assured by currying favor with the US: "No country can win brownie points with great powers. Great powers follow their own national interests and we should follow ours." Hugh White, professor of strategic studies, believes that unless the US is prepared to re-examine its exceptionalism and share power with China as an equal partner, conflict, even nuclear war, is possible.[82]

Many Americans see a basic incompatibility with China. Aaron Friedberg describes China as "inherently untrustworthy and dangerously prone to external aggression," and considers a warm trusting relationship with China impossible.[83] Beijing, he warns, is biding its time to become the dominant power in East Asia.[84] Samuel Huntington predicts that China will follow in the footsteps of Britain, France, Germany, Japan, the US and Soviet Union and pursue hegemony after economic growth.[85] "Red China" is seen as something dangerous and characterized by "sheer size, cunning, brutality and ideological fanaticism."[86] The success of China's political economy is an affront to orthodox American theories,[87] and Stefan Halper warns that China "poses the most serious challenge to the United States since the half-century Cold War struggle with the Soviets."[88] Some fear China will outflank the US in multilateral institutions, that it will not embrace Western ways of thinking,[89] and that "indulgence and accommodation" could embolden "bad behavior."[90] Friedberg puts it plainly: "Stripped of diplomatic niceties, the ultimate aim of the American strategy is to hasten a revolution, albeit a peaceful one, that will sweep away China's one-party authoritarian state and leave a liberal democracy in its place."[91]

To be sure, not all Americans think alike. But those who disagree enjoy little foreign policy influence. Henry Kissinger laments the American "ideological predisposition to battle with the entire nondemocratic world."[92] Zbigniew Brzezinski thinks the US fails to recognize that it can no longer impose security by force.[93] He believes it should avoid military confrontation and instead help to reconcile Asian neighbors, particularly China and Japan.[94] Ron Paul believes that Asians should be left to work things out without US interference. He argued that the two Koreas would be one country today if not for American troops stationed in South Korea. Americans, he pointed out,

> think nothing of saying there's a problem over there and we are going over there to show them our might and set all these rules. But if there was a conflict on the US-Mexican border and China thought it was in their interest to forge an alliance with Hugo Chavez in Venezuela and conducted war games in Gulf of Mexico, Americans would be hysterical.[95]

Dismissing American exceptionalism as a myth, Harvard professor Stephen Walt argues that what America needs is "a more realistic and critical assessment of [its] true character and contributions,"[96] and as Samuel Huntington pointed out: "The West won the world not by the superiority of its ideas or values or religion ... but rather by its superiority in applying organized violence."[97]

China's perspective on international security

The "century of humiliation" is the most important reference point in China's modern worldview. Mao's proclamation in 1949 that the Chinese people had "stood up" was a defining moment for the people's republic.[98] Having regained national sovereignty, it was time to rebuild the nation. But the process is far from complete. On assuming the presidency in 2012, Xi Jinping spoke of "transforming the impoverished and backward Old China into the New China."[99] To develop the country, China needs peace, not war. But a recent Chinese defense white paper warned that "international strategic competition and contradictions are intensifying, global challenges are becoming more prominent, and security threats are becoming increasingly integrated, complex and volatile."[100] At the 18th Party Congress, Hu Jintao noted "signs of increasing hegemonism, power politics and neo-interventionism" but assured his audience that China would "unswervingly follow the path of peaceful development and firmly pursue an independent foreign policy of peace."[101] The Chinese quest for relations based on the *Five Principles of Peaceful Coexistence* have not always been well received.[102] On the 10th anniversary of the normalization of relations with the US, Zi Zhongyun of the Chinese Academy of Social Sciences summed up Chinese frustration:

> As long as both sides follow the Five Principles, the US and China ought to enjoy friendly relations despite differences in systems, political culture and founding philosophy. China believes that state-to-state relations trumps ideology and social systems. Based on postwar experience, China's leaders are determined not to allow social system and ideology to define friend or foe, good or evil, and China has abided by this principle. In relating to China, the US too acts according to pragmatic national interests but relatively speaking, US foreign policy still bears a strong ideological slant. The ultimate aim of US foreign policy is to promote American values, system and political ideology. In advancing its own interests, the US as a superpower does not always respect the interests of others. Besides the Taiwan question, it uses "human rights," Tibet, and population control to interfere in China's internal affairs.[103]

Chinese leaders repeatedly stress the desire for stable ties. Marking the 40th anniversary of Nixon's visit to China, Foreign Minister Yang Jiechi noted:

> Because of globalization, nations have become more interdependent, and the US and China share wide-ranging interests as well as responsibilities. The development of US-China relations bears great import not only on the welfare of their citizens but also on world peace, stability and prosperity.[104]

But senior party theorist Zheng Bijian laments the American lack of appreciation for endogenous synergy. The US warms up only when it needs Chinese support against exogenous threats such as the Soviet Union or Islamic insurgents.[105] Once the threats recede, it treats China as an enemy.

Although it opposes US unilateralism, China seldom votes against the US in the Security Council. Since the inception of the Security Council, China has cast its veto six times (the US, eighty-nine times). Since 1984, it has used its veto on three occasions (the US, 43 times).[106] Yang welcomed US efforts to enhance regional peace but hoped the US would respect Chinese core interests, and observe the *Three Joint Communiqués* with regard to Taiwan and Tibet.

Taiwan

The reunification of China is the last unfinished chapter of the Chinese Civil War. The Chinese claim to Taiwan dates back to 1662. On defeat in the First

Sino–Japanese War in 1895, however, China was forced to cede the island to Japan. After the Second World War, Britain and the US delayed returning Taiwan to China despite Soviet protest (the UK, the US, the USSR and China were Second World War allies).[107] After losing the civil war in 1949, the Kuomintang (KMT) government evacuated to Taiwan. The US recognized the KMT government in Taipei but switched recognition to Beijing two decades later by the *Three Joint Communiqués* (1972, 1979, 1982). In a diplomatic sleight of hand, however, it signed the *Taiwan Relations Act* (TRA) in 1979 which established *de facto* diplomatic ties with the Taiwan, and promised "to provide Taiwan with arms of a defensive character," and "to resist any resort to force or other forms of coercion that would jeopardize the security, or the social or economic system, of the people on Taiwan." Then in the late 1990s, Congress passed a non-binding resolution giving the TRA greater weight than the Three Communiqués.

Both Beijing and Taipei claim to be the sole legitimate national government but Taiwan has only managed to secure recognition from a handful of states. The island has achieved an economic and political miracle, creating a vibrant democracy with multi-party elections,[108] but society has become deeply divided into two opposing camps, the KMT (国民党) versus the DPP (民进党). To take advantage of lower costs, much of Taiwan's manufacturing has moved over to the mainland where more than 2 million Taiwanese live in the Shanghai area alone.[109] Taiwan has a substantial body of high technology, especially in the IT sector, and in 2010 Taiwanese investments in China reached $200 billion while bilateral trade totaled $100 billion.[110] China has become its largest trading partner, accounting for a whopping 40 percent of Taiwanese exports. In the same year the two sides signed the ground-breaking Economic Cooperation Framework Agreement (ECFA), drastically cutting tariffs and knitting the two economies even more tightly together.[111] In 2013 Taiwan eased investment rules to allow Chinese banks to buy up to a 20 percent stake in Taiwanese banks.[112] China's economic success has drawn Taiwan closer into its orbit. Beijing insists on unification under the "one country, two systems" (一国两制) formula,[113] and relations between Beijing and Taipei have warmed under the Ma Ying-jeou administration; however, the TRA remains a thorn in the side of US–China relations.

Tibet

Tibet, the "Roof of the World," became a unified empire in the seventh century but was split soon after into several territories. The western and central regions were nominally under a government in Lhasa although they often came under Mongol or Chinese suzerainty. The eastern (Kham) and northern (Amdo) regions were more decentralized and often fell under direct Chinese rule, and eventually became incorporated into the Chinese provinces of Sichuan and Qinghai. In 1720 Manchu troops took over Tibet to calm a restive political situation, but remained until the end of the Qing dynasty.[114] The

Manchus who ruled China regarded Tibet as part of their empire and posted officials in Lhasa, but allowed the Tibetans considerable autonomy with their own officials and legal system, and made no attempt to establish Tibet as a Chinese province.[115] At the collapse of the Qing, the Tibetans declared independence in 1913. Under the principle of inheritance, however, the Republic of China, which succeeded the Qing government, regarded the former Qing territories as belonging to China, and in March 1929 went a step further and declared Tibet (along with Xinjiang and Manchuria) a part of the Chinese nation.

Meanwhile, the British, in contest with the Russians, encroached on Tibet. Ignoring Qing sovereignty, they dispatched troops to Tibet in 1904, forced out the Chinese and established control in 1913.[116] While encouraging independence in Tibet, the British systematically suppressed aspirations for the same in India.[117] When the CCP came to power in 1949, it was determined to regain Tibet, and in 1950 the PLA advanced toward Tibet and took Chamdo in the east, but did not occupy Lhasa. Subsequent negotiations produced the Seventeen-Point Agreement in May 1951 reincorporating Tibet into the PRC with autonomy under the central government, which promised not to alter the Tibetan political system or the status, functions, and powers of the Dalai Lama.

True to its word, the CCP did not apply the radical revolutionary reforms implemented in the rest of China. In 1955 the State Council appointed the Dalai Lama as chairman of the Preparatory Committee for the Tibet Autonomous Region but the Americans plotted insurgency. In a memo to the State Department on 12 April 1949, Loy Henderson, the US ambassador to India, recommended that if the "Communists succeed in controlling all of China, ... [the US] should be prepared to treat Tibet as independent to all intents and purposes."[118] In November 1949 American diplomats met with Tibetan officials in New Delhi. Secret talks continued throughout 1950 and 1951, becoming more frequent as the Korean War broke out. In 1951 the CIA established contact with Gyalo Thondup, the Dalai Lama's elder brother, who subsequently became the CIA's key contact.[119] Psychological warfare and paramilitary operations intensified.[120] The objective, according to a 1951 National Security Council memo, was to "foster and support anti-communist elements both outside and within China with a view to developing and expanding resistance in China to the Peiping (the former name of Beijing) regime's control, particularly in South China."[121] By stoking unrest in the rear, the Americans hoped to sap Chinese resolve in Korea. In March 1959, a revolt erupted in Lhasa. The PLA moved in and the Dalai Lama fled to India.

Tibetan independence was never a concern of US policymakers.[122] The sparse Himalayan plateau was but a pawn in the Cold War.[123] The Tibet question has roots in British imperialist expansion in Asia, and is kept alive today by the West. The US is more keen to use Tibet to castigate China in the international media and the United Nations. Historically, it recognized China's suzerainty over Tibet, as a US government document from the early 1950s attests:

For its part, the Government of the United States has borne in mind the fact that the Chinese Government has long claimed suzerainty over Tibet and the Chinese Constitution lists Tibet among areas constituting the territory of the Republic of China. This Government has at no time raised a question regarding either of these claims.[124]

But in May 1991, the US Senate passed Resolution 41 condemning the Chinese "occupation of Tibet":

> Tibet, including those areas incorporated into the Chinese provinces of Sichuan, Yunnan, Gansu, and Qinghai, is an occupied country under the established principles of international law; Tibet's true representatives are the Dalai Lama and the Tibetan Government in exile as recognized by the Tibetan people.[125]

The Dalai Lama has inspired images of Tibet as a land of peace, tranquility, universal nonviolence and sage monks.[126] He paints "old Tibet" as a blissful society whose idyllic days were rudely interrupted by the Chinese.[127] In a speech to the British Parliament in July 1996, he charged that "the destruction of cultural artifacts and traditions coupled with mass influx of Chinese into Tibet amounts to cultural genocide."[128] But the United Nations High Commisioner for Refugees found the allegations untrue.[129] Chinese migration to Tibet is short-term and voluntary. Except in Lhasa, Tibetans remain the majority, not only in the autonomous region but also in the Tibetan areas of Sichuan and Qinghai provinces. While there is zero tolerance to political challenge to CCP rule, claims of genocide against Tibetans are unfounded.[130] The Chinese, however, did ban bonded labor, a Tibetan tradition whereby families were owned by a local lord and bound to his land.[131] (The Dalai Lama argued that the wrongs committed in the course of abolishing feudalism outweighed the feudal injustices themselves.) There is virtually no tax revenue in Tibet, and 90 percent of its fiscal resources comes from Beijing. From 1952 to 1994 the central government poured $4.2 billion into the region, and in 1994 launched sixty-two major infrastructure projects which drew in another $480 million. In 1996 alone, China spent $600 million on Tibet with its sparse population of 2.5 million, compared to the $800 million of US aid to Africa, home to over a billion people.[132] Before the Chinese came in 1951, there were no schools; today there are more than 4,000. The Chinese are deeply suspicious of US intentions toward Tibet. Why does America celebrate Lincoln for opposing secession but condemn the Chinese for doing the same, they ask.[133]

Japan

According to a Chinese legend, the Emperor Qin Shihuang (259–210 BC) sent a mission of 3,000 young men and women to the "East Sea" (东海) in quest of the elixir of life. They never returned, and are said to have settled in Japan.[134] Sino–Japanese relations date back to the first century AD when the Han emperor gave a seal to Japan.[135] In the seventh century Japan sent scholars to China, and adopted many aspects of Chinese culture, including its dress, its writing system, the civil service, Confucianism and Buddhism. The imperial capital Kyoto, built in the eighth century, is a scaled replica of the Tang capital of Chang'an (长安). For centuries China was the dominant civilization in East Asia and its influence parallels that of the Greeks and Romans in the Mediterranean world. Japan and China engaged in trade for centuries but in the sixteenth century Lord Toyotomi Hideyoshi sought to invade China. For this, he needed passage through Korea, a vassal of China, and this led to a brutal invasion of Korea. Hideyoshi's campaign failed and thereafter Japan isolated itself for two and a half centuries under the Tokugawa shoguns (1600–1868) until it was forced open by American warships under the command of Commodore Matthew Perry.[136]

Japan swiftly modernized through reforms during the Meiji period (1868–1912) (*meiji ishin*, 明治維新), transforming itself in less than fifty years into an industrialized society with a modern military.[137] Japan responded to the threat of the West more effectively than China.[138] While the Chinese thought of themselves as the fount of civilization, the Japanese had a clear sense of the plurality of nations.[139] The decentralized and diverse Japanese political system enabled a variety of responses. Japan soon patterned itself after the Europeans and even embarked on its own quest for colonies, which led directly to war with Korea and China. It quickly defeated the Chinese in the First Sino–Japanese War (1894–1895) and won control over Korea and Taiwan. The success boosted Japanese confidence but it was its stunning victory over Russia, a European state, in 1905 that firmly established Japan as a great power.

After the First World War, the victorious Allies gave control of the German concessions in Shandong to Japan, a betrayal that provoked outrage in China.[140] Emboldened, the Japanese pressed on in Manchuria (China's northeast) and occupied the province by 1931. The following year they created the puppet state of *Manchukuo* and gained control of the province's vast resources. Japanese ambition did not stop there, and in 1937, following a clash between Chinese and Japanese troops near Peking, war broke out. In Tokyo, hawks gained the upper hand and policies became more bellicose. The war in China reflected differences in moral assumptions.[141] While the Japanese saw their position in China as a matter of national destiny and economic need, the Chinese saw themselves as victims of a long pattern of foreign bullying. As fighting spread, the Japanese hoped for a quick knockout against the Kuomintang government in Nanjing. On December 13, 1937 Nanjing fell to the Japanese Army, which proceeded to punish the city with six weeks of wanton slaughter. Japanese troops massacred 300,000 civilians and raped 80,000 women. The Rape of Nanjing stands as a bitter testimony to Japanese brutality.[142] Emperor Hirohito authorized the 'three alls' – kill all, burn all, loot all – *sanko sakusen* (三光作戰) policy which led to the death of over 2.7

million Chinese civilians.[143] Japanese units competed against each other on ruthlessness, a practice they took throughout Southeast Asia, especially against the Chinese diaspora.

The war left deep scars across East Asia. Some scholars attribute Japanese ruthlessness to its unique bushido or warrior creed. Confucianism was introduced to Japan in the sixth century, and grew during the peaceful years of aristocratic rule, but following the Genpei War (1180–1185), the Kamakura samurai regime preferred the arts of war over Confucian moral virtue and ritual refinement.[144] After lying dormant for centuries, it made a comeback in the Edo period (1603–1867) only to be eclipsed by Europeanization during the Meiji period (1868–1912). But Confucianism in Japan had over the centuries evolved. In the 1930s and 1940s, writers such as Inoue Tetsujiro (1833–1944) fused selected Confucian virtues such as loyalty and filial piety into a nationalistic blend to serve the interests of Japanese militarists.[145] In place of benevolence, they preached *bushido*. Confucius regarded benevolence (仁, ren) as the highest virtue but the Japanese were instilled first with loyalty, ceremony, bravery, faith and frugality. This emphasis on loyalty over benevolence is peculiar to Japanese Confucianism.[146]

For its inhumanity, Japan paid in full with blood. Allied firebombing obliterated dozens of first- and second-tier Japanese cities. American bombing claimed more civilian lives in Tokyo than the atom bombs dropped on Nagasaki and Hiroshima. For accuracy, planes loaded with incendiary bombs and napalm flew in low at 5,000–9,000 feet (modern jetliners cruise at 30,000 to 40,000 feet). Japanese homes were constructed of wood and paper, and in the raid on Tokyo after midnight on March 9, 1945, 325 B-29 bombers dropped 1,665 tons of incendiary bombs over three and half hours, killing 100,000 civilians and destroying 250,000 buildings. Aircrews reported the stench of burnt human flesh over the target.[147] General Curtis Lemay, who planned the merciless attacks, famously said that if the US had lost the war, he expected to be tried for war crimes.[148]

By war's end, Japan lay in utter ruin, and the Chinese government relinquished its right to war reparations so as not to add to the suffering of that prostrate nation. The war cost an estimated 15 million Chinese and 3 million Japanese lives. In the aftermath, pacifist sentiments surged, with calls by the Japanese public, who considered the Allied list too short, for Japan to produce its own list of war criminals and conduct its own trials.[149] One could say the scores were settled, and that all sides were ready to start afresh.

Revisionist history

After the war, however, the Allied high command under General Douglas MacArthur, judging that preserving the imperial family would facilitate Allied occupation, invented the fiction that the Emperor Hirohito was a powerless figurehead not responsible for wartime decision-making.[150] The myth sowed the seeds of future discord.[151] It was as problematic as if the

Allies had exonerated Hitler, and, unlike Germany, Japan has therefore never fully owned up to its past. In the first few years of the occupation, leftist American administrators established universal suffrage (women were allowed to vote for the first time), allowed labor unions and even the communist party to form but by 1950, with the outbreak of the Korean War and the rise of McCarthy in the US, there came an abrupt swing to the right, and leftist organizations and public protests were brutally suppressed. Once the Cold War got underway, America's former adversary became a vital ally. It now became expedient to forget Japan's past and demonize China – a shift that derailed Japan's reconciliation with its neighbors.

From the Japanese perspective, their crime was never the brutal invasion of China but their success at wresting colonial turf from the Western powers. They were, after all, only practicing what the Europeans had been doing all along.[152] The atom bomb attacks on Hiroshima and Nagasaki which killed 300,000, mostly civilians, and the savage fire bombing of their cities left the Japanese feeling more like victims than perpetrators of war. The victors were equally guilty of war crimes, and Justice Radha Binod Pal, one of only two Asian judges at the Tokyo War Crimes Trials, denounced the tribunal as a form of victor's justice and revenge.[153]

The Japanese government did on repeated occasions apologize for the war[154] but Japanese prime ministers and politicians continue to pay homage at the Yasukuni Shrine which honors Japanese war dead, including convicted war criminals.[155] The visits would be comparable to German politicians paying tribute at a Nazi SS cemetery.[156] Rubbing salt on old wounds, officials such as Tokyo's mayor, Ishihara Shintaro, and Nagoya's mayor, Takashi Kawamura, deny the Nanjing massacre; while others including Prime Minister Yoshihiko Noda and Osaka's Mayor Toru Hashimoto deny the use of "comfort women" or sex slaves, mostly Chinese and Korean girls, forced to serve Japanese soldiers in the field.[157] In the *New History Textbook*, the Nanking Massacre is dismissed as a controversial "incident," the war of invasion is no longer termed an invasion, and references to comfort women are dropped.[158] For daring to assert that Emperor Hirohito bore responsibility for the Japanese conduct of World War II, Mayor Hitoshi Motoshima of Nagasaki was shot and wounded by a rightwing group in 1990.[159] In December 2012 Prime Minister Shinzo Abe declared his intention to rescind the landmark 1995 apology by Prime Minister Tomiichi Murayama[160] for the suffering caused in World War II.[161] Without sincere reconciliation with its neighbors, distrust will only persist. Recent polls show that 87 percent of the Chinese public holds a negative opinion of Japan.[162]

Japan's foreign policy

When Japan defeated Russia in 1905, it was seen as Asia's leading light and gave new hope to Asian countries that they too could cast off the Western yoke. In a speech in Kobe in 1924, Sun Yat-sen noted:

> In former days, the colored races in Asia, suffering from the oppression of the Western peoples, thought that emancipation was impossible. We regarded that Russian defeat by Japan as the defeat of the West by the East. We regarded the Japanese victory as our own victory. It was indeed a happy event ... Since the day of Japan's victory over Russia, the peoples of Asia have cherished the hope of shaking off the yoke of European oppression, a hope which has given rise to a series or independence movements in Egypt, Persia, Turkey, Afghanistan, and finally in India. Therefore, Japan's defeat of Russia gave rise to a great hope for the independence of Asia.[163]

But instead of solidarity with Asia, Japan joined the West against its Asian kin. Proud of accession to the white man's club, many Japanese consider themselves, the Yamato race, special and display condescension toward other Asians.[164]

Its constitution, written by Americans in 1947, disarmed Japan. According to Article 9, the Japanese people "renounce war as a sovereign right of the nation and the threat or use of force as means of settling international disputes" and "land, sea and air forces, as well as other war potential will never be maintained."[165] But as the Cold War gathered pace the US rearmed Japan, which now boasts the fifth best-funded military in the world. Its 2011 budget of $58.4 billion surpasses that of Russia, Germany, and India.[166] Its troops are highly trained and its navy is one of the best.[167] Its helicopter carriers are larger (27,000 tons) than the British Invincible-class carriers (21,000 tons) and can quickly be adapted to carry fixed-wing aircraft or the vertical take-off F-35B fighter jets, even though carriers are offensive weapons prohibited under the Constitution.[168] The country spends a further $2.3 billion a year to host US troops.

But Japan enjoys great power status without great power leadership. Not since the end of the Second World War has Japan taken a firm stand against the US.[169] Because of the "subordinate independence" built into the unequal US–Japan Treaty of Mutual Cooperation and Security, Japan engages in foreign relations without an independent foreign policy, and its ability to act as a world leader is hamstrung by its wartime record.[170] Six decades after the end of World War II, there are still 48,000 US troops stationed on Japanese soil.[171] Prime Minister Yukio Hatoyama's endeavor to put US–Japan relations on an equal footing and improve ties with China faltered and faded barely two months after he took office.[172] Six months later he resigned, offering as reason his failure to remove the US marine base from Okinawa.

Sino–Japanese peace

So deep is the trauma of the Sino–Japanese War that it is easy to forget that China and Japan had rarely clashed in the long centuries before. Except for the failed attempts by the Mongol ruler Kublai Khan to invade Japan in the thirteenth century, China never sought to conquer Japan. Japan, on its part, tried to invade China in the sixteenth century but failed. Both sides closed their doors to the outside for long periods. Compared to the wars fought between France and England, Sino–Japanese relations were pacific. In Europe the Hundred Years' War alone (1337–1453) boasted no less than forty-five campaigns and battles over 116 years at places like Hastings, Agincourt, Crécy and Orléans, during which medieval warfare with its attendant epidemics and famines wiped out as much as half the population of France. The Thirty Years' War in central Europe (1614–1648), one of the most destructive and longest continuous wars in modern history, resulted in over 8 million casualties, and reduced the population of the German states by an estimated 25–40 percent. In the end, fighting ceased out of sheer exhaustion. Indeed, from the Peloponnesian Wars to the Napoleonic Wars, campaigns by one European state against another were far more frequent than interstate conflict in East Asia. Too little credit has been given to the abiding peace between China and Japan before the advent of the West.[173]

It is not necessary for nations to become captive to the past. The European Union was formed despite Europe's bloody history, and China may need to forgive Japan whether or not that island nation shows genuine remorse. But reinventing wartime history undermines the Peace Constitution and could pave the way to a new Japanese militarism. Prime Minister Shinzo Abe, who rejects what nationalists call a "masochistic view of history," upgraded the Defense Agency to a full-fledged ministry in 2006 and has expressed interest in rewriting the Constitution.[174] Sino–Japanese relations are complicated by Japan's alliance with the United States, a Western power seeking to sustain its hegemony in Asia.[175] Closer Sino–Japanese ties are patently not in America's favor. To contain China, the US must perpetuate a distance between the two Asian neighbors. Unless Japan steers a more Asia-centric course, tension with China may increase.

Territorial dispute

Territorial dispute is the most likely trigger to armed conflict between the US and China. Although the US has no territorial claims against China, disputes between China and its neighbors could lead to a "new Peloponnesian War."[176] Arguing that every great power seeks "to maximize its share of world power and eventually dominate the system," John Mearsheimer predicts that the rise of China will not be peaceful.[177] In its 2006 report, the US–China Economic and Security Review Commission declared that China might "take advantage of a more advanced military to threaten use of force, or actually use force, to facilitate desirable resolutions ... of territorial claims."[178] The Chinese are frequently accused in the Western media of "grabbing resources" in developing countries and "bullying behavior" in the South China Sea. Hillary Clinton has warned China against the use of "coercion, intimidation and threats" to resolve the disputes in the South China Sea.[179]

The record shows, however, that the Chinese have been more cooperative and less prone to use force to resolve territorial disputes.[180] Since the founding of the People's Republic in 1949, they have offered compromise and concessions in 17 out of 24 territorial disputes. The compromises have been substantial, with China accepting less than half the territory contested. It abandoned claims to more than 3.4 million square kilometers of land that were part of the Qing empire, and contested only 238,000 square kilometers or 7 percent of former Qing territory. Although it used force in six territorial disputes (with India, Vietnam, Taiwan and the Soviet Union), it seized little land that it did not control before the outbreak of hostilities.

Douglas Paal points out that the recent flare-ups over islands in the South China Sea originate outside China but people notice the strong reactions in China more than the actions by the Philippines, Vietnam and Japan to provoke the disputes.[181] Historically, the islands attracted little attention because they were navigation hazards on which ships could run aground and sink, but in the 1970s speculation arose about oil and gas reserves although subsequent drilling yielded modest results. The rising demand for seafood could be a more immediate reason behind the claims.[182] China's internal waters are badly polluted while its coastal areas have been overfished.[183] Vietnam and Taiwan too have depleted their coastal waters, and are compelled to venture farther afield.

Despite its offer to act as honest broker, the US can hardly be expected to mediate impartially because, as Su Xiaohui of the China Institute of Strategic Studies (CISS), points out, the disputes stem from the San Francisco Treaty (1952) and the Okinawa Reversion Agreement (1971), two documents drafted by the US turning the islands over to Japan.[184] While the American public cares little about the islands, they are of immense nationalistic importance to the claimants. Territory is a delicate matter but Chinese sensitivity is heightened by the violence suffered at the hands of the Japanese, and American interference only serves to rile Beijing. According to a Pew Global Attitude Survey in 2012, the Chinese voiced increasing reservations about the US.[185] Over the two previous years, the percentage who characterized the US–China relationship as one of cooperation plummeted from 68 percent to 39 percent; 26 percent now say that the relationship is one of hostility, up from 8 percent two years before. A comparable Chinese poll in 2012 showed that 27 percent of government officials surveyed considered the US an "enemy" while 68 percent thought of it as a "competitor."

The dispute can also be considered in a wider context.[186] The UN Convention on the Law of the Sea (UNCLOS) enacted in 1983 allows countries to claim an economic exclusion zone (EEZ) of 200 nautical miles from their coastline. China is a signatory of the convention, and the South China Sea dispute centers on the extent of the EEZ that China claims compared to those of rival claimants. Importantly, the UNCLOS entitles islands to the same 200-nautical mile rule as land territory. Although most Western colonies were dismantled after the Second World War, numerous islands remain as colonies or under the control of high-income countries. The EEZs of the US, France and the UK vastly exceed their home territories. Many of these territories consist of groups of small islands such as British Indian Ocean Territory, the French Kerguelan Islands and the US North Mariana Islands, that allow these countries to claim sole access to the resources within their vast economic exclusion zones. The US, France, the UK, Australia, New Zealand and Russia boast the largest economic exclusion zones. They have a combined population of 604 million, less than half of China's 1.3 billion, but an EEZ of 54 million square kilometers., three-quarters of which is separate from their home territories; China's undisputed EEZ is 0.9 million square kilometers or about the size of one of the smaller overseas EEZ areas of the US, France or the UK. If it were to succeed in all its disputed claims, its EEZ would not exceed 3 million square kilometers. Apart from its claims in the South China Sea, China has no overseas island territories.

Unlike the West, China did not build an overseas empire, and this has profoundly affected the distribution of property rights over the oceans' resources. The US has by far the largest EEZ of 12.236 million square kilometers, 80 percent of which consists of overseas territory. The disparity is even more stark when one considers that much of the territory, home and overseas, was acquired through violence against the indigenous populations, the conquest of North America by white settlers being only one example.[187] Hawaii too was a sovereign kingdom before being annexed by the US in a coup in 1893. Up until the sixteenth century, the South China Sea was China's backyard but soon became European turf when the French took Indochina; the British appropriated Hong Kong, Malaya, Singapore and Borneo; the Spanish, and later the Americans, seized the Philippines while the Dutch colonized Indonesia. The Chinese can perhaps be forgiven for detecting a note of hypocrisy when the Western media criticize them for making indignant claims in the South China Sea. As Nolan observes:

> The West's preoccupation with Beijing's involvement in the South China Sea contrasts sharply with the complete absence of discussion of the West's vast exclusive economic zones in the region, deriving from colonial conquest ... It is as though the Western media have succeeded in focusing the minds of their populations on a mouse, when a mighty elephant stands behind them unnoticed."[188]

Empathy

The greatest lesson of Vietnam, according to Robert McNamara, was to know one's enemy, to empathize with him.[189]

> What went wrong was a basic misunderstanding or misevaluation of the threat to our security represented by the North Vietnamese. It led President Eisenhower in 1954 to say that if Vietnam were lost, or if Laos

and Vietnam were lost, the dominoes would fall. I am certain we exaggerated the threat. We didn't know our opposition. We didn't understand the Chinese; we didn't understand the Vietnamese, particularly the North Vietnamese. So the first lesson is know your opponents. I want to suggest to you that we don't know our potential opponents today.[190]

But McNamara's warning fell on deaf ears, and the mistakes of Vietnam were repeated in Iraq and Afghanistan where Americans, ignoring social, economic and historical factors, invaded in the faith that military technology alone would overcome any opponent. The commanding officer at Fort Benning, Major General H. R. McMaster, who led the Third Armored Cavalry Regiment in Iraq in 2005 and 2006, lamented his country's poor record of learning from previous experience; one reason being that "we apply history simplistically or ignore it altogether."[191] Sadly, Americans, on the whole, exhibit a shallow understanding of the outside world. The parochialism is reflected in the school curriculum, and in the media where foreigners are happily caricatured. The percentage of Americans who travel abroad is remarkably low, and many politicians are proud of their lack of overseas exposure. Cerebral as he is, President Bill Clinton was famously disinterested in foreign policy.[192] But even more worrying is the fact that the agency created in 1947 to inform the president of what is happening in the world provides surprisingly little useful intelligence. In *Legacy of Ashes*, Tim Weiner concluded:

> For sixty years tens of thousands of clandestine service officers have gathered only the barest threads of truly important intelligence – and that is the CIA's deepest secret ... [We] Americans still do not understand the people and the political forces we seek to contain and control. The CIA has yet to become what its creators hoped it would be.[193]

Part of the agency's problem is the pressure to fit the preconceptions of presidents. To survive as an institution, it has to have the president's ear but it is risky to tell him what he does not want to hear. The CIA learned to march in lockstep, and by conforming to conventional wisdom, misunderstands and misjudges the intentions and capabilities of potential enemies. Despite aggressive efforts to hack into foreign computer networks to steal information or sabotage enemy systems, the agency lacks cross-cultural talent, officers with a deep understanding of foreign lands.[194] Many of its analysts, deskbound in Washington, possess no prolonged overseas experience. Few speak Arabic, Persian, Korean or Chinese.[195] Wary of uncertain loyalty, the agency rarely recruits foreign-born citizens with the linguistic skills the agency so badly needs. With exceptions like J. Christopher Stevens, the CIA and the State Department are staffed by men and women poor at blending in or empathizing with the locals in Karachi, Abidjan, Suzhou or Mandalay.[196]

Gone are the days of the China hands – diplomats, journalists and soldiers with intimate knowledge of the language, culture and people of China. John Service (1909–1999), who correctly predicted the defeat the Kuomintang armies by the PLA, was born to missionary parents in China and spoke the Sichuan dialect fluently.[197] David Barrett (1892–1977) learned Mandarin in Beijing, caught a passion for the language and won the admiration of the Chinese by his ability to quote the Confucian classics. Colonel Barrett, who led the Dixie Mission to establish ties with the CCP, spent almost his entire career in China.[198]

But what about Chinese diplomats and intelligence officers? Little has been written about their work due to censorship, but also because there is simply less to tell. The Chinese have not been known to establish distant colonies, station troops abroad or overthrow governments around the world. Compared to the British, French, Americans, Russians or Israelis, they boast few foreign adventures thanks to a policy of non-interference informed by a very long history.[199] In this sense, the competence of Chinese diplomats and intelligence officers may be less consequential.

Are the Chinese biding their time, patiently waiting for the day when they will be strong enough to dominate the world? No one knows the future with certitude but the past offers a few clues. Chinese borders waxed and waned, but the emperors rarely sought to control non-Han areas. The Great Wall testifies to their traditional defensive posture, and they do not share many of the precepts of US foreign policy such as the need to maintain military supremacy. Chas Freeman believes they are not interested in dominating Asia, much less the world.[200] Edward Steinfeld argues that China's rise does not threaten the West[201] but China wants to be China, not an honorary member of the West.[202] It wants to share this century as co-equals with the US but will rely on economic rather than military power. It deserves empathy, not enmity, which could bring about the very crisis America fears, concludes Will Hutton.[203]

It is worth noting that US and Chinese security concerns are actually compatible in a number of areas. As the two largest trading nations, they share a concern for the safety of navigation along the world's sea lanes, and China has joined the US in a multinational task force patrolling the Gulf of Aden against piracy.[204] China is bordered by three nuclear powers – India, Pakistan and Russia. Like the US, it opposes nuclear proliferation although it prefers direct talks over sanctions to curb proliferation.[205] It hosts the six-party talks to restrain North Korean nuclear weapons development (the six parties being China, Japan, North Korea, Russia, South Korea, and the United States),[206] and participates in the Geneva P5+1 nuclear talks with Iran (the P5+1 being the five permanent members of the UN Security Council plus Germany).

While the US worries about Al-Qaeda, China faces Uighur unrest, and is flanked on its west by Afghanistan and Pakistan. Instability in the Middle East poses potentially more danger to China than to the United States thousands of miles away. China is home to 8.5 million Uighurs, a Turkic Muslim minority, living mainly in the Xinjiang Autonomous Region, an area bordering Central Asia that is three times the size of France. Another 10.5 million Hui, Han Muslims with traces of Arabic, Persian and Central Asian features, live in all large cities but predominantly in the provinces of Gansu, Ningxia, and Yunnan.[207] The Hui have been part of Chinese society since the seventh century and speak Chinese. The Chinese government classes them as ethnic minority, and like all ethnic minorities, they enjoy certain privileges such as bonus points to enter university and exemption from the one-child policy. They live peacefully among the Han but in recent years tensions have flared between Han and Uighurs, which the authorities ascribe to the separatist East Turkestan Islamic Movement. Han–Hui harmony suggests that Han–Uighur tension is ethnic and socio-economic rather than religious. Muslims make up less than 2 percent of the Chinese population and, like Catholics, do not all practice their faith. But because they are part of the *ummah* (أمة) or supranational community of believers, Islamic solidarity and support from abroad cannot be ruled out.

US–Chinese security cooperation is not without precedent. Mired in Vietnam, the US sought Chinese help to quit the war. President Nixon's historic visit to Beijing in 1972 helped pave the way to the Paris Peace Accords of 1973, which implemented a ceasefire to allow American troops to withdraw the same year. The US urged Chinese cooperation to counter Soviet influence and even sold arms to China. The two sides worked against Soviet intervention in Afghanistan but once the Soviet Union fell, the picture changed, and despite common security concerns, US–Chinese collaboration has since become tentative at best. Even as the US prosecutes its global war on terror, it does not equate Uighur strife with terrorism.[208] Instead, it argues that the Uighurs are victims of Han colonization and repression.[209] As for halting weapons of mass destruction, the Chinese refuse to back the use of force and, in contrast to the US preference for regime change, adhere to the Five Principles of Peaceful Coexistence, which include non-interference in the internal affairs of sovereign states. Some have called on the Chinese to shoulder a bigger burden of public goods such as the safety of sea lanes, yet Chinese plans to build a blue-water navy are greeted with suspicion.

Conclusion

The military balance is overwhelmingly in America's favor. The armed forces of the United States are much more potent than China's, and the gap is widening. American combat troops are poised on China's doorstep, and more are on the way.[210] Many American leaders express undisguised contempt for the Chinese government and would welcome a regime change.[211] The German news weekly *Der Spiegel* noted:

Never before in modern history has a country dominated the earth so totally as the United States does today ... America is now the Schwarzenegger of international politics: showing off muscles, obtrusive, intimidating ... The Americans, in the absence of limits put on them by anybody or anything, act as if they own a kind of blank check in their "McWorld."[212]

Trust between states depends on History, Interests, Structures, and Empathy – HISE – but the US has a grim record of intrigue[213] as Amnesty International testifies: "Throughout the world, on any given day, a man, woman or child is likely to be displaced, tortured, killed or 'disappeared,' at the hands of governments or armed political groups. More often than not, the United States shares the blame."[214] In his aptly titled book, William Blum documents how US military and CIA interventions kill the hope of millions, and serve the powerful vested interests behind US foreign policy.[215] The link between foreign policy and class interests is an age-old one, as Joseph Schumpeter records:

There was no corner of the known world where some interest was not alleged to be in danger or under actual attack. If the interests were not Roman, they were those of Rome's allies; and if Rome had no allies, the allies would be invented. When it was utterly impossible to contrive such an interest – why, then it was the national honor that had been insulted. The fight was always invested with an aura of legality. Rome was always being attacked by evil-minded neighbors ... The world was pervaded by a host of enemies, it was manifestly Rome's duty to guard against their indubitably aggressive designs ... Even less than in the cases that have already been discussed, can an attempt be made here to comprehend these wars of conquest from the point of view of concrete objectives. Here there was neither a warrior nation in our sense, nor, in the beginning, a military despotism or an aristocracy of specifically military orientation. Thus there is but one way to an understanding; scrutiny of domestic class interests, the question of who stood to gain.[216]

British historian Arnold Toynbee did not fail to recognize the striking parallel between America and Rome:

America is today the leader of a worldwide anti-revolutionary movement in the defense of vested interests. She now stands for what Rome stood for. Rome consistently supported the rich against the poor in all foreign communities that fell under her sway; and, since the poor, so far, have always and everywhere been far more numerous than the rich, Rome's policy made for inequality, for injustice, and for the least happiness of the greatest number.[217]

America is a plutocracy,[218] and one of its core interests is the arms industry.[219] With the end of the Cold War, the munitions merchants needed a new threat, and the Chinese became the convenient foe. China's unexpected revival threatens American mastery and generates deep disquiet in a world order marked by enduring structures of race, identity and power, as John Dower observes:

> Euro-Americans never questioned their manifest destiny to dominate the global political economy. "Hegemony" is a benign term, a kid glove of a word that tends to hide the iron fingers of imperialism, colonialism, exploitation, and racial and cultural condescension. Whether rationalized idealistically (the "civilizing mission"), or self-righteously (the "white man's burden") or paternalistically (obligation to "little brown brothers"), or contemptuously (mocking for example, the "little yellow men") the Euro-American global domination that existed from the time of Columbus and his fellow captains to the present rested on the assumption that nonwhites and non-Christians are inherently inferior. This conceit – seemingly confirmed by the physical and material domination of the non-Western world – is not easily dissipated.[220]

The full significance of changing hegemonies in modern times lies not just in the end of the "American century" but in the close of five centuries of Western and Caucasian global domination. It marks the conclusion of white supremacy. Hegemonic decline is unsettling, and the US may feel compelled to act while it has a window of opportunity by launching a preventive war to preserve the status quo.[221]

Notes

1 Graham Allison, "Thucydides's Trap Has Been Sprung in the Pacific," *Financial Times*, August 21, 2012, www.ft.com/cms/s/0/5d695b5a-ead3-11e1-984b-00144fea b49a.html#axzz24Ft4mczq.
2 Ibid.
3 Christopher Layne, "The Global Power Shift from West to East," *The National Interest*, April 28, 2012, http://nationalinterest.org/article/the-global-power-shift-west-east-6796?page=1.
4 Vaclav Smil, *Global Catastrophes and Trends: The next Fifty Years* (Cambridge, MA: MIT Press, 2008).
5 Brett Arends, "IMF Bombshell: Age of America Nears End," Market Watch, *Wall Street Journal*, April 25, 2011, http://articles.marketwatch.com/2011-04-25/ commentary/30714377_1_imf-chinese-economy-international-monetary-fund.
6 Ian Katz, "U.S. Government Debt Reaches $16 Trillion for First Time," *Bloomberg*, September 4, 2012, www.bloomberg.com/news/2012-09-04/u-s-go vernment-debt-reaches-16-trillion-for-first-time.html.
7 Giacomo Luciani, "The Economic Content of Security," *Journal of Public Policy* 8, no. 2 (1989): 151–73.
8 Laurence Martin, "Can There Be National Security in an Insecure Age?," *Encounter* 60, no. 3 (March 1983): 11–19.

9   Frank N. Trager and Frank L. Simonie, "An Introduction to the Study of National Security," in *National Security and American Society* (Lawrence: University Press of Kansas, 1973), 36.

10 Barry Buzan, *People, States and Fear: An Agenda for International Security Studies in the Post-Cold War Era*, 2nd edn. (London: Harvester Wheatsheaf, 1991), 16–7.

11 Richard L. Kugler and Ellen L. Frost, *The Global Century: Globalization and National Security*, vol. 2 (Washington, DC: National Defense University Press, 2001).

12 Amitai Etzioni, "Who Authorized Preparations for War with China?," *Yale Journal of International Affairs*, 2013, www.gwu.edu/~sigur/assets/docs/Etzioni_article.pdf.

13 "Timeline of Media Mega Mergers (1986–2004)," *Globalization101*, accessed July 17, 2013, www.globalization101.org/timeline-of-media-mega-mergers-1986-2004; Edward S. Herman and Noam Chomsky, *Manufacturing Consent: The Political Economy of the Mass Media* (New York: Pantheon Books, 2002); C. Edwin Baker, *Media Concentration and Democracy* (New York: Cambridge University Press, 2007); Ben H. Bagdikian, *The New Media Monopoly* (Boston, MA: Beacon Press, 2004).

14 International Institute for Strategic Studies, *The Military Balance* (London: Institute for Strategic Studies, 2013).

15 Winslow Wheeler, "Decoding the Defense Budget," in *The Pentagon Labyrinth* (Washington, DC: Center for Defense Information, 2011), 88.

16 Tim Weiner, *Blank Check: The Pentagon's Black Budget* (New York: Warner Books, 1991).

17 "Tim Weiner, *Blank Check: The Pentagon's Black Budget*," Interview by Brian Lamb, October 21, 1990, www.booknotes.org/Watch/14257-1/Tim+Weiner.aspx.

18 "The Black Budget: Top Secret U.S. Intelligence Funding – Interactive Graphic," *Washington Post*, August 31, 2013, www.washingtonpost.com/wp-srv/special/national/black-budget/.

19 "The Diversified Employment of China's Armed Forces," *PRC Ministry of National Defense*, April 16, 2013, http://eng.mod.gov.cn/TopNews/2013-04/16/content_4442750.htm; Tom Phillips, "China Lays Bare Its Military Might with an Attack on US Ambition," *Telegraph.co.uk*, April 16, 2013, world news section, www.telegraph.co.uk/news/worldnews/asia/china/9998111/China-lays-bare-its-military-might-with-an-attack-on-US-ambition.html.

20 David Shambaugh, "China's Post-Deng Military Leadership," in *China's Military Faces the Future*, ed. James R. Lilley and David L Shambaugh (Armonk, NY: M. E. Sharpe, 1999), 23.

21 International Institute for Strategic Studies, *The Military Balance 2012*, Pap./Chrt (Abingdon and New York: Routledge, 2012), 213.

22 David Shambaugh, *Modernizing China's Military* (Berkeley: University of California Press, 2002), 328–330.

23 The 7.9 magnitude Sichuan earthquake killed 70,000 people.

24 Tai Ming Cheung, "Reforming the Dragon's Tail," in *China's Military Faces the Future*, ed. James R. Lilley and David L. Shambaugh (Armonk, NY: M. E. Sharpe, 1999), 228.

25 Ibid., 238.

26 Robert S. Ross, "China's Naval Nationalism: Sources, Prospects, and the U.S. Response," *International Security* 34, no. 2 (September 30, 2009): 46–81, doi:10.1162/isec.2009.34.2.46.

27 The *Liaoning*, bought from the Ukraine in 1998, remains largely an experimental craft.

28 朱峰 Zhu Feng and Robert S. Ross, "中国和平崛起⊠与单极的关系," in 中国的崛起⊠理论与政策的视角 *China's Peaceful Rise: Theory and Policy Perspective* (Shanghai: Shanghai Renmin Press 上海人民出版社, 2008), 46–7.

29 Wendy Frieman, "The Understated Revolution in Chinese Science and Technology," in *China's Military Faces the Future* ed. James R. Lilley and David L. Shambaugh (Armonk, NY: M. E. Sharpe, 1999), 257.

30 James Wilsdon and James Keeley, *China: The Next Science Superpower?* (London: Demos, 2007); Martin Jacques, *When China Rules the World: The Rise of the Middle Kingdom and the End of the Western World* (London: Allen Lane, 2009), 175.

31 "78.8%受访者认为人情关系复杂阻碍优秀人才回国 Survey Shows Complex Social Relations Keeps Talent from Returning Home to China," *Xinhua Online* 新华网, September 6, 2013, http://news.xinhuanet.com/hr/2013-09/06/c_125335728.htm.

32 David Shambaugh, "China's Post-Deng Military Leadership," in *China's Military Faces the Future*, ed. James R. Lilley and David L. Shambaugh (Armonk, NY: M. E. Sharpe, 1999), 32.

33 In 2008 alone the Iraq and Afghanistan wars cost US$189.3 billion.

34 David Vine, *Island of Shame: The Secret History of the U.S. Military Base on Diego Garcia* (Princeton, NJ: Princeton University Press, 2009).

35 "美军重启一连串旧基地包围中国 防主基地被摧毁 US Revitalizes a String of Old Island Bases to Encircle China," *Tencent News* 腾讯新闻, August 22, 2013, http://news.qq.com/a/20130822/004123.htm; John Reed, "Surrounded: How the US Is Encircling China with Military Bases," *Foreign Policy*, August 20, 2013.

36 Matthew Harper, "Chinese Missiles and the Walmart Factor," *U.S. Naval Institute, Proceedings Magazine*, July 2011, www.usni.org/magazines/proceedings/2011-07/chinese-missiles-and-walmart-factor.

37 Martin E. Dempsey, "Joint Operational Access Concept" (Washington, DC: Department of Defense, January 17, 2012), www.defense.gov/pubs/pdfs/JOAC_Jan%202012_Signed.pdf.

38 Dwight D. Eisenhower, "Military-Industrial Complex Speech," 1960, www.h-net.org/~hst306/documents/indust.html.

39 Andrew Cockburn, "Follow the Money," in *The Pentagon Labyrinth* (Washington, DC: Center for Defense Information, 2011), 78.

40 Carol Giacomo, "How Mitt Romney Would Force-Feed the Pentagon," *New York Times*, August 25, 2012, Opinion/Sunday Review section, www.nytimes.com/2012/08/26/opinion/sunday/how-mr-romney-would-force-feed-the-pentagon.html.

41 Jeremy Scahill, *Blackwater: The Rise of the World's Most Powerful Mercenary Army* (London: Serpent's Tail, 2008).

42 Anna Fifield, "US Bill to Rebuild Iraq Reaches $138bn," *Financial Times*, March 18, 2013, www.ft.com/cms/s/0/7f435f04-8c05-11e2-b001-00144feabdc0.html#axzz2Nt10rkoG.

43 David Barstow, "One Man's Military-Industrial-Media Complex," *New York Times*, April 20, 2008, https://mail-attachment.googleusercontent.com/attachment/?ui=2&ik=925828fbf3&view=att&th=1380e4a89aa76ca1&attid=0.2&disp=safe&zw&saduie=AG9B_P8M-pEX1ScT_7aJrn_zjECe&sadet=1340270910037&sads=yUWzPwhWF-VM4aoebIv8hVC9tZA.

44 David Barstow, "Behind TV Analysts, Pentagon's Hidden Hand," *New York Times*, April 20, 2008, https://mail-attachment.googleusercontent.com/attachment/?ui=2&ik=925828fbf3&view=att&th=1380e4a89aa76ca1&attid=0.1&disp=safe&zw&saduie=AG9B_P8M-pEX1ScT_7aJrn_zjECe&sadet=1340271062750&sads=vmhcCz6wR4qRdXw44Q6ZqP4Crmk.

45 Anne H. Cahn, *Killing Detente: The Right Attacks the CIA* (University Park: Pennsylvania State University Press, 1998).

46 Tim Weiner, "Military Accused of Lies over Arms," *New York Times*, June 28, 1993, www.nytimes.com/1993/06/28/us/military-accused-of-lies-over-arms.html.

47 Barstow, "Behind TV Analysts, Pentagon's Hidden Hand."

48 *SIPRI Yearbook 2013: Armaments, Disarmament and International Security* (Stockholm, Sweden: Stockholm International Peace Research Institute, 2013), www.sipri.org/yearbook/2013/files/SIPRIYB13Summary.pdf; Robert S. Mcnamara, "Apocalypse Soon," *Foreign Policy*, May 5, 2005, www.foreignpolicy.com/articles/2005/05/05/apocalypse_soon?wp_login_redirect=0.

49 "China Sticks to No-First-Use of Nuclear Weapons: White Paper," *Xinhua News*, March 31, 2011, http://news.xinhuanet.com/english2010/china/2011-03/31/c_13806909.htm; Gregory Kulacki, "China Still Committed to No First Use of Nuclear Weapons," *Union of Concerned Scientists: All Things Nuclear*, April 23, 2013, http://allthingsnuclear.org/china-still-committed-to-no-first-use-of-nuclear-weapons/.

50 David E. Sanger, "Obama Ordered Wave of Cyberattacks Against Iran," *New York Times*, June 1, 2012, World/Middle East section, www.nytimes.com/2012/06/01/world/middleeast/obama-ordered-wave-of-cyberattacks-against-iran.html.

51 Sara Sorcher, "Senators Blast Publicity of Cyberattack on Iran," *NationalJournal.com*, June 5, 2012, www.nationaljournal.com/daily/senators-blast-publicity-of-cyberattack-on-iran-20120605.

52 David E. Sanger, "U.S. Accuses China's Military in Cyberattacks," *New York Times*, May 6, 2013, World/Asia Pacific section, www.nytimes.com/2013/05/07/world/asia/us-accuses-chinas-military-in-cyberattacks.html; "U.S. Report Accuses China, Russia of Cyber Attacks," *Washington Post*, November 3, 2011, www.washingtonpost.com/world/us-report-accuses-china-russia-of-cyber-attacks/2011/11/03/gIQAuT2djM_video.html.

53 "互联网应急中心:中国遭受严重来自美国网络攻击 CNCERT: China Is Victim of Hacking Attacks from the US," *China Daily* 中国日报网, June 6, 2013, www.chinadaily.com.cn/language_tips/news/2013-06/06/content_16575578.htm.

54 Matthew M. Aid, "The NSA's Data Haul Is Bigger Than You Can Possibly Imagine," *Foreign Policy*, August 15, 2013, www.foreignpolicy.com/articles/2013/08/15/the_nsas_data_haul_is_bigger_than_you_can_possibly_imagine; Glenn Greenwald, "XKeyscore: NSA Tool Collects 'Nearly Everything a User Does on the Internet,'" *The Guardian*, July 31, 2013, www.theguardian.com/world/2013/jul/31/nsa-top-secret-program-online-data.

55 Lana Lam and Stephen Chen, "Exclusive: Snowden Reveals More US Cyber-spying Details," *South China Morning Post*, June 23, 2013, www.scmp.com/news/hong-kong/article/1266777/exclusive-snowden-safe-hong-kong-more-us-cyberspying-details-revealed?page=all.

56 Stephen Kinzer, *Overthrow: America's Century of Regime Change from Hawaii to Iraq*, Reprint (New York: Times Books, 2007); William Blum, *Rogue State: A Guide to the World's Only Superpower* (Monroe, ME: Common Courage Press, 2000), ch. 17.

57 Sam Gustin, "Game Changers," *Time*, September 2, 2011, www.time.com/time/specials/packages/article/0,28804,2091589_2091591_2091592,00.html; *eDiplomacy at the U.S. Department of State*, 2012, www.youtube.com/watch?v=oVTtm7d6EiE&feature=youtube_gdata_player.

58 "US Security Strategy for the East Asia-Pacific Region" (Washington, DC: Department of Defense, Office of International Security Affairs, February 1995).

59 The US entered into mutual defense treaties with Japan (1951), South Korea (1953), Australia (1951), the Philippines (1951) and Thailand (1954).

60 "US Security Strategy for the East Asia-Pacific Region," 9.

61 Joseph S. Nye, "The 'Nye Report': Six Years Later," *International Relations of the Asia-Pacific* 1 (2001): 95–103.

62 Condoleeza Rice, "Promoting the National Interest," *Foreign Affairs* 79, no. 1 (2000): 45.

63 Condoleeza Rice, "Rethinking the National Interest: American Realism for a New World," *Foreign Affairs* 87, no. 4 (2008): 2–26.

64 Condoleeza Rice, "Rice's Remarks at the Republican National Convention, August 2012," August 29, 2012, www.cfr.org/us-election-2012/rices-remarks-rep ublican-national-convention-august-2012/p28896.

65 Rice claimed that under the Clinton administration, military readiness had declined, moral plummeted and equipment cannibalized to keep planes flying and ships afloat.

66 Rice, "Rethinking the National Interest: American Realism for a New World."

67 Close economic ties between Germany and Britain in 1914 did not ensure peace.

68 Robert B. Zoellick, "A Republican Foreign Policy," *Foreign Affairs* 79, no. 1 (January/February 2000): 63–78. www.jstor.org/stable/10.2307/20049614.

69 "Statement of Principles," *Project for the New American Century*, June 3, 1997, www.newamericancentury.org/statementofprinciples.htm.

70 Jeffrey Goldberg, "Hillary Clinton: Chinese System Is Doomed, Leaders on a 'Fool's Errand,'" *The Atlantic*, May 10, 2011, www.theatlantic.com/internationa l/archive/2011/05/hillary-clinton-chinese-system-is-doomed-leaders-on-a-fools-err and/238591/.

71 Hillary Clinton, "America's Pacific Century," *Foreign Policy*, November 2011, www.foreignpolicy.com/articles/2011/10/11/americas_pacific_century.

72 Ibid.

73 Kenneth Lieberthal, "The American Pivot to Asia," *Foreign Policy*, December 21, 2011, www.foreignpolicy.com/articles/2011/12/21/the_american_pivot_to_asia.

74 Ibid.

75 Jagdish Bhagwati, "US Pacific Trade Pact Aims to Exclude China," *Shanghai Daily*, January 6, 2012, www.china.org.cn/opinion/2012-01/06/content_24339500. htm.

76 Craig Whitlock, "U.S., Australia to Broaden Military Ties amid Pentagon Pivot to SE Asia," *Washington Post*, March 27, 2012, World section, www.washing tonpost.com/world/national-security/us-to-expand-ties-with-australia-as-it-aims-t o-shift-forces-closer-to-se-asia/2012/03/19/gIQAPSXlcS_story.html?hpid=z1.

77 An Australian government review urges expansion of the Stirling naval base in Perth to accommodate the US Navy.

78 "Sustaining US Global Leadership: Priorities for 21st Century Defense" (Pentagon, January 2012).

79 *National Security Strategy* (Washington, DC: The White House, 2010), www. whitehouse.gov/sites/default/files/rss_viewer/national_security_strategy.pdf.

80 Kent Klein, "Obama: US 'The One Indispensable Nation in World Affairs,'" *Voice of America*, May 23, 2012, www.voanews.com/content/obama_tells_air_ force_academy_us_is_one_indispensable_country_world_affairs/940158.html.

81 Malcolm Fraser, "Australia-US Relations in the 'Asian Century': To Avoid Unnecessary and Ill Advised Conflict," Speech, Melbourne University, September 25, 2012.

82 Hugh White, *The China Choice: Why America Should Share Power* (Oxford: Oxford University Press, 2013).

83 Aaron L. Friedberg, *A Contest for Supremacy: China, America, and the Struggle for Mastery in Asia*, 1st edn. (New York: W.W. Norton, 2011).

84 韬光养晦 *taoguang yanghui*: stay out of the limelight, 摸着石头过河 *mozhe shitou guohe*: touch the stones (on the river bed) as you cross the river.

85 Samuel Huntington as qouted in Friedberg, *A Contest for Supremacy*, 159.

86 Ibid., 69.

87 Henry A. Kissinger, "The Future of U.S.–Chinese Relations," *Foreign Affairs*, March 1, 2012, www.foreignaffairs.com/articles/137245/henry-a-kissinger/the-future-of-us-chinese-relations.

88 Stefan Halper, *The Beijing Consensus* (New York: Basic Books, 2010).

89 Friedberg, *A Contest for Supremacy*.

90 Jeffrey A. Bader, *Obama and China's Rise: An Insider's Account of America's Asia Strategy* (Washington, DC: Brookings Institution Press, 2013), 20.

91 Friedberg, *A Contest for Supremacy*, 184.

92 Kissinger, "The Future of U.S.–Chinese Relations."

93 Zbigniew Brzezinski, *Strategic Vision: America and the Crisis of Global Power* (New York: Basic Books, 2012), 190.

94 Ibid., 189.

95 *Ron Paul Interview in Congress, 2010*, 9:30, www.youtube.com/watch?v=bAYvv2xT8yI&feature=youtube_gdata_player. Remarks made about US foreign policy during an interview about the fiscal budget.

96 Stephen M. Walt, "The Myth of American Exceptionalism," *Foreign Policy*, November 2011, www.foreignpolicy.com/articles/2011/10/11/the_myth_of_american_exceptionalism.

97 Samuel P Huntington, *The Clash of Civilizations and the Remaking of World Order* (London: Free Press, 2002), 51.

98 Zheng Wang, *Never Forget National Humiliation: Historical Memory in Chinese Politics and Foreign Relations* (New York: Columbia University Press, 2012); William A. Callahan, "National Insecurities: Humiliation, Salvation, and Chinese Nationalism," *Alternatives: Global, Local, Political* 29, no. 2 (2004): 199–218.

99 习近平 Xi Jinping, "China's New Party Chief Xi Jinping's Speech," *BBC News*, November 15, 2012, www.bbc.co.uk/news/world-asia-china-20338586.

100 "China's National Defense in 2010," *Xinhua English.news.cn*, March 31, 2011, http://news.xinhuanet.com/english2010/china/2011-03/31/c_13806851_3.htm.

101 "Report of Hu Jintao to the 18th CPC National Congress," *China.org.cn*, November 16, 2012, section XI, www.china.org.cn/china/18th_cpc_congress/2012-11/16/content_27137540_11.htm.

102 The Five Principles of Peaceful Coexistence: 1. mutual respect for each others' sovereignty and territorial integrity 2. mutual non-aggression 3. mutual non-interference in each other's internal affairs 4. equality and mutual benefit 5. peaceful coexistence.

103 资中筠 Zi Zhongyun, "利益的汇合:国家关系的基础 – 写在中美建交十周年之际 Convergence of Interests: Basis for Relations among Nations," 美国研究 *American Studies Quarterly*, no. 2 (1989).

104 杨洁篪 Yang Jiechi, "杨洁篪在中美关系研讨会上发表, Speech by Yang Jiechi at US–China Relations Conference 2012," 中国新闻网 *China News Online*, March 8, 2012, www.chinanews.com/gn/2012/03-08/3727598.shtml.

105 郑必坚 Zheng Bijian, "China's Peaceful Rise and US-China Relations," in 郑必坚论集 *Zheng Bijian Collection of Speeches*, vol. 3 (上海人民出版社 Shanghai: People's Press, 2005), 1357.

106 "UN Security Council: Resolutions, Presidential Statements, Meeting Records, SC Press Releases," accessed March 27, 2013, https://www.un.org/Depts/dhl/resguide/scact.htm.

107 According to the 1951 Treaty of San Francisco.

108 Robert Ash, John W. Garver, and Penelope Prime, eds, *Taiwan's Democracy: Economic and Political Challenges* (Abingdon and New York: Routledge, 2011).

109 There are heavy Taiwanese investments concentrated in the Pearl River Delta too.

110 "Taiwan and China at Crossroads," *BBC News*, May 21, 2010, www.bbc.co.uk/news/10122592.

111   Zheng Fei, "Beijing to Expand RQFII Program to Taiwan Investors," *Caixin Online*, January 30, 2013, http://english.caixin.com/2013-01-30/100487895.html.

112   "Taiwan to Ease Rules for Chinese Banks," *Financial Times*, April 2, 2013, www.ft.com/cms/s/0/9a3c8598-9b2c-11e2-97ad-00144feabdc0.html?ftcamp=published_links%2Frss%2Fworld_asia-pacific_china%2Ffeed%2F%2Fproduct&ftcamp=crm/email/201342/nbe/ChinaBusiness/product#axzz2PJLUuTbj.

113   朱镕基答记者问 *Zhu Rongji Answers to Journalists' Questions* (Beijing: People's Press 人民出版社, 2009), 48.

114   The Qing was a dynasty of Manchus who ruled China from 1644 to 1912 when it was overthrown by the Chinese republican revolution.

115   Colin P. Mackerras, "PRC: Background Paper on the Situation of the Tibetan Population," Writenet (Geneva: UNHCR, February 2005), www.unhcr.org/cgi-bin/texis/vtx/refworld/rwmain/opendocpdf.pdf?docid=423ea9094.

116   No Chinese government has ever signed the Simla Convention.

117   Gardiner Harris, "Cameron Calls Colonial-Era Massacre in India 'Shameful,'" *New York Times*, February 20, 2013, World/Asia Pacific section, www.nytimes.com/2013/02/21/world/asia/cameron-calls-colonial-era-massacre-in-india-shameful.html.

118   John Kenneth Knaus, *Orphans of the Cold War: America and the Tibetan Struggle for Survival* (New York: Public Affairs, 1999), 39.

119   *Foreign Relations of the United States 1955–1957*, vol. 3, n.d., 669 (Washington, DC: Government Printing Office; Dawa Norbu, *China's Tibet Policy*, Durham East Asia Series (Richmond: Curzon Press, 2001), 268.

120   Harry August Rositzke, *The CIA's Secret Operations: Espionage, Counter-espionage, and Covert Action* (Boulder, CO: Westview Press, 1988), 173.

121   Steve Weissman, *Last Tangle in Tibet* (East Palo Alto, CA: Pacific Studies Center, 1973), 5.

122   A. Tom Grunfeld, "Tibet and the United States," in *Contemporary Tibet*, ed. Barry Sautman and June Teufel Dreyer (Armonk, NY: M. E. Sharpe, 2006), 325.

123   Knaus, *Orphans of the Cold War*, 40.

124   Charles F. Romanus and Riley Sunderland, *Stilwell's Mission to China* (Washington, DC: Office of the Chief of Military History, Dept of the Army, 1953), 287.

125   Xu Mingfu and Yuan Feng, "The Tibet Question: A New Cold War," in *Contemporary Tibet*, ed. Barry Sautman and June Teufel Dreyer (Armonk, NY: M. E. Sharpe, 2006), 310.

126   Grunfeld, "Tibet and the United States," 341.

127   Barry Sautman, "'Demographic Annihilation' and Tibet," in *Contemporary Tibet*, ed. Barry Sautman and June Teufel Dreyer (Armonk, NY: M. E. Sharpe, 2006), 230–31.

128   Mackerras, *PRC: Background Paper on the Situation of the Tibetan Population*, 18.

129   Ibid., 19.

130   Sautman, "'Demographic Annihilation' and Tibet," 246.

131   Sam Van Schaik, *Tibet: A History* (New Haven, CT: Yale University Press, 2011), 242.

132   Peter Hessler, "Tibet Through Chinese Eyes," *The Atlantic*, February 1999, www.theatlantic.com/magazine/archive/1999/02/tibet-through-chinese-eyes/306395/.

133   Xu Mingfu and Yuan Feng, "The Tibet Question: A New Cold War."

134   It is improbable that Chinese are ancestors of the Japanese, given the linguistic differences between the two. Their syntax, grammar and vocabulary are quite distinct. Chinese belongs to the Sino-Tibetan family whereas Japanese is a Turkic-Altaic language.

135   The event is recorded in the *Book of Later Han* (后汉书) in which Japan was called by its traditional name *Wa* (和).

136 The Japanese referred to the black steamships as *kurofune* (黒船)

137 The Meiji Restoration (明治維新) ended the Tokugawa Shogunate and restored imperial rule in 1868.

138 John K. Fairbank, Edwin Oldfather Reischauer, and Albert Morton Craig, *East Asia: Tradition and Transformation*. Revised edn. (Boston, MA: Houghton Mifflin, 1989), 490.

139 Shogo Suzuki, *Civilization and Empire: China and Japan's Encounter with European International Society* (London and New York: Routledge, 2009).

140 China, like Japan, joined the Allied Powers in the First World War but was granted derisory rewards at the Paris Peace Conference of 1919, while Japan was treated as a great power.

141 Fairbank *et al.*, *East Asia*, 714.

142 Iris Chang, *The Rape of Nanking: The Forgotten Holocaust of World War II*. New edn. (London: Penguin, 1998).

143 Herbert P. Bix, *Hirohito and the Making of Modern Japan*. 1st Perennial edn. (New York and London: HarperCollins, 2001).

144 John Tucker, "Japanese Confucian Philosophy," in *The Stanford Encyclopedia of Philosophy*, ed. Edward N. Zalta, Summer 2012, p. 11. http://plato.stanford.edu/archives/sum2012/entries/japanese-confucian/.

145 Ibid., 34.

146 Michio Morishima, *Why Has Japan "Succeeded"?: Western Technology and the Japanese Ethos* (Cambridge: Cambridge University Press, 1982), 2–6.

147 John Buckley, *Air Power in the Age of Total War* (London: UCL Press, 1999).

148 Lemay boasted that his bombers were "driving [the Japanese] back to the stone age."

149 John W. Dower, *Embracing Defeat: Japan in the Wake of World War II*. New edn. (New York: W. W. Norton, 2000), 475.

150 Dower, *Embracing Defeat*; John W. Dower, *Ways of Forgetting* (New York: The New Press, 2011).

151 At his first meeting with General Douglas MacArthur after Japan's defeat in 1945, Emperor Hirohito said: "I come before you to offer myself to the judgment of the powers you represent, as one to bear sole responsibility for every political and military decision taken by my people in the conduct of the war." (*Economist*, 21 August 1993).

152 Dower, *Embracing Defeat*, 471.

153 The tribunal's "best evidence rule" allowed simple hearsay with no secondary support to be used as evidence against the accused.

154 Jane Yamazaki, *Japanese Apologies for World War II: A Rhetorical Study* (London and New York: Routledge, 2005).

155 At a memorial event marking the 67th anniversary of Japan's surrender, Prime Minister Yoshihiko Noda acknowledged that Japan started the war which inflicted severe damage and deep pain on people throughout Asia; but at about the same time three members of his cabinet visited the Yasukuni Shrine.

156 "German Historian: Japan's Shrine Visit a Great Mistake," *CCTV News*, October 19, 2012, http://english.cntv.cn/program/newsupdate/20121019/101756.shtml.

157 "China Upset over Japan Comments," *BBC News*, February 22, 2012, www.bbc.co.uk/news/world-asia-17125934.

158 Philip J. Cunningham, "Japan's Revisionist History," *Los Angeles Times*, April 11, 2005, http://articles.latimes.com/2005/apr/11/opinion/oe-cunningham11; Norimitsu Onishi, "Japan's Textbooks Reflect Revised History," *New York Times*, April 1, 2007, International/Asia Pacific section, www.nytimes.com/2007/04/01/world/asia/01japan.html.

159   David E. Sanger, "Mayor Who Faulted Hirohito Is Shot," *New York Times*, January 19, 1990, www.nytimes.com/1990/01/19/world/mayor-who-faulted-hir ohito-is-shot.html?sec=.

160   "Statement by Prime Minister Tomiichi Murayama 'On the Occasion of the 50th Anniversary of the War's End,'" *Ministry of Foreign Affairs of Japan*, August 15, 1995, www.mofa.go.jp/announce/press/pm/murayama/9508.html.

161   "Japan PM Abe Wants to Replace Landmark War Apology," *Reuters*, December 31, 2012, http://uk.reuters.com/article/2012/12/31/uk-japan-apology-i dUKBRE8BU03020121231; Robert Whiting, "Saying UnSorry," *Foreign Policy*, January 30, 2013.

162   Adam Westlake, "Chinese Survey Reveals 87% of Nation's Public Has Negative Opinion of Japan," *Japan Daily Press*, December 27, 2012, http://japandailyp ress.com/chinese-survey-reveals-87-of-nations-public-has-negative-opinion-of-jap an-2720499/; John Hofilena, "Anti-Japan Sentiment Sharply Growing in China, South Korea according to Polls," *Japan Daily Press*, July 12, 2013, http://japa ndailypress.com/anti-japan-sentiment-sharply-growing-in-china-south-korea-acco rding-to-polls-1232229/.

163   孙中山 Sun Yat-sen, "Pan Asianism 大亚细亚主义" (Speech, Kobe, Japan, November 28, 1924).

164   John W. Dower, *Japan in War and Peace: Essays on History, Culture and Race* (London: Fontana, 1996), 315.

165   Article 9 of the Japanese Constitution.

166   International Institute for Strategic Studies, *The Military Balance 2012*, Pap./ Chrt (Abingdon and New York: Routledge, 2012), 31.

167   Christopher Hughes, "Japan: Military Modernization in Search of a 'Normal Security Role,'" in *Military Modernization in an Era of Uncertainty* (Washington, DC: National Bureau of Asian Research, 2005).

168   Associated Press, "Japan Unveils New Carrier-like Warship, the Largest in Its Navy since World War II," *Washington Post*, August 6, 2013, www.washingtonp ost.com/world/asia_pacific/japan-unveils-new-carrier-like-warship-the-largest-in-it s-navy-since-world-war-ii/2013/08/06/8fae14d8-fe79-11e2-8294-0ee5075b840d_sto ry.html; "日本准'航母'将于6日下水 排水量超英意航母 Japan Launches Aircraft Carrier on August 6 with Displacement Greater than UK Aircraft Carrier," *Tencent News* 腾讯新闻, August 4, 2013, http://news.qq.com/a/20130804/000261. htm.

169   Arnold Toynbee, Daisaku Ikeda, and Richard L. Gage, *Choose Life: A Dialogue*. British Commonwealth edn. (London: Oxford University Press, 1976), 182.

170   Dower, *Japan in War and Peace*, 318–19.

171   Bader, *Obama and China's Rise*, 147.

172   "Obama Meets Hatoyama in Japan," *Bloomberg Businessweek*, November 27, 2009, www.businessweek.com/globalbiz/content/nov2009/gb20091113_321964. htm.

173   David Kang, *East Asia Before the West: Five Centuries of Trade and Tribute* (New York: Columbia University Press, 2012).

174   Onishi, "Japan's Textbooks Reflect Revised History."

175   Marcie Kagawa, "Oliver Stone Likens Japan to U.S. Vassal," *Japan Times*, June 15, 2013, www.japantimes.co.jp/news/2013/06/15/national/oliver-stone-likens-japa n-to-u-s-vassal/#.UgygplOE42E.

176   Peter Nolan, *A New Peloponnesian War: China, the West and the South China Seas* (Cambridge: Cambridge University Press, 2012).

177   J. J. Mearsheimer, "The Rise of China Will Not Be Peaceful at All," *The Aus- tralian*, November 18, 2005, www.ou.edu/uschina/SASD/SASD2005/2005rea dings/Clash%20of%20the%20Titans.pdf.

178 *2006 Report to Congress of the US–China Economic and Security Review Commission*, November 2006.

179 Nolan, *A New Peloponnesian War: China, the West and the South China Seas.*

180 M. Taylor Fravel, *Strong Borders, Secure Nation: Cooperation and Conflict in China's Territorial Disputes*, Princeton Studies in International History and Politics (Princeton, NJ: Princeton University Press, 2008), 1–6.

181 Douglas Paal, "Territorial Disputes in Asian Waters," *Carnegie Endowment for International Peace*, October 16, 2012, http://carnegieendowment.org/2012/10/16/territorial-disputes-in-asian-waters/e1ex##.

182 Emiko Terazono, "Global Fish Prices Leap to All-Time High," *Financial Times*, June 18, 2013, www.ft.com/cms/s/0/af42937a-d811-11e2-9495-00144feab7de.html#axzz2WPcGmvo8.

183 Liang Jialin and Jiang Han, "Overfishing Pushes 80% of Chinese Fishermen towards Bankruptcy," 中外对话 *Chinadialogue*, October 19, 2012.

184 苏晓晖 Su Xiaohui, "China Should Have No Illusion That the US Will Help Resolve the Dispute," *China Institute of International Studies*, October 17, 2012, www.ciis.org.cn/english/2012-10/17/content_5408981.htm.

185 J. Stapleton Roy, "Strategic Challenges for the US–China Relationship" (East-West Center in Hawaii, February 13, 2013), https://vimeo.com/59754895.

186 Peter Nolan, *China, Western Colonialism and the UN Convention on the Law of the Sea* (Cambridge: Cambridge University Press, 2012).

187 John Grenier, *The First Way of War: American War Making on the Frontier, 1607–1814*, 1st edn. (Cambridge: Cambridge University Press, 2008).

188 Peter Nolan, "Imperial Archipelagos," *New Left Review* II, no. 80 (April 2013): 77–95.

189 Errol Morris, *The Fog of War: Eleven Lessons from the Life of Robert McNamara*, DVD (Sony Pictures Home Entertainment, 2004).

190 Tim Weiner, "Robert S. McNamara, Architect of a Futile War, Dies at 93," *New York Times*, July 7, 2009, US section, www.nytimes.com/2009/07/07/us/07mcnamara.html?pagewanted=6&_r=1&th&emc=th.

191 H. R. McMaster, "Pipe Dream of Easy Wars," *International Herald Tribune*, July 22, 2013, op. edn.

192 M. Elliot and B. Cohn, "A Head for Diplomacy? Clinton: One Year In, He's Still Struggling to Get His Mind around Foreign Policy," *Newsweek*, March 28, 1994; Charles F. Allen and Jonathan Portis, *The Comeback Kid: The Life and Career of Bill Clinton* (New York: Citadel Press, 1992).

193 Tim Weiner, *Legacy of Ashes: The History of the CIA* (London: Allen Lane, 2007), 514.

194 Barton Gellman and Greg Miller, "U.S. Spy Network's Successes, Failures and Objectives Detailed in 'Black Budget' Summary," *Washington Post*, August 30, 2013, www.washingtonpost.com/world/national-security/black-budget-summary-details-us-spy-networks-successes-failures-and-objectives/2013/08/29/7e57bb78-10ab-11e3-8cdd-bcdc09410972_story.html.

195 Weiner, *Legacy of Ashes*, 510.

196 Steven Erlanger, "An American Ambassador Who Plunged Into Arab Life," *New York Times*, September 15, 2012, World/Middle East section, www.nytimes.com/2012/09/16/world/middleeast/us-ambassador-to-libya-knew-the-ways-of-the-arab-street.html.

197 John S. Service, *Lost Chance in China: The World War II Despatches of John S. Service.*, ed. Joseph Esherick, 1st. ed. (New York: Random House, 1974).

198 John N. Hart, *The Making of an Army "Old China Hand": A Memoir of Colonel David D. Barrett*, vol. 27, China Research Monograph (Berkeley: Institute of East Asian Studies, University of California–Berkeley, Center for Chinese Studies, 1985).

199   Rowan Callick, "Malcolm Fraser Praises China's 'Stability and Sense of Purpose,'" *The Australian*, September 26, 2012, www.theaustralian.com.au/national-affairs/foreign-affairs/malcolm-fraser-praises-chinas-stability-and-sense-of-purpose/story-fn59nm2j-1226481377406.

200   Chas Freeman, *Interesting Times: China, America, and the Shifting Balance of Prestige* (Charlottesville, VA: Just World Books, 2013).

201   Edward S. Steinfeld, *Playing Our Game: Why China's Rise Doesn't Threaten the West* (New York: Oxford University Press, 2010); Peter Nolan, *Is China Buying the World?* (Cambridge: Polity Press, 2012).

202   Graham Allison, Robert D. Blackwill, and Ali Wyne, *Lee Kuan Yew: The Grand Master's Insights on China, the United States, and the World* (Cambridge, MA: MIT Press, 2013), 3, 7.

203   Will Hutton, *The Writing on the Wall: China and the West in the 21st Century* (London: Abacus, 2008).

204   Jamil Anderlini and Lucy Hornby, "China Overtakes US as World's Largest Goods Trader," *Financial Times*, January 10, 2014, www.ft.com/cms/s/0/7c2dbd70-79a6-11e3-b381-00144feabdc0.html?ftcamp=crm/email/2014110/nbe/ChinaBusiness/product&siteedition=uk#axzz2pzbVmj1p.

205   "China Warning over Iran Sanctions," *BBC News*, February 4, 2010, http://news.bbc.co.uk/1/hi/world/middle_east/8497876.stm.

206   Liang Xiaodong, "The Six-Party Talks at a Glance," *Arms Control Association*, May 2012, www.armscontrol.org/factsheets/6partytalks.

207   The Han are the dominant ethnic group and constitute about 92 percent of China's population.

208   Shirley A. Kan, *U.S.–China Counterterrorism Cooperation: Issues for U.S. Policy*, CRS Report for Congress (Washington, DC: Congressional Research Service, July 15, 2010), www.fas.org/sgp/crs/terror/RL33001.pdf.

209   Chien-Peng Chung, "China's 'War on Terror': September 11 and Uighur Separatism," *Foreign Affairs*, accessed January 12, 2014, www.foreignaffairs.com/articles/58030/chien-peng-chung/chinas-war-on-terror-september-11-and-uighur-separatism; Preeti Bhattacharji, "Uighurs and China's Xinjiang Region," *Council on Foreign Relations*, May 29, 2012, www.cfr.org/china/uighurs-chinas-xinjiang-region/p16870.

210   Mark E. Manyin, Stephen Dagget, Ben Dolven, Susan V. Lawrence, Michael F. Martin, Ronald O'Rourke, and Bruce Vaughn, *Pivot to the Pacific? Obama Administration's "Rebalancing" toward Asia*, CRS Report for Congress (Washington, DC: Congressional Research Service, March 28, 2012), www.fas.org/sgp/crs/natsec/R42448.pdf.

211   Goldberg, "Hillary Clinton: Chinese System Is Doomed."

212   Erich Follath, "Baden Wir in Unserem Ruhm (We're Bathing in Our Glory)," *Der Spiegel*, September 1, 1997, www.spiegel.de/spiegel/print/d-8777161.html.

213   Gore Vidal, *Perpetual War for Perpetual Peace: How We Got to Be so Hated – Causes of Conflict in the Last Empire* (Forest Row: Clairview, 2002).

214   Amnesty International USA Washington Office, *Human Rights and US Security Assistance* (London: Amnesty International Publications, 1996), 1; Jeremy Scahill, *Dirty Wars: The World Is a Battlefield* (London: Serpent's Tail, 2013).

215   William Blum, *Killing Hope: U.S. Military and CIA Interventions since World War II* (Monroe, ME: Common Courage Press, 1995).

216   Joseph A. Schumpeter, *Imperialism and Social Classes*, ed. Paul M. Sweezy, trans. Heinz Norden (Oxford: Oxford University Press, 1951).

217   Arnold Toynbee, *America and the World Revolution; Public Lectures Delivered at the University of Pennsylvania, Spring 1961* (London: Oxford University Press, 1962), 16.

218 Glenn Greenwald, *With Liberty and Justice for Some: How the Law Is Used to Destroy Equality and Protect the Powerful*, Reprint ed. (London: Picador, 2012); Joseph E. Stiglitz, "Of the 1%, by the 1%, for the 1%," *Vanity Fair*, May 1, 2011, www.vanityfair.com/society/features/2011/05/top-one-percent-201105.
219 Jon Swaine, "Automatic for the People," *Telegraph.co.uk*, July 10, 2013, http://s.telegraph.co.uk/graphics/ar-15/index.html; Philip Rucker, "Biden, in Connecticut, Makes Fiery Plea for Gun Control in Speech near Newtown," *Washington Post*, February 21, 2013, www.washingtonpost.com/politics/a-fiery-biden-shames-lawmakers-worried-about-political-survival-in-gun-debate/2013/02/21/427025a6-7c3a-11e2-82e8-61a46c2cde3d_story.html?hpid=z1&wpisrc=nl_pmpolitics.
220 Dower, *Japan in War and Peace*, 320.
221 Jack S. Levy, "Declining Power and the Preventive Motivation for War," *World Politics* 40, no. 1 (1987): 82–107.

Bibliography

"78.8%受访者认为人情关系复杂阻碍优秀人才回国 Survey Shows Complex Social Relations Keeps Talent from Returning Home to China." *Xinhua Online*新华网, September 6, 2013. http://news.xinhuanet.com/hr/2013-09/06/c_125335728.htm.

2006 Report to Congress of the US–China Economic and Security Review Commission, November2006. Washington, DC: US Government Printing Office.

Aid, Matthew M. "The NSA's Data Haul Is Bigger Than You Can Possibly Imagine." *Foreign Policy*,August 15, 2013. www.foreignpolicy.com/articles/2013/08/15/the_nsas_data_haul_is_bigger_than_you_can_possibly_imagine.

Allen, Charles F., and Jonathan Portis. *The Comeback Kid: The Life and Career of Bill Clinton*. New York: Citadel Press, 1992.

Allison, Graham. "Thucydides's Trap Has Been Sprung in the Pacific." *Financial Times,* August 21, 2012. www.ft.com/cms/s/0/5d695b5a-ead3-11e1-984b-00144feab49a.html#axzz24Ft4mczq.

Allison, Graham, Robert D. Blackwill, and Ali Wyne. *Lee Kuan Yew: The Grand Master's Insights on China, the United States, and the World*. Cambridge, MA: MIT Press, 2013.

Amnesty International USA. *Human Rights and US Security Assistance*. Washington, DC: Amnesty International Publications, 1996.

Anderlini, Jamil, and Lucy Hornby. "China Overtakes US as World's Largest Goods Trader." *Financial Times*, January 10, 2014. www.ft.com/cms/s/0/7c2dbd70-79a6-11e3-b381-00144feabdc0.html?ftcamp=crm/email/2014110/nbe/ChinaBusiness/product&siteedition=uk#axzz2pzbVmj1p.

Arends, Brett. "IMF Bombshell: Age of America Nears End." *Market Watch/Wall Street Journal*, April 25, 2011. http://articles.marketwatch.com/2011-04-25/commentary/30714377_1_imf-chinese-economy-international-monetary-fund.

Ash, Robert. John W. Garver, and Penelope Prime, eds. *Taiwan's Democracy: Economic and Political Challenges*. New York and Abingdon: Routledge, 2011.

Associated Press. "Japan Unveils New Carrier-like Warship, the Largest in Its Navy since World War II." *Washington Post*, August 6, 2013, World section. www.washingtonpost.com/world/asia_pacific/japan-unveils-new-carrier-like-warship-the-largest-in-its-navy-since-world-war-ii/2013/08/06/8fae14d8-fe79-11e2-8294-0ee5075b840d_story.html.

Bader, Jeffrey A. *Obama and China's Rise: An Insider's Account of America's Asia Strategy*. Washington, DC: Brookings Institution Press, 2013.

Bagdikian, Ben H. *The New Media Monopoly*. Boston, MA: Beacon Press, 2004.

Baker, C. Edwin. *Media Concentration and Democracy*. New York: Cambridge University Press, 2007.

Barstow, David. "Behind TV Analysts, Pentagon's Hidden Hand." *New York Times,* April 20, 2008. https://mail-attachment.googleusercontent.com/attachment/?ui=2& ik=925828fbf3&view=att&th=1380e4a89aa76ca1&attid=0.1&disp=safe&zw&sadui e=AG9B_P8M-pEX1ScT_7aJrn_zjECe&sadet=1340271062750&sads=vmhcCz6wR 4qRdXw44Q6ZqP4Crmk.

Barstow, David. "One Man's Military-Industrial-Media Complex." *New York Times*, April 20, 2008. https://mail-attachment.googleusercontent.com/attachment/? ui=2&ik=925828fbf3&view=att&th=1380e4a89aa76ca1&attid=0.2&disp=safe&zw &saduie=AG9B_P8M-pEX1ScT_7aJrn_zjECe&sadet=1340270910037&sads=yUW zPwhWF-VM4aoebIv8hVC9tZA.

Bhagwati, Jagdish. "US Pacific Trade Pact Aims to Exclude China." *Shanghai Daily,* January 6, 2012. www.china.org.cn/opinion/2012-01/06/content_24339500.htm.

Bhattacharji, Preeti. "Uighurs and China's Xinjiang Region." *Council on Foreign Relations*, May 29, 2012. www.cfr.org/china/uighurs-chinas-xinjiang-region/p16870.

Bix, Herbert P. *Hirohito and the Making of Modern Japan*. 1st Perennial edn. New York: HarperCollins, 2001.

Blum, William. *Rogue State: A Guide to the World's Only Superpower*. Monroe, ME: Common Courage Press, 2000.

Blum, William. *Killing Hope: U.S. Military and CIA Interventions since World War II*. Monroe, ME: Common Courage Press, 1995.

Brzezinski, Zbigniew. *Strategic Vision: America and the Crisis of Global Power*. New York: Basic Books, 2012.

Buckley, John. *Air Power in the Age of Total War*. Warfare and History series. London: UCL Press, 1999.

Buzan, Barry. *People, States and Fear: An Agenda for International Security Studies in the Post-Cold War Era*. 2nd edn. London: Harvester Wheatsheaf, 1991.

Callahan, William A. "National Insecurities: Humiliation, Salvation, and Chinese Nationalism." *Alternatives: Global, Local, Political* 29, no. 2(2004): 199–218.

Callick, Rowan. "Malcolm Fraser Praises China's 'Stability and Sense of Purpose.'" *The Australian.*September 26, 2012. www.theaustralian.com.au/national-affairs/for eign-affairs/malcolm-fraser-praises-chinas-stability-and-sense-of-purpose/story-fn59n m2j-1226481377406.

Chang, Iris. *The Rape of Nanking: The Forgotten Holocaust of World War II*. New edn. London: Penguin, 1998.

Cheung, Tai Ming. "Reforming the Dragon's Tail." In *China's Military Faces the Future*, ed. James R. Lilley and David L. Shambaugh, 228–246. Armonk, NY: M. E. Sharpe, 1999.

"China Sticks to No-First-Use of Nuclear Weapons: White Paper." *Xinhua News*, March 31, 2011. http://news.xinhuanet.com/english2010/china/2011-03/31/c_138069 09.htm.

"China Upset over Japan Comments." *BBCNews*, February 22, 2012, www.bbc.co.uk/ news/world-asia-17125934.

"China Warning over Iran Sanctions." *BBC News*, February 4, 2010, http://news.bbc. co.uk/1/hi/world/middle_east/8497876.stm.

"China's National Defense in 2010." *Xinhua/English.news.cn*, March 31, 2011. http:// news.xinhuanet.com/english2010/china/2011-03/31/c_13806851_3.htm.

Chung, Chien-Peng. "China's 'War on Terror': September 11 and Uighur Separatism." *Foreign Affairs.* Accessed January 12, 2014. www.foreignaffairs.com/articles/58030/chien-peng-chung/chinas-war-on-terror-september-11-and-uighur-separatism.

Clinton, Hillary. "America's Pacific Century." *Foreign Policy*, November 2011. www.foreignpolicy.com/articles/2011/10/11/americas_pacific_century.

Cockburn, Andrew."Follow the Money." In *The Pentagon Labyrinth*. Washington, DC: Center for Defense Information, 2011.

Cunningham, Philip J. "Japan's Revisionist History." *Los Angeles Times*, April 11, 2005. http://articles.latimes.com/2005/apr/11/opinion/oe-cunningham11.

Dempsey, Martin E. "Joint Operational Access Concept." Department of Defense, January 17, 2012. www.defense.gov/pubs/pdfs/JOAC_Jan%202012_Signed.pdf.

Dower, John W. *Ways of Forgetting.* New York: The New Press, 2011.

Dower, John W. *Embracing Defeat: Japan in the Wake of World War II.* New edn. New York: W. W. Norton & Co., 2000.

Dower, John W. *Japan in War and Peace: Essays on History, Culture and Race.* London: Fontana, 1996.

eDiplomacy at the U.S. Department of State, Video. 2012. www.youtube.com/watch?v=oVTtm7d6EiE&feature=youtube_gdata_player.

Eisenhower, Dwight D. "Military-Industrial Complex Speech,"1960. www.h-net.org/~hst306/documents/indust.html.

Elliot, M., and B. Cohn. "A Head for Diplomacy? Clinton: One Year In, He's Still Struggling to Get His Mind around Foreign Policy." *Newsweek*, March 28, 1994.

Erlanger, Steven. "An American Ambassador Who Plunged Into Arab Life." *New York Times*, September 15, 2012, World/Middle East section. www.nytimes.com/2012/09/16/world/middleeast/us-ambassador-to-libya-knew-the-ways-of-the-arab-street.html.

Etzioni, Amitai. "Who Authorized Preparations for War with China?" *Yale Journal of International Affairs*, 2013. www.gwu.edu/~sigur/assets/docs/Etzioni_article.pdf.

Fairbank, John K., Edwin Oldfather Reischauer, and Albert Morton Craig. *East Asia: Tradition and Transformation.* Revised edn. Boston, MA: Houghton Mifflin, 1989.

Fifield, Anna. "US Bill to Rebuild Iraq Reaches $138bn." *Financial Times*, March 18, 2013. www.ft.com/cms/s/0/7f435f04-8c05-11e2-b001-00144feabdc0.html#axzz2Nt10rkoG.

Follath, Erich. "Baden Wir in Unserem Ruhm [We're Bathing in Our Glory]." *Der Spiegel*, September 1, 1997. www.spiegel.de/spiegel/print/d-8777161.html.

Foreign Relations of the United States 1955–1957. Vol. 3, n.d. Washington, DC: US Government Printing Office.

Fraser, Malcolm. "Australia–US Relations in the 'Asian Century': To Avoid Unnecessary and Ill Advised Conflict." Speech, Melbourne University, September 25, 2012.

Fravel, M. Taylor. *Strong Borders, Secure Nation: Cooperation and Conflict in China's Territorial Disputes.* Princeton Studies in International History and Politics. Princeton, NJ: Princeton University Press, 2008.

Freeman, Chas. *Interesting Times: China, America, and the Shifting Balance of Prestige.* Charlottesville, VA: Just World Books, 2013.

Friedberg, Aaron L. *A Contest for Supremacy: China, America, and the Struggle for Mastery in Asia.* 1st edn. New York: W.W. Norton, 2011.

Frieman, Wendy. "The Understated Revolution in Chinese Science and Technology." In *China's Military Faces the Future*, 247–267. Armonk, NY: M. E. Sharpe, 1999.

Gellman, Barton, and Greg Miller. "U.S. Spy Network's Successes, Failures and Objectives Detailed in 'Black Budget' Summary." *Washington Post,* August 30, 2013, www.washingtonpost.com/world/national-security/black-budget-summary-det ails-us-spy-networks-successes-failures-and-objectives/2013/08/29/7e57bb78-10ab-11e 3-8cdd-bcdc09410972_story.html.

"German Historian: Japan's Shrine Visit a Great Mistake." *CCTV News,* October 19, 2012. http://english.cntv.cn/program/newsupdate/20121019/101756.shtml.

Giacomo, Carol. "How Mitt Romney Would Force-Feed the Pentagon." *New York Times,* August 25, 2012, Opinion/Sunday Review section. www.nytimes.com/2012/08/26/opinion/sunday/how-mr-romney-would-force-feed-the-pentagon.html.

Goldberg, Jeffrey. "Hillary Clinton: Chinese System Is Doomed, Leaders on a 'Fool's Errand.'" *The Atlantic,* May 10, 2011. www.theatlantic.com/international/archive/2011/05/hillary-clinton-chinese-system-is-doomed-leaders-on-a-fools-errand/238591/.

Greenwald, Glenn. "XKeyscore: NSA Tool Collects 'Nearly Everything a User Does on the Internet.'" *The Guardian,* July 31, 2013. www.theguardian.com/world/2013/jul/31/nsa-top-secret-program-online-data.

Greenwald, Glenn. *With Liberty and Justice for Some: How the Law Is Used to Destroy Equality and Protect the Powerful.* Reprint edn. London and New York: Picador, 2012.

Grenier, John. *The First Way of War: American War Making on the Frontier, 1607–1814.* 1st edn. Cambridge: Cambridge University Press, 2008.

Grunfeld, A. Tom. "Tibet and the United States." In *Contemporary Tibet,* ed. Barry Sautman and June Teufel Dreyer, 205–349. Armonk, NY: M. E. Sharpe, 2006.

Gustin, Sam. "Game Changers." *Time,* September 2, 2011. www.time.com/time/specia ls/packages/article/0,28804,2091589_2091591_2091592,00.html

Halper, Stefan. *The Beijing Consensus.* New York: Basic Books, 2010.

Harper, Matthew. "Chinese Missiles and the Walmart Factor." *U.S. Naval Institute, Proceedings Magazine,* July 2011. www.usni.org/magazines/proceedings/2011-07/chi nese-missiles-and-walmart-factor.

Harris, Gardiner. "Cameron Calls Colonial-Era Massacre in India 'Shameful.'" *New York Times,* February 20, 2013, World/Asia Pacific section. www.nytimes.com/2013/02/21/world/asia/cameron-calls-colonial-era-massacre-in-india-shameful.html.

Hart, John N. *The Making of an Army "Old China Hand": A Memoir of Colonel David D. Barrett.* Vol. 27. China Research Monograph. Berkeley: Institute of East Asian Studies, University of California–Berkeley, Center for Chinese Studies, 1985.

Herman, Edward S., and Noam Chomsky. *Manufacturing Consent: The Political Economy of the Mass Media.* New York: Pantheon Books, 2002.

Hessler, Peter. "Tibet Through Chinese Eyes." *The Atlantic,* February1999. www.thea tlantic.com/magazine/archive/1999/02/tibet-through-chinese-eyes/306395/.

Hofilena, John. "Anti-Japan Sentiment Sharply Growing in China, South Korea according to Polls." *Japan Daily Press,* July 12, 2013. http://japandailypress.com/a nti-japan-sentiment-sharply-growing-in-china-south-korea-according-to-polls-1232229/.

Hughes, Christopher. "Japan: Military Modernization in Search of a 'Normal Security Role.'" In *Strategic Asia 2005–06: Military Modernisation in an Era of Uncertainty,* ed. A. J. Tellis and M. Wills. Washington, DC: National Bureau of Asian Research, 2005, 105–134.

Hutton, Will. *The Writing on the Wall: China and the West in the 21st Century.* London: Abacus, 2008.

International Institute for Strategic Studies. *The Military Balance*. London: Institute for Strategic Studies, 2013.

International Institute for Strategic Studies. *The Military Balance 2012*. Pap/Chrt. Abingdon: Routledge, 2012.

Jacques, Martin. *When China Rules the World: The Rise of the Middle Kingdom and the End of the Western World*. London: Allen Lane, 2009.

"Japan PM Abe Wants to Replace Landmark War Apology." *Reuters*, December 31, 2012. http://uk.reuters.com/article/2012/12/31/uk-japan-apology-idUKBRE8BU0302 0121231.

Kagawa, Marcie. "Oliver Stone Likens Japan to U.S. Vassal." *Japan Times*, June 15, 2013. www.japantimes.co.jp/news/2013/06/15/national/oliver-stone-likens-japan-to-u-s-vassal/#.UgygplOE42E.

Kan, Shirley A. *U.S.-China Counterterrorism Cooperation: Issues for U.S. Policy*. CRS Report for Congress. Congressional Research Service, July 15, 2010. www.fas.org/sgp/crs/terror/RL33001.pdf.

Kang, David. *East Asia Before the West: Five Centuries of Trade and Tribute*. New York: Columbia University Press, 2012.

Katz, Ian. "U.S. Government Debt Reaches $16 Trillion for First Time." *Bloomberg*, September 4, 2012. www.bloomberg.com/news/2012-09-04/u-s-government-debt-reaches-16-trillion-for-first-time.html.

Kinzer, Stephen. *Overthrow: America's Century of Regime Change from Hawaii to Iraq*. Reprint. New York: Times Books, 2007.

Kissinger, Henry A. "The Future of U.S.–Chinese Relations." *Foreign Affairs*, March 1, 2012. www.foreignaffairs.com/articles/137245/henry-a-kissinger/the-future-of-us-chinese-relations.

Knaus, John Kenneth. *Orphans of the Cold War: America and the Tibetan Struggle for Survival*. New York: Public Affairs, 1999.

Kugler, Richard L., and Ellen L. Frost. *The Global Century: Globalization and National Security*. Vol. 2. Washington, DC: National Defense University Press, 2001.

Kulacki, Gregory. "China Still Committed to No First Use of Nuclear Weapons." *Union of Concerned Scientists: All Things Nuclear*, April 23, 2013. http://allthings nuclear.org/china-still-committed-to-no-first-use-of-nuclear-weapons/.

Lam, Lana, and Stephen Chen. "Exclusive: Snowden Reveals More US Cyberspying Details." *South China Morning Post*, June 23, 2013. www.scmp.com/news/hon g-kong/article/1266777/exclusive-snowden-safe-hong-kong-more-us-cyberspying-deta ils-revealed?page=all.

Laris, Karklis. "U.S. Military Expansion in Southeast Asia." *Washington Post*, March 25, 2012. www.washingtonpost.com/world/national-security/2012/03/25/gIQASFQX aS_graphic.html.

Layne, Christopher. "The Global Power Shift from West to East." *The National Interest*, April 28, 2012. http://nationalinterest.org/article/the-global-power-shift-wes t-east-6796?page=1.

Levy, Jack S. "Declining Power and the Preventive Motivation for War." *World Politics* 40, no. 1(1987): 82–107.

Liang Jialin, and Jiang Han. "Overfishing Pushes 80% of Chinese Fishermen towards Bankruptcy." 中外对话 *Chinadialogue*, October 19, 2012.

Liang Xiaodong "The Six-Party Talks at a Glance." *Arms Control Association*, May 2012. www.armscontrol.org/factsheets/6partytalks.

Lieberthal, Kenneth. "The American Pivot to Asia." *Foreign Policy*,December 21, 2011. www.foreignpolicy.com/articles/2011/12/21/the_american_pivot_to_asia.

Luciani, Giacomo. "The Economic Content of Security." *Journal of Public Policy* 8, no. 2(1989): 151–173.

Mackerras, Colin P. "PRC: Background Paper on the Situation of the Tibetan Population." Writenet. UNHCR, February 2005. www.unhcr.org/cgi-bin/texis/vtx/ref world/rwmain/opendocpdf.pdf?docid=423ea9094.

Manyin, Mark E., Stephen Daggett, Ben Dolven, Susan V. Lawrence, Michael F. Martin, Ronald O'Rourke, and Bruce Vaughn. *Pivot to the Pacific? Obama Administration's "Rebalancing" toward Asia*. CRS Report for Congress, March 28, 2012. www.fas.org/sgp/crs/natsec/R42448.pdf.

Martin, Laurence. "Can There Be National Security in an Insecure Age?" *Encounter* 60, no. 3(1983): 11–19.

McMaster, H. R. "Pipe Dream of Easy Wars." *International Herald Tribune*, July 22, 2013, op ed. section.

McNamara, Robert S. "Apocalypse Soon." *Foreign Policy*, May 5, 2005. www.for eignpolicy.com/articles/2005/05/05/apocalypse_soon?wp_login_redirect=0.

Mearsheimer, J. J. "The Rise of China Will Not Be Peaceful at All." *The Australian*, November 18, 2005. www.ou.edu/uschina/SASD/SASD2005/2005readings/Clash% 20of%20the%20Titans.pdf.

Morishima, Michio. *Why Has Japan "Succeeded"?: Western Technology and the Japanese Ethos*. Cambridge: Cambridge University Press, 1982.

Morris, Errol. *The Fog Of War: Eleven Lessons from the Life of Robert McNamara*. *DVD*. Sony Pictures Home Entertainment, 2004.

Nolan, Peter. "Imperial Archipelagos." *New Left Review* II, no. 80(2013): 77–95.

Nolan, Peter. *A New Peloponnesian War: China, the West and the South China Seas*. Cambridge: Cambridge University Press, 2012.

Nolan, Peter. *China, Western Colonialism and the UN Convention on the Law of the Sea*. Cambridge: Cambridge University Press, 2012.

Nolan, Peter. *Is China Buying the World?* Cambridge: Polity Press, 2012.

Norbu, Dawa. *China's Tibet Policy*. Durham East Asia Series. Richmond: Curzon, 2001.

Nye, Joseph S. "The 'Nye Report': Six Years Later." *International Relations of the Asia-Pacific* 1, no. 1(2001): 95–103.

"Obama Meets Hatoyama in Japan." *Bloomberg Businessweek*, November 27, 2009. www.businessweek.com/globalbiz/content/nov2009/gb20091113_321964.htm.

Onishi, Norimitsu. "Japan's Textbooks Reflect Revised History." *New York Times*, April 1, 2007, International/Asia Pacific section. www.nytimes.com/2007/04/01/ world/asia/01japan.html.

Paal, Douglas. "Territorial Disputes in Asian Waters." *Carnegie Endowment for International Peace*, October 16, 2012. http://carnegieendowment.org/2012/10/16/ter ritorial-disputes-in-asian-waters/e1ex##.

Phillips, Tom. "China Lays Bare Its Military Might with an Attack on US Ambition." *Telegraph.co.uk,*April 16, 2013. www.telegraph.co.uk/news/worldnews/asia/china/ 9998111/China-lays-bare-its-military-might-with-an-attack-on-US-ambition.html.

Reed, John. "Surrounded: How the US Is Encircling China with Military Bases." *Foreign Policy*, August 20, 2013.

"Report of Hu Jintao to the 18th CPC National Congress." *China.org.cn*, November 16, 2012. www.china.org.cn/china/18th_cpc_congress/2012-11/16/content_2713 7540_11.htm.

Rice, Condoleeza. "Rice's Remarks at the Republican National Convention, August 2012," August 29, 2012. www.cfr.org/us-election-2012/rices-remarks-republican-na tional-convention-august-2012/p28896.

Rice, Condoleeza. "Rethinking the National Interest: American Realism for a New World." *Foreign Affairs* 87, no. 4(2008): 2–26.

Rice, Condoleeza. "Promoting the National Interest." *Foreign Affairs* 79, no. 1(2000): 45.

Romanus, Charles F., and Riley Sunderland. *Stilwell's Mission to China*. Washington, DC: Office of the Chief of Military History, Dept. of the Army, 1953.

Ron Paul Interview in Congress. Video, 2010. www.youtube.com/watch?v=bAYvv2x T8yI&feature=youtube_gdata_player.

Rositzke, Harry August. *The CIA's Secret Operations: Espionage, Counterespionage, and Covert Action*. Boulder, CO: Westview Press, 1988.

Ross, Robert S. "China's Naval Nationalism: Sources, Prospects, and the U.S. Response." *International Security* 34, no. 2(2009): 46–81.

Roy, J. Stapleton. "Strategic Challenges for the US–China Relationship." East-West Center in Hawaii, February 13, 2013. https://vimeo.com/59754895.

Rucker, Philip. "Biden, in Connecticut, Makes Fiery Plea for Gun Control in Speech near Newtown." *Washington Post*, February 21, 2013. www.washingtonpost.com/p olitics/a-fiery-biden-shames-lawmakers-worried-about-political-survival-in-gun-debate/ 2013/02/21/427025a6-7c3a-11e2-82e8-61a46c2cde3d_story.html?hpid=z1&wpisrc=nl_ pmpolitics.

Sanger, David E. "U.S. Accuses China's Military in Cyberattacks." *New York Times*, May 6, 2013, World/Asia Pacific section. www.nytimes.com/2013/05/07/world/asia/ us-accuses-chinas-military-in-cyberattacks.html.

Sanger, David E. "Obama Ordered Wave of Cyberattacks Against Iran." *New York Times*, June 1, 2012, World/Middle East section. www.nytimes.com/2012/06/01/ world/middleeast/obama-ordered-wave-of-cyberattacks-against-iran.html.

Sanger, David E. "Mayor Who Faulted Hirohito Is Shot." *New York Times*, January 19, 1990. www.nytimes.com/1990/01/19/world/mayor-who-faulted-hirohito-is-shot. html?sec=.

Sautman, Barry. "'Demographic Annihilation' and Tibet." In *Contemporary Tibet*, ed. Barry Sautman and June Teufel Dreyer. Armonk, NY: M. E. Sharpe, 2006, 230–257.

Scahill, Jeremy. *Dirty Wars: The World Is a Battlefield*. London: Serpent's Tail, 2013.

Scahill, Jeremy. *Blackwater: The Rise of the World's Most Powerful Mercenary Army*. London: Serpent's Tail, 2008.

Schumpeter, Joseph A. *Imperialism and Social Classes*. Ed. Paul M. Sweezy. Trans. Heinz Norden. Oxford: Oxford University Press, 1951.

Service, John S. *Lost Chance in China: The World War II Despatches of John S. Service*. Ed. Joseph Esherick. 1st edn. New York: Random House, 1974.

Shambaugh, David. "China's Post-Deng Military Leadership." In *China's Military Faces the Future*, ed. James R. Lilley and David L. Shambaugh, 11–35. Armonk, NY: M. E. Sharpe, 1999.

SIPRI Yearbook 2013: Armaments, Disarmament and International Security. Stockholm, Sweden: Stockholm International Peace Research Institute, 2013. www.sipri. org/yearbook/2013/files/SIPRIYB13Summary.pdf.

Sledge, Matt. "Obama, Romney Both Promise an Increase in Military Spending." *Huffington Post,* October 23, 2012. www.huffingtonpost.com/2012/10/23/military-sp ending-obama-romney_n_2006266.html.

Smil, Vaclav. *Global Catastrophes and Trends: The Next Fifty Years.* Cambridge, MA: MIT Press, 2008.

Sorcher, Sara. "Senators Blast Publicity of Cyberattack on Iran." *NationalJournal. com,* June 5, 2012. www.nationaljournal.com/daily/senators-blast-publicity-of-cy berattack-on-iran-20120605.

"Statement by Prime Minister Tomiichi Murayama 'On the Occasion of the 50th Anniversary of the War's End.'" *Ministry of Foreign Affairs of Japan,* August 15, 1995. www.mofa.go.jp/announce/press/pm/murayama/9508.html.

"Statement of Principles." *Project for the New American Century,* June 3, 1997. www. newamericancentury.org/statementofprinciples.htm.

Steinfeld, Edward S. *Playing Our Game: Why China's Rise Doesn't Threaten the West.* New York: Oxford University Press, 2010.

Stiglitz, Joseph E. "Of the 1%, by the 1%, for the 1%." *Vanity Fair,* May 1, 2011. www.vanityfair.com/society/features/2011/05/top-one-percent-201105.

Sun Yat-sen, 孙中山. "Pan Asianism 大亚细亚主义." Speech, Kobe, Japan, November 28, 1924.

Su Xiaohui, 苏晓晖. "China Should Have No Illusion That the US Will Help Resolve the Dispute." *China Institute of International Studies,* October 17, 2012. www.ciis. org.cn/english/2012-10/17/content_5408981.htm.

Suzuki, Shogo. *Civilization and Empire: China and Japan's Encounter with European International Society.* London: Routledge, 2009.

Swaine, Jon. "Automatic for the People." *Telegraph.co.uk,* July 10, 2013. http://s.tele graph.co.uk/graphics/ar-15/index.html.

"Taiwan and China at Crossroads." *BBC,* May 21, 2010. www.bbc.co.uk/news/ 10122592.

"Taiwan to Ease Rules for Chinese Banks." *Financial Times,* April 2, 2013. www.ft. com/cms/s/0/9a3c8598-9b2c-11e2-97ad-00144feabdc0.html?ftcamp=published_links %2Frss%2Fworld_asia-pacific_china%2Ffeed%2F%2Fproduct&ftcamp=crm/email/ 201342/nbe/ChinaBusiness/product#axzz2PJLUuTbj.

Terazono, Emiko. "Global Fish Prices Leap to All-Time High." *Financial Times,* June 18, 2013. www.ft.com/cms/s/0/af42937a-d811-11e2-9495-00144feab7de.html#a xzz2WPcGmvo8.

"The Black Budget: Top Secret U.S. Intelligence Funding – Interactive Graphic." *Washington Post,* August 31, 2013. www.washingtonpost.com/wp-srv/special/na tional/black-budget/.

"The Diversified Employment of China's Armed Forces." *PRC Ministry of National Defense,* April 16, 2013. http://eng.mod.gov.cn/TopNews/2013-04/16/content_444275 0.htm.

"Timeline of Media Mega Mergers (1986–2004)." *Globalization101.* Accessed July 17, 2013. www.globalization101.org/timeline-of-media-mega-mergers-1986-2004.

Toynbee, Arnold, Daisaku Ikeda, and Richard L. Gage. *Choose Life: A Dialogue.* [British Commonwealth edn]. London: Oxford University Press, 1976.

Toynbee, Arnold. *America and the World Revolution: Public Lectures Delivered at the University of Pennsylvania, Spring 1961.* London: Oxford University Press, 1962.

Trager, Frank N., and Frank L. Simonie. "An Introduction to the Study of National Security." In *National Security and American Society*, ed. Frank N. Trager and Philip S. Kronenberg, 36. Lawrence: University Press of Kansas, 1973.

Tucker, John. "Japanese Confucian Philosophy." In *The Stanford Encyclopedia of Philosophy*, ed. Edward N. Zalta, Summer 2012. http://plato.stanford.edu/archives/sum2012/entries/japanese-confucian/.

"UN Security Council: Resolutions, Presidential Statements, Meeting Records, SC Press Releases." Accessed March 27, 2013. https://www.un.org/Depts/dhl/resguide/scact.htm.

"U.S. Report Accuses China, Russia of Cyber Attacks." *Washington Post,* November 3, 2011. www.washingtonpost.com/world/us-report-accuses-china-russia-of-cyber-attacks/2011/11/03/gIQAuT2djM_video.html.

"US Security Strategy for the East Asia-Pacific Region." Department of Defense, Office of International Security Affairs, February 1995.

Van Schaik, Sam. *Tibet: A History.* New Haven, CT: Yale University Press, 2011.

Vidal, Gore. *Perpetual War for Perpetual Peace: How We Got to Be so Hated – Causes of Conflict in the Last Empire.* Forest Row: Clairview, 2002.

Vine, David. *Island of Shame: The Secret History of the U.S. Military Base on Diego Garcia.* Princeton, NJ: Princeton University Press, 2009.

Wang, Zheng. *Never Forget National Humiliation: Historical Memory in Chinese Politics and Foreign Relations.* New York: Columbia University Press, 2012.

Weiner, Tim. "Robert S. McNamara, Architect of a Futile War, Dies at 93." *New York Times*, July 7, 2009, US section. www.nytimes.com/2009/07/07/us/07mcnamara.html?pagewanted=6&_r=1&th&emc=th.

Weiner, Tim. *Legacy of Ashes: The History of the CIA.* London: Allen Lane, 2007.

Weiner, Tim. *Blank Check: The Pentagon's Black Budget.* New York: Warner Books, 1991.

Weiner, Tim. "Blank Check: The Pentagon's Black Budget. Interview by Brian Lamb," October 21, 1990. www.booknotes.org/Watch/14257-1/Tim+Weiner.aspx.

Weissman, Steve. *Last Tangle in Tibet.* N.p.: Pacific Studies Center, 1973.

Westlake, Adam. "Chinese Survey Reveals 87% of Nation's Public Has Negative Opinion of Japan." *Japan Daily Press*, December 27, 2012. http://japandailypress.com/chinese-survey-reveals-87-of-nations-public-has-negative-opinion-of-japan-2720499/.

Wheeler, Winslow. "Decoding the Defense Budget." In *The Pentagon Labyrinth*, ed. Center for Defense Information. Washington, DC: Center for Defense Information, 2011.

Whiting, Robert. "Saying UnSorry." *Foreign Policy*, January 30, 2013.

Whitlock, Craig. "U.S., Australia to Broaden Military Ties amid Pentagon Pivot to SE Asia." *Washington Post*, March 27, 2012. www.washingtonpost.com/world/national-security/us-to-expand-ties-with-australia-as-it-aims-to-shift-forces-closer-to-se-asia/2012/03/19/gIQAPSXlcS_story.html?hpid=z1.

Wilsdon, James, and James Keeley. *China: The Next Science Superpower?* London: Demos, 2007.

Xi Jinping, 习近平. "China's New Party Chief Xi Jinping's Speech." *BBC News*, November 15, 2012. www.bbc.co.uk/news/world-asia-china-20338586.

Xu Mingfu, and Yuan Feng. "The Tibet Question: A New Cold War." In *Contemporary Tibet*, ed. Barry Sautman and June Teufel Dreyer, 310. Armonk, NY: M. E. Sharpe, 2006.

Yamazaki, Jane. *Japanese Apologies for World War II: A Rhetorical Study*. London: Routledge, 2005.

Yang Jiechi, 杨洁篪. "杨洁篪在中美关系研讨会上发表 Speech by Yang Jiechi at US–China Relations Conference 2012." 中国新闻网 *China News Online,* March 8, 2012. www.chinanews.com/gn/2012/03-08/3727598.shtml.

Zheng Bijian, 郑必坚. "China's Peaceful Rise and US–China Relations." In 郑必坚论集 *Zheng Bijian Collection of Speeches*, vol. 3: 1350–1360. 上海人民出版社 Shanghai: People's Press, 2005.

Zheng Fei. "Beijing to Expand RQFII Program to Taiwan Investors." *Caixin Online*, January 30, 2013. http://english.caixin.com/2013-01-30/100487895.html.

Zhu Feng, 朱锋, and Robert S. Ross. "中国和平崛起:与单极的关系." In 中国的崛起: 理论与政策的视角 *China's Peaceful Rise: Theory and Policy Perspective*, 36–66. Shanghai: Shanghai Renmin Press 上海人民出版社, 2008.

Zi Zhongyun, 资中筠. "利益的汇合:国家关系的基础 – 写在中美建交十周年之际 Convergence of Interests: Basis for Relations among Nations." 美国研究 *American Studies Quarterly*, no. 2(1989). http://ias.cass.cn/en/show_mgyj.asp?id=826

Zoellick, Robert B. "A Republican Foreign Policy." *Foreign Affairs* 79, no. 1(2000): 63–78. www.jstor.org/stable/10.2307/20049614.

"互联网应急中心:中国遭受严重来自美国网络攻击 CNCERT: China Is Victim of Hacking Attacks from the US." *China Daily* 中国日报网, June 6, 2013. www.chinadaily.com.cn/language_tips/news/2013-06/06/content_16575578.htm.

"日本准'航母'将于6日下水 排水量超英意航母 Japan Launches Aircraft Carrier on August 6 with Displacement Greater than UK Aircraft Carrier." *Tencent News* 腾讯新闻, August 4, 2013. http://news.qq.com/a/20130804/000261.htm.

朱镕基答记者问 *Zhu Rongji Answers to Journalists' Questions*. Beijing: People's Press 人民出版社, 2009.

"美军重启一连串旧基地包围中国 防主基地被摧毁 US Revitalizes a String of Old Island Bases to Encircle China." *Tencent News* 腾讯新闻, August 22, 2013. http://news.qq.com/a/20130822/004123.htm.

6 Conclusion

The General Secretary of the Chinese Communist Party is killed by a sniper while officiating the opening of the Three Gorges Dam. Despite an intensive manhunt, the assassin escapes. The southern provinces, reacting against the crackdown that follows, declare independence which prompts a military response from Beijing. Taiwan intervenes and captures a nuclear missile base in the south. As fighting rages, the Taiwanese forces launch a missile which lands in Russia by mistake. Russia and the US respond by wiping out the entire Chinese strategic nuclear force. A nuclear winter follows and 500 million people leave the country to survive. The refugee tidal wave makes its way into Russia and Europe, while others flee to Australia and Latin America. A lone surviving Chinese submarine at sea fires its nuclear missiles in revenge. So goes the plot of *China Tidal Wave*, originally titled *Yellow Peril* (黃禍), the 1991 novel by Wang Lixiong still deemed too provocative to publish in China.[1] Although fictional, the events are not implausible. They depict the all too familiar pattern of misperceptions, miscalculations and unexpected twists that lead to a cataclysm none could have anticipated. As A. J. P. Taylor pointed out, great events have small causes.[2] Accidents are more likely to occur when there is a lack of trust.

Trust is predicated on history, interests, structures and empathy. Because it relates ultimately to notions of ethics, trust necessarily involves the history of one country's dealings with another, the nature of vested interests and power structures, as well as the quality of empathy from each side. Aggression and duplicity rarely foster trust, and infringement on the sovereignty and welfare of other states is often animated by interests and structures seeking to enlarge their own influence. Such ambitions, however, may be tempered by empathy and a sober regard for other nations. The preceeding chapters explored US–China trust with respect to climate change, financial crisis and international security, and found it wanting in each instance.

Climate change

The climate is a global common, and for the first time humanity has been called upon to take collective action against a threat transcending national borders. Carbon dioxide in the atmosphere has passed the long-feared threshold of 400 parts per million (ppm), promising large changes in the climate and to sea levels.[3] CO_2 concentration continues to rise by 2 ppm each year and, on the present course, will reach 800 ppm by the end of the century. Without concerted action, the planet faces climate chaos.[4] But both sides suffer constraints and fear that climate action will impede growth and hurt employment. Some US states and municipalities have adopted bold measures even as Washington remains conflicted. The energy lobby undermines American resolve while the shale gas revolution and the discovery of new oil sources[5] soothe the urgency to act.[6] China has made significant improvements in energy and carbon efficiency, and plans to cap carbon nationwide by 2016.[7] Technology is a key factor in the battle against global warming. The US owns 47.3 percent of key technologies compared to China's 0.34 percent.[8] The US government offers little aid but American companies sell a range of energy-saving products to China. Chinese leaders have signaled an end to the emphasis on growth, and seem committed to developing a new mode of economic life.[9]

Financial crisis

The Global Financial Crisis highlighted the central importance of finance. The crisis can be traced to the ideology of the Washington Consensus. Based on the belief that markets are self-regulating, the US government deregulated financial markets, and allowed debt securitization which changed the nature of banking. Instead of relationship banking, banks now made their money through making and trading bonds. This led to a decline in mortgage lending standards and paved the way for the collapse. Too big to fail, the banks were bailed out by the government. Wall Street began to push for deregulation in the 1980s and continues to resist reform even in the wake of the GFC.[10] Greed and human drama lay behind the crisis.[11] Financial crisis is a crisis of capitalism, and some question whether democracies can thrive with financial systems that are out of control and lack a larger sense of purpose.[12] Market fundamentalism, warns George Soros, is today a greater threat to an open society than any totalitarian ideology.[13] Many have called for institutional restraints on global capitalism[14] but five years after the crisis, reform has yet to materialize, and the top banks are bigger than before. The crisis is as much about politics as it is about economics, observes Andrew Gamble.[15]

International security

Despite mutually compatible security concerns such as the safety of navigation, nuclear proliferation, and terrorism, collaboration between the US and China is hobbled by fundamental differences of principle and approach. To counter nuclear proliferation in Iran and North Korea, the US applies economic sanctions and does not rule out the use of force, whereas the Chinese urge direct talks. Counter-terrorism cooperation is virtually non-existent because the US is sympathetic to the cause of China's ethnic separatist groups.[16] As for sharing maritime patrols, the US may not welcome the rise of a Chinese blue-water navy. Because the US is the world hegemon and China is an emerging force, power transition theorists predict a new Peloponnesian War. US foreign policy is motivated by powerful interests and structures but also by a belief in American exceptionalism. Sharing power with China runs counter to America's vision of itself and its role in the world. America enjoys overwhelming military supremacy, and to contain China, it is shifting additional military resources to East Asia and strengthening alliances with China's neighbors. Washington would welcome a regime change in China. Japan is a key factor in regional stability but its alliance with the US determines its foreign policy. Closer Sino–Japanese ties are not to Washington's advantage, and historical revisionism could pave the way to constitutional change and a remilitarized Japan. To develop, China needs peace, not war, but America may act to preserve the status quo. The ongoing anti-Chinese media campaign may be the prelude, and an incident, perhaps in the South China Sea, could provide grounds to intervene.

Linkages

Climate change, financial crisis and international security are linked, and a relentless quest for pecuniary gain appears to be the common thread. For the sake of profits, energy companies oppose decarbonization; banks resist prudential regulation; and defense contractors welcome war. In addition to supporting US foreign policy objectives, the US military and intelligence services guard the overseas interests of American big business.[17] Financial crisis, by triggering economic crisis, causes unemployment, hardship and social unrest. The GFC, by setting off the worst recession since the Great Depression, weakened America's will to decarbonize, threatened its military budget,[18] and deepened angst about China. It discredited the Washington Consensus, vindicated the Chinese political economy and inspired rethinking about global capitalism.[19] Climate change intensifies floods, draughts, storms and extreme weather conditions, causing food shortages, hunger, social dislocation and migration, which translate sooner or later into security threats.

Asymmetric knowledge

At the same time, the three global challenges reveal an asymmetry in empathy. In his first press conference as president, Xi Jinping declared the need for China to learn more about the world, and for the world to learn more about China.[20] Judging from their school curriculum, and the success of American soft power (Disney's *Iron Man 3* broke Chinese box office records), the Chinese are keen to learn about the West.[21] America is consistently the destination of choice for Chinese students, of whom 220,000 studied in the US in 2012 compared to 15,000 American students in China.[22] Official figures show that 79 percent of science and engineering graduates do not return home to China.[23] Never before have the Chinese ventured abroad in such numbers in search of learning. They outnumber Americans at Cambridge (962 versus 757 enrolled in 2013)[24] and at virtually every university outside North America. Many top Chinese academics earned their doctorates in the West, and almost all theories taught at Chinese universities come from the West. Many Chinese parents spare no expense (倾家荡产) to have their children master English but the reverse is seldom the case.[25] In Cambridge, around a dozen enroll to study Chinese each year compared to eighty who study ancient Greek and Latin literature.

The asymmetry is problematic. How we construe ourselves and the world matters because our intuition shapes our fears, impressions and relationships.[26] Writing in the 1960s, sinologist Raymond Dawson confessed that for many in the West, China is "mainly associated with such trivialities as pigtails, slant eyes, lanterns, laundries, pidgin English, chopsticks, and bird's nest soup."[27] Although the "whimsical notions of a quaint civilization in a setting which resembles the design on a willow-pattern plate" have since been updated by increased trade and travel, many racial and political stereotypes live on. John Fairbank warned early on that Chinese society is very different from America, and that US policymakers would fail unless they took the difference into account.[28] To be sure, there are empathic voices in America that seek to widen understanding. Billionaire Steven Schwarzman is establishing a $300 million fund for a master's program at Tsinghua University bringing together students from around the globe.[29] Schwarzman's stated goal is to reduce tensions between China and the West by educating the world's future leaders.[30] But why is the program necessary when there are already legions of Chinese studying in America? Friendship between American and Chinese students remains limited even when they live in the same dormitories and sit together in the same classroom. While proud of their international composition, most universities have not managed to facilitate engagement, especially when the media are replete with negative images of the Chinese.

Perception and trust

Trust is based on perception but the Chinese have not told their story well. Despite improvements, the state lacks media savvy. International media outlets are controlled by the West but, equally importantly, Chinese soft power seems ill defined and poorly articulated. Chinese universalism was an important force in history when China's neighbors adopted Chinese values and institutions, but today there is no universalism to be heard of in the national discourse. Unlike the West, the Chinese are hesitant to proffer universalist ideals or vision.[31] They have come to see universalism as a form of intervention or imperialism. They consider their conditions (国情) unique, and make no universalist claims about governance and development.[32] "Harmonious society" (和谐社会) and the "Chinese dream" (中国梦) are domestic visions, and "socialism with Chinese characteristics" (中国特色社会主义) is home grown. The Chinese are multilateralist and believe that each country should find its own way according to its own needs. Yet some believe the Chinese to be promoting a "Beijing Consensus" to outflank the Washington Consensus.[33]

Many Americans disapprove of the Chinese government because of its lack of ballot box legitimacy but "one man, one vote" is by no means the only form of legitimacy. Confucian scholar Jiang Qing contends that competence and meritocracy can be a source of legitimacy, a stance that finds resonance in Plato's *Republic*.[34] Liberal democracy is a young experiment. The Chinese believe that basic economic needs and social stability must come first. Zhang Weiwei of Fudan University points out that sixty years ago, China stood at the same level of development as India, the world's most populous democracy, but today its economy is four times larger and its life expectancy ten years longer than India's.[35] Andrew Sheng, president of the Fung Global Institute, observed that one-party rule brought political stability in many Asian countries including Japan, Singapore and Malaysia.[36] South Korea, Taiwan, Thailand and Indonesia too practiced one-party rule that facilitated economic growth before political transformation. Russia stands as a sober reminder of the hazards of hasty reform. Gorbachev's bold strategy brought political chaos and economic failure: "Communist party rule collapsed, ethnic conflicts erupted, the Soviet Union disintegrated, the command economy came to a standstill, and market reform went nowhere," wrote Susan Shirk.[37]

According to the US Social Security Administration, over 40 percent of American workers earn less than today's equivalent of the 1968 minimum wage.[38] In other words, real wages have shrunk for many since the 1960s. The US Census Bureau reports that middle-class income makes up 23.8 percent of national income, the lowest proportion since 1980.[39] At the same time, 46 million Americans live in poverty and over 50 million have no health insurance,[40] while the richest 1 percent takes nearly a quarter of the national income, and controls 40 percent of the nation's wealth.[41] The gulf between the richest 1 percent and the rest of the population is the widest since the 1920s.[42] Stiglitz describes the US polity as the rule "of the one percent, by the one percent, for the one percent,"[43] and Fukuyama, who famously proclaimed the triumph of liberal democracy,[44] now concedes that US democracy has little to teach China.[45] Some call Washington a "Wall Street government."[46] While affirming America's position as the world's hegemon, Lee Kuan Yew expressed dismay at the vagaries of its political system where gridlock exists on virtually every major issue.[47] An NBC poll showed that 83 percent of the public disapproved of Congress, with 6 in 10 saying they would vote out every member of Congress.[48]

By attacking China without mentioning the country's brighter achievements, the media presents a skewed image. Sidney Rittenberg who lived in China from 1944 to 1979, testifies that the Chinese are intensely pragmatic: "If they see that something isn't working, they sit down and try to figure out why it isn't working and change it."[49] The party is not static and has evolved from its early role of championing the working class to representing a broad spectrum of society. The party formally renounced class struggle in 1978,[50] and the theory of the Three Represents (三个代表) announced in 2002 embraced the capitalist class (先进生产力). Less than 10 percent of Party membership today consists of workers, while factory middle managers make up over 25 percent.[51] The National People's Congress includes wealthy entrepreneurs.[52] Chinese tourists to London visit Karl Marx's grave and shop at Prada (and spend three times more than the average tourists).[53] They have become the biggest source of global tourism income, spending $102 billion in 2012, an increase of 40 percent over the previous year, putting them well ahead of Germany and the US, the next two highest spending countries.[54] In the same year, the Chinese bought a quarter of the world's luxury goods by value.[55] The number of private yachts in the country is expected to rise from 3,000 in 2012 to 100,000 by 2020, reaching an estimated value of $8.16 billion.[56] Xi Jinping has shown commitment to reform by confronting entrenched interest groups.[57]

Such subtleties are lost on American politicians, who hold deep-seated anti-Chinese sentiments and fail to appreciate important currents. They take exception to communist atheism even while secularism and "new atheism" become established trends in the West.[58] Many are unaware that despite earlier suppression, the state has relaxed its stance on religion, and Christianity is enjoying a boom in China with an estimated 100 million believers including leading intellectuals and party members.[59] Citizens are allowed to worship as much as they like as long as they do not challenge the state's authority.[60] While it once restricted Bibles, China has since become the world's largest Bible press, printing 10 million copies a year albeit by a sole publisher (which produced its 100 millionth copy in November 2012).[61] Misconceptions about China have grown in the last decade, Rittenberg observes, and

> one of the primary misconceptions is China is a land of darkness, like Nazi Germany almost. If you say one word that the Chinese leadership doesn't like, you are thrown into a dungeon somewhere or even worse. Whereas in fact China is a country where the average individual has more individual liberties than at any time in history.[62]

In short, the question of political legitimacy is not a straightforward one, but the Chinese have not managed to speak persuasively to the West. The reticence may stem from culture, as a passage from the Dao De Jing (道德经) suggests:

> The sage manages affairs without action, and spreads doctrines without words. All things arise, and he does not turn away from them. He produces them but does not take possession of them. He acts but does not rely on his own ability. He accomplishes his task but does not claim

credit for it. It is precisely because he does not claim credit that his accomplishment remains with him.[63]

Trade friction is yet another area where the Chinese voice is not heard. The US does have a big trade deficit with China, but it has a large trade deficit with the rest of the world too. In fact, the proportion of US deficit coming from Asia, including China, has hardly changed in the last ten years, notes John Frisbie, president of the US–China Business Council.[64] The US deficit against China increased mainly because components from Japan, South Korea, Taiwan, Singapore and other Asian countries are now bundled into products assembled in China. Because the final product is "made in China," its value, including the foreign components within, is declared in trade statistics as a Chinese export.[65] In other words, Japanese and other Asian exports are embedded in Chinese exports. Only $10 of the $150 value of the Apple Ipod is contributed by China; the rest is re-exportation. According to Pascal Lamy, director-general of the WTO, if trade statistics were adjusted to reflect the actual value contributed by different countries, the size of the US trade deficit with China would halve.[66]

Allegations of US jobs moving to China have been equally misleading. It is simply not competitive for American businesses to manufacture everything in the US for export to China. Instead, many US companies manufacture in China to sell directly to the Chinese market. Surveys consistently show that more than 90 percent of US companies invest in China primarily to serve the Chinese market, not to outsource production and export back to the United States.[67] At the same time, China has been America's fastest-growing export market for ten consecutive years. US exports to China have grown 542 percent since 2000, while US exports to the rest of the world increased by only 80 percent in the same period. Bilateral trade amounts to almost $500 billion, and each is the second largest trading partner of the other. Between the two countries there are more than ninety inter-governmental exchange mechanisms, coordinating a range of international and regional issues.[68] The dramatic growth in exports to China can only mean more, not less, American jobs.

Accusations about Chinese currency manipulation have proven groundless too, as the renminbi has appreciated by 34 percent since exchange rate reform began in 2005; China unpegged its currency from the dollar on 21 July 2005, and adopted a managed floating exchange rate based on a basket of currencies similar to the European Exchange Rate Mechanism (ERM) before the introduction of the euro.[69] In fact, the US has sought to depress the dollar through quantitative easing since 2008, the latest round of which creates $85 billion a month.[70] Instead of lending to businesses, however, US banks use the massive liquidity to make speculative bets, notes economist Gabriel Palma,[71] and earn enormous profits.[72] Even as the economy remains sluggish,[73] the Dow index hit a record high, rising 19 percent in the first half of 2013 – a sure sign of a bubble in the making.[74] If the Chinese were to succumb as the Japanese did in 1985 to US pressure to rapidly appreciate their currency, they would risk the same stagnation that has bedeviled Japan ever since.[75] All this amounts to saying that the Chinese are the target of gratuitous charges to which they are unable to answer effectively thanks to Western control of the international media.

Trust between states

William Fulbright reasoned that the study of international relations must be grounded in the study of human needs and fears. The question of trust brings social psychology to bear on international relations. Social psychology is the study of how people think about, influence, and relate to one another. Its central themes include how human beings construe their social worlds, and how their intuition guides and sometimes misleads them.[76] It involves questions like "Who are we?" and "Who are they?" and how to transform closed fists into open arms. Social psychology is about life, beliefs, attitudes, and relationships.

One common social-psychological phenomenon is prejudice. Prejudice is a preconceived negative judgment of a group and its members. Gordon Allport calls it "an antipathy based upon a faulty and inflexible generalization."[77] A prejudiced person may dislike those from a different group and behave in a discriminatory manner, believing them to be ignorant and dangerous.[78] Prejudice is an attitude marked by stereotypes. Prejudices spring from different sources and exist in subtle as well as overt forms. Social institutions may foster prejudices, and a group that enjoys economic or military superiority will often use prejudicial beliefs to justify its privileged position.[79] We ascribe human emotions such as love and hope to in-group members but are more reluctant to see the same in out-group members.[80] One reason for prejudice is status. Status is relative, and to perceive ourselves as having higher status, we need people below us.[81] One benefit of prejudice is a feeling of superiority.[82]

Ethnocentrism, according to William Sumner, is "the view of things in which one's group is the center of everything ... and looks with contempt on outsiders."[83] In hard times, it is conducive to identify a group as a scapegoat, and people are attracted to those who offer an ideology for a better world and an enemy who must be crushed to fulfill the ideology.[84] Typically a negative stereotype is fostered to justify ill treatment of that group. The most extreme form of this is dehumanization, wherein the rival is described as less than human, and therefore deserves to be treated accordingly.

Conflicts can occur over resources, values, status and power.[85] They frequently contain a small core of truly incompatible goals, surrounded by a thick layer of misperceptions of the adversary's motives and goals. Conflicting parties often have mirror-image perceptions where both sides believe "We are peace-loving – they are hostile," and each may treat the other in ways that bring about the outcome they expect. Conflicts are easily kindled by competition and misperceptions but contact, communication and conciliation – in short, empathy – can turn suspicion to trust. Contact is especially beneficial when both sides work together to overcome a common threat that overrides differences.[86]

US–China relations demonstrate the importance of History, Interests, Structures and Empathy (HISE) in forging trust. History reflects the past; Interests and Structures constitute the present; Empathy shapes the future. HISE can serve as a framework to understand goodwill between states. As with Porter's model of national advantage[87] or Sen's human development parameters,[88] it draws attention to underlying factors, and could shift thinking from rivalry and contest to trust and goodwill. Kurt Koch calls trust "the basic attitude in a culture of humanity," and the counter-pole of fear.[89] HISE asks: "How much do other states trust us? Why? What can we do about it?" Like a mirror, it may help states to see themselves more clearly.

Notes

1 王力雄 Wang Lixiong, *China Tidal Wave*, English edn. (Folkestone: Global Oriental Ltd, 2008).

2 A. J. P. Taylor, *The First World War: An Illustrated History* (London: Hamish Hamilton, 1963).

3 Justin Gillis, "Carbon Dioxide Level Passes Long-Feared Milestone," *New York Times*, May 10, 2013, Science/Environment section, www.nytimes.com/2013/05/11/science/earth/carbon-dioxide-level-passes-long-feared-milestone.html.

4 Michael Le Page, "Climate Change: It's Even Worse than We Thought," *New Scientist*, 2013, www.newscientist.com/special/worse-climate; Martin Wolf, "Why the World Faces Climate Chaos," *Financial Times*, May 14, 2013, www.ft.com/cms/s/s/0/c926f6e8-bbf9-11e2-a4b4-00144feab7de.html#axzz2TUh8pTrh; Martin Wolf, "Living with Limits: Growth, Resources, and Climate Change," *Climate Policy* 12, no. 6 (2012): 772–83, doi:10.1080/14693062.2012.695464.

5 Deborah Gordon, "The World's Growing Oil Resources," *Carnegie Endowment for International Peace*, 2013, http://carnegieendowment.org/2013/04/17/world-s-growing-oil-resources/fzzj.

6 Anna Fifield, "Who's Who of Obama Lobbyists Pushes Keystone Pipeline," *Financial Times*, May 30, 2013, www.ft.com/cms/s/0/91300bf0-c80e-11e2-be27-00144feab7de.html#axzz2UQTUsz3u.

7 Jane Qiu, "China Gets Tough on Carbon," *Nature* 498, no. 7453 (June 12, 2013): 145–46, doi:10.1038/498145a.

8 KISTEP, *Korea Main Science and Technology Indicators 100*, vol. 2012 (Seoul: Korea Institute of Science and Technology Evaluation and Planning, 2013), http://m.kistep.re.kr/global/filelink.jsp?fileKey=save.policy.data&fileName=scientific%20technique_result(2012).pdf; "韩媒称韩技术水平正被中国追赶 差距持续缩小 China Closes Technology Gap with South Korea," *Global Times*, August 12, 2013, http://world.huanqiu.com/exclusive/2013-08/4235959.html.

9 "习近平:不能照搬发达国家现代化模式 Xi Jinping: China Should Not Follow Developed Countries' Modernization Model," *Tencent News* 腾讯新闻, July 22, 2013, http://news.qq.com/a/20130722/012112.htm.

10 Charles Ferguson, *Predator Nation: Corporate Criminals, Political Corruption, and the Hijacking of America* (New York: Crown, 2013).

11 Gillian Tett, *Fool's Gold: How Unrestrained Greed Corrupted a Dream, Shattered Global Markets and Unleashed a Catastrophe* (London: Little, Brown, 2009).

12 Zbigniew Brzezinski and Nathan Gardels, "Can Democracies Thrive with Financial Systems That Are Out of Control?," *Christian Science Monitor*, January 24,
   2012, www.csmonitor.com/Commentary/Global-Viewpoint/2012/0124/Brzezinski-C
   an-democracies-thrive-with-financial-systems-that-are-out-of-control.
13 George Soros, *The Crisis of Global Capitalism: Open Society Endangered*, 1st ed.
   (Boston/London: Little, Brown, 1998).
14 Peter Nolan, *Re-Balancing China: Essays on the Global Financial Crisis, Industrial
   Policy and International Relations* (New York: Anthem Press, 2014).; Tom
   Braithwaite and Patrick Jenkins, "Bob Diamond Calls for Bank Rules Shake-Up,"
   Financial Times, September 15, 2013, www.ft.com/cms/s/0/9e256f5a
   -1bb8-11e3-b678-00144feab7de.html?siteedition=uk#axzz2ez3edruQ.
15 Andrew Gamble, *The Spectre at the Feast: Capitalist Crisis and the Politics of
   Recession* (Basingstoke: Palgrave Macmillan, 2009).
16 Shirley A. Kan, *U.S.-China Counterterrorism Cooperation: Issues for U.S. Policy*,
   CRS Report for Congress (Washington, DC: Congressional Research Service, July
   15, 2010), www.fas.org/sgp/crs/terror/RL33001.pdf.
17 Stephen C. Schlesinger and Stephen Kinzer, *Bitter Fruit: The Untold Story of the
   American Coup in Guatemala*, Reprint (New York: Anchor Books, 1990).
18 "Pentagon to Reduce Troops and Cut Spending," *France 24*, January 26, 2012, www.
   france24.com/en/20120126-us-pentagon-military-spending-cuts-panetta-budget-war
   -republicans.
19 Nolan, *Re-Balancing China*.
20 习近平 Xi Jinping, "China's New Party Chief Xi Jinping's Speech," *BBC News*,
   November 15, 2012, sec. China, www.bbc.co.uk/news/world-asia-china-20338586.
21 "'Iron Man 3' Breaks China's Box Office Record," *China.org.cn*, May 2, 2013,
   www.china.org.cn/arts/2013-05/02/content_28714797.htm.
22 Raisa Belyavina, *US Students in China: Meeting the Goals of the 100,000 Strong
   Initiative* (International Institute of Education, January 2013), www.iie.org/
   ~/media/Files/Corporate/Publications/US-Students-in-China.ashx.
23 "78.8%受访者认为人情关系复阻碍优秀人才回国 Survey Shows Complex Social
   Relations Keeps Talent from Returning Home to China," *Xinhua Online* 新华网,
   September 6, 2013, http://news.xinhuanet.com/hr/2013-09/06/c_125335728.htm.
24 Professor Richard Penty quoting figures from the Cambridge University International Office at an education forum on 30 July 2013.
25 Clarissa Ward and Enjoli Francis, "China Pushes English Language," *ABC News*,
   November 15, 2010, http://abcnews.go.com/WN/China/china-pushes-english-la
   nguage/storynew?id=12154435; Joseph Lo Bianco, Jane Orton, and Gao Yihong,
   China and English: Globalisation and the Dilemmas of Identity (Bristol: Multilingual Matters, 2009); Bob Adamson, *China's English: A History of English in
   Chinese Education* (Hong Kong: Hong Kong University Press, 2004).
26 David G. Myers, *Social Psychology*, 11th edn. (New York: McGraw-Hill, 2013), 6.
27 Raymond Stanley Dawson, *The Legacy of China*, The Legacy Series (Oxford:
   Clarendon Press, 1964), 2.
28 John K. Fairbank, *The United States and China* (Cambridge, MA: Harvard University Press, 1948), 310.
29 Henny Sender, "Blackstone CEO Donates Money to Tsinghua," *Financial Times*,
   April 21, 2013, www.ft.com/cms/s/0/391c5cda-aa3f-11e2-bc0d-00144feabdc0.htm
   l#axzz2Qi87uNr1.
30 Keith Bradsher, "U.S. Financier Backs China Scholarship Program," *New York
   Times*, April 20, 2013, World/Asia Pacific section, www.nytimes.com/2013/04/21/
   world/asia/us-financier-backs-china-scholarship-program.html.
31 Sameh El-Shahat, "China Needs to Sell Its Dreams to an Increasingly Skeptical
   World," *Globaltimes*, May 14, 2013, www.globaltimes.cn/content/781570.shtml#.
   UZO3aII8zuU.

32 张维为 Zhang Weiwei, *The China Wave: Rise of a Civilizational State* 中国震撼：一个"文明型国家"的崛起, trans. Anton Platero (New York: World Century Publishing Corporation, 2012), www.amazon.co.uk/The-China-Wave-Civilizational-ebook/dp/B007T72B7C.

33 Stefan Halper, *The Beijing Consensus* (New York: Basic Books, 2010).

34 Plato, *The Republic of Plato*, trans. Francis Macdonald Cornford, Reprint. (Oxford: Clarendon Press, 1948).

35 Zhang Weiwei, *The China Wave: Rise of a Civilizational State* 中国震撼：一个"文明型国家"的崛起; Amartya Sen, "Why Is China Ahead of India?," *The World Bank*, June 20, 2013, http://live.worldbank.org/china-ahead-india-amartya-sen.

36 Andrew Sheng, *From Asian to Global Financial Crisis: An Asian Regulator's View of Unfettered Finance in the 1990s and 2000s* (Cambridge: Cambridge University Press, 2009), 292.

37 Susan L Shirk, *The Political Logic of Economic Reform in China*, California Series on Social Choice and Political Economy, 24 (Berkeley: University of California Press, 1993), 333.

38 "4成美国工人收入低于1968年最低工资 40 Percent of US Workers Earn Less than 1968 Minimum Wage," *Tencent News* 腾讯新闻, August 6, 2013, http://finance.qq.com/a/20130806/010185.htm.

39 徐长银 Xu Changyin, "美国人口普查局数据表明美国贫富差距在扩大 U.S. Census Bureau Data Shows Widening Wealth Gap," *People's Daily Online* 人民网, September 30, 2012, http://world.people.com.cn/n/2012/0930/c157278-19158695.html?prolongation=1.

40 US Census Bureau, *Income, Poverty, and Health Insurance Coverage in the United States: 2009* (Washington, DC: US Department of Commerce, September 2010), 22.

41 Robert Pear, "States' Policies on Health Care Exclude Poorest," *New York Times*, May 24, 2013, U.S. section, www.nytimes.com/2013/05/25/us/states-policies-on-health-care-exclude-poorest.html.

42 Paul Wiseman, "Richest 1 Percent Earn Biggest Share Since '20s," *ABC News*, September 10, 2013, http://abcnews.go.com/US/wireStory/top-percent-record-share-2012-us-income-20213135.

43 Joseph E. Stiglitz, "Of the 1%, by the 1%, for the 1%," *Vanity Fair*, May 1, 2011, www.vanityfair.com/society/features/2011/05/top-one-percent-201105.

44 Francis Fukuyama, *The End of History and the Last Man* (London: Hamish Hamilton, 1992).

45 Francis Fukuyama, "US Democracy Has Little to Teach China," *Financial Times*, January 17, 2011, www.ft.com/cms/s/0/cb6af6e8-2272-11e0-b6a2-00144feab49a.html#axzz2TumrMKHo.

46 Charles Ferguson, *Inside Job: The Financiers Who Pulled Off the Heist of the Century* (London: Oneworld Publications, 2012).

47 Graham Allison, Robert D. Blackwill, and Ali Wyne, *Lee Kuan Yew: The Grand Master's Insights on China, the United States, and the World* (Cambridge, MA: MIT Press, 2013).

48 Mark Murray, "NBC/WSJ Poll: Faith in DC Hits a Low; 83 Percent Disapprove of Congress," *NBC News*, July 24, 2013, http://firstread.nbcnews.com/_news/2013/07/24/19644154-nbcwsj-poll-faith-in-dc-hits-a-low-83-percent-disapprove-of-congress.

49 *CRI Interview with Sidney Rittenberg*, 2011, www.youtube.com/watch?v=tU_oXb_OrCc&feature=youtube_gdata_player.

50 Guangyuan Yu, Steven I. Levine, and Ezra F. Vogel, *Deng Xiaoping Shakes the World: An Eyewitness Account of China's Party Work Conference and the Third Plenum (November-December 1978)* (New York: EastBridge, 2004).

51 J. Stapleton Roy, "Strategic Challenges for the US-China Relationship" (East-West Center in Hawaii, February 13, 2013), https://vimeo.com/59754895.

52   Bloomberg News, "China's Billionaire People's Congress Makes Capitol Hill Look Like Pauper," *Bloomberg*, accessed May 24, 2013, www.bloomberg.com/news/2012-02-26/china-s-billionaire-lawmakers-make-u-s-peers-look-like-paupers.html.

53   "British Visas 'Should Be Easier,'" *BBC News*, February 4, 2013, www.bbc.co.uk/news/uk-england-21323534.

54   "Chinese Tourists Top Spending League," *BBC News*, April 5, 2013, www.bbc.co.uk/news/business-22037233.

55   Andrew Hill, "Kering Takes New Luxe to China," *Financial Times*, June 12, 2013, www.ft.com/cms/s/0/db847778-d1bd-11e2-b17e-00144feab7de.html#axzz2VteL03Xw.

56   Wang Wen and Li Fangfang, "Yacht Industry Sails Ahead," *China Watch*, June 14, 2013, http://chinawatch.washingtonpost.com/2013/06/yacht-industry-sails-ahead.php.

57   "Xi's Speech Underlines Commitment to Reform," *People's Daily Online* 人民网, July 29, 2013, http://english.peopledaily.com.cn/90785/8343641.html.

58   "Catholicism's Fading Appeal in France," *BBC News*, March 10, 2013, www.bbc.co.uk/news/21732437; "Italy's Dwindling Catholic Congregation," *BBC News*, March 6, 2013, www.bbc.co.uk/news/world-europe-21694860.

59   David Aikman, *Jesus in Beijing*, 2nd revised ed. (Cincinatti, OH: Monarch Publications, 2006); Christopher Marsh, *Religion and the State in Russia and China: Suppression, Survival, and Revival* (London: Continuum, 2011).

60   Jason Kindopp and Carol Lee Hamrin, *God and Caesar in China: Policy Implications of Church-State Tensions* (Washington, DC: Brookings Institution Press, 2004).

61   Li Yao, "100 Millionth Bible Printed," *Chinadaily.com.cn*, November 10, 2012, www.chinadaily.com.cn/china/2012-11/10/content_15906773.htm.

62   *CRI Interview with Sidney Rittenberg*.

63   陈荣捷 Chan Wing-Tsit, trans., *The Way of Lao Tzu (Tao-Te Ching)* 道德经, vol. 139, Library of Liberal Arts (Indianapolis: Bobbs-Merrill, 1963).

64   John Frisbie, "Best Way to Deal with China Is to Heal Ourselves," *Columbus Dispatch*, October 17, 2012, www.dispatch.com/content/stories/editorials/2012/10/17/best-way-to-deal-with-china-is-to-heal-ourselves.html.

65   Y. Xing and N. Detert, *How the Iphone Widens the United States Trade Deficit with the People's Republic of China*, ADB Working Paper Series (Asian Development Bank Institute, December 2010), http://papers.ssrn.com/sol3/papers.cfm?abstract_id=1729085.

66   "Obsolete Way of Measuring Trade Inflates China's Trade Surplus," *China Daily Europe*, January 3, 2011, http://europe.chinadaily.com.cn/business/2011-01/03/content_11790607.htm.

67   Frisbie, "Best Way to Deal with China Is to Heal Ourselves."

68   "引领中美关系向前迈进 A Forward Thrust in Sino-US Relations," *People's Daily Online* 人民网, June 8, 2013, http://english.people.com.cn/90883/8278304.html.

69   "China's Yuan Gains 34% against USD in Past 8 Years," *People's Daily Online* 人民网, July 22, 2013, http://english.peopledaily.com.cn/90778/8336176.html.

70   Ross Heard, "QE: A Timeline of Quantitative Easing in the US," *Open Democracy*, July 6, 2013, www.opendemocracy.net/openeconomy/ross-heard/qe-timeline-of-quatitative-easing-in-us; John Paul Rathbone and Jonathan Wheatley, "Brazil's Finance Chief Attacks US over QE3," *Financial Times*, September 20, 2012, www.ft.com/cms/s/0/69c0b800-032c-11e2-a484-00144feabdc0.html#axzz26iBCYxBa.

71   Remarks by Gabriel Palma at the Rethink Economics Conference at Birkbeck College, University of London, June 28, 2013.

72   "US Banks See Profits Rise Sharply," *BBC News*, January 16, 2013, www.bbc.co.uk/news/business-21044121; "US Banking Giants See Profits Jump," *BBC News*, July 12, 2013, www.bbc.co.uk/news/business-23286901; "Citigroup Reports $4.2bn in Second Quarter Net Income," *Financial Times*, July 15, 2013; "JP Morgan

Chase Reports Net Income of $6.5bn," *Financial Times*, July 13, 2013; "Goldman Sachs Reports Strong Earnings," *Financial Times*, July 16, 2013.

73 "Oil Prices Slip on Disappointing U.S. Jobs Data," *Xinhua* 新华/*English.news. cn*, August 3, 2013, http://news.xinhuanet.com/english/business/2013-08/03/c_1251 10241.htm.

74 Hibah Yousuf, "Dow, S&P 500 Close at Record Highs, up 19% in 2013," *CNNMoney*, July 18, 2013, http://money.cnn.com/2013/07/18/investing/stocks-ma rkets/index.html; "S&P Breaks Milestone Level, Dow Sets Record High on Encouraging Data," *Xinhua* 新华/*English.news.cn*, August 2, 2013, http://news. xinhuanet.com/english/business/2013-08/02/c_125104288.htm.

75 Jonathan Shaw, "Japan's 'Lost Decades' – and Economic Stagflation in the U.S.," *Harvard Magazine*, August 2010, http://harvardmagazine.com/2010/07/an-afterma th-to-avoid.

76 Myers, *Social Psychology*, 9.

77 Gordon W. Allport, *The Nature of Prejudice* (Cambridge, MA: Addison-Wesley, 1954), 9.

78 J. H. Duckitt, *The Social Psychology of Prejudice* (New York: Praeger, 1992).

79 Myers, *Social Psychology*, 325.

80 Stéphanie Demoulin, Vassilis Saroglou, and Matthieu Van Pachterbeke, "Infra-Humanizing Others, Supra-Humanizing Gods: The Emotional Hierarchy," *Social Cognition* 26, no. 2 (2008): 235–47.

81 Jacques-Philippe Leyens, B. P. Cortes, S. Demoulin, J. Dovidio, S. T. Fiske, and R. Gaunt, "Emotional Prejudice, Essentialism, and Nationalism," *European Journal of Social Psychology* 33, no. 6 (2003): 703–17.

82 Jacques-Philippe Leyens, P. M. Paladino, S. Demoulin, J. Vaes, and R. Gaunt, "Infra-Humanization: The Wall of Group Differences," *Social Issues and Policy Review* 1, no. 1 (2007): 139–72.

83 William Graham Sumner, *Folkways: A Study of the Sociological Importance of Usages, Manners, Customs, Mores, and Morals* (Boston, MA: Ginn & Company, 1906), 12.

84 Ervin Staub, *The Roots of Evil: The Origins of Genocide and Other Group Violence* (Cambridge: Cambridge University Press, 1992).

85 Ronald J. Fisher, "Needs Theory, Social Identity and an Eclectic Model of Conflict," in *Conflict: Human Needs Theory*, ed. J. Burton (New York and London: St. Martin's Press/Macmillan, 1990), 89–112.

86 Muzafer Sherif, *In Common Predicament: Social Psychology of Intergroup Conflict and Cooperation* (Boston, MA: Houghton Mifflin, 1966).

87 Michael E. Porter, *The Competitive Advantage of Nations* (Cambridge, MA: Harvard Business School Management Programs, 1993); Michael E. Porter, *Competitive Strategy: Techniques for Analyzing Industries and Competitors* (New York and London: Free Press, 1980).

88 Amartya Sen, *Development as Freedom* (Oxford: Oxford University Press, 2001).

89 Cardinal Kurt Koch, "Trust as the Basic Attitude in a Culture of Humanity," Speech, Woolf Institute, Cambridge, February 26, 2013.

Bibliography

"4成美国工人收入低于1968年最低工资 40 Percent of US Workers Earn Less than 1968 Minimum Wage." *Tencent News* 腾讯新闻, August 6, 2013. http://finance.qq. com/a/20130806/010185.htm.

"78.8%受访者认为人情关系复杂阻碍优秀人才回国 Survey Shows Complex Social Relations Keeps Talent from Returning Home to China." *Xinhua Online* 新华网, September 6, 2013. http://news.xinhuanet.com/hr/2013-09/06/c_125335728.htm.

Adamson, Bob. *China's English: A History of English in Chinese Education*. Hong Kong University Press, 2004.

Aikman, David. *Jesus in Beijing*. 2nd revised ed. New York: Monarch Publications, 2006.

Allison, Graham, Robert D.Blackwill, and Ali Wyne. *Lee Kuan Yew: The Grand Master's Insights on China, the United States, and the World*. Cambridge, MA: MIT Press, 2013.

Allport, Gordon W. *The Nature of Prejudice*. Cambridge, MA: Addison-Wesley, 1954.

Belyavina, Raisa. "US Students in China: Meeting the Goals of the 100,000 Strong Initiative." International Institute of Education, January 2013. www.iie.org/~/media/Files/Corporate/Publications/US-Students-in-China.ashx.

Bianco, Joseph Lo, JaneOrton, and Gao Yihong. *China and English: Globalisation and the Dilemmas of Identity*. Clevedon: Multilingual Matters, 2009.

Bradsher, Keith. "U.S. Financier Backs China Scholarship Program." *New York Times*, April 20, 2013, World/Asia Pacific section. www.nytimes.com/2013/04/21/world/asia/us-financier-backs-china-scholarship-program.html.

Braithwaite, Tom, and Patrick Jenkins. "Bob Diamond Calls for Bank Rules Shake-Up." *Financial Times*, September 15, 2013. www.ft.com/cms/s/0/9e256f5a-1bb8-11e3-b678-00144feab7de.html?siteedition=uk#axzz2ez3edruQ.

"British Visas 'Should Be Easier.'" *BBC News,* February 4, 2013. www.bbc.co.uk/news/uk-england-21323534.

Brzezinski, Zbigniew, and Nathan Gardels. "Can Democracies Thrive with Financial Systems That Are Out of Control?" *Christian Science Monitor*, January 24, 2012. www.csmonitor.com/Commentary/Global-Viewpoint/2012/0124/Brzezinski-Can-democracies-thrive-with-financial-systems-that-are-out-of-control.

"Catholicism's Fading Appeal in France." *BBC News*, March 10, 2013. www.bbc.co.uk/news/21732437.

Chan Wing-Tsit, 陈荣捷, trans. *The Way of Lao Tzu (Tao-Te Ching)* 道德经. Vol. 139. Library of Liberal Arts. Indianapolis: Bobbs-Merrill, 1963.

"China's Billionaire People's Congress Makes Capitol Hill Look Like Pauper." *Bloomberg*. Accessed May 24, 2013. www.bloomberg.com/news/2012-02-26/china-s-billionaire-lawmakers-make-u-s-peers-look-like-paupers.html.

"China's Yuan Gains 34% against USD in Past 8 Years." *People's Daily Online* 人民网, July 22, 2013. http://english.peopledaily.com.cn/90778/8336176.html.

"Chinese Tourists Top Spending League." *BBC News*, April 5, 2013. www.bbc.co.uk/news/business-22037233.

"Citigroup Reports $4.2bn in Second Quarter Net Income." *Financial Times*, July 15, 2013.

CRI Interview with Sidney Rittenberg, 2011. www.youtube.com/watch?v=tU_oXb_OrCc&feature=youtube_gdata_player.

Dawson, Raymond Stanley. *The Legacy of China*. The Legacy Series. Oxford: Clarendon Press, 1964.

Demoulin, Stéphanie, Vassilis Saroglou, and Matthieu Van Pachterbeke. "Infra-Humanizing Others, Supra-Humanizing Gods: The Emotional Hierarchy." *Social Cognition* 26, no. 2(2008): 235–247.

Duckitt, J. H. *The Social Psychology of Prejudice*. New York: Praeger, 1992.

El-Shahat, Sameh. "China Needs to Sell Its Dreams to an Increasingly Skeptical World." *Globaltimes*, May 14, 2013. www.globaltimes.cn/content/781570.shtml#. UZO3aII8zuU.

Ferguson, Charles. *Inside Job: The Financiers Who Pulled Off the Heist of the Century.* London: Oneworld Publications, 2012.

Ferguson, Charles. *Predator Nation: Corporate Criminals, Political Corruption, and the Hijacking of America.* New York: Crown Pub, 2013.

Fifield, Anna. "Who's Who of Obama Lobbyists Pushes Keystone Pipeline." *Financial Times*, May 30, 2013. www.ft.com/cms/s/0/91300bf0-c80e-11e2-be27-00144feab7de. html#axzz2UQTUsz3u.

Fisher, Ronald J. "Needs Theory, Social Identity and an Eclectic Model of Conflict." In *Conflict: Human Needs Theory*, ed. J. Burton. New York and London: St. Martin's Press/Macmillan, 1990, 89–112.

Frisbie, John. "Best Way to Deal with China Is to Heal Ourselves." *Columbus Dispatch*, October 17, 2012. www.dispatch.com/content/stories/editorials/2012/10/17/best-way-to-deal-with-china-is-to-heal-ourselves.html.

Fukuyama, Francis. "US Democracy Has Little to Teach China." *Financial Times*, January 17, 2011. www.ft.com/cms/s/0/cb6af6e8-2272-11e0-b6a2-00144feab49a.html#axzz2TumrMKHo.

Fukuyama, Francis. *The End of History and the Last Man.* London: Hamish Hamilton, 1992.

Gamble, Andrew. *The Spectre at the Feast: Capitalist Crisis and the Politics of Recession.* Basingstoke: Palgrave Macmillan, 2009.

Gillis, Justin. "Carbon Dioxide Level Passes Long-Feared Milestone." *New York Times*, May 10, 2013, Science/Environment section. www.nytimes.com/2013/05/11/science/earth/carbon-dioxide-level-passes-long-feared-milestone.html.

"Goldman Sachs Reports Strong Earnings." *Financial Times*, July 16, 2013.

Gordon, Deborah. "The World's Growing Oil Resources." *Carnegie Endowment for International Peace*, 2013. http://carnegieendowment.org/2013/04/17/world-s-growing-oil-resources/fzzj.

Halper, Stefan. *The Beijing Consensus.* New York: Basic Books, 2010.

Heard, Ross. "QE: A Timeline of Quantitative Easing in the US." *Open Democracy*, July 6, 2013. www.opendemocracy.net/openeconomy/ross-heard/qe-timeline-of-quatitative-easing-in-us.

Hill, Andrew. "Kering Takes New Luxe to China." *Financial Times*, June 12, 2013. www.ft.com/cms/s/0/db847778-d1bd-11e2-b17e-00144feab7de.html#axzz2VteL03Xw.

"'Iron Man 3' Breaks China's Box Office Record." *China.org.cn*, May 2, 2013. www.china.org.cn/arts/2013-05/02/content_28714797.htm.

"Italy's Dwindling Catholic Congregation." *BBC News*, March 6, 2013. www.bbc.co.uk/news/world-europe-21694860.

"JP Morgan Chase Reports Net Income of $6.5bn." *Financial Times*, July 13, 2013.

Kan, Shirley A. *U.S.-China Counterterrorism Cooperation: Issues for U.S. Policy.* CRS Report for Congress. Congressional Research Service, July 15, 2010. www.fas.org/sgp/crs/terror/RL33001.pdf.

Kindopp, Jason, and Carol Lee Hamrin. *God and Caesar in China: Policy Implications of Church–State Tensions.* Washington, DC: Brookings Institution Press, 2004.

KISTEP. *Korea Main Science and Technology Indicators 100.* Vol. 2012. Seoul: Korea Institute of Science & Technology Evaluation and Planning, 2013. http://m.kistep.re.

kr/global/filelink.jsp?fileKey=save.policy.data&fileName=scientific%20technique_res
ult(2012).pdf.

Koch, Cardinal Kurt. "Trust as the Basic Attitude in a Culture of Humanity." Speech,
Woolf Institute, Cambridge, February 26, 2013.

Le Page, Michael. "Climate Change: It's Even Worse than We Thought." *New Scientist*, 2013. www.newscientist.com/special/worse-climate.

Leyens, Jacques-Philippe, Brezo Cortes, Stéphanie Demoulin, John F. Dovidio, Susan
T. Fiske, Ruth Gaunt, Maria-Paola Paladino, Armando Rodriguez-Perez, Ramon
Rodriguez-Torres, and Jeroen Vaes. "Emotional Prejudice, Essentialism, and
Nationalism." *European Journal of Social Psychology* 33, no. 6(2003): 703–717.

Leyens, Jacques-Philippe, Stéphanie Demoulin, Jeroen Vaes, Ruth Gaunt, and Maria
Paola Paladino. "Infra-Humanization: The Wall of Group Differences." *Social
Issues and Policy Review* 1, no. 1(2007): 139–172.

Li Yao. "100 Millionth Bible Printed." *Chinadaily.com.cn*, November 10, 2012. www.
chinadaily.com.cn/china/2012-11/10/content_15906773.htm.

Marsh, Christopher. *Religion and the State in Russia and China: Suppression, Survival,
and Revival*. London: Continuum, 2011.

Murray, Mark. "NBC/WSJ Poll: Faith in DC Hits a Low; 83 Percent Disapprove of
Congress." *NBC News*, July 24, 2013. http://firstread.nbcnews.com/_news/2013/07/
24/19644154-nbcwsj-poll-faith-in-dc-hits-a-low-83-percent-disapprove-of-congress.

Myers, David G. *Social Psychology*. 11th ed. New York: McGraw-Hill, 2013.

Nolan, Peter. *Re-Balancing China: Essays on the Global Financial Crisis, Industrial
Policy and International Relations*. New York: Anthem Press, 2014.

"Obsolete Way of Measuring Trade Inflates China's Trade Surplus." *China Daily
Europe,* January 3, 2011. http://europe.chinadaily.com.cn/business/2011-01/03/con
tent_11790607.htm.

"Oil Prices Slip on Disappointing U.S. Jobs Data." *Xinhua* 新华/*English.news.cn*,
August 3, 2013. http://news.xinhuanet.com/english/business/2013-08/03/c_12511024
1.htm.

Pear, Robert. "States' Policies on Health Care Exclude Poorest." *New York Times*,
May 24, 2013, U.S. section. www.nytimes.com/2013/05/25/us/states-policies-on-hea
lth-care-exclude-poorest.html.

"Pentagon to Reduce Troops and Cut Spending." *France 24*, January 26, 2012. www.fra
nce24.com/en/20120126-us-pentagon-military-spending-cuts-panetta-budget-war-rep
ublicans.

Plato. *The Republic of Plato*. Trans. Francis Macdonald Cornford. Reprint. Oxford:
Clarendon Press, 1948.

Porter, Michael E. *The Competitive Advantage of Nations*. Cambridge, MA: Harvard
Business School Management Programs, 1993.

Porter, Michael E. *Competitive Strategy: Techniques for Analyzing Industries and
Competitors*. New York and London: Free Press, 1980.

Qiu, Jane. "China Gets Tough on Carbon." *Nature* 498, no. 7453(2013): 145–146.
doi:10.1038/498145a.

Rathbone, John Paul, and Jonathan Wheatley."Brazil's Finance Chief Attacks US over
QE3." *Financial Times*, September 20, 2012. www.ft.com/cms/s/0/69c0b800-032c-11e
2-a484-00144feabdc0.html#axzz26iBCYxBa.

Roy, J. Stapleton."Strategic Challenges for the US-China Relationship." Video. East-
West Center in Hawaii, February 13, 2013. https://vimeo.com/59754895.

Schlesinger, Stephen C., and Stephen Kinzer. *Bitter Fruit: The Untold Story of the American Coup in Guatemala*. Reprint. New York: Anchor Books, 1990.

Sen, Amartya. "Why Is China Ahead of India?" *The World Bank*, June 20, 2013. http://live.worldbank.org/china-ahead-india-amartya-sen.

Sen, Amartya. *Development as Freedom*. Oxford: Oxford University Press, 2001.

Sender, Henny. "Blackstone CEO Donates Money to Tsinghua." *Financial Times*, April 21, 2013. www.ft.com/cms/s/0/391c5cda-aa3f-11e2-bc0d-00144feabdc0.html#a xzz2Qi87uNr1.

Shaw, Jonathan. "Japan's 'Lost Decades' – and Economic Stagflation in the U.S." *Harvard Magazine*, August2010. http://harvardmagazine.com/2010/07/an-aftermat th-to-avoid.

Sheng, Andrew. *From Asian to Global Financial Crisis: An Asian Regulator's View of Unfettered Finance in the 1990s and 2000s*. Cambridge: Cambridge University Press, 2009.

Sherif, Muzafer. *In Common Predicament: Social Psychology of Intergroup Conflict and Cooperation*. Boston, MA: Houghton Mifflin, 1966.

Shirk, Susan L. *The Political Logic of Economic Reform in China*. California Series on Social Choice and Political Economy, 24. Berkeley: University of California Press, 1993.

Soros, George. *The Crisis of Global Capitalism: Open Society Endangered*. 1st edn. Boston, MA: Little, Brown, 1998.

"S&P Breaks Milestone Level, Dow Sets Record High on Encouraging Data." *Xinhua* 新华/*English.news.cn*, August 2, 2013. http://news.xinhuanet.com/english/business/ 2013-08/02/c_125104288.htm.

Staub, Ervin. *The Roots of Evil: The Origins of Genocide and Other Group Violence*. Cambridge: Cambridge University Press, 1992.

Stiglitz, Joseph E. "Of the 1%, by the 1%, for the 1%." *Vanity Fair*, May 1, 2011. www.vanityfair.com/society/features/2011/05/top-one-percent-201105.

Sumner, William Graham. *Folkways: A Study of the Sociological Importance of Usages, Manners, Customs, Mores, and Morals*. Boston, MA: Ginn & Company, 1906.

Taylor, A. J. P. *The First World War: An Illustrated History*. London: Hamish Hamilton, 1963.

Tett, Gillian. *Fool's Gold: How Unrestrained Greed Corrupted a Dream, Shattered Global Markets and Unleashed a Catastrophe*. London: Little, Brown, 2009.

"US Banking Giants See Profits Jump." *BBC News*, July 12, 2013. www.bbc.co.uk/ news/business-23286901.

"US Banks See Profits Rise Sharply." *BBC News*, January 16, 2013. www.bbc.co.uk/ news/business-21044121.

US Census Bureau. *Income, Poverty, and Health Insurance Coverage in the United States: 2009*. Washington, DC: US Department of Commerce, September 2010.

Wang Lixiong, 王力雄. *China Tidal Wave*. English ed. Beijing: Global Oriental Ltd, 2008.

Wang Wen, and Li Fangfang. "Yacht Industry Sails Ahead." *China Watch*, June 14, 2013. http://chinawatch.washingtonpost.com/2013/06/yacht-industry-sails-ahead.php.

Ward, Clarissa, and Enjoli Francis. "China Pushes English Language." *ABC News*, November 15, 2010. http://abcnews.go.com/WN/China/china-pushes-english-langua ge/storynew?id=12154435.

Wiseman, Paul. "Richest 1 Percent Earn Biggest Share Since '20s." *ABC News*, September 10, 2013. http://abcnews.go.com/US/wireStory/top-percent-record-share-2012 -us-income-20213135.

Wolf, Martin. "Why the World Faces Climate Chaos." *Financial Times*, May 14, 2013. www.ft.com/cms/s/0/c926f6e8-bbf9-11e2-a4b4-00144feab7de.html#axzz2TUh8pTrh.

Wolf, Martin. "Living with Limits: Growth, Resources, and Climate Change." *Climate Policy* 12, no. 6(2012): 772–783. doi:10.1080/14693062.2012.695464.

Xi Jinping, 习近平. "China's New Party Chief Xi Jinping's Speech." *BBC News*, November 15, 2012. www.bbc.co.uk/news/world-asia-china-20338586.

Xing, Y., and N. Detert. *How the Iphone Widens the United States Trade Deficit with the People's Republic of China*. ADB Working Paper Series. Asian Development Bank Institute, December 2010. http://papers.ssrn.com/sol3/papers.cfm?abstract_id= 1729085.

"Xi's Speech Underlines Commitment to Reform." *People's Daily Online* 人民网, July 29, 2013. http://english.peopledaily.com.cn/90785/8343641.html.

Xu Changyin, 徐长银. "美国人口普查局数据表明美国贫富差距在扩大 U.S. Census Bureau Data Shows Widening Wealth Gap." *People's Daily Online* 人民网, September 30, 2012. http://world.people.com.cn/n/2012/0930/c157278-19158695.html? prolongation=1.

Yousuf, Hibah. "Dow, S&P 500 Close at Record Highs, up 19% in 2013." *CNNMoney*, July 18, 2013. http://money.cnn.com/2013/07/18/investing/stocks-markets/index. html.

Zhang Weiwei, 张维为. *The China Wave: Rise of a Civilizational State* 中国震撼: 一 个"文明型国家"的崛起. Trans. Anton Platero. Beijing: World Century Publishing Corporation, 2012. www.amazon.co.uk/The-China-Wave-Civilizational-ebook/dp/ B007T72B7C.

"习近平:不能照搬发达国家现代化模式 Xi Jinping: China Should Not Follow Developed Countries' Modernization Model." Tencent News 腾讯新闻, July 22, 2013. http://news.qq.com/a/20130722/012112.htm.

"引领中美关系向前迈进 A Forward Thrust in Sino–US Relations." People's Daily Online 人民网, June 8, 2013. http://english.people.com.cn/90883/8278304.html.

"韩媒称韩技术水平正被中国追赶 差距持续缩小 China Closes Technology Gap with South Korea." *Global Times*, August 12, 2013. http://world.huanqiu.com/exclusive/ 2013-08/4235959.html.

Index

Abe Shinzo 155, 157
Afghanistan 106, 137, 160–62
aggression 8 - 15, 139, 144, 147, 185
AIG 103
Allison, Graham 8, 73, 137
Arawak 1
Aristotle 5, 6, 7
Asian Financial Crisis 45, 105–7
Athens 38, 137
attachment theory 8

Bank of America 103, 118–20, 122
Barrett, David 161
Bartolome de las Casas 2
Bear Stearns 103, 110
benevolence 6, 7, 44, 154
Bernanke, Ben 106, 110, 112, 119
Big Oil 13, 70
Blanchard, Olivier 122
Bowlby, John 8
Brzezinski, Zbigniew 36, 42, 148
Buck, Pearl S. 42
Buddhism 153
Bush, George W. 10, 28, 74, 116, 146

capitalism 38, 47, 49, 87, 106, 108, 115,
    145, 186
Carr, E.H. 11
Catholic 29, 162
Cheney, Dick 11, 73, 143
Chiang Kai-shek 14
China Banking and Regulatory Com-
    mission 105, 124
Chinese Academy of Social Sciences 47,
    49, 86, 149
Christian 28, 164, 190
CIA 139, 151, 160, 163
Citigroup 117, 120, 122
climate change 28, 69–90, 187

Clinton, Bill 43, 79, 116, 140, 144–46,
    160
Clinton, Hilary 34, 38, 73, 157
coal 69, 76, 80, 82, 83, 88–9
Columbus 1
communist 14, 31, 40, 42, 48, 85, 144,
    151, 155, 185, 189
Confucianism 153–54
Cultural Revolution 39, 45, 47
cyber warfare 144

Dalai Lama 151–52
Dao De Jing 5
Darwin, Charles 7
Darwinism 42
defense contractors 142, 187
Deng Xiaoping 45, 47, 104
Diamond, Jared 79
Dodd-Frank 117
Dower, John 163

Economic Exclusion Zone (EEZ) 158–59
education 4, 5, 29, 30, 32, 48, 53, 108,
    140
Emerson, Ralph Waldo 11
emission 70–5, 77–90
empathy 6, 8, 11, 12, 14, 15, 159, 161,
    186, 193
energy 46–7, 69–90, 111, 186–87

Fairbank, John K. 27, 42, 188
Fannie Mae 103, 107, 112
Federal Reserve Board 103, 107, 112, 115
Feldstein, Martin 111, 116
Five Principles of Peaceful Coexistence
    149
Five-Year Plan 45, 80–2, 89, 90,
foreign direct investment 46, 50
fracking 75–6, 83

Fraser, Malcolm 147
free market fundamentalism 103, 108, 113–15
Freeman, Chas 42, 161
Fromm, Erich 9
Fukuyama, Francis 189
Fulbright, William 9, 28, 37, 41, 192

Galbraith, Kenneth 103
Geithner, Timothy F. 117
Gini coefficient 47
Global Financial Crisis 49, 109, 119, 137
global imbalances 106, 113–14
global warming 69–75, 77, 80–1, 85, 88–90, 186
globalization 35, 42, 46, 80, 108, 114, 117, 123, 149
Golden Age of Gas 76–7
Gore, Al 74
greenhouse gas 69–71, 74–5, 77, 82, 85
Greenspan, Alan 104, 107, 109–10, 112, 117

Hardin, Russell 2, 3, 12, 13
harmonious society 48
Hatoyama Yukio 156
hegemony 36, 43, 146–47, 157, 164
Hirohito 153–55
HISE 11, 15, 70, 103, 138, 163, 193
history 5, 9, 12, 14–5, 27, 32, 35, 38, 41, 43–4, 46, 50, 52, 105, 109, 121–22, 154–55, 157, 160–61, 163, 185, 188, 190, 193
Hobbes, Thomas 9
Holocaust 52
Hu Jintao 69, 80, 148
Hui 162
Huntington, Samuel 28, 37, 39, 147, 148

identity 28–9, 41, 164
IMF 104–7, 113, 119, 121–23, 136
imperialism 28, 41, 52, 147, 164, 188
Industrial and Commercial Bank 105, 121
interests 12–15, 36, 42, 45, 49–51, 70–1, 73, 85–6, 90, 114, 116, 119, 122–23, 140, 145–47, 149, 154, 163–64, 185, 187, 193
Intergovernmental Panel on Climate Change 70
International Energy Agency 71
international relations 1, 8, 9, 10, 11, 192
Iraq 51, 53, 107, 137, 146, 160

Japan 51, 145, 150–161, 187
Jiang Zemin 78
Johnson, Simon 113–17
Johnston, Alastair 42
JP Morgan Chase 103

Kennedy, John 10, 52
Kennedy, Paul 36
Kennedy, Robert 10–1
Khrushchev, Nikita 11
Kissinger, Henry 148
Krugman, Paul 73, 111, 113–16
Kuomintang 14, 150, 153, 161
Kupchan, Charles 12
Kyoto Protocol 72–7, 86, 88

Lee Kuan Yew 37, 189
Lehman Brothers 104, 110, 112, 119
Lemay, Curtis 154
Lin, Justin 104, 106
Lorenz, Konrad 9
love 3, 6, 7, 8, 192
Lovelock, James 69, 72

MacArthur, Douglas 154
Mann, Michael 13
Mao Zedong 27, 45, 54, 148
Marx, Karl 47, 87, 104, 137, 190
McCarthy 155
McNamara, Robert 11, 143, 159, 160
Mearsheimer, John 157
media 13, 29, 39, 41, 49, 50, 73–4, 103, 111, 138, 143, 151, 157, 159–60, 187–89, 192
Meiji 31, 153–54
Mencius 5, 6, 7, 12, 44
Mercer, Jonathan 10
Merrill Lynch 103, 119
militarism 42, 157
military balance 138, 162
Mullen, Mike 42, 51
Murayama Tomiichi 155
Myrdal, Gunnar 34

Nanjing 153, 155
national security 13, 36, 50
National Security Agency (NSA) 144
New York Civil Liberties Union 35
Nolan, Peter 44, 82, 121, 159
Nye, Joseph 36, 144–45

Obama, Barack 31, 35, 43, 69, 73–5, 88
Okinawa Reversion Agreement 158
one country, two systems 150

Oppenheimer, Franz 10
Osgood, Charles 10

Paulson, Henry 103, 110, 116
Peloponnesian Wars 157, 187
Pentagon 138, 141, 143
People's Liberation Army 139–41, 144, 151, 161
Pew Survey 28–9, 47, 158
philosophy 5, 28, 44–5, 116, 149
population 47, 71, 79, 80–4, 89
Protestant 28, 34
Puritans 29, 30, 32
Putnam, Robert 4

racism 10, 32, 40
Radha Binod Pal 155
Rajan, Raghuram 113, 115–16
Raymond, Lee 72
Reagan, Ronald 11, 28, 38, 139
regulation 105, 107–9, 112, 187
Rice, Condoleeza 145
Rittenberg, Sidney 189–90
Roach, Stephen 111
Rumsfeld, Donald 10, 146
Russia 12, 39, 83, 138, 140, 147, 153, 155–56, 159, 189

Sachs, Jeffrey 113, 115–16
Said, Edward 41
San Francisco Treaty 158
savings glut 106, 107, 112, 123
Schumpter, Joseph 163
SDR 106, 123
Service, John 161
shale gas 70, 75–6, 83, 88, 186
Shiller, Robert 115
Shirk, Susan 43, 189
Smith, Adam 6, 7
Snow, Edgar 42
Snowden, Edward J. 144
socialism 45–8, 189
Soviet 12, 36, 38, 51, 140, 143–44, 147, 149, 158, 162, 189
Sparta 38, 137
Stern, Nicholas 80, 86
Stiglitz, Joseph 113–15, 121, 189
structures 12–15, 70, 90, 114, 122–23, 163–64, 185, 187, 193
subprime 103, 105, 110, 112–14
Summers, Lawrence 112, 116, 117

Taiwan 15, 53, 107, 140, 150, 153, 185, 189, 191
Taiwan Relations Act (TRA) 141, 150
Taylor, A.J.P. 8, 185
think tanks 13, 72–3, 109, 111
Thompson, Llewellyn 11
Three Joint Communiques 149–50
Thucydides 137
Tibet 44, 149–52
Toynbee, Arnold 163
trade 15, 28, 36, 38–9, 42, 44, 46, 50, 73, 90, 106–7, 111, 123, 145, 150, 191
    Transpacific Partnership (TPP) 146
transportation 75, 80, 84, 140
Treaty of Mutual Cooperation and Security 156
Triffin Dilemma 105

Uighur 161–62
UN Convention of the Law of the Sea (UNCLOS) 158
USCESRC 78, 110–11
Uslaner, Eric 3

Vietnam War 29, 37–8, 41, 51, 54
violence 13, 29, 32, 49, 73, 147–48, 158–59
Volcker, Paul 115–16

Walmart 42, 53
Wang Lixiong 185
Washington Consensus 108–9, 119, 186–87
Weiner, Tim 139, 160
Wen Jiabao 48, 106
Wendt, Alexander 12
Wolf, Martin 122
Wolfowitz, Paul 146
World Bank 105–6
WTO 46, 78, 106, 120, 123, 191

Xi Jinping 40, 48, 85, 123, 148, 187, 190
Xinjiang 138, 151, 162
    Yan Xuetong 48
Yasukuni Shrine 155
Yellow Peril 41, 79, 185

Zheng Bijian 46, 89, 149
Zheng He 44
Zhou Xiaochuan 105, 123
Zinn, Howard 32
Zoellick, Robert 145–46

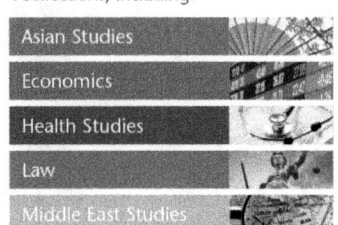

For Product Safety Concerns and Information please contact our EU
representative GPSR@taylorandfrancis.com
Taylor & Francis Verlag GmbH, Kaufingerstraße 24, 80331 München, Germany

www.ingramcontent.com/pod-product-compliance
Lightning Source LLC
Chambersburg PA
CBHW070414270326
41926CB00014B/2807